DATE DUE

PRINTED IN U.S.A.

SOMETHING ABOUT THE AUTHOR

ISSN 0276-816X

SOMETHING ABOUT THE AUTHOR

Facts and Pictures about Authors
and Illustrators of Books for Young People

EDITED BY
ANNE COMMIRE

VOLUME 48

GALE RESEARCH COMPANY
BOOK TOWER
DETROIT, MICHIGAN
48226

Editor: Anne Commire

Associate Editors: Agnes Garrett, Helga P. McCue

Senior Assistant Editor: Dianne H. Anderson

Assistant Editors: Elisa Ann Ferraro, Eunice L. Petrini, Linda Shedd

Sketchwriters: Marguerite Feitlowitz, Rachel Koenig

Researcher: Catherine Ruello

Editorial Assistants: Kathleen Betsko, Catherine Coray, Joanne J. Ferraro, Nigel French

Permissions Assistant: Susan Pfanner

In cooperation with the Young People's Literature staff

Editor: Joyce Nakamura

Assistant Editor: Heidi Ellerman

External Production Manager: Mary Beth Trimper

External Production Assistants: Linda Davis, Michael Vargas

Internal Production Associate: Louise Gagné

Internal Senior Production Assistant: Sandy Rock

Layout Artist: Elizabeth Lewis Patryjak

Art Director: Arthur Chartow

Special acknowledgment is due to the members of the *Contemporary Authors* staff
who assisted in the preparation of this volume.

Chairman: Frederick G. Ruffner

President: J. Kevin Reger

Publisher: Dedria Bryfonski

Associate Editorial Director: Ellen T. Crowley

Director, Biography Division: Christine Nasso

Senior Editor, Something about the Author: Adele Sarkissian

Contents

Introduction

As the only ongoing reference series that deals with the lives and works of authors and illustrators of children's books, *Something about the Author (SATA)* is a unique source of information. The *SATA* series includes not only well-known authors and illustrators whose books are most widely read, but also those less prominent people whose works are just coming to be recognized. *SATA* is often the only readily available information source for less well-known writers or artists. You'll find *SATA* informative and entertaining whether you are:

—a student in junior high school (or perhaps one to two grades higher or lower) who needs information for a book report or some other assignment for an English class;

—a children's librarian who is searching for the answer to yet another question from a young reader or collecting background material to use for a story hour;

—an English teacher who is drawing up an assignment for your students or gathering information for a book talk;

—a student in a college of education or library science who is studying children's literature and reference sources in the field;

—a parent who is looking for a new way to interest your child in reading something more than the school curriculum prescribes;

—an adult who enjoys children's literature for its own sake, knowing that a good children's book has no age limits.

Scope

In *SATA* you will find detailed information about authors and illustrators who span the full time range of children's literature, from early figures like John Newbery and L. Frank Baum to contemporary figures like Judy Blume and Richard Peck. Authors in the series represent primarily English-speaking countries, particularly the United States, Canada, and the United Kingdom. Also included, however, are authors from around the world whose works are available in English translation, for example: from France, Jean and Laurent De Brunhoff; from Italy, Emanuele Luzzati; from the Netherlands, Jaap ter Haar; from Germany, James Krüss; from Norway, Babbis Friis-Baastad; from Japan, Toshiko Kanzawa; from the Soviet Union, Kornei Chukovsky; from Switzerland, Alois Carigiet, to name only a few. Also appearing in *SATA* are Newbery medalists from Hendrik Van Loon (1922) to Sid Fleischman (1987). The writings represented in *SATA* include those created intentionally for children and young adults as well as those written for a general audience and known to interest younger readers. These writings cover the spectrum from picture books, humor, folk and fairy tales, animal stories, mystery and adventure, science fiction and fantasy, historical fiction, poetry and nonsense verse, to drama, biography, and nonfiction.

Information Features

In *SATA* you will find full-length entries that are being presented in the series for the first time. This volume, for example, marks the first full-length appearance of Sergio Aragonés, Betsy Bang, Federico Castellon, Margaret Drabble, Edward Frascino, Dick Gackenbach, Michael Hague, Leslie H. Morrill, Willard Price, and Cynthia Voigt.

Brief Entries, first introduced in Volume 27, are another regular feature of *SATA*. Brief Entries present essentially the same types of information found in a full entry but do so in a capsule form and without illustration. These entries are intended to give you useful and timely information while the more time-consuming process of compiling a full-length biography is in progress. In this volume you'll find Brief

Entries for Sue Ann Alderson, Susan Bonners, Suzy Kline, Dale Messick, Robert N. Munsch, Michael J. Pellowski, Meredith Ann Pierce, Pat Ross, and Lawrence Weinberg, among others.

Obituaries have been included in *SATA* since Volume 20. An Obituary is intended not only as a death notice but also as a concise view of a person's life and work. Obituaries may appear for persons who have entries in earlier *SATA* volumes, as well as for people who have not yet appeared in the series. In this volume Obituaries mark the recent deaths of Jesse Jackson, Eleanor Frances Lattimore, Patricia Miles Martin, Noel Streatfeild, and others.

Revised Entries

Since Volume 25, each *SATA* volume also includes newly revised and updated entries for a selection of *SATA* listees (usually four to six) who remain of interest to today's readers and who have been active enough to require extensive revision of their earlier biographies. For example, when Beverly Cleary first appeared in *SATA* Volume 2, she was the author of twenty-one books for children and young adults and the recipient of numerous awards. By the time her updated sketch appeared in Volume 43 (a span of fifteen years), this creator of the indefatigable Ramona Quimby and other memorable characters had produced a dozen new titles and garnered nearly fifty additional awards, including the 1984 Newbery Medal.

The entry for a given biographee may be revised as often as there is substantial new information to provide. In this volume, look for revised entries on Alice Childress, Helen Cresswell, E. L. Konigsburg, and Joseph Krumgold.

Illustrations

While the textual information in *SATA* is its primary reason for existing, photographs and illustrations not only enliven the text but are an integral part of the information that *SATA* provides. Illustrations and text are wedded in such a special way in children's literature that artists and their works naturally occupy a prominent place among *SATA*'s listees. The illustrators that you'll find in the series include such past masters of children's book illustration as Randolph Caldecott, Kate Greenaway, Walter Crane, Arthur Rackham, and Ernest L. Shepard, as well as such noted contemporary artists as Maurice Sendak, Edward Gorey, Tomie de Paola, and Margot Zemach. There are Caldecott medalists from Dorothy Lathrop (the first recipient in 1938) to Richard Egielski (the latest winner in 1987); cartoonists like Charles Schulz, ("Peanuts"), Walt Kelly ("Pogo"), Hank Ketcham ("Dennis the Menace"), and Georges Rémi ("Tintin"); photographers like Jill Krementz, Tana Hoban, Bruce McMillan, and Bruce Curtis; and filmmakers like Walt Disney, Alfred Hitchcock, and Steven Spielberg.

In more than a dozen years of recording the metamorphosis of children's literature from the printed page to other media, *SATA* has become something of a repository of photographs that are unique in themselves and exist nowhere else as a group, particularly many of the classics of motion picture and stage history and photographs that have been specially loaned to us from private collections.

Indexes

Each *SATA* volume provides a cumulative index in two parts: first, the Illustrations Index, arranged by the name of the illustrator, gives the number of the volume and page where the illustrator's work appears in the current volume as well as all preceding volumes in the series; second, the Author Index gives the number of the volume in which a person's biographical sketch, Brief Entry, or Obituary appears in the current volume as well as all preceding volumes in the series. These indexes also include references to authors and illustrators who appear in *Yesterday's Authors of Books for Children*. Beginning with Volume 36, the *SATA* Author Index provides cross-references to authors who are included in *Children's Literature Review*.

Starting with Volume 42, you will also find cross-references to authors who are included in the *Something about the Author Autobiography Series*. This companion series to *SATA* is described in detail below.

What a *SATA* Entry Provides

Whether you're already familiar with the *SATA* series or just getting acquainted, you will want to be aware of the kind of information that an entry provides. In every *SATA* entry the editors attempt to give as complete a picture of the person's life and work as possible. In some cases that full range of information may simply be unavailable, or a biographee may choose not to reveal complete personal details. The information that the editors attempt to provide in every entry is arranged in the following categories:

1. The "head" of the entry gives

   —the most complete form of the name,
   —any part of the name not commonly used, included in parentheses,
   —birth and death dates, if known; a (?) indicates a discrepancy in published sources,
   —pseudonyms or name variants under which the person has had books published or is publicly known, in parentheses in the second line.

2. "Personal" section gives

   —date and place of birth and death,
   —parents' names and occupations,
   —name of spouse, date of marriage, and names of children,
   —educational institutions attended, degrees received, and dates,
   —religious and political affiliations,
   —agent's name and address,
   —home and/or office address.

3. "Career" section gives

   —name of employer, position, and dates for each career post,
   —military service,
   —memberships,
   —awards and honors.

4. "Writings" section gives

   —title, first publisher and date of publication, and illustration information for each book written; revised editions and other significant editions for books with particularly long publishing histories; genre, when known.

5. "Adaptations" section gives

   —title, major performers, producer, and date of all known reworkings of an author's material in another medium, like movies, filmstrips, television, recordings, plays, etc.

6. "Sidelights" section gives

   —commentary on the life or work of the biographee either directly from the person (and often written specifically for the *SATA* entry), or gathered from biographies, diaries, letters, interviews, or other published sources.

7. "For More Information See" section gives

   —books, feature articles, films, plays, and reviews in which the biographee's life or work has been treated.

How a *SATA* Entry Is Compiled

A *SATA* entry progresses through a series of steps. If the biographee is living, the *SATA* editors try to secure information directly from him or her through a questionnaire. From the information that the biographee supplies, the editors prepare an entry, filling in any essential missing details with research. The author or illustrator is then sent a copy of the entry to check for accuracy and completeness.

If the biographee is deceased or cannot be reached by questionnaire, the *SATA* editors examine a wide variety of published sources to gather information for an entry. Biographical sources are searched with the aid of Gale's *Biography and Genealogy Master Index*. Bibliographic sources like the *National Union*

Catalog, the *Cumulative Book Index, American Book Publishing Record*, and the *British Museum Catalogue* are consulted, as are book reviews, feature articles, published interviews, and material sometimes obtained from the biographee's family, publishers, agent, or other associates.

For each entry presented in *SATA*, the editors also attempt to locate a photograph of the biographee as well as representative illustrations from his or her books. After surveying the available books which the biographee has written and/or illustrated, and then making a selection of appropriate photographs and illustrations, the editors request permission of the current copyright holders to reprint the material. In the case of older books for which the copyright may have passed through several hands, even locating the current copyright holder is often a long and involved process.

We invite you to examine the entire *SATA* series, starting with this volume. Described below are some of the people in Volume 48 that you may find particularly interesting.

Highlights of This Volume

ALICE CHILDRESS......American playwright, novelist, and children's author, who was born in Charleston, South Carolina, but reared "on the poorest blocks in Harlem, New York." In 1941, Childress joined the American Negro Theatre in Harlem, where she acted and directed for eleven years. By the end of the decade, she was writing plays for the black theatre. Encouraged by children's editor and author, Ferdinand Monjo, who was familiar with her work as a playwright, Childress wrote her first young adult book, *A Hero Ain't Nothin' but a Sandwich*. Although the book was critically acclaimed and the recipient of numerous awards, it was one of nine books that went to the Supreme Court in a book-banning case. "We do not have to read or accept a book at all," acknowledged Childress, "but to ban it is wrong." Despite her achievements in the theatre and in the literary world, Childress admits that, "I don't like the writing process. I like writing when I have completed it."

HELEN CRESSWELL......English author who began writing at age seven by creating stories for adults. In her teens, Cresswell preferred to write poetry, imitating such favorite poets as Hopkins, Spenser, and Keats. After graduation from Kings College in London, she held a variety of jobs, including work as a teacher, a tutor, and a secretary, while trying to establish herself as a writer. Since her first book, which was published in 1960, this prolific author has written over sixty books, several television plays for children, and numerous magazine articles. The main body of her work is fantasy because, "a much deeper level of truth can be reached through fantasy than by any other form of writing (except poetry, of course)."

EDWARD FRASCINO......cartoonist, author, and illustrator who was greatly influenced in his early years by radio, movies, and comics. Hating school, Frascino played "hooky every chance I got." Until he went to Parsons School of Design, Frascino could not develop a rapport with other students. There he learned "basic technique," and gained "a confidence in...work that was totally new." He began his professional art career as a designer of greeting cards, working later as a draftsman and in advertising until becoming a free-lance cartoonist. In 1968, Frascino illustrated his first children's book, discovering that cartoons and illustration "are similar in many ways." Ten years later he found that he could write and sketch his own book when he produced *Eddie Spaghetti*. Subsequently, Frascino has written other books for children, and admits that he "must work spontaneously," making "exciting discoveries in the course of working."

MICHAEL HAGUE......California-born children's author and illustrator who demonstrated "a talent for drawing as early as kindergarten." Besides "rendering illustrations of my own creations," Hague admitted that he "was always reading" as a child. In his teen years, he had developed an interest in sports, especially baseball, and didn't seriously take up drawing until college. After graduating with a B.F.A. degree, Hague worked for Hallmark Greeting Cards. "Glad though I was to have a job," he recalled, "I was determined to eventually work in publishing." After five years of showing his portfolio to publishers, he was hired to illustrate a cover for *Cricket* magazine. He has since illustrated his own stories and numerous children's classics, including *The Wind in the Willows, The Reluctant Dragon, The Lion, the Witch and the Wardrobe*, and *Alice's Adventures in Wonderland*. "I know I haven't reached my potential," he confessed. "I'm hoping by the time I'm fifty I'll be in my stride."

E. L. KONIGSBURG......an author and illustrator of children's books who holds the distinction of being the only author to have a Newbery honor book and to win the Newbery Medal during the same year in

1968. Growing up in small Pennsylvania mill towns, Konigsburg learned self-reliance and developed a self-consciousness "about one's education and exposure, both of which tend to be limited." Although she was interested in writing and illustrating, Konigsburg majored in chemistry in college because "there would be jobs waiting when I finished." Consequently, her writing career didn't begin until her youngest child was in school. Using her three children as models, Konigsburg wrote and illustrated her first two books, which were both recognized for their excellence with numerous literary awards, including the 1968 Newbery Medal for *From the Mixed-Up Files of Mrs. Basil E. Frankweiler.* She confesses that it takes at least a year to finish a book because, "writing for children demands a kind of excellence."

JOSEPH KRUMGOLD......novelist, film producer, and author of children's books, including two Newbery Medal winners. Inspired by his father, a motion picture exhibitor, and his older brother, a music supervisor for Paramount studios, Krumgold took an early interest in filmmaking, deciding on a motion-picture career at the age of twelve. After completing his education, he went to Hollywood where he worked as a writer, producer, and press agent for major movie companies. Subsequently, he formed his own companies and began to make documentary films: "the real thing—instead of actors and fake scenery." It was one of Krumgold's documentaries that led to his book ...*And Now Miguel* and to his first Newbery Medal in 1954. When asked why he writes books for children, Krumgold answered that he finds the writing "therapeutic" because his books help him "to learn to grow again."

CYNTHIA VOIGT......grew up in southern Connecticut and remembers her childhood as being "very close to perfect." Voigt, who was always interested in reading and writing, decided to become a writer in the ninth grade. Continuing her education at Smith College, she took creative writing courses, "but considered them real bombs." From 1971 to 1979 Voigt was department chairman at The Key School in Annapolis, Maryland, where she is currently a part-time teacher. Although her first book, *Homecoming* (1981), was well received by the critics, she feels that the acceptance of that first manuscript for publication was her most important award. *Dicey's Song* was written as a "natural ending" to *Homecoming.* In her cover letter to her editor Voigt added, "I don't know that you will want this, but I think you will love reading it." In 1983, *Dicey's Song* won the distinguished Newbery Medal.

These are only a few of the authors and illustrators that you'll find in this volume. We hope you find all the entries in *SATA* both interesting and useful.

Something about the Author Autobiography Series

You can complement the information in *SATA* with the *Something about the Author Autobiography Series (SAAS),* which provides autobiographical essays written by important current authors and illustrators of books for children and young adults. In every volume of *SAAS* you will find about twenty specially commissioned autobiographies, each accompanied by a selection of personal photographs supplied by the authors. The wide range of contemporary writers and artists who describe their lives and interests in the *Autobiography Series* includes Joan Aiken, Betsy Byars, Leonard Everett Fisher, Milton Meltzer, Maia Wojciechowska, and Jane Yolen, among others. Though the information presented in the autobiographies is as varied and unique as the authors, you can learn about the people and events that influenced these writers' early lives, how they began their careers, what problems they faced in becoming established in their professions, what prompted them to write or illustrate particular books, what they now find most challenging or rewarding in their lives, and what advice they may have for young people interested in following in their footsteps, among many other subjects.

Autobiographies included in the *SATA Autobiography Series* can be located through both the *SATA* cumulative index and the *SAAS* cumulative index, which lists not only the authors' names but also the subjects mentioned in their essays, such as titles of works and geographical and personal names.

The *SATA Autobiography Series* gives you the opportunity to view "close up" some of the fascinating people who are included in the *SATA* parent series. The combined *SATA* series makes available to you an unequaled range of comprehensive and in-depth information about the authors and illustrators of young people's literature.

Please write and tell us if we can make *SATA* even more helpful to you.

Acknowledgments

Grateful acknowledgment is made to the following publishers, authors, and artists
for their kind permission to reproduce copyrighted material.

AMECUS STREET. Illustration by Harold Henriksen from *Dan Moves Up* by Paul J. Deegan. Copyright © 1975 by Amecus Street. Reprinted by permission of Amecus Street.

ATHENEUM PUBLISHERS, INC. Illustration by E. L. Konigsburg from *A Proud Taste for Scarlet and Miniver* by E. L. Konigsburg. Copyright © 1973 by E. L. Konigsburg./ Illustration by E. L. Konigsburg from *Jennifer, Hecate, Macbeth, William McKinley, and Me, Elizabeth* by E. L. Konigsburg. Copyright © 1967 by E. L. Konigsburg./ Jacket illustration by E. L. Konigsburg from *From the Mixed-Up Files of Mrs. Basil E. Frankweiler* by E. L. Konigsburg. Copyright © 1967 by E. L. Konigsburg./ Frontispiece illustration by E. L. Konigsburg from *About the B'nai Bagels* by E. L. Konigsburg. Copyright © 1969 by E. L. Konigsburg./ Illustration by Alvin Smith from *Henry 3* by Joseph Krumgold. Copyright © 1967 by Joseph Krumgold./ Illustration by Leslie Morrill from *Morgan's Zoo* by James Howe. Copyright © 1984 by James Howe./ Illustration by Judith Gwyn Brown from *Shyster* by Elizabeth-Ann Sachs. Text copyright © 1985 by Elizabeth-Ann Sachs. Illustrations copyright © 1985 by Atheneum Publishers, Inc./ Jacket illustration by Michael Garland from *The Runner* by Cynthia Voigt. Text copyright © 1985 by Cynthia Voigt. Jacket illustration copyright © 1985 by Michael Garland./ Jacket illustration by James Shefcik from *A Solitary Blue* by Cynthia Voigt. Text copyright © 1983 by Cynthia Voigt. Jacket illustration copyright © 1983 by James Shefcik./ Jacket illustration by Michael Garland from *Tell Me If the Lovers Are Losers* by Cynthia Voigt. Text copyright © 1982 by Cynthia Voigt. Jacket illustration copyright © 1982 by Michael Garland./ Jacket illustration by James Shefcik from *Dicey's Song* by Cynthia Voigt. Text copyright © 1982 by Cynthia Voigt. Jacket illustration copyright © 1982 by James Shefcik./ Jacket illustration by Ted Lewin from *Homecoming* by Cynthia Voigt. Text copyright © 1981 by Cynthia Voigt. Jacket illustration copyright © 1981 by Ted Lewin./ Jacket illustration by Judith Gwyn Brown from *The Callender Papers* by Cynthia Voigt. Text copyright © 1983 by Cynthia Voigt. Jacket illustration copyright © 1983 by Judith Gwyn Brown. All reprinted by permission of Atheneum Publishers, Inc.

BANTAM BOOKS, INC. Illustration by Leslie Morrill from *The Wind in the Willows* by Kenneth Grahame. Illustrations copyright © 1982 by Leslie Morrill. Reprinted by permission of Bantam Books, Inc.

BEAUFORT BOOKS, INC. Jacket illustration by Michael Garland from *Minerva's Stepchild* by Helen Forrester. Copyright © 1981 by Jamunadevi Bhatia./ Jacket illustration by Troy Howell from *The Shadows of Jeremy Pimm* by Betsy Haynes. Copyright © 1981 by Betsy Haynes. Both reprinted by permission of Beaufort Books, Inc.

BERKLEY PUBLISHING GROUP. Cover illustration by G. D. Lang from *I'm Not Your Other Half* by Caroline B. Cooney. Copyright © 1984 by Caroline B. Cooney. Reprinted by permission of Berkley Publishing Group.

BLACKIE & SON LTD. Jacket illustration by Bob Harvey from *Megastar* by Jean Ure. Reprinted by permission of Blackie & Son Ltd.

BOBBS-MERRILL CO., INC. Illustration by Maureen Eckersley from *Pietro and the Mule* by Helen Cresswell. Text copyright © 1965 by Helen Rowe. Illustrations copyright © 1965 by Oliver & Boyd Ltd. Reprinted by permission of Bobbs-Merrill Co., Inc.

JONATHAN CAPE LTD. Illustrations by Pat Marriott from *Tiger Adventure* by Willard Price. Text copyright © 1979 by Willard Price. Illustrations copyright © 1979 by Jonathan Cape Ltd./ Sidelight excerpts from *My Own Life of Adventure* by Willard Price./ Illustration by Pat Marriott from *Safari Adventure* by Willard Price. Text copyright © 1966 by Willard Price. Illustrations copyright © 1966 by Jonathan Cape Ltd./ Illustration by Pat Marriott from *Cannibal Adventure* by Willard Price. Text copyright © 1972 by Willard Price. Illustrations copyright © 1972 by Pat Marriott./ Illustration by Pat Marriott from *Diving Adventure* by Willard Price. Text copyright © 1970 by Willard Price. Illustrations copyright © 1970 by Pat Marriott./ Illustration by Pat Marriott from *South Sea Adventure* by Willard Price. First published 1952./ Illustration by Pat Marriott from *Elephant Adventure* by Willard Price. Copyright © 1964 by Willard Price. All reprinted by permission of Jonathan Cape Ltd.

CHILDRENS PRESS. Illustration by Tom Dunnington from *The Story of Old Ironsides* by Norman Richards. Copyright © 1967 by Childrens Press. Reprinted by permission of Childrens Press.

COWARD, McCANN & GEOGHEGAN, INC. Jacket illustration by Jerry Pinkney from *Rainbow Jordan* by Alice Childress. Copyright © 1981 by Alice Childress./ Jacket illustration by David Brown from *A Hero Ain't Nothin' but a Sandwich* by Alice Childress. Copyright © 1973 by Alice Childress./ Illustration by Charles Lilly from *When the Rattlesnake Sounds* by Alice Childress. Copyright © 1975 by Alice Childress. All reprinted by permission of Coward, McCann & Geoghegan, Inc.

CREATIVE EDUCATION SOCIETY, INC. Illustration by John Keely from *Elton John* by Paula Taylor. Copyright © 1975 by Creative Educational Society, Inc./ Illustration by Dick Brude from *Elvis Presley* by Paula Taylor. Copyright © 1978 by Creative Educational Society, Inc. Both reprinted by permission of Creative Education Society, Inc.

THOMAS Y. CROWELL CO. Illustration by Michael Hampshire from *The Most Terrible Turk* by Joseph Krumgold. Text copyright © 1969 by Joseph Krumgold. Illustrations copyright © 1969 by Michael Hampshire./ Illustration by Jean Charlot from *...And Now Miguel* by Joseph Krumgold. Copyright 1953 by Joseph Krumgold./ Illustration by Symeon Shimin from *Onion John* by Joseph Krumgold. Copyright © 1959 by Joseph Krumgold./ Illustration by Clare Romano Ross from *God Wash the World and Start Again* by Lorenz Graham. Text copyright 1946 by Lorenz Graham. Illustrations copyright © 1971 by Clare Romano Ross. All reprinted by permission of Thomas Y. Crowell Co.

CROWN PUBLISHERS, INC. Illustration by Paula Winter from *The Bear and the Fly* by Paula Winter. Copyright © 1976 by Paula Winter. Reprinted by permission of Crown Publishers, Inc.

THE JOHN DAY CO. Photograph by Willard Price from *Roaming Britain* by Willard Price. Copyright © 1958 by Willard Price./ Photograph from *Odd Way Round the World* by Willard Price. Copyright © 1969 by Willard Price./ Photograph from *I Cannot Rest from Travel* by Willard Price. Copyright 1951 by Willard Price. All reprinted by permission of The John Day Co.

DELACORTE PRESS. Illustration by Leslie Morrill from *The Winter Worm Business* by Patricia Reilly Giff. Text copyright © 1981 by Patricia Reilly Giff. Illustrations copyright © 1981 by Leslie Morrill./ Illustrations by Leslie Morrill from *Fourth-Grade Celebrity* by Patricia Reilly Giff. Text copyright © 1979 by Patricia Reilly Giff. Illustrations copyright © 1979 by Leslie Morrill./ Jacket illustration by Robert Tannenbaum from *Corky and the Brothers Cool* by P. J. Petersen. Text copyright © 1985 by P. J. Petersen. Illustrations copyright © 1985 by Robert Tannenbaum./ Jacket illustration by Paul Bachem from *Here's to the Sophomores* by P. J. Petersen. Text copyright © 1984 by P. J. Petersen. Jacket illustration copyright © 1984 by Paul Bachem. All reprinted by permission of Delacorte Press.

ANDRE DEUTSCH LTD. Illustration by Charlotte Firmin from *Alex and Roy* by Mary Dickinson. Text copyright © 1981 by Mary Dickinson. Illustrations copyright © 1981 by Charlotte Firmin. Reprinted by permission of Andre Deutsch Ltd.

DILLON PRESS, INC. Illustration by Inese Jansons from *The Sea Wedding and Other Stories from Estonia* by Selve Maas and Peggy Hoffman. Copyright © 1978 by Dillon Press, Inc. Reprinted by permission of Dillon Press, Inc.

DODD, MEAD & CO. Illustration by Betsy Lewin from *The Strange Thing That Happened to Oliver Wendell Iscovitch* by Helen Kronberg Olson. Copyright © 1983 by Helen Kronberg Olson. Reprinted by permission of Dodd, Mead & Co.

DOUBLEDAY & CO., INC. Illustration by Priscilla Hillman from *The Merry-Mouse Schoolhouse* by Priscilla Hillman. Copyright © 1982 by Priscilla Hillman./ Illustration by Jane Johnson from *Sybil and the Blue Rabbit* by Jane Johnson. Copyright © 1979 by Jane Johnson. Both reprinted by permission of Doubleday & Co., Inc.

E. P. DUTTON, INC. Sidelight excerpts from an article "An Interview with John and Faith Hubley" by John D. Ford in *The American Animated Cartoon: A Critical Anthology*, edited by Danny Peary and Gerald Peary./ Sidelight excerpts from an article "Memories of Mr. Magoo" by Howard Rieder in *The American Animated Cartoon: A Critical Anthology*, edited by Danny Peary and Gerald Peary./ Illustration by Leslie Morrill from *Mouse Six and the Happy Birthday* by Miska Miles. Text copyright © 1978 by Miska Miles. Illustrations copyright © 1978 by Leslie Morrill. All reprinted by permission of E. P. Dutton, Inc.

FUNK & WAGNALLS, INC. Illustration by Ati Forberg from *Where the Wind Blows* by Helen Cresswell. Text copyright © 1968 by Elizabeth Helen Rowe. Illustrations copyright © 1968 by Ati Forberg. Reprinted by permission of Funk & Wagnalls, Inc.

GROSSETT & DUNLAP, INC. Illustrations by Federico Castellon from *The Story of John J. Audubon* by Joan Howard. Copyright 1954 by Joan Howard./ Illustrations by Federico Castellon from *The Story of Madame Curie* by Alice Thorne. Copyright © 1959 by Alice Thorne. All reprinted by permission of Grosset & Dunlap, Inc.

HAMISH HAMILTON LTD. Illustration by Karen Heywood from *The Wild Man of the Four Winds* by John Broughton. Text copyright © 1982 by John Broughton. Illustrations copyright © 1982 by Karen Heywood. Reprinted by permission of Hamish Hamilton Ltd.

HARCOURT BRACE JOVANOVICH, INC. Illustration by Bernard Most from *Whatever Happened to the Dinosaurs?* by Bernard Most. Copyright © 1984 by Bernard Most. Reprinted by permission of Harcourt Brace Jovanovich, Inc.

HARPER & ROW, PUBLISHERS, INC. Illustrations by Rose O'Neill from *The Biography of a Boy* by Josephine Daskam Bacon. Copyright 1910 by Harper and Brothers./ Illustration by Edward Frascino from *Gladys Told Me to Meet Her Here* by Marjorie Weinman Sharmat. Text copyright © 1970 by Marjorie Weinman Sharmat. Illustrations copyright © 1970 by Edward Frascino./ Illustration by Edward Frascino from *Delilah* by Carole Hart. Text copyright © 1973 by Carole Hart. Illustrations copyright © 1973 by Edward Frascino./ Illustration by Edward Frascino from *The Trumpet of the Swan* by E. B. White. Text copyright © 1970 by E. B. White. Illustrations copyright © 1970 by Edward Frascino./ Illustration by Edward Frascino from *The Dragons of the Queen* by Mary Stolz. Copyright © 1969 by Mary Stolz./ Illustration by Edward Frascino from *Crystal Is My Friend* by Shirley Gordon. Text copyright © 1978 by Shirley Gordon. Illustrations copyright © 1978 by Edward Frascino./ Illustration by Dick Gackenbach from *I Hate My Brother Harry* by Crescent Dragonwagon. Text copyright © 1983 by Crescent Dragonwagon. Illustrations copyright © 1983 by Dick Gackenbach./ Illustration by Dick Gackenbach from *Hattie Rabbit* by Dick Gackenbach. Copyright © 1976 by Dick Gackenbach./ Illustration by Dick Gackenbach from *McGoogan Moves the Mighty Rock* by Dick Gackenbach. Copyright © 1981 by Dick Gackenbach./ Illustration by Charles Robinson from *The Boy Who Wanted a Family* by Shirley Gordon. Text copyright © 1980 by Shirley Gordon. Illustrations copyright © 1980 by Charles Robinson./ Illustration by Faith Hubley from *Skydance* by Elizabeth Swados. Text copyright © 1981 by Elizabeth Swados. Illustrations copyright © 1978, 1981 by Faith Hubley./ Illustration by N. Scott Momaday from *The Gourd Dancer* by N. Scott Momaday. Copyright © 1976 by N. Scott Momaday./ Photograph reproductions by Jim Kalett from *The Names: A Memoir* by N. Scott Momaday. Copyright © 1976 by N. Scott Momaday./ Illustration by Leigh Grant from *It Can't Hurt Forever* by Marilyn Singer. Text copyright © 1978 by Marilyn Singer. Illustrations copyright © 1978 by Leigh Grant. All reprinted by permission of Harper & Row, Publishers, Inc.

WILLIAM HEINEMANN LTD. Illustration by Joanna Troughton from *The Smallest Man in England* by Julia Dobson. Text copyright © 1977 by Julia Dobson. Illustrations copyright © 1977 by William Heinemann Ltd. Reprinted by permission of William Heinemann Ltd.

HOLIDAY HOUSE, INC. Illustration by Dick Gackenbach from *Amanda and the Giggling Ghost* by Steven Kroll. Text copyright © 1980 by Steven Kroll. Illustrations copyright © 1980 by Dick Gackenbach./ Illustration by Leslie Morrill from *Judge Benjamin: Superdog* by Judith Whitelock McInerney. Text copyright © 1982 by Judith Whitelock McInerney. Illustrations copyright © 1982 by Leslie Morrill. Both reprinted by permission of Holiday House, Inc.

HENRY HOLT & CO. Illustration by Michael Hague from *The Velveteen Rabbit; or, How Toys Become Real* by Margery Williams. Illustrations copyright © 1983 by Michael Hague./ Illustration by Michael Hague from "The Ugly Duckling" in *Michael Hague's Favourite Hans Christian Andersen Fairy Tales,* selected by Michael Hague. Special edited text copyright © 1981 by Holt, Rinehart & Winston. Illustrations copyright © 1981 by Michael Hague./ Illustration by Michael Hague from "The Town Mouse and the Country Mouse" in *Aesop's Fables,* selected by Michael Hague. Special edited text copyright © 1985 by Holt, Rinehart & Winston. Illustrations copyright © 1985 by Michael Hague./ Illustration by Michael Hague from *The Wind in the Willows* by Kenneth Grahame. Copyright © 1980 by Ariel, Inc./ Illustration by Michael Hague from *Alice's Adventures in Wonderland* by Lewis Carroll. Illustrations copyright © 1985 by Michael Hague./ Illustration by Michael Hague from *The Wizard of Oz* by L. Frank Baum. Copyright © 1982 by Michael Hague. All reprinted by permission of Henry Holt & Co.

THE HORN BOOK, INC. Sidelight excerpts from an article "Newbery Award Acceptance" by E. L. Konigsburg, August, 1968 in *Horn Book*./ Sidelight excerpts from an article

"Acceptance Paper" by Joseph Krumgold in *Newbery Medal Books: 1922-1955,* edited by Bertha Mahony Miller and Elinor Whitney Field. Copyright © 1955 by The Horn Book, Inc./ Sidelight excerpts from *Illustrators of Children's Books: 1946-1956* by Bertha M. Miller and others. Copyright © 1958 by The Horn Book, Inc./ Sidelight excerpts from an article "Newbery Award Acceptance" by Joseph Krumgold in *Newbery and Caldecott Medal Books: 1956-1965.* Copyright © 1965 by The Horn Book, Inc./ Sidelight excerpts from an article "Cynthia Voigt" by Elise K. Irving, August, 1983 in *Horn Book.* All reprinted by permission of The Horn Book, Inc.

HOUGHTON MIFFLIN CO. Illustration by Dick Gackenbach from *Harry and the Terrible Whatzit* by Dick Gackenbach. Copyright © 1977 by Dick Gackenbach./ Illustration by Dick Gackenbach from *Claude and Pepper* by Dick Gackenbach. Copyright © 1976 by Dick Gackenbach./ Illustration by Michael Hague from *The Hobbit; or, There and Back Again* by J. R. R. Tolkien. Copyright © 1966 by J. R. R. Tolkien. Illustrations copyright © 1984 by Oak, Ash & Thorn Ltd./ Illustration by Robert Andrew Parker from *Beautiful My Mane in the Wind* by Catherine Petroski. Text copyright © 1983 by Catherine Petroski. Illustrations copyright © 1983 by Robert Andrew Parker. All reprinted by permission of Houghton Mifflin Co.

ALFRED A. KNOPF, INC. Jacket illustration by Muriel Nasser from *The Middle Ground* by Margaret Drabble. Copyright © 1980 by Margaret Drabble. Reprinted by permission of Alfred A. Knopf, Inc.

LERNER PUBLICATIONS CO. Photograph by Art Thomas from *Archery Is for Me* by Art Thomas. Copyright © 1981 by Lerner Publications Co. Reprinted by permission of Lerner Publications Co.

J. B. LIPPINCOTT CO. Illustration by W. T. Mars from *The Piemakers* by Helen Cresswell. Copyright © 1967 by Helen Cresswell. Illustrations copyright © 1968 by J. B. Lippincott Co./ Sidelight excerpts from *A Sense of Story* by John Rowe Townsend. Both reprinted by permission of J. B. Lippincott Co.

MACMILLAN PUBLISHING CO. Jacket illustration by Lino Saffioti from *Dear Shrink* by Helen Cresswell. Text copyright © 1982 by Helen Cresswell. Illustrations copyright © 1982 by Macmillan Publishing Co./ Illustration by Shirley Felts from *The Secret World of Polly Flint* by Helen Cresswell. Text copyright © 1982 by Helen Cresswell. Illustrations copyright © 1982 by Shirley Felts./ Jacket illustration by Trina Schart Hyman from *Bagthorpes Versus the World: Being the Fourth Part of the Bagthorpe Saga* by Helen Cresswell. Copyright © 1979 by Helen Cresswell./ Jacket illustration by Trina Schart Hyman from *Absolute Zero* by Helen Cresswell. Copyright © 1978 by Helen Cresswell./ Illustration by Gareth Floyd from *The Night-Watchmen* by Helen Cresswell. Copyright © 1969 by Helen Cresswell./ Illustration by Ati Forberg from *A Game of Catch* by Helen Cresswell. Copyright © 1969 by Helen Rowe. Copyright © 1977 by Macmillan Publishing Co./ Illustration by Michael Hague from *The Lion, the Witch and the Wardrobe* by C. S. Lewis. Copyright 1950 by C. S. Lewis Pte. Ltd. Copyright © 1981 by Macmillan Publishing Co. All reprinted by permission of Macmillan Publishing Co.

JULIAN MESSNER. Illustration from *Is There a Loch Ness Monster? The Search for a Legend* by Gerald S. Snyder. Copyright © 1977 by Gerald S. Snyder. Reprinted by permission of Julian Messner.

WILLIAM MORROW & CO., INC. Illustration by Leslie Morrill from *Animals and Their Niches: How Species Share Resources* by Laurence Pringle. Text copyright © 1977 by Laurence Pringle. Illustrations copyright © 1977 by Leslie Morrill. Reprinted by permission of William Morrow & Co., Inc.

NORTH WINDS PRESS. Illustration by Ron Berg from *Wynken, Blynken and Nod* by Eugene Field. Text copyright © 1985 by Scholastic-TAB Productions Ltd. Illustration copyright © 1985 by Ron Berg./ Illustration by Ron Berg from *The Owl and the Pussycat* by Edward Lear. Text copyright © 1984 by Scholastic-TAB Publications Ltd. Illustrations copyright © 1984 by Ron Berg. Both reprinted by permission of North Winds Press.

OXFORD UNIVERSITY PRESS. Sidelight excerpts from the "Preface" of *The Oxford Companion to English Literature* by Margaret Drabble. Copyright © 1985 by Oxford University Press and Margaret Drabble. Reprinted by permission of Oxford University Press.

PRENTICE-HALL, INC. Illustration by Edward Frascino from *My Cousin the King* by Edward Frascino. Copyright © 1985 by Edward Frascino./ Illustration by Quentin Blake from *Smelly Jelly, Smelly Fish* by Michael Rosen. Text copyright © 1986 by Michael Rosen. Illustrations copyright © 1986 by Quentin Blake. Both reprinted by permission of Prentice-Hall, Inc.

RANDOM HOUSE, INC. Illustration by Fred Castellon from *The Man Who Changed China: The Story of Sun Yat-sen* by Pearl Buck. Copyright 1953 by Pearl S. Buck. Reprinted by permission of Random House, Inc.

SCOTT, FORESMAN & CO. Illustration from *Scott, Foresman Beginning Dictionary* by E. L. Thorndike and Clarence L. Barnhart. Copyright © 1976, 1979, 1983 by Scott, Foresman & Co. Reprinted by permission of Scott, Foresman & Co.

CHARLES SCRIBNER'S SONS. Illustration by Virginia Kahl from *Whose Cat Is That?* by Virginia Kahl. Copyright © 1979 by Virginia Kahl. Reprinted by permission of Charles Scribner's Sons.

SEABURY PRESS. Jacket illustration "The Last of England" by Ford Madox Brown from *For Queen and Country* by Margaret Drabble. Text copyright © 1978 by Margaret Drabble. Reprinted by permission of Seabury Press.

SHEED ANDREWS McMEEL, INC. Illustrations from *A Doonesbury Special: A Director's Notebook* by Garry Trudeau. Copyright © 1978 by Garry Trudeau. Reprinted by permission of Sheed Andrews McMeel, Inc.

TERRA MAGICA. Illustration by Leonie Kooiker from *Met de grote vogel mee* by Leonie Kooiker. Reprinted by permission of Terra Magica.

TYNDALE HOUSE PUBLISHERS, INC. Cover illustration from *Teddy Jo and the Ragged Beggars* by Hilda Stahl. Copyright © 1984 by Hilda Stahl. Reprinted by permission of Tyndale House Publishers, Inc.

FREDERICK WARNE LTD. Illustration by Andrew Glass from *The Fido Frame-Up* by Marilyn Singer. Text copyright © 1983 by Marilyn Singer. Illustrations copyright © 1983 by Andrew Glass. Reprinted by permission of Frederick Warne Ltd.

ALBERT WHITMAN & CO. Illustration by Joelle Shefts from *Casey the Nomad* by Susan Sussman. Text copyright © 1985 by Susan Sussman. Illustrations copyright © 1985 by Joelle Shefts. Reprinted by permission of Albert Whitman & Co.

Sidelight excerpts from an article "The Watercolor Series," May, 1949 in *American Artist.* Copyright © 1949 by Billboard Publishers, Inc. Reprinted by permission of *American Artist.*/ Sidelight excerpts from an article "The Complete Clare Romano and John Ross" by Clare Romano, August 16, 1981 in *American Artist.* Reprinted by permission of *American Artist.*/ Sidelight excerpts from an article "Beyond Pigs and Bunnies" by John Hubley, Spring, 1975 in *The American Scholar.* Copyright © 1975 by John Hubley. Reprinted by permission of *The American Scholar.*/ Sidelight excerpts from an article "Mad Magazine's Sergio Aragonés," August, 1970 in *Cartoonist Profiles,* edited by Jud Hurd. Reprinted by permission of *Cartoonist Profiles.*/ Sidelight excerpts from an article "An Interview with Michael Rosen," in *Language Matters.* Reprinted by permission of The Centre for Language in Primary Education./ Sidelight excerpts from an article "If It's Someone from Porlock, Don't Answer the Door" by Helen Cresswell, March, 1971 in *Children's Literature in Education.* Reprinted by permission of *Children's Literature in Education.*/ Sidelight excerpts from an article "An Interview with Margaret Drabble" by Nancy S. Hardin, Autumn, 1973 in *Contemporary Literature.* Reprinted by permission of *Contemporary Literature.*/ Illustrations by Sergio Aragonés from *A Mad Look at Winter* by Sergio Aragonés, Summer, 1982 in *Mad.* Copyright © 1976, 1977, 1981 by E. C. Publications Inc./ Illustrations by Sergio Aragonés from *A Mad Look at Santa* by Sergio Aragonés, January, 1964 in *Mad.* Reprinted by permission of E. C. Publications, Inc.

Illustrations by Sergio Aragonés from *A Mad Look at. . .Air Travel* by Sergio Aragonés, April, 1981 in *Mad.* Copyright © 1981 by E. C. Publications, Inc. Reprinted by permission of E. C. Publications, Inc./ Sidelight excerpts and photograph from *Federico Castellon: His Graphic Works 1936-1971* by August L. Freundlich. Copyright © 1973 by College of Visual and Performing Arts, Syracuse University. Both reprinted by permission of August L. Freundlich./ Sidelight excerpts from the "Afterword" in *The Wizard of Oz* by Michael Hague. Copyright © 1982 by Michael Hague. Reprinted by permission of Michael Hague./ Sidelight excerpts from an article "Sprezzatura: A Kind of Excellence" by E. L. Konigsburg, June, 1976 in *Horn Book.* Reprinted by permission of E. L. Konigsburg./ Sidelight excerpts from an article "Looking Toward the Future with Faith Hubley" by Susan King, April 8, 1985 in *Los Angeles Herald Examiner.* Reprinted by permission of *Los Angeles Herald Examiner.*/ Illustration by Dick Gackenbach from *Harry and the Terrible Whatzit* by Dick Gackenbach. Copyright © 1977 by Dick Gackenbach. Reprinted by permission of McIntosh & Otis, Inc./ Sidelight excerpts from an article "Those Were the Days, My Friend" by Alice Childress, Dec. 3, 1972 in *Sunday News.* Amended by Alice Childress. Copyright © 1972 by New York News, Inc. Reprinted by permission of New York News, Inc.

Sidelight excerpts from an article "At the Movies" by Chris Chase, November 4, 1983 in *New York Times*. Copyright © 1983 by The New York Times Co. Reprinted by permission of The New York Times Co./ Sidelight excerpts from an article "Discovering the Land of Light" by N. Scott Momaday, March 17, 1985 in *New York Times Magazine*. Copyright © 1985 by The New York Times Co. Reprinted by permission of The New York Times Co./ Cover illustration from *Down Timberland Trail: A Tale of Upper Canada* by Bernice Callaway. Copyright © 1969 by Prairie Bible Institute. Reprinted by permission of Prairie Bible Institute./ Sidelight excerpts from an article "Animation Learns a New Language" by John Hubley and Zachary Schwartz, July, 1946 in *Film Quarterly*. Copyright 1946 by The Regents of the University of California. Reprinted by permission of The Regents of the University of California./ Sidelight excerpts from an article "Newbery Medal Acceptance" by Cynthia Voigt, August, 1983 in *Horn Book*. Reprinted by permission of Cynthia Voigt./ Sidelight excerpts from an article "Cynthia Voigt" by Elise K. Irving, August, 1983 in *Horn Book*. Reprinted by permission of Cynthia Voigt./ Sidelight excerpts from an article "Mr. Magoo's Creator Finds His Children's Hour" by Christopher Sharp, July 7, 1975 in *Women's Wear Daily*. Reprinted by permission of *Women's Wear Daily*.

PHOTOGRAPH CREDITS

Sergio Aragonés: Jim Ruth; Alice Childress: Joseph Abeles and Sy Friedman; Caroline B. Cooney: John Goodwin Cooney; Margaret Drabble: Jerry Bauer; Joan Kahn: Judy Kemp; Michael Kurland: Paul Nelson; John S. Marr (with Gwyneth Cravens): Henry Korman; N. Scott Momaday: Jim Kalett; Alan E. Nourse: Irene Fury; Catherine Petroski: Copyright © 1985 by Alice Adams; Clare Ross: Rhoda F. Sidney; Susan Sussman: EPS Studios, Inc.; Cynthia Voigt: Walter Voigt; Betty Jane Wylie: Gerald Campbell Studios (Toronto, Canada).

something ABOUT the Author

ALDERSON, Sue Ann 1940-

BRIEF ENTRY: Born September 11, 1940. An author of children's books, Alderson grew up in New York City, spending summers with her sister and psychologist parents in a community of noted psychologists on a 160-acre New Hampshire farm. While attending Antioch College, from which she received a B.A. in 1962, Alderson spent a year as an assistant preschool teacher and later studied child development and education. She earned a master's degree in English from Ohio State University and taught English courses at several colleges before becoming an assistant professor in the creative writing department at the University of British Columbia in 1980. Alderson has worked as a volunteer kindergarten teacher and editorial assistant of *Parent's Magazine* and has spoken at conferences and conducted workshops in creative writing.

Influenced by experiences with her own children, Alderson's writing illuminates childhood difficulties without being overtly didactic, according to Irma McDonough in *Profiles 2*. Alderson's daughter Rebecca serves as the role model for the unnamed protagonist of *The Finding Princess* (Fforbez, 1977), in which an unsatisfied princess who has all that money can buy leaves home and finds what makes her happy—a seashell, a ring around the moon, and dancing barefoot in the grass. Likewise, Alderson's son Kai is the prince who overcomes several obstacles with the help of an ivory staff, a tall hat with a feather, and a golden yo-yo in *The Adventures of Prince Paul* (Fforbez, 1977). Character Bonnie McSmithers asserts her independence with catchy rhyme in *Bonnie McSmithers You're Driving Me Dithers* (Tree Frog, 1974; published in French as *Anne-Marie Maginol, tu me rends folle*, Tree Frog, 1981), *Hurry Up, Bonnie!* (Tree Frog, 1976), and *Bonnie McSmithers Is at It Again!* (Tree Frog, 1979). Alderson uses the same light style in her two books for older children: *Comet's Tale* (Tree Frog, 1983) and *The Not Impossible Summer* (Irwin, 1983).

FOR MORE INFORMATION SEE: Irma McDonough, editor, *Profiles 2*, Canadian Library Association, 1982.

ANFOUSSE, Ginette 1944-

BRIEF ENTRY: Born in 1944, in Quebec, Canada. French-Canadian children's author and illustrator Anfousse has read and drawn for as long as she can remember. She became interested in engraving while attending the Montreal School of Fine Arts and later continued to engrave on her own while working as an illustrator for Radio-Quebec. It was not until 1970, when she moved to a village in the Laurentians with her husband and daughter, that she began working with children, running a school of dance and plastic arts. Anfousse's picture books have been published in both French and English. Her first two, *La cachette (Hide-and-Seek)* and *Mon ami Pichou (My Friend Pichou)*, written in 1972 and first published in French in 1976, introduced the child Jiji (Jojo) and Pichou, her "honest-to-goodness-baby-aardvark-who-really-eats-ants." These characters appear in nearly all of Anfousse's books—cajoling the reader to play hide-and-seek in *La cachette*, helping each other through a bout of chicken pox in *La varicelle (Chicken Pox)*, and fighting and making up with another child in *La chicane (The Fight)*.

Two later books, *L'hiver, ou le bonhomme sept heures* and *Le savon (Winter* and *The Bath)*, also feature the pair. *Sophie, Pierrot et un crapaud (Sophie, Pierrot and a Toad)* introduces new characters who explore traditional male-female roles. "Anfousse's stories are whimsical and slightly sassy," according to *Quill & Quire*. "The illustrations show talent and careful work and they are truly captivating," noted *Canadian Children's Literature*. "Everything she writes and draws relates entirely to a child's-eye view of the world." Anfousse received the Canada Council Children's Literature Prize in 1978 and the Canada Council Award for Children's Literature in 1979, for *La chicane* and *La varicelle*. *La cachette* and *La chicane* were named to the International Board on Books for Young People Honor List in 1978 and 1979, respectively. Anfousse is also the author of several untranslated juvenile works, including *L'ecole, La fête, Un loup pour Rose,* and *Une nuit au pays des malices. Residence:* Val-David, Quebec, Canada.

FOR MORE INFORMATION SEE: Irma McDonough, editor, *Profiles 2,* Canadian Library Association, 1982.

ARAGONÉS, Sergio   1937-

PERSONAL: Born September 6, 1937, in Castellon, Spain; came to the United States in 1962; son of Pascual (a movie producer) and Isabel (Domenech) Aragonés; married Lilio Chomette (a teacher), September 14, 1962. *Education:* Attended University of Mexico; studied mime with Marcel Marceau. *Office:* Mad, 485 Madison Ave., New York, N.Y. 10022.

CAREER: Comic book and magazine cartoonist. Began career as contributor of cartoons and drawings to the Mexican humor magazine *Ja Ja,* and to a variety of other Mexican magazines, including *Mañana,* 1953; *Mad* magazine, New York, N.Y., regular contributor of cartoon features and drawings, 1962—; National Periodical Publications, contributor of pantomime cartoons, writer of comic book stories, and collaborator for a short time on the strip ''Bat Lash,'' beginning 1967. Has also worked as an architect's assistant, as a professional pantomimist, and has done several documentary films. *Military service:* Mexican Navy. *Member:* Academy of Comic Book Arts, American Federation of Television and Radio Artists (AFTRA), Cartoonist Guild, Comic Art Professional Society (vicepresident, 1980-81), National Cartoonists Society, Screen Actors Guild, Writers Guild of America. *Awards, honors:* Reubens Award from the National Cartoonists Society and various international awards for cartoons.

WRITINGS—Of interest to young adults, except as noted; all self-illustrated; all cartoon books: *Viva Mad,* 7th edition, New American Library, 1968; *Mad about Mad,* 4th edition, New American Library, 1970; *Aunts in Your Pants: Memoirs of a Dirty Old Woman* (adult), Kanrom, 1972; *Mad-ly Yours,* Warner Books, 1972; *In Mad We Trust,* Warner Books, 1974; *Mad Marginals,* Warner Books, 1974; *Mad as the Devil,* Warner Books, 1975; *Incurably Mad,* Warner Books, 1977; *Sergio*

Aragonés on Parade, edited by Albert B. Feldstein and Jerry DeFuccio, Warner Books, 1979, published as *Mad's Sergio Aragonés on Parade,* 1982; *Sergio Aragonés' Mad as a Hatter,* Warner Books, 1981; *Mad Menagerie,* Warner Books, 1983; *More Mad Marginals,* Warner Books, 1985. Also coauthor of television special ''It's a Wacky World.''

Illustrator: Betty Rollin, *Mothers Are Funnier than Children* (adult satire), Doubleday, 1964; Edward J. Hegarty, *The Seven Secrets of Sales Success* (adult), McGraw-Hill, 1966; John De Coursey, *Up Your Lexicon* (adult humor), Kanrom, 1966; Henry Blankfort, *Henry, the Smiling Dog* (juvenile), Putnam, 1967; David M. (pseudonym of David Miller), *The World's Best Dirty Limericks* (adult), L. Stuart, 1982. Also illustrator of more than fifteen additional books for both children and adults; has executed drawings for several television specials.

SIDELIGHTS: **September 6, 1937.** Born in Castellon, Spain. ''I was born in Spain, . . . but on account of the civil war, my family had to leave the country when I was six months old and go to a refugee camp in France where we stayed for a few years. After that we went to Mexico City where I grew up. In elementary school and in high school I was always drawing cartoons. My father's brother, who had a great sense of humor, kept me supplied with all the cartoon magazines, and I owe the fact that I'm now a cartoonist to his encouragement. I read the cartoons in Spanish newspapers, such as *La Codorniz,* which is one of the oldest ones, and many of the American daily comics—'Blondie,' 'The Katzenjammer Kids,' and others, which were translated in Mexico.

''I even made my first cartoon money in the third grade when the teacher wanted the class to make little drawings to illustrate lessons in Biology, Zoology, etc. It seems that nobody in the class knew how to draw so I started charging—probably the equivalent of half a penny—to make the pictures for the various children. All in all, I guess I made 23 pesos, or somewhere around two or three dollars.

''Finally my teacher caught on and said that each child would have to draw his own pictures. Later on, in high school, I was

SERGIO ARAGONÉS

(From "A Mad Look at Winter" in *Mad* by Sergio Aragonés. Illustrated by the author.)

drawing all day long and the teachers were always mad at me. One day a girl classmate, who had an enormous collection of my cartoons that I'd given her, told me that I should try and sell them professionally to some magazine. Some weeks after that, she came up to me with a very happy expression on her face and showed me some cartoons of mine in a little magazine—called *Ja Ja*—to which she had submitted them without my knowing anything about it. I remember I got $1 a cartoon, and, with the proceeds, I invited a girl—my benefactress—out to dinner for the first time. This was about 1953 and from then on I submitted cartoons regularly in Mexico." ["*Mad Magazine's Sergio Aragonés*," *Cartoonist Profiles*, edited by Jud Hurd, Volume 2, number 7, August, 1970.[1]]

Aragonés attended architectural school largely because his family encouraged him to become a professional. "I never intended to be an architect but the idea was to have that professional title framed on the wall—and I figured that my family would be very proud of me—that's all they dreamed about—having an architect in the family. The first three years were interesting—the story of art and architecture—but after the third year the course became quite technical, and involved the study of materials and processes of construction that I wasn't really interested in at all. However, I did draw a daily mural cartoon which showed what was happening in the school—and this was put up on the wall of a school corridor each day. I drew this in huge size with a big magic marker and developed a real velocity in turning them out. Students got mad when this mural

newspaper didn't appear, by the way. At this time, too, I was doing a weekly page for a magazine called *Mañana*. I did six cartoons, containing no words, on a different theme each week."[1]

While Aragonés was a university student, he studied mime under the world famous pantomimist Marcel Marceau, an experience that he later credited as a major influence on his wordless cartoons. "I loved acting—my father was a movie producer—(before he passed away he had made over 100 films in Mexico) and I was delighted when Marcel Marceau, the world-famous French pantomimist, came to Mexico City, gave a few lectures, and then opened a school of pantomime there. I attended his workshops several times a week, spent almost every day practicing my acting, and later worked professionally with a group of mimes. I was working as an architect's assistant during the day and as a clown on weekends."[1]

1962. Came to the United States, where he made the rounds of publishers, attempting to sell his cartoons. "I arrived in New York with $8 and found that the hotel I went to wanted more money for the night than I had. So I walked down to Greenwich Village which had seemed a very exciting place in my imagination. It was the era of the Beatniks—and at night the characters and the scenes were fantastic. I kept my luggage in a locker in a bus station and, fortunately, a man who owned

(From "A Mad Look at Santa" in *Mad* by Sergio Aragonés. Illustrated by the author.)

(From "A Mad Look at Santa" in *Mad* by Sergio Aragonés. Illustrated by the author.)

one of the coffee houses saw that I needed money and gave me a chance to sing at his place. I would sing Mexican songs, recite flamenco poetry and then pass the bucket. And I slept in the coffee house during this period. My first contacts with the American cartoon market were very discouraging. I thought that the syndicates distributed cartoons to all the magazines, for instance. Before long I met a cartoonist who was working for one of the girlie cartoon magazines which paid about $9 a cartoon, so I went around there too. Apparently they liked my ideas but not my drawings, because they gave me a few American cartoons and wanted me to copy the style. I was desperate at this point and went to see an agent. I left his office crying because he said he didn't understand my pantomime cartoons, that my characters looked like Martians, and that I should go back to Mexico.

"My girl friend—now my wife—sent me $200 from California because I wasn't making any money. Finally, a friend in the Village told me not to take my cartoons to the little magazines but, rather, to the top ones. So I said, 'I'm going to the biggest one I know—*Mad!*' I had been a *Mad* fan for many years and I had even published a poor imitation of the magazine in Mexico. The first man I met there was Antonio Prohias who does the 'Spy vs. Spy' feature. He exclaimed, 'My Brother!'—and immediately we started talking about Cuba and Mexico. I asked him if he could introduce me to the editors, to which he replied, 'You'll have to introduce *yourself* because I don't speak *English!*' At that, Jerry DeFuccio, an Associate Editor, came in and again Prohias shouted, 'My brother—my brother!' I remember Jerry saying, 'Oh, you're Prohias' brother—glad to meet you.'

"Well, I had a whole series of cartoons about astronauts with me—the astronaut boom was just starting. Jerry took them inside and, from my seat in the conference room, I could hear everybody laughing. Pretty soon, Al Feldstein, the Editor, came out and asked me if I wanted to sell the cartoons. I said, 'I'll *give* them to you if you want them!' Al said, 'We like them very much—here's a check for $200.' Wow! I couldn't believe it!

"These cartoons eventually appeared in *Mad* #76, entitled 'A Mad Look at the U.S. Space Effort.' Jerry DeFuccio told me to come to the office often and to make it my home—he knew I didn't have anybody or anything. So I spent a lot of hours there, watching, etc. After a while I started drawing ideas for covers—they liked a few of them and I sold three in a row. Another thing—I had never understood the little marginal things that *Mad* had in the corners of the pages—they were very American—takeoffs on words, etc. And I had always dreamed that if there were little *cartoons* instead, *everybody* would understand them. So one day I pasted up a page of tiny cartoons and they liked the idea. There was a good reaction and I've continued doing them ever since. . . . John Putnam, the *Mad* Art Director took me to parties in the Village, and I met all the cartoonists who gave me hints about where to go.

"I started selling cartoons to *Gourmet* magazine—a man wanted me to illustrate a book and I was off to a pretty good start.''[1]

Aragonés's first illustrated book, an adult satire, was published in 1964. Three years later he illustrated the children's book *Henry, the Smiling Dog* by Henry Blankfort. He has written

(From "A Mad Look at Winter" in *Mad* by Sergio Aragonés. Illustrated by the author.)

and illustrated several cartoon books for young adults since 1968.

As one of *Mad* magazine's star cartoonists, Aragonés maintains a rigorous work schedule. "I like to work at night—after 6—and when things are relaxed and quiet. I pick a subject—a theme—and start elaborating on it until 5 or 6 o'clock in the morning. After that I get some sleep, wake up, relax and spend the day doing other things. If I've picked a theme such as some sport, I first visualize the sport mentally, write down various words that occur to me in connection with it, and then ideas seem to unreel in my head like a film—I'm watching all kinds of scenes and situations pertaining to that particular sport.

"First of all, I do doodles very fast—no particular size—sometimes in the corner of a sheet—very rough as the ideas come to me. When you're hot, the ideas start rolling, and after a night session, I may come up with 20 or more ideas—I've even done 40. Before I submit my ideas to *Mad*, I eliminate all those which aren't funny. Then I take a sheet of regular typewriter paper and make the roughs of the good ones.

"If I think a theme is good for, say, four pages in the magazine, that will require 17 to 20 cartoons—so I'll submit about 40 ideas from which the *Mad* editors can choose the ones they want.

"As for my marginal cartoons, about 20 are used in a typical issue, and I draw them 2 and 1/2 times the size they appear. I submit a month of them at a time."[1]

Aragonés works directly in ink without preliminary drawings. "A lot of people put too much stress on materials—they're not important—use what you're comfortable with. If it feels comfortable to use a ballpoint, use it. Sometimes when I'm traveling, I just go to a store and buy any kind of tablet that merely won't blot ink—generally I don't even know the name of the paper. However, I always carry two particular pens in my jacket pocket wherever I go. One is an Ultraflex India Ink Fountain Pen which I can not only sketch with but with which I make my finished cartoons also. It's made by the Ropex Company in New York City. For my little marginal, and other small cartoons, I use a new pen—the Pelikan Technos.

"It's filled by inserting drawing ink cartridges and has a number (21) of interchangeable points. The Ultraflex pen, by the way, is filled with a dropper which comes with it. So, with these two pens, I can carry my studio in my jacket pocket. I have no favorites among pencils. Strathmore is a good paper. You need enough thickness so your cartoons aren't folded in the mail. I never use a brush except to fill in large spaces of black.

"I believe in the sketch as the final form of art—the spontaneity of the drawing—when you have to pencil and ink, you lose a lot of this spontaneity. I often do cartoons containing hundreds of figures and I start right in with ink. . . ."[1]

An avid traveller, Aragonés believes that cartoonists should be aware of many kinds of humor from other parts of the world. "The more the cartoonist knows about anything, the better he can get. If you know everything that's happening around, and how everything looks, when you do a cartoon about a foreign country, you know what you're doing."[1]

Besides having an awareness of the different kinds of humor in the world, Aragonés believes that cartoonists should be educated, and advises would-be cartoonists to first receive a well-rounded education. "Get a good college education in all subjects. I have very fixed ideas about culture. If you put all your time on the technical aspects of becoming an artist, you may neglect your general education and then you will always have to draw just what people tell you to do.

"An artist should be a creator also. Read—complete a course in literature—develop a good culture and then you can be a writer-artist. Study everything—music, art—get everything you can in all subjects. You have your whole life to be a cartoonist—get the education first. Then you'll know how to communicate ideas to a wider public. If you have just an elementary education, your work will reflect this and your cartoons will be mediocre for only basic people.

"With a thorough education, you can reach the total range of people—any level—sophisticated magazines, those which are distributed internationally, etc. A cartoonist does cartoons of what he knows—if he knows very little, then he does cartoons

(From "A Mad Look at...Air Travel" in *Mad* by Sergio Aragonés. Illustrated by the author.)

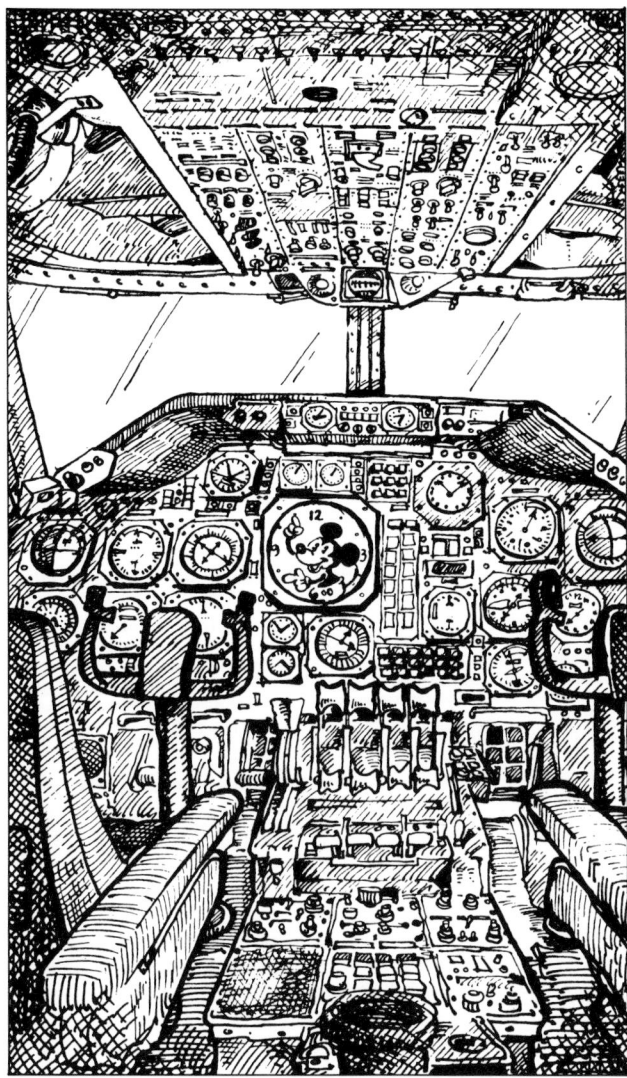

(From "A Mad Look at...Air Travel" in *Mad* by Sergio Aragonés. Illustrated by the author.)

about very little. If you want to do cartoons about psychiatrists and you don't know anything about the profession, how can you do them? You'll wind up doing just what you've heard about psychiatrists—you'll be copying another cartoonist's cartoons—just doing cliches. A cartoonist doesn't have to go to art school—the majority of people don't care about the style of the cartoon—the *idea* is what counts."[1]

HOBBIES AND OTHER INTERESTS: Pantomime, traveling, sailing, and scuba diving.

FOR MORE INFORMATION SEE: Cartoonist Profiles, Volume 2, number 7, August, 1970; Nick Meglin, *The Art of Humorous Illustration,* Watson-Guptill, 1973; Maurice Horn, editor, *The World Encyclopedia of Comics,* Volume 1, Chelsea House, 1976.

Still sits the school-house by the road,
   A ragged beggar sleeping;
Around it still the sumachs grow
   And blackberry-vines are creeping.
               —John Greenleaf Whittier

BACON, Josephine Dodge (Daskam) 1876-1961
(Josephine Dodge Daskam; Ingraham Lovell)

PERSONAL: Born February 17, 1876, in Stamford, Conn.; died July 29, 1961; daughter of Horace Sawyer and Anne (Loring) Daskam; married Selden Bacon (a lawyer), July 25, 1903 (died July 25, 1946); children: Anne, Deborah, Selden, Jr. *Education:* Smith College, B.A., 1898. *Religion:* Episcopalian.

CAREER: Writer. Member of Girl Scout National Executive Board, 1914-24; public health worker. Participant in amateur theatricals. *Wartime service:* Broadcaster for recruiting and salvage campaigns and writer of war slogans and special articles for Writers War Board, 1941-44. *Member:* Onteora Club (founder and curator of collection, "A Hundred Years of American Art"), Colony Club, Women's Cosmopolitan Club.

JOSEPHINE DODGE BACON

Awards, honors: League of Nations Association prize, 1935, for "Hymn of the Nations."

WRITINGS—Juvenile: (Under name Josephine Dodge Daskam) *Sister's Vocation, and Other Girls' Stories,* Scribner, 1900; *Ten to Seventeen: A Boarding-School Diary,* Harper, 1908; *While Caroline Was Growing,* Macmillan, 1911; *Luck of Lowry* (illustrated by Joan Esley), Longmans, Green, 1931; *The Girl at the Window* (illustrated by Clara Elsene Peck), Appleton, 1934; *The Room on the Roof: A Mystery Novel for Girls* (illustrated by C. E. Peck), Appleton, 1935; *Girl Wanted!* (illustrated by C. E. Peck), Appleton, 1936.

Fiction; under name Josephine Dodge Daskam; reprints under name Josephine Dodge Bacon: *Smith College Stories,* Scribner, 1900, reprinted, Books for Libraries, 1969; *Fables for the Fair,* Scribner, 1901, new edition (illustrated by Robert Tallon), Holt, 1968; *The Imp and the Angel* (illustrated by Bernard J. Rosenmeyer), Scribner, 1901, reprinted, Books for Libraries, 1969; *The Madness of Philip, and Other Tales of Childhood* (illustrated by F. Y. Cory), McClure, Phillips, 1902, reprinted, Books for Libraries, 1969; *Whom the Gods Destroyed,* Scribner, 1902, reprinted, Books for Libraries, 1970; *Middle Aged Love Stories,* Scribner, 1903, reprinted, Books for Libraries, 1971; *Her Fiancé: Four Stories of College Life* (illustrated by Elizabeth Shippen Green), Altemus, 1904, re-

THE TALL, GAUNT, SILENT WOMAN . . . STRIDING THROUGH THE PASTURES

Hester had never guessed it, never in fact turned her back when once started. ■ (From *Margarita's Soul: The Romantic Recollections of a Man of Fifty* by Ingraham Lovell. Illustrated by J. Scott Williams with Whistler's "butterfly" decoration.)

printed, Books for Libraries, 1970; *The Memoirs of a Baby* (illustrated by F. Y. Cory), Harper, 1904.

Fiction; under name Josephine Daskam Bacon, except as noted: *The Domestic Adventurers,* Scribner, 1907; *An Idyll of All Fools' Day* (illustrated by R. M. Crosby), Dodd, 1908; *In the Border Country* (illustrated by C. E. Peck), Doubleday, 1909, reprinted, Books for Libraries, 1970; (under pseudonym Ingraham Lovell) *Margarita's Soul: The Romantic Recollections of a Man of Fifty* (illustrated by J. Scott Williams), Lane, 1909; *The Biography of a Boy* (illustrated by Rose O'Neill), Harper, 1910.

The Inheritance, Appleton, 1912; *The Luck o' Lady Joan: A Fairy Tale for Women* (illustrated by C. E. Williams), F. G. Browne, 1913; *The Strange Cases of Dr. Stanchon,* Appleton, 1913; *To-day's Daughter* (illustrated by C. D. Williams), Appleton, 1914; *Open Market* (illustrated by A. I. Keller), Appleton, 1915; *The Twilight of the Gods,* Kennerly, 1915; *On Our Hill* (illustrated by T. M. Bevans and M. T. Bevans), Scribner, 1918; *Square Peggy,* Appleton, 1919; *Blind Cupid,* Appleton, 1923; *Medusa's Head,* Appleton, 1926; *Counterpoint,* John Day, 1927; *Kathy* (illustrated by J. Esley), Longmans, Green, 1934; *The House by the Road* (illustrated by Harvé Stein), Appleton, 1937; *Cassie-on-the-Job* (illustrated by Harley Ennis Stivers), Appleton, 1937; *The Root and the Flower,* Appleton, 1939; *The Door in the Closet,* Viking, 1940; *The World in His Heart,* Appleton, 1941.

Poems: (Editor, under name Josephine Dodge Daskam) *The Best Nonsense Verses,* Lord, 1901; (under name Josephine Dodge Daskam) *Poems,* Scribner, 1903; *Truth o' Women: Last Words from Ladies Long Vanished,* Appleton, 1923.

Author of lyrics of "Hymn for the Nations," and "Processional of the Seven Nations." Contributor of articles, stories, and poems to magazines, including *Collier's, Harper's Bazaar, Ladies' Home Journal, American Girl,* and *Saturday Evening Post.* Compiler of *Girl Scout National Handbook,* 1920.

SIDELIGHTS: **February 17, 1876.** Born in Stamford, Conn. "When I was thirteen, my life, like everybody's, as I supposed, was divided into two compartments—the things I wanted to do, and the things I had to do. There seemed to be no connection between the two, and I don't remember that it ever occurred to me that there might be.

"Wherever I turned I met a person larger and older than I was, who seemed to have a mania for telling me what to do. If this person talked to me in a church, he was a clergyman; if in a schoolroom, she was a teacher; if at home, they were parents and assorted relatives. They were all quite different from each other, but they had one remarkable resemblance: they were all directly inspired with a profound and exact knowledge of what I ought to do in any and all circumstances. If I wanted any time for my own concerns, it was almost necessary to run directly counter to their advice in order to accomplish anything at all!

"I don't remember, in those days, taking any notice of girls five or ten years older than I. I never seemed to meet them. At school they were the 'old girls,' stuck-up, scornful creatures, whispering and giggling over their own affairs. I don't recall a single instance of asking one of them for advice or sympathy. Children and grown-ups were the only people with whom I dealt.

"It is most interesting to me now to remember that the first use we made of our leisure was to form clubs and societies of our own. They were 'secret societies' with elaborate passwords and mysterious initials. We met in retired spots and elected with great pomp a president, a secretary and a treasurer. We considered eligibles and tempestuously excluded undesirables from our band. We pledged eternal loyalty and deathless devotion to each other and to our 'society.' We consecrated pocket-money to mysterious emblems which we wore around our necks on ribbons, defying the world to interpret them. We proved, in fact, that man is the organizing animal.

"But all the societies withered away and failed. We wondered why, and energetically formed new ones; but it was no use, for they withered and failed in their turn. We thought it was because the girls were horrid or the meeting-places unfortunate or the dues too much or too little. I know now that none of these was the reason.

"I know better than the grown-ups of my own day, who used to ask impatiently, when I held forth at length on the tiresomeness and nondependability of the other girls, 'Well, but what do you have these clubs *for,* anyway? What do you *do?*. The trouble with you is, you want to boss everything!'

"I know better than to criticize any young people in this way, because, though the criticism in all its parts is and was perfectly just, it is not very constructive or helpful. There *wasn't* any real reason for our clubs and societies, except the great, fundamental need for 'gang' amusement, for some kind of cooperation with our equals which didn't depend on those arbiters of our destiny, the home, the school and the church. We *hadn't* anything to do, and we didn't know how to invent anything. We wanted a thing of our own and a good time, but we had no skeleton of occupation to build on and we had no leader. I *did* 'want to boss everything': there are just so many natural bosses in the world and they begin young. But I didn't know how. The spirit of leadership is a more complicated thing among girls than anything that the boys' gang-tyrant ever confronts, and whether this is rooted in a fundamental difference between the sexes or the mere lack of training in teamwork among women, the fact remains that infinitely more tact is needed in dealing with so many individualists. But as a self-imposed leader I could not hold them." [Josephine Daskam

Bacon, "When I was a Little Girl," *The Delineator,* November, 1921.[1]]

While attending Smith College in the late 1890s, Bacon contributed articles to magazines. Two years after graduation, in 1900, she had her first literary success with the publication of *Smith College Stories.* Almost every year, from 1900 to 1960, saw her work published. She was a versatile writer, producing stories for young children, poetry, a number of Girl Scout books and other stories for girls, adult novels, comedy and satire.

In 1903 Bacon married lawyer Selden Bacon. The couple had three children. She continued to write and work on community projects after her marriage, managing a family and household in Westchester, New York. She was an ardent spokeswoman for the education of women in home economics. "The only 'cause' which interests me at all in connection with women is the systematic education for duties and responsibilities inevitably assumed by the great majority of them. I firmly believe that the result of such education, insisted upon in public and private schools and colleges, would eliminate the over-whelmingly greater part of the domestic service problem in this country, and would, moreover, allow women time and excuse for dealing with the socialistic, politic and economic sides of the question, their attempts to settle which at present appear to me premature. I am quite convinced that many of the greatest problems in the country—the liquor question, child labor, factory questions, all manner of working-girl reforms, public health, and ultimately, of course, good government—will be completely, or at any rate largely, solved by the training of one generation of women, of all classes, for the complicated duties they now assume without the preparation of the average milliner's apprentice for her trade. I know of no profession or trade open to either sex which requires the versatility, poise, judgment, self-control, imagination and physical endurance, combined, required of the administrator of the average family; and until the training of such administrators is regarded seriously, all attempts at correcting the enormous evils resulting from the neglect so to train them must be, and should be, only slightly and sporadically successful." [Josephine Daskam Bacon, "A Question of Values," *Good Housekeeping Magazine,* October, 1911.[2]]

I'll begin directly," Aunt Emma interposed. ■ (From *The Memoirs of a Baby* by Josephine Daskam. Illustrated by F. Y. Cory.)

From 1914 to 1924, Bacon was an active member of the National Girl Scout Executive Committee, edited the *Girl Scout Magazine* (now the *American Girl* magazine), and also edited the official handbooks of the Girl Scouts. ''I do not know the number of American girls whose parents can afford to give them six weeks of open-air life every year under such pleasant older sisters, but I do know that there are one hundred and seven thousand girls in the United States who want just such help for fifty-two weeks of every year. They are the Girl Scouts, and I have seen them grow from six thousand to nearly twenty times that number in a few years. They call their 'counselors' captains, and lieutenants, and if they could be sure of ten thousand good ones to-day, I think that they would be represented in every town of America, as they are now in every State!

''The hikes, the swims, the First-Aid drills, the badges for domestic accomplishments, the important little business meetings, the fascinating outdoor cookery, the honors for excellence of every kind, the outlet for applied patriotism, the responsibilities and dignities of civic welfare work, all appeal to the girl and stimulate her sense of power and responsibility.''[1]

When asked how she managed to combine her housekeeping profession with her writing profession, Bacon responded: ''. . . There is but one answer: system. If any woman answers otherwise she is untruthful or incredibly ignorant of her own business. It is quite unimportant which system be employed: it is quite unimportant whether the system be inherited, or taught in a college of household economy, or evolved through a bitter experience; it is quite unimportant whether or not the system appears consistent or valuable to an outsider: what is important is that there should be a system. And if you look carefully, you will always find it.

''Mind you, I do not say that the woman herself must understand and apply the system by which her household is maintained; far from it. I have one friend who fills her large leisure with what appear to me to be the most fatiguing and unprofitable schemes. I never meet her that she has not embarked in some new line of work, each quite distinct from what seem to me to be her natural duties. When I ask her why she does these things, she says: 'Why, one must do something! The house runs itself and I have so much energy.'

''Now of course it is perfectly obvious to any practical person that a large country house miles from a station emphatically does *not* 'run itself.' It couldn't. No architect has ever included the necessary mechanism for that in his blue prints, nor will Mr. Edison ever invent it. So I cast about for an explanation, and found it. It was very simple: the servants ran the house. They ran it pretty well, too, and they were delighted to do it, as they were all overpaid and quite unquestioned. And the butler had evolved a very good system, as indeed he was forced to do, in order to get any leisure for himself. Anyone in such a position who wants any leisure will evolve a system, and if he or she is an able person, will enforce it. For without the system there will be no leisure. Whether one employs the leisure thus gained in writing for the magazines or playing auction bridge is greatly a matter of choice.

''. . . Housekeeping, if it is anything, is a combination of providing food and all supplies; sanitation and cleanliness; accurate accounts; and the hiring, discipline and dismissal of servants. . . . The professional-domestic woman must be ready

Dr. Boskowitz was wonderfully interesting. ■ (From *The Biography of a Boy* by Josephine Daskam Bacon. Illustration by Rose O'Neill.)

to do what, as a matter of fact, she has always done—a little of her own work and a great deal of other people's!''[2]

During the course of her writing profession Bacon experimented with many literary genres: short story, poetry, mystery, comedy, and satire. She wrote fiction for both adults and children, and in the majority of cases, her central characters were women.

In some ways Bacon's work foreshadows that of present-day feminist writers, since many of her stories deal with women seeking a place for themselves in a male-dominated world. Cassie, for example, in *Cassie-on-the-Job,* is faced with the challenge of earning a living after the death of her father. The heroine of *Kathy* is a college girl making her way by working in a tearoom, and the girls in *Domestic Adventurers* pursue single lives while sharing a Greenwich Village apartment. Both *In the Border Country* and *The Root and the Flower* take serious looks at the female role as they trace the lives and attitudes of different generations of American women.

Bacon's books are by no means all serious. Many of her plots have the added element of mystery, and she has written tongue-in-cheek fables, rhymes, and satires. Her book *The Memoirs of a Baby,* for example, is a satire on child care which became a national best seller.

In 1935 Bacon won the League of Nations Association prize for an international hymn by an American poet. Her song, ''Hymn for the Nations,'' was written to the first sixteen bars of Beethoven's ''Ode to Joy.'' During World War II she was a broadcaster and a writer of war slogans and articles for the Writers War Board.

For many years Bacon lived in New York City, spending summers in the Catskills. She enjoyed rural life, with farming and outdoor sports occupying her leisure time.

Making a collar of kisses. ■ (From *The Biography of a Boy* by Josephine Daskam Bacon. Illustrated by Rose O'Neill.)

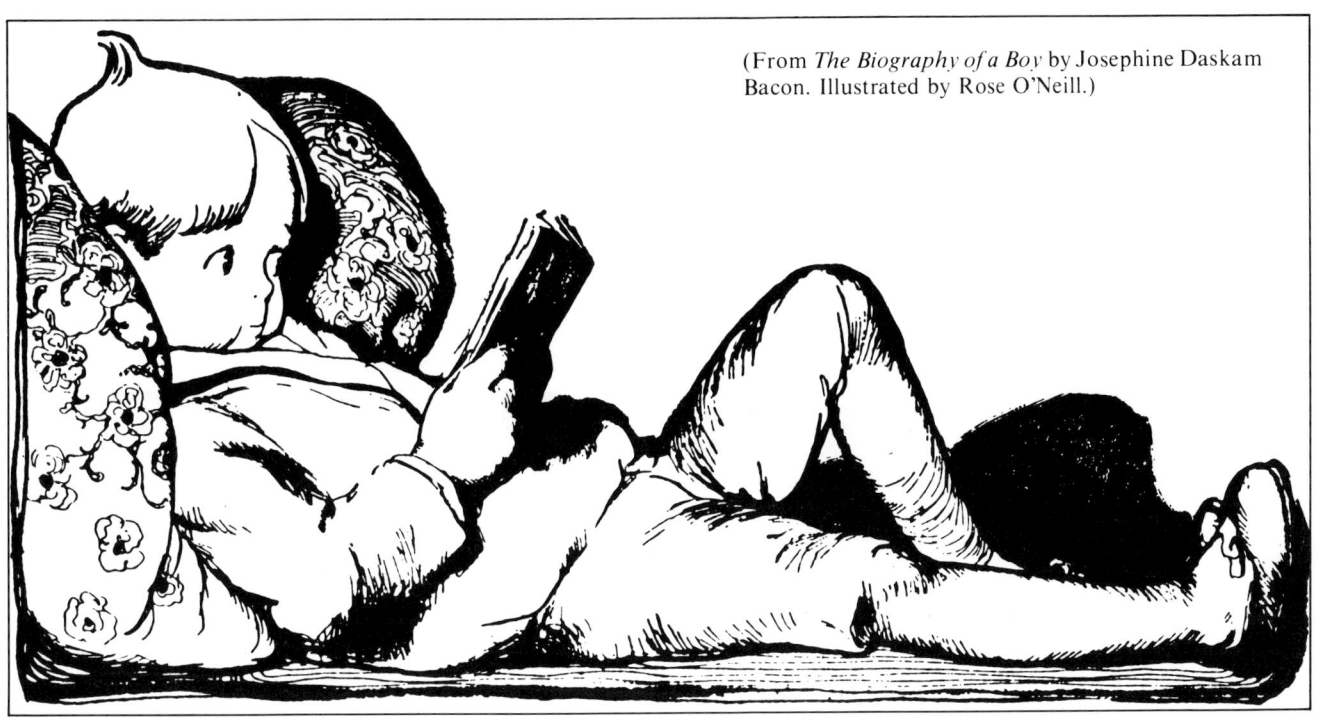

(From *The Biography of a Boy* by Josephine Daskam Bacon. Illustrated by Rose O'Neill.)

She died on **July 29, 1961** at the age of eighty-four. "... In my judgment, the more important to the scheme of this world a person is, the less that person can do as he pleases."[2]

HOBBIES AND OTHER INTERESTS: Farming, outdoor sports, stock breeding, amateur dramatics, music.

FOR MORE INFORMATION SEE: Good Housekeeping Magazine, October, 1911; *The Delineator,* November, 1921; Stanley J. Kunitz and Howard Haycraft, editors, *Twentieth Century Authors,* H. W. Wilson, 1942. Obituaries: *New York Times,* July 31, 1961; *Publishers Weekly,* August 28, 1961.

BANG, Betsy (Garrett) 1912-

PERSONAL: Born July 9, 1912, in South Carolina; daughter of Francis Walton (a tax expert) and Estelle (Edwards) Garrett; married Frederik Barry Bang (a physician and professor), June 1, 1940; children: Caroline Bang Moyer, Molly Garrett Bang-Campbell, Axel F. II. *Education:* George Washington University, B.A., 1933; Johns Hopkins University, diploma in Art, 1937. *Politics:* Independent Democrat. *Religion:* Episcopal. *Home:* 76 Lillie Rd., Woods Hole, Mass. 02543. *Office:* Marine Biological Laboratory, Woods Hole, Mass. 02543.

CAREER: American Museum of Natural History, New York City, illustrator in comparative anatomy, 1935-37; associated with New York Postgraduate Medical School, New York City, 1938-40; Johns Hopkins University, Baltimore, Md., research associate in pathobiology, 1958-85, worked at Center for Medical Research, Calcutta, India, 1962-74. Associated with Macausland Orthopedic Clinic, 1938-40. Past president of Maryland Prisoners Aid Association. Member of Baltimore Criminal

BETSY BANG

Justice Commission, police commissioner's advisory panel, and Health and Welfare Council. *Member:* American Association for the Advancement of Science, Marine Biological Association, Maryland Mental Health Association.

WRITINGS—Translator and adapter: *The Old Woman and the Red Pumpkin: A Bengali Folktale* (illustrated by daughter, Molly Garrett Bang), Macmillan, 1976; *The Old Woman and the Rice Thief: Adapted from a Bengali Folktale* (illustrated by M. G. Bang), Greenwillow, 1977; *Tuntuni the Tailorbird: Adapted from a Bengali Folktale* (illustrated by M. G. Bang), Greenwillow, 1978; *The Cucumber Stem: Adapted from a Bengali Folktale* (illustrated by Tony Chen), Greenwillow, 1979; *The Demons of Rajpur: Five Tales from Bengal* (illustrated by M. G. Bang), Greenwillow, 1980. Contributor of about fifty articles to scientific journals.

SIDELIGHTS: Bang received her B.A. from George Washington University and a diploma in Art as Applied to Medicine from Johns Hopkins University. She became a free-lance surgical illustrator, an illustrator in comparative anatomy, and was a research associate in pathology at Johns Hopkins University until 1985. With her husband, Frederik Bang, a physician, Bang worked at the Center for Medical Research in Calcutta from 1962 to 1974. "We became interested in effects of malnutrition on respiratory infections and worked on these interactions in a program in India directed by my physician husband." [Sally Holmes Holtze, editor, *Fifth Book of Junior Authors and Illustrators,* H. W. Wilson, 1983.[1]]

Bang's interest in "folk literature and art as representative of the historic roots of current beliefs and social attitudes" led her to translating and adapting several children's folktales from Bengali. Several of her books have been illustrated by her daughter Molly Garrett Bang. In Calcutta "we all responded to the magic of story time at dusk when lamps are lit and shadows cloak innumerable beings that are perfectly believable.

"Bengali is one of the most beautiful, expressive and musical of languages and, like all non-mother-tongue languages, is best learned by nursery rhymes and folktales. At first I translated them for sheer fun, and later as vehicles for Molly's sketches of Bengal village life in all its age-old talent for making simple tasks graceful and common implements beautiful."[1]

FOR MORE INFORMATION SEE: Sally Holmes Holtze, editor, *Fifth Book of Junior Authors and Illustrators,* H. W. Wilson, 1983.

BARKHOUSE, Joyce 1913-

BRIEF ENTRY: Born May 3, 1913, in Woodville, Nova Scotia, Canada. Educated at Dalhousie University and the Thomas Moore Institute, Barkhouse taught at elementary schools in Nova Scotia and Montreal until 1966. She had begun contributing articles, short stories, and poems to textbooks, anthologies and periodicals in the 1930s. According to Barkhouse, her first two juvenile biographies reflect her desire "to help Canadian children to know themselves and their country—to give them a sense of identity." A lack of ready information drove her to write *George Dawson: The Little Giant* (Clarke, Irwin, 1974), about the Canadian geologist who contributed to the mapping of Canada and became director of the Geological Survey of Canada in 1895. *Saturday Night* observed: "Children will respond sympathetically to the ravages of

George's childhood illness and thrill to his recovery. They'll feel sad about his resulting hunchback, but exuberant about his scholastic prizes and his contributions to the mapping of this country."

Similarly, *Abraham Gesner* (Fitzhenry & Whiteside, 1980) resulted from Barkhouse's desire to know more about the native Nova Scotian who invented the process for making kerosene. Her third biography, *A Name for Himself: A Biography of Thomas Head Raddall* (Irwin, 1986) was written for classroom use at the junior high school level. Barkhouse also writes fiction, such as *The Witch of Port LaJoye* (Ragweed Press, 1983), the eighteenth-century legend of a healing stone, a serpent, and a beautiful girl who was arrested as a heretic and burned at the stake. Barkhouse collaborated with her niece, Margaret Atwood, on the children's story *Anna's Pet* (Lorimer, 1980), which was reissued as a reader for first and second graders. *Residence:* Halifax, Nova Scotia, Canada.

FOR MORE INFORMATION SEE: K. A. Hamilton, editor, *Canada Writes!,* Writers' Union of Canada, 1977; *Contemporary Authors,* Volumes 93-96, Gale, 1980; Irma McDonough, editor, *Profiles 2,* Canadian Library Association, 1982; *Quill & Quire,* May, 1986.

BARNHART, Clarence L(ewis) 1900-

PERSONAL: Born December 30, 1900, near Plattsburg, Mo.; son of Franklin Chester (a farmer) and Frances (a housewife; maiden name, Eliot) Barnhart; married Frances Knox, February 21, 1931; children: Robert K., David K. *Education:*
University of Chicago, Ph.B., 1930, graduate study, 1934-37. *Home:* 26 Latimer Lane, Bronxville, N.Y. 10708. *Office:* 75 Main St., Cold Spring, N.Y. 10516.

CAREER: Scott, Foresman & Co., Chicago, Ill., editor, 1929-45; U.S. War Department, editor, 1943; Random House, New York, N.Y., editor, 1945-48; Clarence L. Barnhart, Inc. (reference books), Bronxville, N.Y., editor and owner, 1948-73; free-lance editor and author of reference books and a magazine, 1974—. Honorary research associate, Institute of Psychological Research, Columbia University, 1945-46.

MEMBER: American Name Society (past president), American Dialect Society, International Linguistic Association, American Association for the Advancement of Science, Linguistic Society of America, Modern Language Association of America, National Council of Teachers of English, University Club (New York City), Century Association (New York City), Authors' Club (London), Phi Beta Kappa. *Awards, honors:* U.S. War Department Certificate of Appreciation, 1946, for *Dictionary of United States Army Terms.*

WRITINGS—Editor, except where indicated: *Thorndike Century Junior Dictionary,* Scott, Foresman, 1935, revised edition (co-author with E. L. Thorndike), published as *Thorndike-Barnhart Junior Dictionary,* Scott, Foresman, 1952; *Thorndike Century Senior Dictionary,* Scott, Foresman, 1941, revised edition (co-author with E. L. Thorndike), published as *Thorndike-Barnhart High School Dictionary,* Scott, Foresman, 1952; *Dictionary of United States Army Terms,* U.S. Government Printing Office, 1943; *Thorndike Century Beginning Dictionary,* Scott, Foresman, 1945; *American College Dictionary,* Random House, 1947.

CLARENCE L. BARNHART

Thorndike-Barnhart Comprehensive Desk Dictionary, Double-day, 1951; *Thorndike-Barnhart Handy Pocket Dictionary,* Doubleday, 1951; *New Century Cyclopedia of Names,* 3 volumes, Appleton, 1954; *New Century Handbook of English Literature,* Appleton, 1956; *Thorndike-Barnhart Concise Dictionary,* Scott, Foresman, 1956; *Thorndike-Barnhart Advanced Junior Dictionary,* Scott, Foresman, 1957.

(Editor with Leonard Bloomfield) *Let's Read: A Linguistic Approach,* Wayne State University Press, 1961; (co-author with L. Bloomfield) *Let's Read,* Clarence L. Barnhart, Inc., 9 volumes, 1963-66; *World Book Encyclopedia Dictionary,* Field Enterprises Educational Corp., 1963, revised edition with co-editor, son, Robert K. Barnhart, published as *The World Book Dictionary,* two volumes, 1986.

(Co-author with R. K. Barnhart and S. Steinmetz) *The Barnhart Dictionary of New English Since 1963,* Harper, 1973; (co-author with E. L. Thorndike), *Scott, Foresman Beginning Dictionary,* Scott Foresman, 1976; (co-author with R. K. Barnhart and S. Steinmetz) *The Second Barnhart Dictionary of New English,* 1980. Editor, *The Barnhart Dictionary Companion* (a quarterly record of new words in English), 1982—. Contributor to professional journals, including *Teachers College Record, Language, American Speech,* and *Word.*

WORK IN PROGRESS: Lexicographical papers.

SIDELIGHTS: "My work from the beginning in 1929 until now has been the editing of standard English dictionaries at

(From *Scott, Foresman Beginning Dictionary* by E. L. Thorndike and Clarence L. Barnhart.)

various levels, encyclopedias of names and English literature, and the adapting of Leonard Bloomfield's system of teaching primary reading for use in American schools. My first dictionary (*Thorndike Century Junior Dictionary*) was a fourth-grade dictionary but I have made dictionaries for the entire school system, from third grade through college. I have also made dictionaries for Doubleday, particularly the *Thorndike-Barnhart Comprehensive Desk Dictionary* and *The World Book Dictionary.* My largest dictionary, *The World Book Dictionary,* is a family dictionary with over 250,000 entries. It is made with a graded vocabulary so that the terms looked up by children can be understood.

"In order to keep the dictionaries up to date in later years, I have specialized in the collection of neologisms with the result that I have collected a large and extensive file of the words that have come into the English language that are not now recorded in the dictionaries. Since new words and meanings accumulate at the rate of 10,000 or more a year, I have continued publishing new words in a quarterly magazine instead of in books.

"My work generally has been the explaining of the vocabulary of standard English language for different types of users and the recording of standard English as now used in the periodicals of various countries that use standard English as their first language."

BENHAM, Leslie 1922-

PERSONAL: Surname is pronounced Ben-am; born April 29, 1922, in Cambridge, Galt, Ontario, Canada; son of William Charles and Mabel (Hays) Benham; married Lois Irene Dakin (a writer), July 31, 1950; children: Arlene Alison. *Education:* Attended Galt Collegiate Institute and Vocational School. *Religion:* Presbyterian. *Home:* 14 Hillcrest Dr., Cambridge, Galt, Ontario, Canada N1S 3L5.

CAREER: Babcock & Wilcox Canada Ltd., Cambridge, Ontario, systems analyst, 1947-79. *Military service:* Royal Canadian Air Force, 1942-45, aero engine mechanic; became leading aircraftsman. *Member:* Colour Photographic Association of Canada, Galt Camera Club (president, 1959-60).

WRITINGS: (With wife, Lois Benham) *The Heroine of Long Point* (juvenile), Macmillan of Canada, 1963; (with L. Benham) *Sergeant Stanley* (juvenile historical novel; illustrated by Frank J. O'Connor), Highway Book Shop (Canada), 1980.

WORK IN PROGRESS: An adult romance novel under pseudonym Alda Barron; another adult novel; a juvenile novel.

SIDELIGHTS: "As a young boy in the early 1930s, I lived a block from the limits of Cambridge, Galt, Ontario, a very small city at that time. There were opportunities to explore the nearby tranquil rural countryside, the patches of forest, and the creeks of the Grand River watershed. When I was twelve years old, my father lost his life in an automobile accident, and I spent my studious teen years with my mother and grandmother, trying to fill the role of the man about the house.

"It was during this period that my aging grandmother told me about her big, strong, heroic Aunt Abigail who lived on Long Point and frequently visited my grandmother's family in Port Rowan, Ontario. While I had little interest in writing or history at that time, the stories were later to spark research into the life of Abigail Becker and the history of her time.

LESLIE BENHAM

"In my final year of high school, World War II broke out, and at age twenty I joined the Royal Canadian Air Force to become an aero engine mechanic. It was during this time that a chance encounter exposed me to reporting events for a Royal Canadian Air Force station magazine, my first attempts at writing.

"When the war ended, I resumed my civilian trade as a draftsman, which led to other engineering and business related duties. These covered a period of thirty-four years in the machinery and steam power equipment industries. As those years passed, my wife and I became interested in amateur photography. This led to reporting the bi-monthly activities of the Galt Camera Club for the local newspaper, and writing articles for the *Colour Photographic Association of Canada Photography Journal.*

"In 1962, Macmillan of Canada sponsored a competition for 'budding Canadian authors.' Encouraged by my wife, the old stories of my grandmother's Aunt Abigail evolved into a juvenile book entitled *The Heroine of Long Point.* Inspired by the success of the first novel, we produced two more juvenile book manuscripts, but it was not until April, 1978, that we succeeded in interesting a Canadian publisher, the Highway Book Shop, in publishing *Sergeant Stanley.*

"*Sergeant Stanley* is a tale of two fictitious Canadian boys who lived in Kingston, Ontario, during the incredible War of 1812. Their adventures are set in a background of military action and historical detail encompassing the American naval attack and capture of Fort York in Toronto.

"Both books attempt to document Canadian heritage in a form and at a level suitable for young readers, to make *dry* history most palatable."

HOBBIES AND OTHER INTERESTS: Writing, photography, art, leathercraft and wood carving.

FOR MORE INFORMATION SEE: Canadiana, April, 1963.

BENHAM, Lois (Dakin) 1924-

PERSONAL: Born March 19, 1924, in Cambridge, Galt, Ontario, Canada; daughter of Harry (a plumber and electrician) and Alice E. (Atkinson) Dakin; married Leslie Benham (a systems analyst and writer), July 31, 1950; children: Arlene Alison. *Education:* Attended Galt Collegiate Institute and Vocational School, and Canada Business College, summer, 1946; McMaster University, B.A. (with honors), 1946. *Religion:* Presbyterian. *Home:* 14 Hillcrest Dr., Cambridge, Galt, Ontario, Canada N1S 3L5.

CAREER: McMaster University, Hamilton, Ontario, secretary to director of extension courses, 1946-48; Shurly-Dietrich-Atkins Ltd., secretary, Cambridge, Galt, Ontario, 1948-50. *Member:* Colour Photographic Association of Canada, Galt Camera Club (treasurer 1957-64). *Awards, honors:* Numerous award ribbons in Canadian photographic competitions.

LOIS BENHAM

WRITINGS: (With husband, Leslie Benham) *The Heroine of Long Point* (juvenile), Macmillan of Canada, 1963; (with L. Benham) *Sergeant Stanley* (juvenile historical novel; illustrated by Frank J. O'Connor), Highway Book Shop, 1980. Contributor of "Camera Club News" to *Cambridge Reporter* for several years; also co-author of humorous articles contributed to the *Colour Photographic Association of Canada Photography Journal.*

WORK IN PROGRESS: Editing adult romance novel written by her husband, Leslie Benham.

SIDELIGHTS: "Since childhood I have felt a desire to write books, or songs, or letters—or 'something.' While in public school I wrote a first-person adventure tale, in a make-believe farm setting, about my Boston terrier and her animal and human friends. I still keep that manuscript as a treasure. That was the extent of my youthful writing, other than a few fanciful school essays.

"The desire to write remained through the years, however, and in recent years I enjoyed writing reports of the Galt Camera Club meetings for the local newspapers, as well as co-authoring the whimsical articles for the *Colour Photographic Association of Canada Photography Journal.* The latter usually stemmed from actual incidents, often minor, which happened to us in our photographic endeavors, and then expanded through joint brain-storm sessions in which we exchanged ideas and elaborated on the theme. We shared many good laughs during these sessions, regardless of what our readers may have thought of the finished articles.

"It was an entirely different exercise to capture our amusing ideas in print, requiring tedious work in editing sessions to convey our exact meaning to others.

"In writing *The Heroine of Long Point* and *Sergeant Stanley,* the laborious editing was even more pronounced. My husband would carry out the research, write the rough draft of the story, and then we would spend innumerable, tiring hours of editing together to attain the level of our youthful audience.

"One of the more pleasurable aspects of the research phase for our two books was visiting story locales to mentally capture the mood. In the Port Rowan Library we discovered a tiny book written by Margaret Becker, daughter of Abigail Becker (*The Heroine of Long Point*). Her purpose in writing was to correct several errors in newspaper reports and document the truth about her mother's heroism. Thus we were able to establish authenticity in our story. Before we began writing *Sergeant Stanley,* we visited Kingston and explored the trail followed by the British Army on their march to York.

"Let's hope we never decide to write about an adventure on the moon!"

HOBBIES AND OTHER INTERESTS: "I share my husband's interests in writing, photography (particularly table-top and creative), and oil painting."

FOR MORE INFORMATION SEE: Canadiana, April, 1963.

Three wise men of Gotham
Went to sea in a bowl;
If the bowl had been stronger
My story had been longer.

                      —Mother Goose

BERG, Ron 1952-

PERSONAL: Born April 10, 1952, in Niagara-on-the-Lake, Ontario, Canada; son of John (a chemist in the auto industry) and Susan (a bank loan officer; maiden name, Rempel) Berg; married Josie (an artist and designer), November 20, 1976; children: Jennifer, Christopher. *Education:* Sheridan Community College, Oakville, Ontario, diploma in graphic design, 1972; Ontario College of Art, Toronto, diploma in fine art, 1976. *Home and office:* 71 Hewitt Ave., Toronto, Ontario, Canada M6R 1Y4.

CAREER: Ginn and Co., Toronto, Ontario, in-house artist, 1976—; free-lance illustrator, 1979—. Creator of the poster "Canadian Historical Fiction" for the "Bookmarks and Banners" series published by the Children's Book Centre. *Exhibitions:* Dinsmore Gallery, Toronto, 1982. *Member:* Canadian Society of Children's Authors, Illustrators and Performers, Canadian Association of Photographers and Illustrators in Communications. *Awards, honors: Michi's New Year* was a runner-up for the Amelia Frances Howard-Gibbon Award, 1981.

ILLUSTRATOR: Mary Alice Downie, *The King's Loon,* Kids Can Press, 1979; Mary Hamilton, *The Tin-Lined Trunk,* Kids Can Press, 1980; M. A. Downie and George Rawlyk, *A Proper Acadian,* Kids Can Press, 1980; Shelley Tanaka, *Michi's New Year,* PMA Books, 1980; Geoffrey Bilson, *Goodbye Sarah,* Kids Can Press, 1981; Edward Lear, *The Owl and the Pussycat,* Scholastic-TAB, 1984; Eugene Field, *Wynken, Blynken and Nod,* Scholastic-TAB, 1985.

SIDELIGHTS: Canadian illustrator Ron Berg was born in 1952 in Niagara-on-the-Lake, Ontario. Although they were uncertain that he would be able to support himself as an artist, Berg's parents were always supportive of his career choice. One problem that young Berg had to overcome, however, was the lack of opportunity for art instruction in school. "I was always dabbling in art, I always had an interest in being by myself and working with my hands in some way. I'm an only child and so I got used to being alone a lot of the time. I got my masters in daydreaming.

RON BERG

**The old Moon laughed
and sang a song
As they rocked in the wooden shoe....**

■ (From *Wynken, Blynken and Nod* by Eugene Field. Illustrated by Ron Berg.)

...And were married next day by the Turkey who lives on the hill. ■ (From *The Owl and the Pussycat* by Edward Lear. Illustrated by Ron Berg.)

"There wasn't a peer group interested in what I was doing until I got to college. I was shy, and there weren't many people I could associate with anyway. Because of this, my kind of sensibilities didn't seem to be legitimate. I was doing a balancing act, not knowing where I was supposed to belong. In our high school, art was taught at first by an English teacher and later by the metal shop teacher. It wasn't until the last year that we had an art room and an art teacher."

Berg's first formal art instruction occurred when he enrolled in Saturday morning art classes. He continued his studies at Sheridan Community College in Oakville, Ontario, receiving a diploma in graphic design. "Technically, I learned a great deal at Sheridan. I had decided to take design, because I wasn't sure where I was going. Spiritually it was a high for me. All of a sudden I met lots of people who were interested in what they were doing and what I was doing. All of a sudden I had friends. . . . I could talk to them about sensitive matters."

He continued his art education at Ontario College of Art in Toronto, receiving a diploma in fine art in 1976. After graduation Berg began his art career by free-lancing for magazines, newspapers and a number of educational publishers. Beginning with the illustrations for the historical children's novel *The King's Loon* in 1979, Berg has illustrated a number of books for Canadian publisher Kids Can Press. Working on historical novels has lead Berg to make full use of research for his illustrations. "I dig myself into a library—actually three or four libraries—and I try to get as much information as I can. A lot of the information is scarce, and I'm usually working against a deadline. I probably could spend more time than I'm able to."

Berg's more recent books, *The Owl and the Pussycat* and *Wynken, Blynken and Nod*, are fantasy oriented. "The research I did for these books was of a different nature. In *Wynken, Blynken and Nod* for example, the room in the story is an interpretation of the rooms we have in our house. The flying bed is a recreation of my daughter's bed. The houses that I used in the illustrations are very much like the houses in our neighbourhood. I also used photographs of my daughter, Jennifer, and some of her stuffed animals as models for the main

characters. The visual interpretation of the book was that of a very personal creative process rather than that of one researched at a library.

"I love illustrating stories or poems that have interesting characters and exotic settings. So when Scholastic Publications approached me with the well-loved poem 'The Owl and the Pussycat,' it seemed the perfect vehicle for my interests and style of illustration.

"The first thing I had to do was to set the stage for the two lovers. Together, Scholastic and I decided to make the pea-green boat a magnificent ocean liner. I loved the idea and right away I had visions of beautiful luxury liners floating on the high seas. From then on it was easy to make up the setting. I looked through my reference library and found the Edwardian era to represent the kind of elegant mood I was after. I studied the architecture, furniture and clothing designs. Even the mass consciousness of the Edwardian people seemed to suit the personalities of the Owl and the Pussycat.

"Next came the task of getting all the ideas into an organized visual form. I began by making thumbnail sketches. These are quick illustrative memos where I can jot down my ideas quickly without worrying about detail.

"I then use the thumbnail sketches to develop my roughs. This is when I begin dealing with all the details that I want to introduce into the drawings. Here is where I concern myself with proportion, perspective, layout and design. To create the characters, I searched my mind for all the various personalities I have known in the past. Some are drawn directly from people I've known either personally or through the media, and others are composites improvised from my imagination. As people read the book, they tell me that the characters are all familiar to them. That is what I intended. I do the roughs over and over until I am completely satisfied with them.

"After completing the roughs I trace them onto watercolour paper. Then the painting process begins. I put on colour, layer by layer, until I achieve the depth that makes the characters and scenes come alive. I also use tiny brush strokes to create texture and to further define the images.

"The whole process of producing illustrations is a lot of fun and also a lot of hard work. I find it to be a fully rewarding and invigorating experience."

Working as a free-lance artist produces a special kind of life style. Berg is able to work in his studio at home where he can enjoy time with his family. "Freelancing suits my personality. I enjoy going out to talk to editors and art directors but the bulk of my work is done in my studio where I can be with myself and my creativity."

BESTALL, Alfred (Edmeades) 1892-1986

OBITUARY NOTICE: Born in 1892 in Mandalay, Burma; died January 15, 1986, in Wales. Illustrator, cartoonist, and author, Bestall was best known as the author and illustrator of a popular British comic strip about a bear named Rupert. A longtime feature of the London *Daily Express,* the cartoon was created by Mary Tourtel in 1920. Bestall, who took over the strip in 1935 when Tourtel's failing eyesight forced her to retire, worked on the "Rupert" series for thirty years. Before joining the *Daily Express,* Bestall worked as an illustrator for *Tatler* and *Punch* magazines and drew most of the color cover drawings for *Schoolgirls' Own Annuals* in the 1920s. He wrote and illustrated several works, such as *Boys and Girls Book, Daily Express Rupert Annuals, Rupert Adventure Series, Adventure Books, Rupert Colour Library,* and collaborated with writer George Perry on *A Bear's Life: Rupert.* In addition, Bestall provided illustrations for more than fifty books, including *Myths and Legends of Many Lands, The Spanish Goldfish,* and *Folk Tales of Wales.*

FOR MORE INFORMATION SEE: Who's Who in Art, 20th edition, Art Trade Press, 1982; *Twentieth-Century Children's Writers,* St. Martin's, 1983. *Obituaries: Facts on File,* January 24, 1986.

BEZENCON, Jacqueline (Buxcel) 1924-

PERSONAL: Born January 4, 1924, in Romainmôtiers, Vaud, Switzerland; daughter of Raymond (a teacher) and Nelly (Zahnd) Buxcel; married Paul Bezencon (a painter and art teacher), November 23, 1946; children: Philippe, Nicolas. *Education:* Ecole Cantonale des Beaux-Arts, Lausanne, Switzerland, diploma, 1945. *Home:* En Cuvillard, 1302 Vufflens-la-Ville, Lausanne, Switzerland.

CAREER: Painter and illustrator. Teacher of painting and drawing, 1954—; *Mon Ami Pierrot* (children's magazine), Lausanne, Switzerland, illustrator, 1972-84. Book illustrator for publishers Pierrot, Lusanne, Switzerland, 1980-82, and for Ipomee, Moulins, France, 1985. *Exhibitions:* F. de Bologna, Italy, 1975, 1976, 1977; La Chaux-De-Fonds, 1978; Sion, Switzerland, 1979; Lausanne, Switzerland, 1980, 1986; Geneva, Switzerland, 1982; Delémont, Switzerland, 1983; Porrentruy, Switzerland, 1983; Vevey, Switzerland, 1983; Lyon, France, 1985; Moutreux, Switzerland, 1986.

ILLUSTRATOR: Ghislaine Vautier, *Quand brillant les etoiles,* Pierrot (Switzerland), 1980, published as *The Shining Stars: Greek Legends of the Zodiac,* adapted by Kenneth McLeish, Cambridge University Press, 1981; G. Vautier, *Les lois du*

JACQUELINE BEZENCON

ciel, Pierrot, 1982, published as *The Way of the Stars,* adapted by K. McLeish, Cambridge University Press, 1982; Ulrike Blatter, *Les trois cognées: d'après fable d'Esope* (title means "The Three Axes: Aesop's Fable"), Ipomee (France), 1985.

SIDELIGHTS: "Teaching art is an exchange. I like to teach painting and drawing. I especially appreciate the sensitivity and the effort of which the students are capable. I finally chose to draw and to paint for children because it is a gratifying exchange of feelings and perceptions. I graduated from the Cantonale School of Fine Arts in Lausanne (Switzerland) and I have been teaching basic drawing and painting classes with great pleasure for the past thirty years. I have collaborated on a children's magazine *Mon Ami Pierrot.*

"The things that I did not have time to teach my own children when they were little, I would love to convey to other children. I was seduced by the modest aspect of illustration. My aim is to communicate tenderness, poetry, joy, and my own passion for colors.

"My ambition is to be able to illustrate popular fairy tales, fables, and especially to work with contemporary authors with whom I could collaborate.

"My last work, *Les trois cognées,* based on an Aesop fable, allowed me to use a forest as a frame for the story. I wanted

(From an unpublished work, "Allan Is Gone." Illustrated by Jacqueline Bezencon.)

to make children aware of the great beauty of the forests. Will I be able to accomplish this? (Today the death of many forests is a problem.) With a lot of talent, the children's writer Ulrike Blatter developed and composed this fable. Our collaboration was perfect. To continue being creative under those ideal conditions is a dream.

"My techniques are classical: pen, charcoal, china ink, gouache paint, and other techniques for colors."

HOBBIES AND OTHER INTERESTS: Fine arts, history of art, literature, music.

FOR MORE INFORMATION SEE: Catalogue des illustrateurs Suisse, Foire du Livre (Bologna), 1975, 1976, 1977.

BLY, Robert W(ayne) 1957-

BRIEF ENTRY: Born July 21, 1957, in Paterson, N.J. A freelance copywriter and industrial and high-tech advertising consultant, Bly also writes technical "how-to" books for adults and children on such topics as computers, advertising, and writing. Bly earned a B.S. degree from the University of Rochester and is a member of the American Institute of Chemical Engineers and Business/Professional Advertising Association. Both fiction and nonfiction, his juvenile books include *A Dictionary of Computer Words* (Banbury, 1983), *Ronald's Dumb Computer* (Standish, 1983), the story of two teenagers' attempt to program a robot to do tasks like cleaning their rooms and doing their homework, and *Computers: Pascal, Pac-Man, and Pong* (Banbury, 1984). Of *Computers: Cookies, Marbles, and Games* (Banbury, 1984), which explains data bases to elementary-school children, *School Library Journal* noted: "This

slight, appealing book, with its fun illustrations, makes the complex topic of computers understandable and interesting."

With Gary Blake, Bly co-authored *Technical Writing: Structure, Standards, and Style* (McGraw, 1982), *How to Promote Your Own Business* (New American Library, 1983), and *Dream Jobs: A Guide to Tomorrow's Top Careers* (Wiley, 1983). *Dream Jobs* profiles nine careers such as computers, employee training and development, biotechnology, advertising, and public relations and describes the nature of the work, training, qualifications, and sources of information for each. Bly's solo works include *The Personal Computer in Advertising: Using Technology to Increase Creativity* (Banbury, 1984), and *The Copywriter's Handbook: A Step-by-Step Guide to Writing Copy That Sells* (Dodd, 1985). Bly also contributes articles to magazines including *Business Marketing, Chemical Engineering, Cosmopolitan,* and *Direct Marketing. Home and office:* 174 Holland Ave., New Milford, N.J. 07646.

FOR MORE INFORMATION SEE: Contemporary Authors, Volume 117, Gale, 1986.

BONESTELL, Chesley 1888-1986

OBITUARY NOTICE: Born in 1888; died June 11, 1986, in Carmel, Calif. Architect, artist, illustrator, and author. A successful architect who helped design the Golden Gate Bridge, Bonestell developed an interest in astronomy and later turned to painting astral scenes. Bonestell illustrated numerous articles for magazines such as *Colliers, Life, Look,* and *Scientific American.* He also worked as a matte artist in Hollywood, where he created special effects and background paintings for such motion pictures as "Citizen Kane," "War of the Worlds," "When Worlds Collide," and "Swiss Family Robinson." Among his most notable art works is a forty-foot mural of "A Trip to the Moon," completed in 1957 and exhibited in museums and observatories around the United States.

Collaborating with rocket pioneer Wernher von Braun and science writer Willie Ley in 1949, Bonestell illustrated the book *Conquest in Space,* which, according to the *Los Angeles Times,* is "still considered a perfect pattern for the melding of science and art." The three men also worked together on *Beyond the Solar System* and *The Exploration of Mars.* In addition, Bonestell published *Beyond Jupiter: The Worlds of Tomorrow* with Arthur C. Clarke, the author of *2001: A Space Odyssey. The Solar System,* a children's book which first appeared in 1961, was both written and illustrated by Bonestell.

Highly esteemed in his field, Bonestell received numerous awards for his achievements. He became an inspiration to many astronomers and scientists; well-known astronomer and author Carl Sagan attributed his own fascination with the cosmos to the artist "whose early paintings did so much to convey that other worlds are places in some sense like our own." Paying tribute to his work, the international Planetary Society of Pasadena named an asteroid after Bonestell prior to his death.

FOR MORE INFORMATION SEE: Space World, December, 1985; *Encyclopedia of Science Fiction: An Illustrated A to Z,* Grenada, 1979. Obituaries: *Los Angeles Times,* June 26, 1986; *Facts on File,* July 11, 1986.

The one real object of education is to have a man in the condition of continually asking questions.
—Bishop Mandell Creighton

BONNERS, Susan

BRIEF ENTRY: Born in Lake Hiawatha, N.J. A children's book illustrator and author, Bonners learned to draw from her mother, a commercial artist, and later studied illustration in New York City. *Panda* (Delacorte, 1978), the first picture book she wrote as well as illustrated, describes the eating, sleeping, growth, and mating habits of the panda in poetic, hand-lettered text. Bonners illustrated the book in shades of blue watercolor, using blurred edges to create soft pictures. The same style enhances *A Penguin Year* (Delacorte, 1981), which received the American Book Award for children's non-fiction in 1982. This book focuses on the life cycle of the penguin, specifically the mating, nest-building, and raising of the young of Brush-tail and his mate, Scarred Wing.

In a review of Joanne Ryder's *Inside Turtle's Shell, and Other Poems of the Field* (Macmillan, 1985), *Booklist* observed: "Bonners' soft, exquisite pencil drawings show us the world through a mist, suggesting how a forest appears to a turtle, or tall grass to a leaping mouse. . . ." Bonners depicts mountain and forest scenes with soft-edged black-and-white illustrations in James R. Newton's *Rain Shadow* (Crowell, 1983). She also has illustrated Seymour Simon's *Animals in Your Neighborhood* (Walker & Co., 1976), an edition of Robert Louis Stevenson's *A Child's Garden of Verses* (Western Publishers, 1978), Newton's *A Forest Is Reborn* (Crowell, 1982), Louise Fitzhugh's *I Am Four* (Delacorte, 1982), Barbara J. Esbensen's *Cold Stars and Fireflies: Poems of the Four Seasons* (Crowell, 1984), and others. *Residence:* Brooklyn, New York.

BRADFORD, Karleen   1936-

PERSONAL: Born December 16, 1936, in Toronto, Ontario, Canada; daughter of Karl H. (an accountant) and Eileen (a housewife; maiden name, Ney) Scott; married James C. Bradford (a Canadian foreign service officer) August 22, 1959; children: Donald, Kathleen, Christopher. *Education:* University of Toronto, B.A., 1959. *Home:* Blumenaustrasse 14, 5300 Bonn 2, Federal Republic of Germany.

CAREER: T. Eaton Co., Toronto, Ontario, advertising copywriter, 1959; West Toronto Young Women's Christian Association, Toronto, Ontario, social worker, 1959-63; writer, 1963—. *Member:* Writers Union of Canada (curriculum chairperson, 1984-85), Canadian Authors Association, Canadian Society of Children's Authors, Illustrators and Performers, PEN. *Awards, honors:* Grant from Ontario Arts Council, 1977; first prize in juvenile writing from Canadian Authors Association, 1978, for short story "A Wish about Freckles"; first prize from CommCept Canadian KiddLit Competition, 1980, for novel *The Other Elizabeth;* Canada Council grant, 1983 and 1985.

WRITINGS—For young people; all novels: *A Year for Growing* (illustrated by Charles Hilder), Scholastic-TAB, 1977, revised edition published as *Wrong Again, Robbie,* 1983; *The Other Elizabeth* (illustrated by Deborah Drew-Brook), Gage, 1982; *I Wish There Were Unicorns* (illustrated by Greg Ruhl), Gage, 1983; *The Stone in the Meadow* (illustrated by G. Ruhl),

KARLEEN BRADFORD

Gage, 1984; *The Haunting at Cliff House,* Scholastic-TAB, 1985; *The Nine Days Queen,* Scholastic-TAB, 1986.

Work represented in anthologies, including *Beyond Belief,* Clarke, Irwin, 1980; *Starting Points in Reading,* Ginn, 1981; *Barefoot Island,* Ginn, 1982. Editor of *Our Books in the Curriculum,* three volumes, Writers' Union of Canada, 1985, and of the *Canadian Authors Association Newsletter,* Ottawa Branch, 1984-85. Contributor to magazines, including *Cricket, Canadian Children's Magazine, Jabberwocky,* and *Instructor,* and to newspapers. Editor of *American College Women's Newsletter,* Manila, Philippines, 1978-79.

ADAPTATIONS: "The Other Elizabeth" (record), Talking Books for the Blind (Canada), 1985.

WORK IN PROGRESS: A book set on a small lighthouse island, amongst the inshore fishermen and their families of the southern Nova Scotia coast, tentatively titled *The Tide Will Rise.*

SIDELIGHTS: "Because of my husband's career, I have spent the last twenty-three years of my life travelling from country to country—an experience that has proven to be wonderfully stimulating for me both as a person and as a writer. We have lived in Southeast Asia, South America, England, and now Germany. Probably the country which has had the most influence on my writing, so far, other than Canada, has been England. During the time we lived there we found that two of our favourite places were Cornwall and Wales, and two of my books take place in those locales: *The Stone in the Meadow* (Cornwall), and *The Haunting at Cliff House* (Wales).

"Both of these books, as well as *The Other Elizabeth,* which is set in Canada, have a 'back to the past' theme. In *The Stone in the Meadow* a young Canadian girl visiting her uncle is magically transported back to 300 B.C., a time when Britain was occupied by warring tribes of Celts and their Druid priests. In *The Other Elizabeth,* a modern day girl, Elizabeth, enters an old building in Upper Canada Village—a pioneer village in Ontario—and suddenly finds herself back in the year 1813, during the war between the United States of America and Canada. *The Haunting at Cliff House* concerns a Canadian girl who has accompanied her father, a novelist and university professor, on his sabbatical to a small town in Wales. They move into an old house on the coast which he has inherited, and the heroine finds that it is haunted by the ghost of another girl who lived there over a hundred years before. They're concerned with events that happened in the past, and the possibility of altering these events in such a way that the future, as well, is altered. It's a theme that has fascinated me for a long time.

"My other two books, *Wrong Again, Robbie* and *I Wish There Were Unicorns,* are both set in present-day Canada and deal with contemporary themes of learning to get along with other people and to adjust to difficult situations.

"History, as well, is a passion of mine. I received a Canada Council Grant in 1983 which enabled me to return to England to research a fictional biography of Lady Jane Grey, who was Queen of England for nine days when she was fifteen years old, and who was then executed on Tower Green. It's this love of history which I can feel taking over again now that we have returned to Europe. Walking around castles, exploring ruins, hiking in the mountains—there are a wealth of possibilities to be explored here. I can positively feel a new book lurking around the corner!

"In the meantime I am working on a novel which is set amongst the lighthouse keepers and inshore fishermen of the southern coast of Nova Scotia. Our last four years back in Canada have allowed me to spend a good deal of time rediscovering my own country. Again, thanks to a Canada Council Grant, I was able to go in the spring of 1985 and live on a small lighthouse island for a while. There I found a peace and a strength that I have not found anywhere else, and I want very much to write about it.

"I've often been asked why I write for children rather than adults. In fact, I was once asked why a thirteen year old who could read at adult level would need a 'children's' book at all.

"My answer to that particular question was that a thirteen year old who was capable of reading at an adult level did not necessarily *want* to read about adults and adult concerns all of the time. Often, that young person would like to read about other young people of the same age, with the same interests and concerns. For that reason I write for them—in an adult manner, but about *them,* about the problems and complexities that face *them.* And I hope that through my writing I can offer these young people—if not solutions—at least understanding, perhaps some ideas of how to cope, and most important of all, a sense of humor about the whole business."

HOBBIES AND OTHER INTERESTS: Flying, scuba diving, reading ("of course!").

BERNICE CALLAWAY

CALLAWAY, Bernice (Anne) 1923-

PERSONAL: Born November 23, 1923, near Hamilton, Ontario, Canada; daugher of E. Wray (a carpenter) and Muriel (a homemaker; maiden name, Pearson) Marr; married Victor L. Callaway (secretary of Prairie Bible Institute), December 19, 1942; children: David, Daniel, Timothy, Ruth Callaway MacKenzie, Philip. *Education:* Attended Prairie Bible Institute. *Politics:* "Conservative." *Religion:* Evangelical Free Church. *Home and office:* 29 Mobile Dr., Three Hills, Alberta, Canada T0M 2A0.

CAREER: Homemaker, writer.

WRITINGS: Down Timberland Trail: A Tale of Upper Canada (illustrated by Brian Parlane), Prairie Press, 1969; *Tell Us a Story* (illustrated by Alastair Parlane and B. Parlane), Prairie Press, 1973; *Tell Us a Missionary Story* (illustrated by B. Parlane), Prairie Press, 1976; *To Mothers . . . with Love,* Prairie Press, 1978; *From a Mother's Heart,* G. R. Welch, 1982.

Also author of two plays; contributor of weekly column, "Prairie Campus" to local newspaper, *Three Hills Capital,* 1980—; contributor of monthly stories and articles to Evangelical magazines for children and adults.

WORK IN PROGRESS: Our Prairie Pioneers, a history of the Prairie Bible Institute's roots in story form.

SIDELIGHTS: "A child of the Depression years, we were rich in good books, which I read avidly. At age thirty-nine, during a prolonged illness, having never 'written' (except long, descriptive, almost weekly letters, mostly to dear parents 2,000 miles away in Ontario), a short article for a cookbook was needed. Result? 'Bernice, you have a talent there. You had better use it. God has given it to you.' Our children's magazine, *Young Pilot,* needed children's stories—it was sheer joy to write. Before that I sent a 400-word article to *Power Paper* (Sunday School adult paper) in Wheaton, Illinois—my first attempt. It was accepted and the first check arrived! A busy, not-strong mother of five (the youngest only one-and-a-half), my motivation was basically to write, not only interesting, wholesome stories for children and young people, but to challenge readers to commit theirs lives to the Saviour of the world. Books had so influenced my life as a child . . . (*The Wide, Wide World* and *Ministering Children,* along with *Uncle Tom's Cabin, Little Women,* etc.), that I longed that each story/book— each page—would bless and challenge and inform my readers. Very deeply was I, and continue to be, aware that I am accountable to my Creator God and will someday stand before Him who saved my soul as a teenager and has in loving kindness and tender mercy been with me, and mine, ever since.

"My first book, *Down Timberland Trail,* was published in serial form during Canada's centennial year (during another bout with illness) and is a historical novel centered around the War of 1812, set in my childhood home area in southern Ontario. It has gone through several printings and is due for another. My *Tell Us a Story* and *Tell Us a Missionary Story* pair followed. The former is a collection of either true stories from our family life or based on such; the latter all true. These also are ready for another reprint. My last two books are especially for mothers—parts taken from articles published in various periodicals—as were the *Tell Us* books.

"As my dear husband (who served in the Canadian army for four years, then returned to school, and for the past twenty-five years has served here as public relations director, then secretary) nears retirement, perhaps most of my writing is

(From *Down Timberland Trail: A Tale of Upper Canada* by Bernice Callaway.)

done. It has definitely been a wonderful experience (though always secondary to my family, who are a continuing, growing source of joy) and a surprising one as my second interest was always music! I thank God for the privilege of writing, and my prayer will continue to be that He will be honored by all of it and readers will be challenged to live their lives with eternity's values in view."

CARLSTROM, Nancy White 1948-

BRIEF ENTRY: Born August 4, 1948, in Washington, Pa. From the time she was in high school and working in the children's section of the local library, Carlstrom knew that she wanted to write children's books. Following her graduation from Wheaton College in 1970, she taught at elementary schools in Pennsylvania and Massachusetts before returning to the classroom herself as a student of art and children's literature. She and her husband then relocated to Yucatán, where she was involved in a school for Down's syndrome children. Upon their return to the United States, the couple settled in Seattle, Washington. There, in 1977, Carlstrom became owner and manager of The Secret Garden Children's Bookshop. Proceeds from this shop not only benefitted the school in Mexico, but also St. Vincent's School for Handicapped Children in Port-au-Prince, Haiti. Carlstrom's first child, Jesse, was the inspiration for her first picture book; as she dressed her son, she would sing a song that was later translated into the catchy rhyme of *Jesse Bear, What Will You Wear?* (Macmillan, 1986). According to *School Library Journal,* "There's much for a child to recognize in this book; not just physical objects but attitudes, habits and relationships, too.'' Carlstrom sold her bookshop in 1983 to devote more time to her family—including a second son, Joshua—and her writing. Among her anticipated children's books are *The Moon Came Too, Wild Wild Sunflower Child Anna,* and *Blow Me a Kiss Miss Lilly. Residence:* Seattle, Wash.

CASTELLON, Federico 1914-1971

PERSONAL: Born September 14, 1914, in Alhabia, Almeria, Spain; came to the United States in 1921, naturalized in 1943; died July 29, 1971, in New York, N.Y.; married Hilda Green-

FEDERICO CASTELLON

field, October 21, 1940; children: Paul. *Education:* Attended high school in Brooklyn, N.Y. *Residence:* New York, N.Y.

CAREER: Artist and illustrator. Worked as a commercial artist, beginning 1936; commissioned by International Graphic Arts Society to execute two prints; lecturer in art, Teachers College at Columbia University, 1946-61, Pratt Institute, 1951-61 and 1964-71, Queens College, 1964, National Academy of Design, beginning 1964, and the New School for Social Research; traveled for Department of State, International Education Exchange Program, 1954. *Awards, honors:* Received a four-year traveling fellowship from the Spanish Republic, 1934.

EXHIBITIONS—One-man: Weyhe Gallery, New York City, 1934, 1936, 1939-41; Raymond and Raymond Gallery, New York City, 1934; Prado De Almeria, Almeria, Spain, 1934; American Federation of Arts Traveling Exhibition, 1938-39; Phildelphia Art Alliance, Pa., 1941; Princeton Print Club, N.J., 1946; Associated American Artists Gallery, New York City, 1947-52, 1965, 1966; Mercerburg Art Gallery, Pa., 1952; University of Maine, Orono, 1953, 1966; American Embassies in Buenos Aires, Argentina, Las Paz, Bolivia, Santiago, Chile, Bogota, Columbia, Asuncion, Paraguay, Montivedeo, Uruguay, and Caracas, Venezuela, 1954-55; Society of Illustrators, New York City, 1958.

Gallery 10, New Hope, Pa., 1961; Philadelphia Print Club, Pa., 1964; Dintenfass Gallery, New York City, 1964; Great Neck Library, Mich., 1964; Hudson Guild Gallery, Great Neck, N.Y., 1965; Los Angeles County Museum, Calif., 1968; Storm King Art Center, Mountainville, N.Y., 1968; Slater Memorial Museum, Norwich, Conn., 1968-69; Lunn Gallery, Washington, D.C., 1971; American Academy of Arts and Letters, New York City, 1972; Graphics Gallery, Toronto, Ontario, 1976, 1977.

Group shows: Weyhe Gallery, New York City, 1933, 1934, 1936-40; Upton Gallery, New York City, 1934; Raymond and Raymond Gallery, New York City, 1934; Casa Valasque, Madrid, Spain, 1934; College D'Espagne (Cite de Universitaire), Paris, France, 1935; Art Institute of Chicago, Ill., 1937, 1940; Ritsforbundet for Bilande Kunst, 1937-38; Whitney Museum of Art, New York City, 1937, 1938, 1945, 1970; Pennsylvania Academy of Fine Arts, Philadelphia, 1938, 1940, 1942, 1969; Springfield Museum of Fine Arts, Mass., 1939.

Philadelphia Art Alliance, Pa., 1941, 1947; Carnegie Institute of Art, Pittsburgh, Pa., 1942, 1943, 1947; Alexandria Library, Va., 1943; National Academy, New York City, 1944-45; Associated American Artists Gallery, New York City, 1946, 1952, 1965, 1973, 1974; Philadelphia Art Alliance, Pa., 1947; Brooklyn Museum, N.Y., 1947, 1949, 1968; J. B. Speed Art Museum, Louisville, Ky., 1948.

American Embassy, Bombay, India, 1950; Cheltenham Township Art Centre, Pa., 1951; Metropolitan Museum of Art, New York City, 1952, 1953; Mercerburg Art Gallery, Pa., 1952; Galerie Jungst der Gegenwart, Salzburg, Austria, 1952; Succession Gallery, Vienna, Austria, 1952; Walker Art Center, Milwaukee, Wis., 1954; New Jersey State Museum, Trenton, 1956; University of Illinois, Urbana, 1957.

Gallery 10, New Hope, Pa., 1961; Pepsi-Cola Exhibition Gallery, New York City, 1963; Princeton Print Club, N.J., 1964; Dintenfass Gallery, New York City, 1964; Pratt Graphic Art Center, New York City, 1964; Gallery Ten, Woodstock, N.Y., 1964; Visual Arts Gallery (School of Visual Arts), New York City, 1964; World's Fair, New York City, 1964-65; Drexel Institute of Technology, Philadelphia, Pa., 1965; Dorsky Gal-

He remembered a ride through a stormy night. ∎ (From *The Story of John J. Audubon* by Joan Howard. Illustrated by Federico Castellon.)

lery, New York City, 1965; Galerie des Peintres Graveurs, Paris, France, 1965; Madison Art Center, Wis., 1966; Depauw University Art Center, Chicago, Ill., 1966; NYS Development of Fine and Applied Arts, Grossinger, N.Y., 1967; New York Public Library, New York City, 1968; Rijksakademie Van Beelende Kunsen, Amsterdam, 1968; Slater Memorial Museum, Norwich, Conn., 1968; 1969; Los Angeles County Museum, Calif., 1968; Storm King Art Center, Mountainville, N.Y., 1969.

Biennale International de L'Estampe Epinal, Paris, France, 1971; Lunn Gallery, Washington, D.C., 1971; Minnesota Museum of Art, St. Paul, 1972; Housatonic Community College, Bridgeport, Conn., 1977.

Permanent collections: Brooklyn Museum of Art, N.Y.; Butler Institute of American Art, Youngstown, Ohio; Art Institute of Chicago, Ill.; Columbia University, New York City; Dartmouth College, Hanover, N.H.; Georgia University, Athens; University of Illinois, Urbana; Kalamazoo Institute of Art, Mich.; Library of Congress, Washington, D.C.; Los Angeles County Museum, Calif.; Madison Art Center, Wis.; Metropolitan Museum of Art, New York City; University of Minnesota, Chaska; Montclair State College, Montclair, N.J.; Munson Williams Proctor Institute, Utica, N.Y.

Museum of Modern Art, New York City; National Institute of Arts and Letters, New York City; New York Public Library, New York City; Newark Public Library, N.J.; Norwich Free Academy, Conn.; Pennsylvania Academy of Fine Arts, Pa.; Princeton University, N.J.; Nelson A. Rockefeller Collection; Jonathan Sax Collection; Slater Memorial Museum, Norwich, Conn.; Syracuse University, N.Y.; Tucson Public School, Ariz.; Stella Elkins Tyler School of Art, Philadelphia, Pa.; Whitney Museum of American Art, New York City; Yale University Collection, New Haven, Conn. *Military service:* World War II, 1943-46; served as a member of the Office of Strategic Services in China and India.

MEMBER: National Academy of Design (associate member), National Institute of Arts and Letters, Society of American Graphic Artists, Century Club. *Awards, honors:* Fellowship from the Spanish Republic, 1934-36; Mr. and Mrs. Frank C. Logan Prize from the Art Institute of Chicago, 1939, and Alice McFadden Eyre Medal from Pennsylvania Academy of Fine Arts, 1940, both for ''Rendezvous in a Landscape''; Guggenheim Fellowships, 1940, 1949; Lambert Fund Purchase Prize,

"**Please, please, take care of yourself,**" Bronya begged.
■ (From *The Story of Madame Curie* by Alice Thorne. Illustrated by Federico Castellon.)

1943; First Annual National Print Competition, Associated American Artists, first prize, 1946, for ''The Family''; Second Annual National Print Competition, Associated American Artists, Purchase Prize, 1947, for ''The Groom''; National Print Competition, Associated American Artists, first prize, 1948; grant from the National Institute of Arts and Letters, 1949; Pennell Purchase Prize from the Library of Congress, 1949.

Mary S. Collins Prize from the Print Club of Philadelphia, 1964, for ''The Traveller''; prize from the Society of American Graphic Artists, 1964; Madison Art Center, First Purchase Prize, 1966, for ''The Onus''; elected member to the National Institute of Arts and Letters, 1968; purchase prize from the Seventh Dublin National Print and Drawing Competition, 1971.

WRITINGS: (Editor) Henry Cliffe, *Lithography: Techniques of Lithography,* Watson-Guptill, 1965.

Illustrator: Delmore Schwartz, *Shenandoah* (play), New Directions, 1941; Thomas Bulfinch, *Mythology: The Age of Fable; or, Stories of Gods and Heroes,* Doubleday, 1948; Pearl S. Buck, *Man Who Changed China: The Story of Sun Yat-Sen* (young adult), Random House, 1953; Olive Price, *The Story of Marco Polo* (juvenile), Grosset, 1953; Antoine de Saint Exupéry, *The Little Prince,* Macmillan, 1954; Charlotte Mary Yonge, *The Little Duke: Richard the Fearless* (juvenile), Macmillan, 1954; Joan Howard (pseudonym of Patricia Gordon), *The Story of John J. Audubon* (juvenile), Grosset, 1954; Alice D. Thorne, *The Story of Madame Curie* (juvenile), Grosset, 1959; Gerald Abraham, *A Hundred Years of Music,* Grosset, 1961; Daniel Defoe, *Robinson Crusoe* (young adult; with an afterword by Clifton Fadiman), Macmillan, 1962; Alice C. Desmond, *Your Flag and Mine* (juvenile), Macmillan, 1967; Walter Scott, *The Talisman,* Limited Editions, 1967; Edgar Allan Poe, *The Mask of the Red Death,* Aquarius Press, 1969; H. Roskolenko, *I Went into the Country,* Black Faun Press, 1972. Contributor of illustrations to numerous periodicals, including *Abbott Laboratories Medical Journals, Life,* and *M.D.*

She would study in her bare, unheated room until two in the morning. ■ (From *The Story of Madame Curie* by Alice Thorne. Illustrated by Federico Castellon.)

SIDELIGHTS: **September 14, 1914.** Born in Almeria, Spain, Castellon immigrated with his family to his lifetime home in Brooklyn, New York in 1921. Sketching became his form of self expression, much encouraged by his teachers. "They weren't people with any exceptional talent or perceptiveness, but I understood from their reactions to the work that I was doing, that I had attained a certain degree of respect in the teacher's eye which was reflected again in my classmates eyes.... As a rejected foreign child who wanted to earn some degree of acceptance, I found that this slight talent gave me a certain little acceptance, a degree of acceptability and notoriety, and I suddenly became very ambitious in this. Especially because it attracted me so much anyhow, that it began to develop, and I think within my grammar school years, it was a kind of nasty conceit. I wanted to prove my value to everybody. I don't know that it moved me as greatly for itself. It probably did or I wouldn't have pursued it as much as I have, but it did indicate to me a way that I could assert myself as a human being." [August L. Freundlich, *Federico Castellon: His Graphic Works, 1936-1971,* College of Visual and Performing Arts, Syracuse University, 1978.[1]]

1933. Graduated from Erasmus Hall High School in Brooklyn, New York. During his student years, Castellon was provided with wall spaces on which to execute his murals. "I was not completely self-taught. Even in high school I had some teachers that were very good guides. They didn't teach me so much in the way that an art school teaches by criticizing the work you do, because they used to leave me alone in the back of the room. They realized that I wasn't going to goof off. I wanted to do more art work than they would ever ask for, so they left me to my own resources. But they did encourage me to go to this gallery, or that museum, and in that sense, they did a lot of beautiful guiding for me."[1]

1934. Granted a four-year fellowship from Spain to study and travel in England, France, and Spain. He stayed in Europe for a year and a half and held a one-man exhibition in the Prado, in Madrid, Spain before returning to New York. Castellon's surrealist lithographs earned him an international reputation by the time he was twenty-two.

October 21, 1940. Married Hilda Greenfield. Granted a Guggenheim fellowship which enabled him to travel through the American southwest.

1943. Served in the United States Army during World War II.

1946-1971. Taught art in the New York metropolitan schools for twenty-five years. Because his own work was so distinctive, many of his students tried to imitate him although Castellon would try to discourage them. "I feel somehow that if they do imitate, it's only because they enjoy my class, because they feel that 'this person understands what I want to do.' Now, what I usually do is to get at the core of their kinship. If there is something spiritual in the student that is very close to mine, I realize that he is an entirely different personality. Let's get down to the difference between us, not our similarities, and try to make him a little more independent, getting him away from any approach too close to mine. It may end up that the germ is still there because we do feel very much the same about many things. And, if classification were applied to his work, they might say 'yes, he works under the influence of,' but you can tell the difference, or at least I hope by the end of the term with me, you can tell the difference."[1]

1948. Illustrated *Bulfinch's Mythology: The Age of Fable; or, Stories of Gods and Heroes* for Doubleday. Throughout his distinguished career, Castellon worked in a variety of media that included oils, lithographs, etchings and resist-ink painting, which is a combination of India ink and tempera colors. "The technique of resist-ink, in description, sounds more complicated and laborious than it really is. As a matter of fact, it is a fairly easy and rapid method of picturemaking. On a rather fine-grained watercolor paper or illustration board, the drawing is sketched in pencil. From this point till the washing of the drawing, the work is done in negative. Just why this is so can only be discovered by actual experimentation. I first use any poster paint which is just off white to paint in the highlights and lighter tones. It is best at this point to keep the brush fairly dry so that a dry-brush technique may be used in getting tones and shading off, but do not allow the paint to become thin. Over this I use black poster paint for the medium gray tones. When the paint is completely dry, I brush an even coat of India ink over the entire surface of the board. The ink should cover poster paint and exposed illustration board. Great care should be taken at this point to prevent the poster paint from being washed off or thinned out by the ink. It is best, therefore, to work on a small portion at a time when inking in, not allowing the brush to become too full or too dry. The poster paint will absorb the ink without allowing it to penetrate to the board, while the exposed parts of the board will get a permanent waterproof coat of ink. When the ink is thoroughly dry, the board is washed under a faucet or hose. The poster paint with the ink on its surface will wash off completely, the black poster paint leaving a medium tone of gray. Where there was no poster paint, the India ink will remain black. Over the resultant black-and-white drawing, add watercolor and, to retain both the richness of the color and the texture of the resist-ink technique, make the color transparent by applying picture wax and rubbing it in." ["The Watercolor Series," *American Artist,* Volume 13, number 5, May, 1949.[2]]

1949. Elected a member of the National Academy. Received a grant from the National Institute of Arts and Letters and was awarded his second Guggenheim Fellowship, which enabled him to travel through Italy.

The schoolmaster was a long gloomy man who told his pupils a great many dull facts. ▪ (From *The Story of John J. Audubon* by Joan Howard. Illustrated by Federico Castellon.)

1951. Taught at Pratt Institute, an experience he described as somewhat easier for his students than his classes at Columbia University had been. "You don't have to make them into geniuses within a month. College curriculum, classes and semesters being what they are, what you have already decided in your own mind is to emphasize his process of development. He may suffer like mad at the beginning, because you're not pushing him into a genius classification within two months. However, in the end he may come to realize the next semester, 'My God, I'm suddenly beginning to see the light, now I understand the reason for these almost infantile lessons that I was getting before.' The disadvantage with college is that it makes one a little unhappy that very often the thought is in the student's mind that, 'I want to be an artist very much, but if that doesn't work out, I'll be a teacher.' You don't wish to be an artist first and then possibly something second. You're either going to be an artist or nothing—you don't look for credits, you don't look for degrees if being an artist is that enormously important, and yet, I've had them in colleges where I have felt that the student should not have selected anything but to be an artist. They were so good, and it hurt that a person with this sensitivity, this talent, should select a college just in case it didn't work out."[1]

During the same year he also began several major commissions for *Life* magazine.

1954. Travelled through South America with an exhibition of his works as a member of the Department of State, International Education Exchange Program.

1961. Moved with his family to Europe.

1963. Returned to the United States; made an academician of the National Academy of Design. Castellon described himself as a surrealist. "... Only in the sense that people find it irrational when they look at it. There is a symbolism involved. Now the symbolism that I use is in the place of the philosophy I mean to put into it, and the philosophy is usually of such an abstract nature that I cannot illustrate with action, so I have to use symbolism. For instance, if you are going to make a painting on suffering as an inward emotion, you cannot identify it with an actuality of some sort of a woman with a dead child at her feet. This is not suffering, this is a very specific type and it is not at all what I mean. I mean suffering in an abstract sense; so I have to arrive at it through symbolism that becomes a little weird to others. To others it appears irrational."[1]

1968. Elected to the National Institute of Arts and Letters. Carl Zigrosser, the art director of Weyhe's Gallery who gave Castellon his first exhibition, described the artist as having "phenomenal technical facility. There is no impression or effect that he cannot achieve in painting, sculpture, drawing, or printmaking. And he has an extraordinary visual memory: he does not draw from an object or a model, he draws from imagination. His technical faculty is matched by his pictorial invention. Graphic ideas come bubbling up in great profusion—ideas that are crystal clear and complete. No need for him to grope or fumble. Such prodigality of accomplishment is refined and heightened by his innate sense of style. It governs his thought, his feeling, and his action. It is possible that his sense of style is derived from his Spanish background, for the Latin temperament, as Santayana and Norman Douglas have pointed out, seems to possess it instinctively. The Latins, having a certain pride in life yet being cognizant of its limitations, know well how to live. Their rule of life is not moral precept, but aesthetic value—a sense of fitness, an awareness of limitation."[1]

The Boxers led a nationwide massacre of white people. ■ (From *The Man Who Changed China: The Story of Sun Yat-Sen* by Pearl Buck. Illustrated by Federico Castellon.)

July 29, 1971. Died in Mount Sinai Hospital, New York City, at the age of fifty-six.

FOR MORE INFORMATION SEE: Art News, November 28, 1936, November 16, 1940, April 15, 1941, July 1, 1946, May, 1947, June, 1949, January, 1952; Carl Zigrosser, *Six Centuries of Fine Printing,* Covici-Friede, 1937; *Coronet,* September, 1938; *Art Digest,* April 1, 1939, May 15, 1939, November 15, 1940, April 15, 1941, April 1, 1942, January 1, 1945, July, 1946, August, 1949; Albert Reese, *American Prize Prints of the Twentieth Century,* American Artists Group, 1949; C. Zigrosser, "Federico Castellon," *American Artist,* May, 1949; Bertha M. Miller and others, compilers, *Illustrators of Children's Books: 1946-1956,* Horn Book, 1958; Daniel A. Mendowitz, *A History of American Art,* Holt, 1961; C. Zigrosser, *The Artist in America: Close-Ups of Contemporary Print Makers,* Knopf, 1962; August L. Freundlich, *Federico Castellon: His Graphic Works 1936-1971,* College of Visual and Performing Arts, Syracuse University, 1978.

Obituaries: *New York Times,* July 30, 1971; *Art News,* September, 1971.

CAUMAN, Samuel   1910-1971

PERSONAL: Surname is pronounced "common"; born June 29, 1910, in Boston, Mass.; died March 6, 1971; son of Meyer (a manufacturer) and Anne (Waldstein) Cauman; married Leigh Davis Steinhardt (an editor), October 13, 1940; children: Thomas Edward, John Henry. *Education:* Attended Massachusetts Institute of Technology, 1929-30; Harvard University, A.B., 1931, A.M., 1940. *Politics:* "Left of center." *Religion:* Jewish. *Residence:* New York, N.Y.

CAREER: Plays, Inc., Boston, Mass., assistant to publisher, 1940-42; Coolidge, Shepley, Bulfinch & Abbot, Boston, architectural draftsman, 1942; Submarine Signal Co., Boston, director of publications, 1943-46; Cauman & Pfeufer, Inc., Boston, creative director, 1946-50; New York University, New York, N.Y., research scientist in graphic arts, 1956-61; Harry N. Abrams, Inc. (publisher), New York, editor, 1958-60; writer, free-lance editor, and typographer. Lecturer in visual design, Boston University. Consultant, American-Scandinavian Foundation.

WRITINGS: The Living Museum, New York University Press, 1958; *Jonah Bondi Wise,* Crown, 1967; (with H. W. Janson and D. J. Janson) *Short History of Art,* Abrams, 1969; (with H. W. Janson) *History of Art for Young People* (young adult), Abrams, 1971; (with H. W. Janson) *A Basic History of Art,* Prentice-Hall, 1973. Assistant editor, *Harper's Encyclopedia of Art.*

WORK IN PROGRESS: Discovering Art, for Abrams; a study and biography of Gyorgy Kepes.

FOR MORE INFORMATION SEE: New York Times, March 7, 1971; *Horn Book,* October, 1972.

CAVANAGH, Helen (Carol)   1939-

PERSONAL: Born December 4, 1939, in Quincy, Mass.; daughter of Wapaa Albert (a construction worker) and Blanche Holmes (a housewife; maiden name, Magnant) Hanninen; married Lawrence Joseph Cavanagh (a corrections officer), June 18, 1960; children: Christopher (deceased), Lawrence Joseph, Jr., Patrick, Carin. *Education:* Attended Bay Path Junior College, 1957-58. *Home and office:* 29 Burgess Ave., Spotswood, N.J. 08884.

CAREER: Writer, Boston, Mass., clerk, 1958-59; WEEI-Radio, Boston, secretary, 1959; *Sentinel,* East Brunswick, N.J., reporter, feature writer, and author of column, "Telling It Like It Is," 1970-78; free-lance writer, 1978—. Spotswood town historian, 1976. Creative writing teacher at Old Bridge Community School. *Member:* Penmeisters. *Awards, honors:* Author Award from New Jersey Institute of Technology, 1979, for both *Second Best* and *Honey.*

WRITINGS—For young adults; all published by Scholastic Book Services, except as noted: *Second Best,* 1979; *Honey,* 1979; *Superflirt,* 1980; *Wildfire Diary,* 1980; *The Easiest Way,* 1980; *My Day by Day Diary with Special Poems for Me,* 1980; *A Place for Me,* 1981; *Just a Summer Girl,* 1982; *Angel,* 1984; *Kiss and Tell,* 1984; *The Candy Papers,* Simon & Schuster, 1985. Contributor of stories and poems to magazines and newspapers, including *True Romance, Down East, Writer's Digest,* and *Co-Ed.*

WORK IN PROGRESS: Salt and Old Silver, a ghost story, "The Soul Journey" series, *Brotherly Loves,* all for young adults; *My Feet Are Longfellows* and *Marla Mushroom,* both for children: *Mad about You, Baby, Behind God's Back, Silk and Sand, Maybe This Time, Outside Our Number,* and *Dream of Paisley,* all for adults; *A Wild Sadness,* an autobiographical novel.

SIDELIGHTS: "It's not just that I remember what it's like to be sixteen years old, or twelve; in my heart I still am! Just as I can look ahead and be eighty, sometimes I can go way back to when I was a year and a half. I can also be my true age when I *have* to be.

"Of course, what's true and what feels true gets all mixed together whenever I sit down to write. Who knows why? Maybe because I'm a mixture myself: part Finn, part French, part New England Yankee. Perhaps too because I'm left-handed (lefties often take liberties with logic). Very possibly it's because I gazed out the window too much when I should have been paying attention to the teacher.

"Daydreamer was a bad thing to be in those days, later, too, and sometimes I notice, even now. Not everyone approves of dreaming and not everyone believed I could be a writer. Except me—I did. Now I know my gazing and my dreaming were necessary and right. I dreamed of becoming a writer and *my dreams came true.*

HELEN CAVANAGH

"I was born on December 4, 1939 in Quincy, Massachusetts, and christened Helen Carol Hanninen. Massachusetts remained my home until I married at age twenty, although I spent many summers in Maine and in Chatham on Cape Cod. I graduated from Newton High School in 1957, and attended Bay Path Junior College in Longmeadow, Massachusetts. My nickname in school was 'Honey' just like the character in my second novel for Scholastic. At Bay Path I was studying art and learning to be an executive secretary, but my heart wasn't in it; I still kept dreaming about being a writer.

"Over the years I've had many jobs, including mother's helper, waitress, salesperson, secretary, model, toy store clerk, and newspaper reporter and columnist. I didn't realize it at the time, but these experiences would be valuable and a necessity when I actually did begin to write steadily and 'seriously,' deciding to make my dream come true.

"Becoming a writer has not been easy; it was hard, often discouraging, painful, and there were lots of moments when I wondered if I was dreaming an impossible dream.

"Which is exactly what I write about: in *Second Best*, I dealt with Shelly's struggles with jealousy and self-doubt, *Honey*'s problems with her mother and father, and *Superflirt* Susan's confusion. Also, Abbie in *The Easiest Way* must struggle and suffer, and so does Colleen in *A Place for Me*. All these girls are me, and I feel their pain, but in my books *we* always win and learn a little more about ourselves, and become better people. If their experiences, the events of their lives are not *exactly* true when I write them, they eventually *become* true. Who's to say that's not the same, or ever closer to the *real* truth? I think it is, but what do I know? I'm a leftie and I still look out the window too much.

"What makes it nicer is that when I do my dreaming now, I have lots of choices of who to be, and how old, and where I want to live. In *Summer Girl* I am Nina on Cape Cod; in *Angel* I'm Angela in deep trouble and in love with a wonderful guy.

"I don't have to live in one place, or be just one person. As a writer I can be in a thousand places, be a thousand people. And more . . . always more ahead."

HOBBIES AND OTHER INTERESTS: Gardening, reading, and people.

FOR MORE INFORMATION SEE: Writer's Digest, May, 1982.

CHILDRESS, Alice 1920-

PERSONAL: Surname is pronounced *Chill*-dress; born October 12, 1920, in Charleston, S.C.; married second husband, Nathan Woodard (a musician); children: (first marriage) Jean (Mrs. Richard Lee). *Education:* Radcliffe Institute for Independent Study, 1966-68. *Residence:* Roosevelt Island, N.Y. 10044. *Agent:* Flora Roberts, Inc., 157 West 57th St., Penthouse A, New York, N.Y. 10019.

CAREER: Actress and director with American Negro Theatre, New York, N.Y., for eleven years; writer. Has made several appearances on Broadway and television. Lecturer at universities and schools. Member of advisory board, Frances Delafield Community City Hospital. *Member:* P.E.N., Dramatists Guild (member of Council), Writers East (member of council), Harlem Writers Guild, American Federation of Television and Radio Artists, Society of Choreographers and Stage Directors.

Awards, honors: Obie Award for best original Off-Broadway play, *Village Voice*, 1956, for "Trouble in Mind"; John Golden Fund for Playwrights grants, 1957; Rockefeller Grant, 1967; one of *New York Times Book Review* Outstanding Books of the Year, 1973, Woodward Park School Book Award, 1974, Jane Addams Children's Book Honor Award for young adult novel, 1974, National Book Award nomination, 1974, Achievement Award, National Association for Negro Business and Professional Women's Clubs, 1975, selected as a Best Young Adult Book by the American Library Association, 1975, and Lewis Carroll Shelf Award, University of Wisconsin, 1975, all for *A Hero Ain't Nothin' but a Sandwich;* named honorary citizen of Atlanta, Ga., 1975, for opening of "Wedding Band"; Virgin Islands film festival award for best screenplay, and Paul Robeson Award for outstanding contributions to the performing arts, Filmmakers Hall of Fame, both 1977, both for "A Hero Ain't Nothin' but a Sandwich"; "Alice Childress Week" officially observed in Charleston, S.C. and Columbia, S.C., 1977, to celebrate opening of "Sea Island Song"; *Rainbow Jordan* was selected one of *School Library Journal*'s "Best Books," 1981, one of *New York Times* Outstanding Books of the Year, 1981, as a notable children's trade book in social studies, 1982, by the National Council for Social Studies and the Children's Book Council, and received honorable mention, Coretta Scott King Award, 1982.

WRITINGS: Like One of the Family: Conversations from a Domestic's Life, Independence Press, 1956; (editor) *Black Scenes: Collections of Scenes from Plays Written by Black People about Black Experience*, Doubleday, 1971; *A Hero Ain't Nothin' but a Sandwich* (young adult novel), Coward, 1973; *A Short Walk* (adult novel), Coward, 1979; *Rainbow Jordan*, Coward, 1981; *Many Closets*, Coward, 1987.

ALICE CHILDRESS

I'm standin here ready to go, waitin for Mayola, our caseworker. I don't wanna go. ■ (Jacket illustration by Jerry Pinkney from *Rainbow Jordan* by Alice Childress.)

Plays: "Florence" (one-act), first produced at American Negro Theatre, directed by A. Childress, 1949; (adapter) Langston Hughes, "Just a Little Simple" (based on L. Hughes's novel, *Simple Speaks His Mind*), first produced in New York City at Club Baron Theatre, September, 1950; "Gold through the Trees," first produced in New York City at Club Baron Theatre, 1952; "Trouble in Mind," first produced Off-Broadway at Greenwich Mews Theatre, directed by A. Childress, November 3, 1955 (published in *Black Theatre: A Twentieth-Century Collection of the Work of Its Best Playwrights,* edited by Lindsay Patterson, Dodd, 1971); *Wedding Band: A Love/Hate Story in Black and White* (first produced in Ann Arbor, Mich. at University of Michigan, December 7, 1966; produced Off-Broadway at New York Shakespeare Festival Theatre, directed by A. Childress and Joseph Papp, September 26, 1972), Samuel French, 1973; "String" (one-act; adapted from Guy de Maupassant's story "A Piece of String"; also see below), first produced Off-Broadway at St. Mark's Playhouse, March 25, 1969; "Mojo: A Black Love Story" (one-act; also see below), produced at New Heritage Theatre, New York, November, 1970; *Mojo* [and] *String* (two one-act plays; produced in Los Angeles at Inner City Cultural Center, 1978), Dramatists Play Service, 1971; *When the Rattlesnake Sounds* (juvenile), Coward, 1975; *Let's Hear It for the Queen* (juvenile), Coward, 1976; "Sea Island Song," produced in Charleston, S.C., 1977, produced as "Gullah," University of Massachusetts—Amherst, 1984; "Moms: A Praise Play for a Black Comedienne," produced by Green Plays, New Lex Theater, 1986.

Screenplays: *Wine in the Wilderness: A Comedy-Drama* (first produced in Boston by WGBH-TV, March 4, 1969), Dra-

matists Play Service, 1970; "Wedding Band," ABC-TV, 1973; "A Hero Ain't Nothin' but a Sandwich" (based on novel of same title), New World Pictures, 1978; "String" (series), PBS-TV, 1979.

Also author of plays "The World on a Hill" (published in *Plays to Remember,* Macmillan, 1968); "Martin Luther King at Montgomery, Alabama," music by Nathan Woodard, 1969; "A Man Bearing a Pitcher," 1969; "The Freedom Drum," music by N. Woodard, retitled "Young Martin Luther King," produced by Performing Arts Repertory Theatre (on tour), 1969-72; and "The African Garden," music by N. Woodard, 1971. Work represented in numerous anthologies, including *Plays to Remember,* Macmillan, 1968; *Black Theatre,* edited by L. Patterson, New American Library, 1971; *The Best Short Plays of 1972,* edited by Stanley Richards, Chilton, 1972; *The Young American Basic Reading Program,* Lyons & Carnaham, 1972; *Success in Reading,* Silver Burdett, 1972; and *Best Short Plays of the World Theatre, 1968-1973,* edited by S. Richards, Crown, 1973. Author of column, "Here's Mildred," *Baltimore Afro-American,* 1956-58. Contributor of plays, articles, and reviews to *Masses and Mainstream, Black World, Freedomways, Essence,* and other publications.

WORK IN PROGRESS: A novel about Paul Laurence Dunbar which takes place in New York City during the 1890s.

SIDELIGHTS: "There is nothing grand, fine or right about going hungry, standing on the receiving end of persecution or being any other kind of loser, except coming through such

I hate for people to lie on me. No matter what they color or creed—I can't stand nobody lyin. ■ (Jacket illustration by David Brown from *A Hero Ain't Nothin' but a Sandwich* by Alice Childress.)

experiences with your head up, ready for the next round. There is nothing noble or romantic about being illiterate, unable to read or write even your own name, except when one so deprived or limited is able to attain, among other things, the almost unattainable—beautiful, tender, fulfilling love relationships without the use of the written word, without the comfort of financial security. I wrote my play *Wedding Band* as a remembrance of the intellectual poor. The poor, genteel and sensitive people who are seamstresses, coal-carriers, candy-makers, sharecroppers, bakers, baby care-takers, housewives, foot soldiers, penny candy sellers, vegetable peelers who are somehow able to sustain within themselves the poet's heart, sensitivity and appreciation of pure emotion, the ability to freely spend tears and laughter without saving them up for a rainy day. I was raised by and among such people living on the poorest blocks in Harlem and have met many more on the boundary lines of the segregated life—the places where black, white, brown, yellow and red sometimes meet—in bus stations, train and plane waiting rooms, on lines where we pay gas, light and telephone bills.

"*Wedding Band* kept coming at me from hidden, unexpected places, the characters called on my mind while I was trying to write something else, demanding attention, getting together, coming into being. It was a play I did not want to write, about people few others wanted to hear from . . . I thought. It somehow seemed to be answering back all the stage and screen

stories about rich, white land owners and their 'octoroon' mistresses.

"Such stories meant nothing in my life. I am a black woman of light complexion, have no white relatives except on the other side of slavery, and have experienced the sweetness, joy and bitterness of living almost entirely within the Harlem community. I really did not wish to beat the drum for an interracial couple and yet there they were in front of me, not giving a damn about public opinion of this day or that past day. It was like being possessed by rebel spirits, ideas clinging, taking over and starting my day for me. Instead of a joyous experience, writing the play became a trial, a rough journey through reams of paper. Characters know, they won't be fooled, not even by their medium, the writer. They *allow* you to write them, pushing you along until they're satisfied that they've done their thing to the utmost of your ability.

"I was born in Charleston, South Carolina, and raised on 118th Street between Lenox and Fifth Avenues in Harlem, New York City. My grandmother and her friends were not ashamed of living: 'Got it to do!' they said. When people were ill, neighbors rallied and brought various home remedies to the bedside, seldom a doctor. Those days are almost gone, thank God. Who wants to live with one foot in hell just for the sake of nostalgia? Our time is forever now! Today our youngsters can freely discuss sex. Soon they will even be able to openly discuss one of the results of sex—life. I also remember death, funerals, just before it went out of style to have the last service within the home instead of at the undertaking parlor. In one corner of the kitchen, a big truckdriver of a man wept tears into a large handkerchief, his shoulders shaking with grief: 'Why did she leave us? Only last week I was talking to her and answered real short: "shut up." I said that to her . . . and now she's gone.' And those there gathered answered him with healing words of comfort: 'Well, God knows you loved her, don't take it so hard, you did your best.' They brought him through that day. Other men, richer and smarter, had to go through three years of therapy to find the reasons why and why and why . . . and to know there's always another why. On our block there was prostitution, but we were so damned blind until even the prostitutes were called 'Miss' Margaret or 'Miss' Beatrice or whatever. And they did not beckon to men until our backs were turned, most of the time. Heroin was not yet King of the Ghetto and a boy would not dream of killing his grandmother or hurting his mamma or her friends in order to pour cooked opium dust through a hole in his arm. But they weren't 'the good old days.' The only good days are ahead. The characters kept chasing me down. Men in love with 'nothing to offer.' Women who couldn't or wouldn't hold back their emotions 'for the sake of the race.' They tap at the brain and move a pen to action to the middle of the night. They are alive, they really are, pushing and shoving interfering creators out of the way. Now, in this slot of time, they return singing old songs about inner discovery. Other characters keep knocking at our doors, pushing, pulling, tearing at seams of life. Poets, novelists, painters, playwrights stand around shifting from foot to foot, trying to keep score. Ordinary people know more about how to live with love and hate than given credit for . . . even though they're never seen on talk shows. I've tried to capture some of them in *Wedding Band*." [Alice Childress, "Those Were the Days, My Friend," *Sunday News* (Leisure Section; N.Y.), December 3, 1972. Amended by Childress.]

The publishing world presented itself to Childress. "I didn't have to fight and struggle as in the theater because, almost by accident, an editor came to me who knew of my playwriting—the late Ferdinand Monjo, he was also a noted children's au-

LENNIE
We all hungry, Celia. Can't you hold out a little more? ■ (From *When the Rattlesnake Sounds*
by Alice Childress. Illustrated by Charles Lilly.)

thor. He said, 'Alice, you've said so much about drugs in your writing, why don't you really put some time into it, and do a book?'' That's how I came to write *A Hero Ain't Nothin' but a Sandwich.* He told me it had to be a young adult book because he was a young adult book editor . . . and young adults needed such a book.

In *A Hero . . .* each chapter represents a different character's point of view: the boy on drugs, the boy's mother, the boy's teacher, etc. ''When I'm writing a character that I see as a villain, I try to take the villain's side and believe in the righteousness of the villainous act. In *A Hero . . .* we pondered long over cutting out the drug pusher's side of the story. [Because it was a book for young people.] The drug pusher is so convincing about the rightness of his acts and the reader feels for him. Monjo was very helpful. After a great deal of talk about it, we decided to leave the character in.''

A Hero . . . went as far as the Supreme Court in a book-banning case, along with books by eight other authors. ''Nine books got to the Supreme Court, and mine was one of them. I don't know if I'm the first or only woman whose book got to the Supreme Court on a banning. In one school, the authorities banned *Romeo and Juliet,* saying the Nurse was a poor role model, because Juliet's parents had hired her to take care of their daughter, and there she was passing notes and arranging liaisons, covering up that Romeo and Juliet were seeing each other. Another school banned *all* of Shakespeare's

plays *except Romeo and Juliet.* But some people have the wrong idea. They say 'I like this book, such a beautiful book shouldn't be banned.' But they don't mind it when a book they *don't* like is banned. I feel we must be against banning regardless of whether we like a book. We do not have to accept its content or quality; we do not have to read or accept a book at all—but to ban it is wrong.

''The theater influences my novel writing. I feel each chapter is a scene, but when writing novels, I find description difficult. With plays, after we've described the set, we're free of that. We don't have to describe the sun rising or the sound of rain. Someone else brings lighting, set, costumes and sound to life for us. Playwrights are specialists in dialogue, situation and conflict, and they must make it all happen within a limited time and space. The novel is more permissive. When I'm writing a book, I visualize it all on a stage. I'm very pleased when critics say my novels feel like plays. I've learned to lean on theater instead of breaking with it. I came to theater first, acted for eleven years with the American Negro Theatre and started writing out of that experience. When writing a novel or a play I act out all the parts. I've actually gotten up, walked around and played out a scene when I've run into difficulty with the writing . . . moved through all the entrances and exits. Making theater is more than how you feel and speak, it's how you move. You have to work it out, act it out, think it out as if on a stage. I also think that way about a book.''

(From the movie "A Hero Ain't Nothin' but a Sandwich," starring Paul Winfield and Cicely Tyson. Copyright © 1977 by New World Pictures.)

(From the stage production of "Wedding Band: A Love/Hate Story in Black and White,"
starring Ruby Dee [left]. Produced at the New York Shakespeare Festival Theatre, 1972.)

Childress feels that "the less a writer understands the faster he or she can write. . . . And you're forgiven for what you don't know. But when you understand your material, you can't shove it along at great speed. When you 'know,' there is a pleasure in taking time, in stopping yourself, in choosing another direction. As my present editor, Refna Wilkins, once said to me, 'Alice, you always pick the hard way.' I ask myself if it's healthy, choosing the more difficult road. I guess the bottom line about writing is that it's a torturous process but the beautiful part is there's a deep, indescribable, inexplicable satisfaction in having written—feeling of elevation and joy afterwards that is greater than the despair of sitting there and doing it. I don't enjoy the writing process. I like writing when I have completed it."

HOBBIES AND OTHER INTERESTS: Traveling.

FOR MORE INFORMATION SEE: New York Times, November 5, 1955, February 2, 1969, October 26, 1972, February 3, 1978, January 11, 1979; *Crises,* April, 1965; Alice Childress, "The Negro Woman in American Literature," *Freedomways,* winter, 1966; Loften Mitchell, *Black Drama: The Story of the American Negro in the Theatre,* Hawthorn, 1966; *Negro Digest,* April, 1967, January, 1968; Langston Hughes and Milton Meltzer, *Black Magic: A Pictorial History of the Negro in American Entertainment,* Prentice-Hall, 1967; Doris E. Abramson, *Negro Playwrights in the American Theatre: 1925-1959,* Columbia University Press, 1969; *Show Business,* April 12, 1969; *Washington Post,* May 18, 1971; *New Yorker,* November 4, 1972; *Nation,* November 13, 1972; *Variety,* December 20, 1972; Theressa G. Rush, Carol Fairbanks, and Esther S. Arata, *Black American Writers Past and Present: A Biographical and Bibliographical Dictionary,* Volume 1, Scarecrow, 1975.

James V. Hatch, *Black Playwrights, 1823-1977*, Bowker, 1977; James A. Page, *Selected Black American Authors: An Illustrated Bio-Bibliography*, G. K. Hall, 1977; John T. Gillespie, *More Juniorplots: A Guide for Teachers and Librarians*, Bowker, 1977; *Lion and the Unicorn*, fall, 1978; *Los Angeles Times*, November 13, 1978; *Village Voice*, January 15, 1979; *New York Times Book Review*, November 11, 1979; *Washington Post Book World*, December 28, 1979; Janet Brown, *Feminist Drama*, Scarecrow, 1979; *Contemporary Literary Criticism*, Gale, Volume XII, 1980, Volume XV, 1980; A. Childress, ''Knowing the Human Condition,'' in *Black American Literature and Humanism*, edited by R. Baxter Miller, University of Kentucky Press, 1981.

COONEY, Caroline B. 1947-

PERSONAL: Born May 10, 1947; daughter of Dexter Mitchell (a purchasing agent) and Martha (a teacher; maiden name, Willerton) Bruce; (divorced); children: Louisa, Sayre, Harold. *Education:* Attended Indiana University, 1965-66, Massachusetts General Hospital School of Nursing, 1966-67, and University of Connecticut, 1968. *Residence:* Westbrook, Conn. *Agent:* Curtis Brown Ltd., 10 Astor Pl., New York, N.Y. 10003.

CAREER: Author, 1978—. Musician (organist). *Member:* Authors' Guild, Mystery Writers of America. *Awards, honors:* North Carolina American Association of University Women's Award for juvenile literature, 1980, for *Safe as the Grave;* Romantic Book Awards, Teen Romance category, 1985, for her body of work.

WRITINGS—Young adult, except as noted: *Safe as the Grave* (juvenile mystery; Junior Literary Guild selection; illustrated by Gail Owens), Coward, 1979; *Rear View Mirror* (adult), Random House, 1980; *The Paper Caper* (juvenile mystery;

CAROLINE B. COONEY

(Cover illustration by G. D. Lang from *I'm Not Your Other Half* by Caroline B. Cooney.)

Junior Literary Guild selection; illustrated by G. Owens), Coward, 1981; *An April Love Story*, Scholastic, 1981; *Nancy and Nick*, Scholastic, 1982; *He Loves Me Not*, Scholastic, 1982; *A Stage Set for Love*, Archway, 1983; *Holly in Love*, Scholastic, 1983; *I'm Not Your Other Half*, Putnam, 1984; *Sun, Sea, and Boys*, Archway, 1984; *Nice Girls Don't*, Scholastic, 1984; *Rumors*, Scholastic, 1985; *Trying Out*, Scholastic, 1985; *Suntanned Days*, Simon & Schuster, 1985; *Racing to Love*, Archway, 1985; *The Bad and the Beautiful*, Scholastic, 1985; *The Morning After*, Scholastic, 1985; *All the Way*, Scholastic, 1985; *Saturday Night*, Scholastic, 1986; *Don't Blame the Music*, Putnam, 1986.

Contributor of stories to juvenile and young adult magazines, including *Seventeen, American Girl, Jack and Jill, Humpty Dumpty,* and *Young World.*

WORK IN PROGRESS: A screenplay; a young adult novel, *The Girl Who Invented Romance,* for Bantam; two sequels to *Saturday Night.*

ADAPTATIONS: ''Rear View Mirror'' (television movie; based on *Rear View Mirror*), starring Lee Remick, 1984.

(From the television movie "Rear View Mirror," starring Lee Remick. Released by Warner Brothers Television Distribution, 1984.)

SIDELIGHTS: "I have been writing exclusively for teenagers for several years now. Most of my books are written to an editor's request: for example, *Don't Blame the Music* was based on my (then) Pacer editor's wish for a book about a girl who craves fame to the point of destroying herself. I also write books in series, having done four 'Cheerleader' books for Scholastic, and two 'Chrystal Falls.' It is exciting to write 'to order.' It often involves an idea or characters I've never thought about before, and I have to tackle it cold like any other assignment. Editors have such good ideas! I also continue to write my own ideas, like *The Girl Who Invented Romance.* 'Romance' is a board game that Kelly designs and the board game will be part of the book.

"My daughters are now fifteen and eighteen, a high school sophomore and a college freshman, and I am pretty well surrounded with teenagers. The town I live in is quiet, and out of the mainstream of social problems and disasters, which my daughters think is too bad—they'd like to live in an exciting city with some action! But it's a good place to think, and watch, and write. My son, who is eleven, is my child who dislikes school and books. It has been a real revelation to me to live with someone who finds all that an annoyance interrupting his *real* life.

"About half the books I write are romances. I believe that to love and to be loved are the most fierce desires any of us will ever have, and young girls can never read enough about it. (Girls *my* age can never read enough about it, either!) One of my daughters loves teen romances and memorizes mine; the other daughter wouldn't be caught dead reading a romance; and my son wants to know, when each book is published, does this mean we have enough money to go to Disney World again?"

CORRIN, Sara 1918-

BRIEF ENTRY: Born August 25, 1918, in London, England. Corrin graduated from the University of London, receiving a teacher's certification in 1956 and an advanced diploma in child development in 1963. She has worked as a senior lecturer in education at the Hertfordshire College of Higher Education. Since the 1960s, Corrin and her husband Stephen have been co-editors of numerous collections of stories and poems for children. These, said Corrin, are inspired by "an unquenchable desire to share great yarns and beautiful tales." The Corrins' books are suitable for children in age groups ranging from under five to ten and older. Beginning in 1964 with *Stories for Seven-Year-Olds and Other Young Readers,* they have presented read-aloud stories such as James Thurber's "Many Moons," Dickens's "The Magic Fishbone" (both in *Stories for Eight-Year-Olds and Other Young Readers*), and Kipling's "The White Seal," along with Greek myths and folktales (all in *Stories for Nine-Year-Olds and Other Young Readers*).

Fourteen years after the first edition, *More Stories for Seven-Year-Olds and Other Young Readers* appeared, with, according to *Times Literary Supplement,* "a wider thematic and geographical range." This collection includes tales from Ireland, Greece, Russia, Italy, and Canada. The Corrins combined two variants of a Brothers Grimm tale to produce a picture book entitled *Mrs. Fox's Wedding* published in 1980. Among the husband-and-wife team's anticipated works are more collections of stories and another picture book retelling, *The Pied Piper of Hamelin. Residence:* London, England.

The glory of young men is their strength.
—Proverbs 20:29

CORRIN, Stephen

BRIEF ENTRY: Born in Tredegar, South Wales. Editor, writer, reviewer, and translator. Corrin and his wife Sara have co-edited a number of anthologies for children in which familiar stories are mixed with retellings of folktales. Tales by authors such as Hans Christian Andersen and the Brothers Grimm are found in *Stories for Seven-Year-Olds and Other Young Readers* (Faber, 1964), while *Stories for Six-Year-Olds and Other Young Readers* (Faber, 1967) features shorter, more modern selections. Subjects other than folk and fairy tales also appear in their anthologies. For example, *Pet Stories for Children* (Faber, 1985) abounds with dogs, cats, ponies, a kangaroo, and a crocodile, while *Round the Christmas Tree* (Faber, 1983) presents familiar and lesser-known Christmas stories. In *Once upon a Rhyme: 101 Poems for Young Children* (Faber, 1982), the Corrins provide what *School Library Journal* described as "a poetry collection in the old style—in the spirit of de la Mare, Untermeyer, and the first edition of Arbuthnot . . . ranging in time from the Renaissance to Silverstein." Corrin, who attended the University of Wales and the Institut Français, has lectured on children's literature and reviewed adult nonfiction and juvenile fiction for the *Times Educational Supplement* and other periodicals. He is an occasional consultant to the British Broadcasting Corporation on children's reading, and has translated works from the French, Russian, Danish, and German. *Residence:* London, England.

CRESSWELL, Helen 1934-

PERSONAL: Born July 11, 1934, in Nottinghamshire, England; daughter of J. E. (an electrical engineer) and A. E. (Clarke) Cresswell; married Brian Rowe (in textiles), April 14, 1962; children: Caroline Jane, Candida Lucy. *Education:* Kings College, University of London, B.A. (with honors), 1955. *Religion:* Church of England. *Home:* Old Church Farm, Eakring, Newark, Nottinghamshire NG22 0DA, England. *Agent:* A. M. Heath & Co. Ltd., 40-42 William IV St., London WC2N 4DD, England.

CAREER: Writer, mainly of books for children. Career up to marriage was varied, including periods as literary assistant to a foreign author, fashion buyer, and teacher, and television work for British Broadcasting Corp. *Member:* International P.E.N., Society of Authors.

AWARDS, HONORS: Nottingham Poetry Society Award for best poem submitted in annual competition, 1950; runner-up, Carnegie Medal, 1967, for *The Piemakers,* 1969, for *The Nightwatchmen,* 1971, for *Up the Pier,* and 1973, for *The Bongleweed;* runner-up, Guardian Award for children's fiction, 1967, for *The Piemakers,* 1968, for *The Signposters;* runner-up for best children's original television drama, Television Writers Guild of Great Britain, 1972, for "Lizzie Dripping"; *Absolute Zero: Being the Second Part of the Bagthorpe Saga* was named "Best Book" by *School Library Journal,* 1978; *Absolute Zero: Being the Second Part of the Bagthorpe Saga* and *Bagthorpes Unlimited: Being the Third Part of the Bagthorpe Saga* were both selected as a "Children's Choice" by the International Reading Association, both 1979; runner-up, Whitbread Literary Award, for best children's novel, 1982, for *The Secret World of Polly Flint.*

WRITINGS—Juvenile: *Sonya-by-the-Shore* (illustrated by Robin Jane Wells), Dent, 1960; *Jumbo Spencer* (illustrated by Clixby Watson), Brockhampton Press, 1963, Lippincott, 1966;

The White Sea Horse (illustrated by Robin Jacques), Oliver & Boyd, 1964, Lippincott, 1965, new edition published as *The White Sea Horse and Other Stories from the Sea* (contains *The White Sea Horse, The Sea Piper,* and *A Tide for the Captain*), Chatto & Windus, 1972.

Jumbo Back to Nature (illustrated by Leslie Wood), Brockhampton Press, 1965; *Pietro and the Mule* (illustrated by Maureen Eckersley), Oliver & Boyd, 1965, Bobbs-Merrill, 1970; *Jumbo Afloat* (illustrated by L. Wood), Brockhampton Press, 1966; *Where the Wind Blows* (illustrated by Peggy Fortnum), Faber, 1966, Funk & Wagnalls, 1968; *The Piemakers* (illustrated by V. H. Drummond), Faber, 1967, Lippincott, 1968, new edition (illustrated by Judith G. Brown), Macmillan 1980; *A Day on Big O* (illustrated by Shirley Hughes), Benn, 1967, Follett, 1968; *A Tide for the Captain* (illustrated by R. Jacques), Oliver & Boyd, 1967; *The Signposters* (illustrated by Gareth Floyd), Faber, 1968; *The Sea Piper* (illustrated by R. Jacques), Oliver & Boyd, 1968; *Jumbo and the Big Dig* (illustrated by L. Wood), Brockhampton Press, 1968; *Rug Is a Bear* (illustrated by Susanna Gretz), Benn, 1968; *Rug Plays Tricks* (illustrated by S. Gretz), Benn, 1968; *The Barge Children* (illustrated by Lynette Hemmant), Brockhampton, 1968; *The Night-watchmen* (illustrated by G. Floyd), Faber, 1969, Macmillan, 1970; *A Game of Catch* (illustrated by G. Floyd), Oliver & Boyd, 1969, (illustrated by Ati Forberg), Macmillan, 1977; *A Gift from Winklesea* (illustrated by Janina Ede), Brockhampton Press, 1969; *A House for Jones* (illustrated by Margaret Gordon), Benn, 1969; *Rug Plays Ball* (illustrated by S. Gretz), Benn, 1969; *Rug and a Picnic* (illustrated by S. Gretz), Benn, 1969.

HELEN CRESSWELL

The shores of the lake were lit by little glowing lamps.
■ (From *The Secret World of Polly Flint* by Helen Cresswell. Illustrated by Shirley Felts.)

The Outlanders (illustrated by Doreen Roberts), Faber, 1970; *Rainbow Pavement* (illustrated by S. Hughes), Benn, 1970; *The Wilkses* (illustrated by G. Floyd), BBC Publications, 1970; *John's First Fish* (illustrated by Prudence Seward), Macmillan, 1970; *At the Stroke of Midnight: Traditional Fairy Tales Retold* (illustrated by Carolyn Dinan), Collins, 1971; *The Bird Fancier* (illustrated by Renate Meyer), Benn, 1971; *Up the Pier* (ALA Notable Book; *Horn Book* honor list; illustrated by G. Floyd), Faber, 1971, Macmillan, 1972; *The Weather Cat* (illustrated by Margery Gill), Benn, 1971; *The Beachcombers* (illustrated by Errol Le Cain), Macmillan, 1972; *Bluebirds over Pit Row* (illustrated by Richard Kennedy), Benn, 1972; *Jane's Policeman* (illustrated by M. Gill), Benn, 1972; *The Long Day* (illustrated by M. Gill), Benn, 1972; *Roof Fall!* (illustrated by R. Kennedy), Benn, 1972; *Short Back and Sides* (illustrated by R. Kennedy), Benn, 1972; *Lizzie Dripping* (illustrated by Jenny Thorne), BBC Publications, 1972; *The Beetle Hunt* (illustrated by Anne Knight), Longman, 1973; *The Bongleweed* (illustrated by Ann Strugnell), Macmillan, 1973; *The Bower Bird* (illustrated by M. Gill), Benn, 1973; *The Key* (illustrated by R. Kennedy), Benn, 1973; *Cheap Day Return* (illustrated by R. Kennedy), Benn, 1974; *Shady Deal* (illustrated by R. Kennedy), Benn, 1974; *The Trap* (illustrated by R. Kennedy), Benn, 1974; *Lizzie Dripping by the Sea* (illustrated by Faith Jacques), BBC Publications, 1974; *Lizzie Dripping and the Little Angel* (illustrated by F. Jacques), BBC Publishing, 1974; *Lizzie Dripping Again* (illustrated by F. Jacques), BBC Publications, 1974; *Two Hoots* (illustrated by Martine Blanc), Benn, 1974, Crown, 1978; *Two Hoots Go to*

Sea (illustrated by M. Blanc), Benn, 1974, Crown, 1978; *More Lizzie Dripping* (illustrated by F. Jacques), BBC Publications, 1974.

Butterfly Chase (illustrated by M. Gill) Kestrel, 1975; *The Winter of the Birds* (ALA Notable Book; *Horn Book* honor list), Faber, 1975, Macmillan, 1976; *Two Hoots in the Snow* (illustrated by M. Blanc), Benn, 1975, Crown, 1978; *Two Hoots and the Big Bad Bird* (illustrated by M. Blanc), Benn, 1975, Crown, 1978; *Two Hoots and the King* (illustrated by M. Blanc), Benn, 1977, Crown, 1978; *Two Hoots Play Hide and Seek* (illustrated by M. Blanc), Benn, 1977, Crown, 1978; *Awful Jack* (illustrated by Joanna Stubbs), Hodder & Stoughton, 1977; *Ordinary Jack: Being the First Part of the Bagthorpe Saga* (ALA Notable Book; *Horn Book* honor list; illustrated by J. Bennet), Macmillan, 1977; *Donkey Days* (illustrated by S. Hughes), Benn, 1977; *Absolute Zero: Being the Second Part of the Bagthorpe Saga* (ALA Notable Book; illustrated by J. Bennet), Macmillan, 1978; *Bagthorpes Unlimited: Being the Third Part of the Bagthorpe Saga* (ALA Notable Book; illustrated by J. Bennet), Macmillan, 1978; *Bagthorpes Versus the World: Being the Fourth Part of the Bagthorpe Saga* (illustrated by J. Bennet), Macmillan, 1979; *The Flyaway Kite* (illustrated by Bridget Clarke), Kestrel, 1979.

My Aunt Polly by the Sea (illustrated by Margaret Gordon), Wheaton, 1980; *Nearly Goodbye* (illustrated by Tony Morris), Macmillan (London), 1980; *Penny for the Guy* (illustrated by

(Jacket illustration by Lino Saffioti from *Dear Shrink* by Helen Cresswell.)

"I know we're the *cleverest* family in England," said Rosie aged nine. ■ (Jacket illustration by Trina Schart Hyman from *Bagthorpes Versus the World: Being the Fourth Part of The Bagthorpe Saga* by Helen Cresswell.)

Nicole Goodwin), Macmillan (London), 1980; *Dear Shrink,* Macmillan, 1982; *The Secret World of Polly Flint,* (illustrated by Shirley Felts), Faber, 1982, Macmillan, 1984; *Bagthorpes Abroad: Being the Fifth Part of the Bagthorpe Saga,* Macmillan, 1984; *Ellie and the Hagwitch* (illustrated by J. Heap), P. Hardy, 1984; *Bagthorpes Haunted: Being the Sixth Part of the Bagthorpe Saga,* Macmillan, 1985; *Whodunnnit?* (illustrated by Caroline Browne), J. Cape, 1986; *Greedy Alice* (illustrated by Martin Honeysett), Deutsch, 1986; *Moondial,* Faber, 1987.

Contributor: M. R. Hodgkin, editor, *Winter's Tales for Children 4,* Macmillan (London), 1968; A. D. Maclean, editor, *Winter's Tales,* Macmillan, 1969; Anne Geraghty, editor, *The World of Ballet,* Collins, 1970; Eileen Colwell, editor, *Bad Boys,* Puffin, 1972; *Author's Choice 2,* Hamish Hamilton, 1973, Crowell, 1974; Leon Garfield, editor, *Bakers Dozen,* Ward, Lock, 1973, Lothrop, 1974; Richard Church and others, *My England,* Heinnemann, 1973; Noel Streatfeild, *Christmas Holiday Book,* Dent, 1973; N. Streatfeild, *Summer Holiday Book,* Dent, 1973; Clifton Fadiman, *Cricket's Choice,* Open Court Publishing, 1974; N. Streatfeild, *Birthday Book,* Dent, 1975; Lance Salway, editor, *The Cat-Flap and the Apple Pie and Other Funny Stories,* W. H. Allen, 1979; L. Salway, editor, *They Wait,* Pepper Press, 1983; *Over the Rainbow,* St. Michael, 1983; Jennifer Kavanagh, editor, *The Methuen Book of Animal Tales,* Methuen, 1983; Aidan Chambers, editor, *Shades of Dark,* Patrick Hardy Books, 1984; L. Salway, editor, *Shivers in the Dark,* Magnet Books, 1984; Kaye Webb, editor, *I Like This Story,* Puffin, 1986. Also contributor of short stories and poetry to *Cornhill Magazine.*

Television plays; all produced by British Broadcasting Corp.: "Dick Whittington" (based on original fairytale), 1974; "For Bethlehem Read Little Thraves" (adult), 1976; "Lizzie Dripping and the Witch," 1977, (stage play) first produced at Unicorn Theater, London, England, 1979; "The Day Posy Bates Made History," 1977; "The Haunted School" (eight-part miniseries), Revcom (France) and Australian Broadcasting Co., 1986.

ADAPTATIONS—Television plays; all produced by British Broadcasting Corp., except as indicated: "The Piemakers," 1967; "The Signposters," 1968; "The Night-watchmen," 1969; "The Outlanders," 1970; "Lizzie Dripping" series, six episodes, 1973, five episodes, 1975; "Jumbo Spencer" series, five episodes, 1976; "The Bagthorpe Saga," 1981; "The Secret World of Polly Flint" series, seven episodes, ITV Central Television, 1986; "Moondial," six-part series, 1987.

SIDELIGHTS: **July 11, 1936.** Born in Nottinghamshire, England, the middle child of three. Nottinghamshire is the birthplace of two other famous English authors, D. H. Lawrence and Lord Byron. Perhaps because of this distinction, Cresswell can't remember a time when she didn't want to become a writer. "I began writing at the age of six or seven, in fact don't remember ever *not* writing, and all my earliest work was verse. I had a tremendous output right through my teens and early twenties. I experimented with countless techniques, and altogether think it a very useful apprenticeship. I think the fantasy I now write is an extension of poetry, and that very

much the same processes are involved in the writing of them. I still think of myself as a poet rather than a novelist, though certain of my books, e.g. the 'Jumbo Spencer' series, clearly are novels. The main body of my work is fantasy. It seems to me that a very much deeper level of truth can be reached through fantasy than by any other form of writing (except poetry, of course)."

1950. Won her first literary prize at the age of fourteen for best poem submitted in the annual competition of the Nottingham Poetry Society. "I probably seem too prolific to some people, but this I cannot help. I started writing a lot too early in life to be able to break the habit now. The passion for words has been the strongest and longest-lasting in my life so far, and I see no possibility of my ever being free from it. With it, equally deep-rooted (and I confess this at the risk of being thought hopelessly out of date) goes a passion for natural beauty and the English countryside, so that the two are almost inseparable. The temptation to launch into descriptive passages is sometimes almost irresistible, but in many ways writing for children has been good discipline, in that it has forced me to find the single evocative word or phrase where I might quite happily have written several paragraphs. I am very conscious of the 'spirit of place' and practically all my books are germinated by this feeling rather than by character, plot, message or anything else." [John Rowe Townsend, *A Sense of Story,* Lippincott, 1971.[1]]

During her childhood and teens Cresswell practiced writing by imitating favorite poets. She would write epics in Spencerian stanza, imitate Gerard Manley Hopkins' sprung rhythm, and write poetry in the style of Keats.

(Jacket illustration by Trina Schart Hyman from *Absolute Zero: Being the Second Part of The Bagthorpe Saga* by Helen Cresswell.)

1955. Graduated with honors from Kings College, University of London. Although her main career goal was to write full time, Cresswell found it necessary to support herself with a variety of jobs including teaching slow readers in English primary schools to working as a fashion buyer. "I have a strong feeling now, as an adult, that I am practically a result of what I read as a child, and yet I am sure that I did not 'understand,' in the sense of being able to formulate as an idea, even a fraction of what I read. But in reading, as in life, ninety per cent of what we experience, we experience as it were through the pores, and it comes to us directly without our translating it at all. We do not go through life constantly saying to ourselves 'I am now looking at the grass' or 'I can now feel a draught blowing on my neck,' but these kinds of things are happening the whole time and are present to us in some way. The whole time things are filtering through direct, as it were, by-passing our conscious awareness. Paradoxically, then, one almost reads the real substance between the lines of a book.

"I have said that I write partly in order to find out, and in a sense I do now know what I mean until I have said it. And in the same way as I am operating on this level as a writer, so the reader too is experiencing things which he recognizes but has no words for. This is partly what any kind of reading does.

"Do you understand, Modestine? Do you?" he pleaded.
■ (From *Pietro and the Mule* by Helen Cresswell. Illustrated by Maureen Eckersley.)

It makes accessible all kinds of floating feelings and attitudes and ideas which probably have never been crystallized before." [Helen Cresswell, "Ancient and Modern and Incorrigibly Plural," *The Thorny Paradise: Writers on Writing for Children,* edited by Edward Blishen, Kestrel Books, 1975.[2]]

Shortly after graduating from college, Cresswell wrote her first children's book "more to amuse myself than anything."

1960. First book published. Over the next ten years Cresswell produced more than twenty books, which had at least two main themes: poetic fantasy, and humor. "Whenever I am called upon to write or talk about why and how I write, I usually find myself using not my own, but other people's words. I quote endlessly—Gide, Russell, Blake, Lichtenberg, Manley Hopkins, Goethe, MacNeice . . . I have even had it recently suggested to me that I should publish a 'Helen Cresswell Commonplace Book,' so it now looks as if people are beginning to notice. In fact it was this suggestion that made *me* notice, and having noticed, think about it.

"I think there is more than one reason why I always quote other people about the writing process. Firstly, it is because I have an instinctive fear of meddling with my own inner mechanisms. I shall quote my (earlier) self on this:

"These days we have a good many impressive terms for magic, all running into polysyllables and having a pleasantly authoritative ring to them. And these terms are all quite valid, and very useful to the psychologist himself and even to the critic. But to the creative writer they spell death—death to magic. The moment a writer becomes aware of his own creative processes, the moment he stands outside them and they become conscious, then they lose their dynamism, and he may as well lay down his pen. He who attempts to analyse magic while at the same time practising it stands in peril of finding symbol turn to cliché, intuition to conscious will, organic growth to mere plotting.

"I stand by this, adding only to clarify my point the analogy of the havoc that can be caused by paying attention to, say, one's own heartbeat.

"Secondly, having all my life been a solitary and dedicated thinker, a muser, an amateur philosopher, I am always delighted whenever I come across an endorsement of my own beliefs from a superior mind. I then quote to give them added weight for myself, as well as for others.

"But the third, and I suspect the real reason, is that whatever I have to say that is of any value whatever, is contained in my work itself. If I could say what I have to say in any other form, then I would do so. And in any case, I do not usually know what I *do* think until I have said it. . . .

"I do not make a habit of thinking about why I write for children. Any thoughts I have had at all on the matter have been a result of a direct question put to me by someone else. The last time I had to give an answer to it in print, this is what I wrote:

"'If you are going to use words (and I have no choice) you have to say something, and gradually you come to find that when you are saying what you really mean you tend to use words best of all, and so it is worth while finding out what you really mean. I am still working on this. With any luck, I shall *never* really be quite sure what I mean, and so I will never have to stop using words in order to find out. I think that may be one reason why my books are for children. They never know for sure what they mean, either. Most adults do. Most adults manage to find an attitude, and when they have found it, it takes them over, and fixes them like a fly in aspic (or whatever the expression is—I'm sure that's not it. Wasp in alabaster? Bee in marble? Fly in ointment . . .? Drop it . . .).'''[2]

1962. Married Brian Rowe. With their two daughters the couple lived in a two-hundred-year-old Georgian farmhouse at the edge of Robin Hood's Sherwood Forest.

1967. Runner-up for the prestigious Carnegie Medal for her children's book, *The Piemakers*, which was also one of the author's favorite books, giving her much pleasure to write. ''I rarely set out with any definite statement to make, and am usually well into a fantasy before I begin myself to see what it is saying. Carefully worked-out symbolism is almost always cliché. You don't choose symbols—they choose you. I'm a great believer in letting things happen as far as possible. This sounds very woolly and undisciplined but is in fact quite dif-

"You've been sleeping rolled up in newspapers!" said Henry, enchanted. "Are they really warm?" ■ (From *The Night-Watchmen* by Helen Cresswell. Illustrated by Gareth Floyd.)

ficult, and needs a particular, very delicate balance between the workings of the conscious and unconscious minds. If I tried to work out a fantasy in advance with all the symbolism neatly tied up, it would be stone dead before I even started. In fact, I doubt whether I could be bothered to write it, because it would not be an exploration, and there would be nothing in it for me (or for anybody).

"All the same, these fantasies do have meanings, they have meanings to begin with and they take on meanings of their own as they progress. If a fantasy *didn't* have a meaning, then there would be no point in publishing it—I mean, one person's fantasy is as good as another's, isn't it?

"My own favourite book is still *The Piemakers,* partly because I think it the most nearly perfect in form (not that it's anywhere near enough) and partly because it marked a turning-point in my writing, and was the first book in which humour and fantasy became fused. Up till then, the humour had gone into the Jumbo books and the fantasy was unleavened with comedy. With *The Piemakers* I suddenly became conscious that I had found my 'voice' if this is not to use too high-flown a term.

For a minute nobody spoke. ■ (From *A Game of Catch* by Helen Cresswell. Illustrated by Ati Forberg.)

I also had more pleasure in the actual writing of this book than in any other before or since. I loved it, and still do.

"As to why I write for children, I have no idea. I think it may partly be because primarily I have always thought of myself as a poet, having written poetry from childhood in enormous quantities, and I think that fantasy is in many ways an extension of poetry. Also, growing older is very often a growing into rigidity, and there is enormous fluidity and freedom of range possible in children's writing which would not be possible in any other form. Also, it is fun. Also, I have a very great respect for childhood, and like to be talking to human beings before they have become capable of pose or hypocrisy or prejudice. I think this is why my writing is for younger children, for real childhood. Also, I have always had a deep-rooted sense of what I can only describe as 'infinite possibility,' a sort of glorious feeling of the unpredictability of things and their unlimited variety (a bit like what Gerard Manley Hopkins is talking about in his poem 'Pied Beauty') and this excites me very much, and keeps me going."[1]

The Piemakers was inspired by a publicity photo of an enormous pie that was made in the village of Danby Dale in Yorkshire. The book was written in the evenings and took less than a month to complete.

1969. "I have been absolutely staggered at the varying reactions to *The Night-watchmen.* I think it's a sort of do-it-yourself book because everybody's done it themselves. They all know what it's about, but they all say different things. One person said to me 'I started reading this book and I felt absolutely let down. I thought this was just going to be a nice jolly really funny story about these two blokes who camped round the country and got moved on by the police and all this sort of thing. But then it went absolutely off the rails.' So to speak. I went home and brooded on that. Another time the mother of two children said how much they'd enjoyed the book. She said 'It was so marvelous because I picked up the book and thought "Oh dear, here's another of those stories about blokes who camp round the country having adventures," when suddenly it was marvelous.' Well, what do you do? This is why I say it's a do-it-yourself book.

"Writing fantasy needs a very delicate balance between conscious control and openness. When I start writing a fantasy I haven't got very much idea either what it's going to be about or how it's going to end. What I get in the first place is a very strong feeling, an essence that I want, as it were, to distil. I must get a very strong feeling of this essence so that it will then permeate the whole book. I can't put it into words. If I could I wouldn't bother going ahead writing the book. It's just very powerful and I must hold it and let it grow, in the meantime gathering images to itself for later when I begin to write. So I have this feeling, and then the feeling that the time is coming ripe, which I can't describe either. Then I go into what I call the naming phase. I have to name my characters and until I've named my characters I don't know who they are, and yet I know which are the right names for them and I can't begin until I know that the names are absolutely right. I spend up to a fortnight thinking up exactly the right name for each character. Then when I've got that I've usually got the title and I've got this strong feeling and I've got these names.

"I then go through the phase where I think of reasons why I shouldn't begin writing this particular book at this particular moment and I then finally go and I shut myself in and I sit down and I write the title and I write the first paragraph. I cannot tell you how I write the first paragraph, but having written the first it then becomes possible to write the second

Once upon a time there was a mill that stood beside a lazy river called Slow. ■ (From *Where the Wind Blows* by Helen Cresswell. Illustrated by Ati Forberg.)

(From *The Piemakers* by Helen Cresswell. Illustrated by W. T. Mars.)

and this is how it goes on. I don't want to give the impression that one is sitting there waiting for the pen to move, as though this was some kind of automatic writing, but you do have to keep a sort of balance where you must not in the early stages of fantasy impose on it any kind of consciously pre-thoughtout plot or shape. You must let it open out. As it begins to develop you do begin to get a more conscious feeling of what's happening and you can start to control it and direct it. It's very difficult to explain but this is invariably the method I use. We all have our odd little ways and this is my odd little way.

"The characters themselves: I have their names but whenever I see them illustrated it's always a shock to me to see them because—I think a lot of other writers agree about this—you don't see your characters visually, you feel them or hear them, without wishing to sound like Joan of Arc, as voices. You write down their voices more or less and you do not see them as an outsider looking in. They are inside you coming out.

"This vague way of working must sound very unsatisfactory, but I do think for a very long time before I start writing and this thinking isn't plotting, it's ruminating, or brooding and it looks to my friends and relations like downright idleness. When I sit for some time in a chair while people are whirling around me in their various activities, I say to them 'I'm thinking,' and there's no answer to that. When I do start to write, though, I write very rapidly indeed. Sometimes I finish the shorter books in as little as six days.... Of course it always makes it sound as if this has just been rushed off and the whole thing is a piece of cake. But it's not like that at all. In any case they vary.

"Now *The Night-watchmen.* I had this idea which was a comic one about these two old boys. We had these men putting in sewerage pipes in our lane—that is, we gathered in the end they were putting in sewerage pipes. They were there for nearly a year doing it and it did occur to me in absolute seriousness, all joking apart, that one could actually get a pickaxe and make a hole and have a hole and a hut of one's own and squat for some considerable length of time without any questions being asked. One almost feels tempted to test this. This was the idea and it was just purely going to be a comic thing and I sat down and I wrote the first chapter more or less as it now stands in *The Night-watchmen.* And when I'd written the first chapter I thought, well, now what? That's all there is to it, I can't write any more, I put it away and more or less forgot about it for a couple of years and wrote other things in the meantime." [Helen Cresswell, "If It's Someone from Porlock, Don't Answer the Door," *Children's Literature in Education 4,* March, 1971.[3]]

1980. After twenty years of writing, Cresswell had achieved substantial success with her profession. She had written over sixty books, several television plays, and contributed articles to magazines. Four of her books were runner-ups for the Carnegie Medal. She wrote five original television plays for children and had six of her books adapted for children and read on the British children's program, "Jackanory." With an Arts Council Grant, Cresswell had also adapted *Lizzie Dripping and the Witch* for the London stage. "If I have an attitude, which I doubt (because attitudes are rigid, and I like things to be flexible), it is one of idealism. I feel bound always to affirm the possibilities for good in any given situation. I am not a sentimentalist. But I have a strenuous faith in the human spirit and the qualities I most admire are those of courage and gaiety. I have never been able to see that to be realistic one must be pessimistic.

"I am never aware that I am writing specifically for children. In fact, I have no idea whom I am trying to 'reach.' Everyone, probably."

Besides writing, Cresswell enjoys gardening, walking, collecting antiques and exploring new places. She is also interested in the study of philosophy, and her books reflect this interest. "... My books are roads, journeys, explorations. I do not know where I am going until I arrive there. I simply set out. I write at the top of a blank sheet the title I have given myself, and set out.

"This is not properly expressed, and I never can find the right words to say it (probably because I do not really wish to.) When I was trying to say it recently to someone who was asking me questions, she said, 'You mean that your books are riddles that you set yourself, and you write them in order to solve them.' Which is more or less right. . . .

"... Each book simply rounds another bend in the road. And the more I read of writers like Jung, Koestler, Roszak, Wilson, Laing and Lyall Watson, the more I see that the road I am travelling is not one that has already been mapped, because it is one for which each traveller must make his *own* map. It is not a wistful, nostalgic tour with an already certain destination, but a *real* one, being travelled here and now by countless thousands of others (most of them young) and with no fixed point of arrival. There never can be a final destination because the meaning of the journey lies in the making of it. In a sense, the moment one sets out, one is there."[2]

HOBBIES AND OTHER INTERESTS: Collecting antiques, walking, visiting the seashore, "ticking"—exploring new places, philosophy, gardening, and "collecting coincidences."

FOR MORE INFORMATION SEE: New York Times Book Review, January 2, 1966, November 8, 1970; *Times Literary Supplement,* May 25, 1967, June 6, 1968, April 4, 1969, June 26, 1969, July 7, 1970, December 3, 1971, November 3, 1972, November 23, 1973, December 5, 1975, April 7, 1978, July 23, 1982; *Play,* Volume 1, number 1, September, 1969; Marcus Crouch, "Helen Cresswell—Craftsman," *Junior Bookshelf,* June, 1970; Helen Cresswell, "If It's Someone from Porlock, Don't Answer the Door," *Children's Literature in Education 4,* March, 1971; Martha E. Ward and Dorothy A. Marquardt, *Authors of Books for Young People,* 2nd edition, Scarecrow Press, 1971; John Rowe Townsend, *A Sense of Story,* Lippincott, 1971; *Books and Bookmen,* February, 1973, November, 1975, June, 1980; *Horn Book,* February, 1973, October, 1978, April, 1981; *Spectator,* October 20, 1973, December 10, 1977; *New Statesman,* November 9, 1973; November 3, 1978; H. Cresswell, "Ancient and Modern and Incorrigibly Plural," *The Thorny Paradise,* edited by Edward Blishen, Kestrel Books, 1975; *Listener,* November 10, 1977; *Washington Post Book World,* April 9, 1978; D. L. Kirkpatrick, *Twentieth-Century Chidren's Writers,* St. Martin's Press, 1978; Doris de Montreville and Elizabeth D. Crawford, editors, *Fourth Book of Junior Authors and Illustrators,* H. W. Wilson, 1978; *Chicago Tribune Book World,* October 10, 1982.

DEEGAN, Paul Joseph 1937-
(Sean O'Reilly)

PERSONAL: Born March 19, 1937, in Mankato, Minn.; son of Ray C. (a civil engineer) and Ellen G. (Coughlin) Deegan; married Dorothy A. Schreiner (a registered nurse), September 24, 1960; children: Lisa, Michael, John. *Education:* University of Minnesota, B.A., 1959. *Religion:* Christian. *Home:* 139 Eastwood Dr., Mankato, Minn. 56001. *Office:* P.O. Box 3089, Mankato, Minn. 56001.

CAREER: Served as a reporter and editor with newspapers in Austin, Mankato, and St. Paul, Minn., 1960-69. Creative Education, Inc., Mankato, editorial director, 1969-80; Children's Book Company, Mankato, editorial director, 1969-80, president, 1980-82, consultant, 1982-83; Deegan Learning Materials, Inc., Mankato, president, 1982; Deegan Associates, Mankato, owner, 1983-86; Total Concept Software, Mankato, chief executive officer, 1985—; MGA Graphics, Inc., Mankato, director of publications services, 1986—. Author of books for young people, 1969. Chairman of the board of education of the Mankato Public Schools, 1978-83.

WRITINGS—Juvenile; all published by Creative Education, except as noted: *A Monastery: Life in a Religious Community* (illustrated with photographs by Bruce Larson), 1970; *Animals of East Africa: Our Vanishing Wildlife* (illustrated with photographs by B. Larson), 1970; *A Hospital: Life in a Medical Center* (illustrated with photographs by B. Larson), 1971; *A Kibbutz: Life on an Israeli Commune* (illustrated with photographs by Yair Shazar), 1971; *Jack Nicklaus* (illustrated by Harold Henriksen), 1974; *O. J. Simpson* (illustrated by H. Henriksen), 1974.

All published by Amécus Street, except where indicated; all illustrated by Harold Henriksen: *Hank Aaron,* 1974; *Kareem Abdul-Jabbar,* 1974, revised edition with Michael Deegan, Children's Book Company, 1981; *Bill Russell,* 1974; *Tom Seaver,* 1974; *Jerry West,* 1974.

All published by Children's Book Company: (With Gary Libman) *Bjorn Borg,* 1979; (with G. Libman) *Catfish Hunter,* 1979; (with G. Libman) *Reggie Jackson,* 1979; (with M. Deegan) *Magic Johnson,* 1981.

"Sports Instructional" series; all published by Creative Education; all illustrated by Harold Henriksen: *Bunting and Baserunning* (baseball), 1975; *Hitting* (baseball), 1975; *Pitching* (baseball), 1975; *The Jump Shot and Lay-Up* (basketball), 1975; *The Set Shot* (basketball), 1975; *Shooting in a Game* (basketball), 1975; *Catching the Football,* 1975; *Passing the Football,* 1975; *Placekicking and Punting* (football), 1975; *Skates and Skating* (hockey), 1976; *Stickhandling and Passing* (hockey), 1976; *The Basic Strokes* (tennis), 1976; *Serving and Returning Serve* (tennis), 1976; *Volleying and Lobs* (tennis), 1976.

"Meet the Players" series; all under pseudonym Sean O'Reilly; all published by Creative Education: *Meet the Centers,* 1977; *Meet the Coaches,* 1977; *Meet the Guards,* 1977; *Meet the Forwards,* 1977.

"Dan Murphy" series; all published by Amécus Street; all illustrated by Harold Henriksen: *Important Decisions,* 1975; *The Team Manager,* 1975; *Almost a Champion,* 1975; *Dan Moves Up,* 1975; *Close But Not Quite,* 1975; *The Tournaments,* 1975.

It had been a pleasant, sunny day. ■ (From *Dan Moves Up* by Paul J. Deegan. Illustrated by Harold Henriksen.)

"Super Bears" series; all published by Abdo & Daughters: *Richard Dent*, 1986; *Mike Ditka*, 1986; *Willie Gault*, 1986; *Jim McMahon*, 1986; *Walter Payton*, 1986; *William Perry*, 1986; *Mike Singletary*, 1986.

Has also edited and/or designed 100 juvenile books published by Creative Education, Amécus Street, The Children's Book Company; and 15 software manuals published by Deegan Learning Materials, Inc., and Total Concept Software.

WORK IN PROGRESS: "A variety of books and other publications as director of publications services at MGA Graphics, Inc. in Mankato, Minn."

SIDELIGHTS: "I grew up in a home where reading, thinking, and discussing were encouraged. My mother was a teacher, though she was only in a classroom for a few years. However, she and my father encouraged my interests in reading. Books were available, newspapers and magazines were plentiful, and the public library was an easy walk or bike-ride away.

"I began writing while still in grade school. I wrote for myself. I would come home after watching a local athletic contest and write a 'newspaper story' on the game. While in high school and college I worked on school newspapers, and I majored in editorial journalism at the University of Minnesota.

"Writing is basically a discipline, and as in the development of other skills, practice may not make perfect, but is in an indispensable ingredient. Other ingredients are an interest in the language arts and familiarity with its various components. You must be comfortable with the language if you are to convey your . . . ideas.

"Writing for children and young adults requires even more discipline. You must hone your skills because extraneous words, lengthy sentences, and multisyllabic words are obstacles for young readers.

"Writing fiction is particularly challenging, even difficult. The six-book 'Dan Murphy' series I wrote brings the books' characters face to face with some of life's realities. Writing fiction is often hard work, but it is very rewarding when a story unfolds which is entertaining, stimulating, and, hopefully, thought-provoking.

"Fiction allows the author to utilize some of the information and posit some of the questions which accumulate over the years. I have always been interested in many topics—history, contemporary events, education, religion, athletics among them. I read constantly to continually broaden my insights.

"Like many raised in an Irish Catholic atmosphere and exposed to competent parochial education in the 1940s and 1950s, I am basically a skeptic. A skeptical person runs the risk of approaching too many things with an overly negative attitude, but has an advantage when seeking information or trying to sort out many of life's riddles.

"My wife, Dorothy, is my best sounding board and my most reliable critic. She is bright yet much more compassionate and patient than I am. My daughter and two sons, all in their early 20s, are delightful companions and friendly critics.

"The 'Sports Instructional' series I developed stemmed from a lack of readable, informative, accurate instructional material for young readers when our children were at an age where such information was useful to them. My goal was to provide a readable and useful book for any youngster interested in learning how to play a sport.

"Writing is almost always an enjoyment for me. However, doing a specific project often remains primarily a matter of keeping the seat in front of the word processor. Whatever skill may be involved, it is the effort that produces a result."

HOBBIES AND OTHER INTERESTS: "I walk, jog, play tennis, and continue to play competitive basketball—last winter my team went undefeated in an open city league. I read a variety of newspapers, books, and magazines on a daily basis. I enjoy watching basketball, football, tennis, and baseball."

DEWEY, Jennifer (Owings)

BRIEF ENTRY: Born in Chicago, Ill. A wildlife artist and illustrator, Dewey spent her childhood in New Mexico and later attended the Rhode Island School of Design and the University of New Mexico. Usually using pen-and-ink but also employing full color, Dewey has illustrated nearly a dozen books for young readers, including Harriett Weaver's *Frosty: A Raccoon to Remember* (Archway, 1977), Howard E. Smith, Jr.'s *Living Fossils* (Dodd, 1982), Edith Thacher Hurd's *Song of the Sea Otter* (Sierra Club/Pantheon, 1983), and Lucia Anderson's *Mammals and Their Milk* (Dodd, 1985). A *Publishers Weekly* review of *Living Fossils* observed that "[the illustrator's] ink drawings are striking and add illumination on the subject," while *Horn Book* noted that "soft black-and-white drawings" in *Song of the Sea Otter* "carry the listener along . . . and are sufficiently detailed to identify the flora and fauna." In 1984, with authors Terry Tempest Williams and Ted Major, Dewey received the New York Academy of Sciences Children's Science Book Award for *The Secret Language of Snow* (Sierra Club/Pantheon, 1984). She has most recently produced a children's book she not only illustrated but wrote as well, titled *Clem: The Story of a Raven* (Dodd, 1986). It describes her family's experiences caring for and raising a baby raven. In addition to book illustration, Dewey has designed and illustrated several projects for the National Park Service. Her artwork has been exhibited regularly in a number of galleries in the western United States.

DICKINSON, Mary 1949-

PERSONAL: Born January 12, 1949, in Brighton, England; daughter of John (a farmer) and Celia (an antiques dealer; maiden name, Vye) Field; married Charles Dickinson (a teacher), May 21, 1969; children: Sam, Charlotte, Rosie. *Education:* Attended University of Leicester, 1967-70. *Residence:* London, England. *Address:* c/o Andre Deutsch, 105 Great Russell St., London WC1, England.

CAREER: Lambeth Library, London, England, part-time storyteller, 1975—; author of children's books, 1980—.

WRITINGS—For children; all illustrated by Charlotte Firmin, except as indicated: *Alex's Bed*, Deutsch, 1980; *Alex and Roy*, Deutsch, 1981; *Alex and the Baby*, Deutsch, 1982; *Alex's Outing*, Deutsch, 1983; *New Clothes for Alex*, Deutsch, 1984; *Jilly, You Look Terrible* (illustrated by Joanna Stubbs), Deutsch, 1985; *Jilly's Boat Trip* (illustrated by J. Stubbs), Deutsch, 1986; *Jilly Makes It Better* (illustrated by J. Stubbs), Deutsch, 1987.

WORK IN PROGRESS: Alex and Roy stories, a collection for six- to eight-year-olds to read themselves.

They painted their car red, with a yellow stripe along one side. ■ (From *Alex and Roy* by Mary Dickinson. Illustrated by Charlotte Firmin.)

SIDELIGHTS: ''I grew up as an only child on a farm and was very lonely. I did a lot of writing then. My father loved poetry so I wrote poetry. As a hobby my father wrote a column about country life in a weekly magazine. The fury and panic that accompanied getting each week's article in on time was so great I vowed I'd never be a writer. So for many years all I wrote were long letters to my friends, telling them of my amazing adventures. Well, I thought they were amazing.

''I wanted to be a social worker so I studied sociology, but gave up after a year—I couldn't stand putting people in boxes (categories). I then studied economics—a mathematical nightmare to me.

''I suppose my career started with my job as a preschool storyteller at the Lambeth libraries. I got the job because I needed the money and I thought it looked easy. There was no vacancy at first so I telephoned the library once a month for six months until they called me in for an interview and gave me the job.

''My job as a children's storyteller put me in contact with children's books. I was disappointed by the lack of good 'everyday' stories. So I sat down and, for the first time since I left school, worked seriously at writing. I was lucky that my first attempt was accepted.

''I don't think of myself as an author or storyteller. First and foremost I am a parent and household manager. Most of my time is spent dealing with the little details of life. I used to be ashamed at parties when asked what I did, and I answered 'only a housewife.' (Household manager I call it now.) I realize now how vital this job is to give me impetus, ideas and a firm base for my writing and storytelling. Writing and storytelling gives me challenges, private income, the opportunity to travel and promote my ideas—that you don't have to be grown up or rich to have a story worth listening to.

''Every time I feel low, I put down what I am doing and lock myself away to write. The washing piles up, so does the dust, the junk begins to ooze from under the furniture. The weeds in the garden are happily untouched. But writing is a lonely job. I'm always pleased to finish a story and return to the living world.

''My books are about a boy and his mother and their relationship. For children I aim to show incidents that they will rec-

MARY DICKINSON

ognize. For adults I hope to show what a difficult job being a parent is. I'd like to raise the status of parenthood.''

HOBBIES AND OTHER INTERESTS: ''Anything that comes my way. I haven't the time at present to go looking for things. When I'm rich I'll go traveling the world in a mobile home, so I can see the everyday life of other peoples.''

DOBSON, Julia 1941-

PERSONAL: Born September 23, 1941, in Tanzania, East Africa; daughter of Kenneth (a civil servant) and Barbara (Phillips) Dobson; married Christopher Tugendhat, April 8, 1967; children: James, Angus. *Education:* Lady Margaret Hall, Oxford, B.A., 1963. *Politics:* Conservative. *Religion:* Church of England. *Home:* 35 Westbourne Park Rd., London W2 5QD, England. *Agent:* Pat White, 11 Mortimer St., London W1N 7RH, England.

CAREER: Grey Coat School for Girls, London, England, history teacher, 1963-64; Peckham Manor School for Boys, Peckham, England, history teacher, 1964-65; *Time,* New York City, secretary, 1965-66; *Town,* London, general writer, 1966-67; Glendower Primary School, London, teacher, 1967-71; writer, 1971—.

WRITINGS—Juvenile; published by Heinemann, except as noted: *The Children of Charles I* (illustrated by David Walker),

1975; *The Smallest Man in England* (illustrated by Joanna Troughton), 1977; *Children of the Tower* (illustrated by Jeroo Roy), 1978; *They Were at Waterloo* (illustrated by J. Roy), 1979; *Mountbatten: Sailor Hero* (illustrated by Michael Ogden), F. Watts, 1982.

Adventure series; all published by Magnet Books, except as indicated: *The Ivory Poachers* (illustrated by Gary Rees), 1981; *The Tomb Robbers* (illustrated by G. Rees), 1981; *The Wreak Finders,* 1982; *Animal Rescuers,* 1982; *Danger in the Magic Kingdom,* Methuen, 1983; *The Chinese Puzzle,* Methuen, 1984.

SIDELIGHTS: ''My writing arose out of my teaching experience. I found that children read too little and too unwillingly about 'boring' subjects like history, so I set out to write educational books that were exciting as well as informative. In so doing, I may have dealt with my historical material too selectively, but I may have succeeded in livening up history.

''My father wrote some novels when he was young, and my great grandfather, Austin Dobson, was a famous biographer and poet. So I guess I have inherited some literary urge from the Dobsons. My chief problem as a writer married to a public figure is finding time for creative thought in a life in which public and social duties play a large part.

''I am at present taking a break from writing in order to train as a family therapist which will, I am sure, open up a new literary avenue for me.''

HOBBIES AND OTHER INTERESTS: ''My avocational interests are largely centered around children.''

JULIA DOBSON

Hearing shouts behind him, he urged his pony faster and faster. ■ (From *The Smallest Man in England* by Julia Dobson. Illustrated by Joanna Troughton.)

DRABBLE, Margaret 1939-

PERSONAL: Born June 5, 1939, in Sheffield, Yorkshire, England; daughter of John Frederick (a judge) and Kathleen Marie (a teacher; maiden name, Bloor) Drabble; married Clive Walter Swift (an actor with Royal Shakespeare Company), June, 1960 (marriage ended, 1975); married Michael Holroyd (a writer), 1982; children: (first marriage) Adam Richard George, Rebecca Margaret, Joseph. *Education:* Newnham College, Cambridge, B.A. (first class honors), 1960. *Agent:* A. D. Peters, 10 Buckingham St., London W.C.1, England.

CAREER: Writer. Lecturer. Instructor at Morley College, London, England. Member of Royal Shakespeare Company, one year. *Member:* National Book League. *Awards, honors:* John Llewelyn Rhys Memorial Award for *The Millstone,* 1966; James Tait Black Memorial Book Prize, for *Jerusalem the Golden,* 1968; E. M. Forster Award, 1973; American Academy of Arts and Letters grant, 1974; D.Litt., University of Sheffield, 1976; Commander of the British Empire, 1980.

WRITINGS—Novels, except as indicated: *A Summer Bird-Cage,* Weidenfeld & Nicolson, 1962, Morrow, 1964; *The Garrick Year,* Weidenfeld & Nicolson, 1964, Morrow, 1965; *The Millstone,* Weidenfeld & Nicolson, 1965, Morrow, 1966, published in America as *Thank You All Very Much,* New American Library, 1969, reissued with new introduction by Drabble and editorial material compiled by Michael Marland, Longman, 1970; *Wordsworth* (criticism), Evans Bros., 1966, Arco, 1969; *Jerusalem the Golden,* Morrow, 1967; *The Waterfall,* Knopf, 1969.

The Needle's Eye, Knopf, 1972; (editor with B. S. Johnson) *London Consequences* (group novel), Greater London Arts Association, 1972; *Virginia Woolf: A Personal Debt,* Aloe Editions, 1973; *Arnold Bennett* (biography), Knopf, 1974; *The Realms of Gold,* Knopf, 1975; (editor) Jane Austen, *Lady Susan, the Watsons and Sanditon,* Penguin (London), 1975; (editor and contributor) *The Genius of Thomas Hardy,* Weidenfeld & Nicolson, 1975, Knopf, 1976; *The Ice Age,* Knopf, 1977; *A Writers' Britain: Landscape in Literature* (illustrated by Jorge Lewinsky), Knopf, 1979; *For Queen and Country: Victorian England* (juvenile), Deutsch, 1978, Seabury, 1979.

The Middle Ground, Knopf, 1980; (editor) *Oxford Companion to English Literature,* Oxford University Press, 1985.

Short fiction published in collections, including: *Winter's Tales 12,* edited by A. D. Maclean, Macmillan (London), 1966; *Winter's Tales 14,* edited by Kevin Crossley-Holland, Macmillan (London), 1968; *Penguin Modern Stories 3,* Penguin, 1969; *Winter's Tales 16,* edited by A. D. Maclean, Macmillan (London), 1970.

MARGARET DRABBLE

(From the movie "Thank You All Very Much," based on the novel *The Millstone* by Margaret Drabble, starring Sandy Dennis. Copyright © 1969 by Columbia Pictures.)

Author of play ''Bird of Paradise,'' produced in London, 1969. Writer of dialog, ''Isadora,'' Universal, 1968. Author of television play, ''Laura,'' produced by Granada Television, 1964. Contributor to British literary journals, including *Punch, Vogue, Guardian, Ms., Saturday Review,* and *Spectator.*

ADAPTATIONS: (Author of screenplay) ''Thank You All Very Much'' (based on *The Millstone*), starring Sandy Dennis and Ian McKellen, Columbia Pictures, 1969, released in Great Britain as ''A Touch of Love,'' Palomar Pictures, 1969.

WORK IN PROGRESS: The Radiant Way to be published in the U.K. and U.S.

SIDELIGHTS: Drabble grew up in a family that loved books. As a youngster she wrote and produced plays with her two sisters. ''I was born in Sheffield in the North of England. My father was a barrister and is now a county court judge. This gives everyone the impression that we were a frightfully grand family. However, this wasn't at all so because both my parents were the first of their families ever to go to a university. They were very much a new generation. I suppose they were, both of them, fairly intellectual. They encouraged us to read. I was the second of three girls and there was a little brother, some years later. So there were four of us altogether. I went to a very old Quaker girls' boarding school, the Mount School, York. Then I went on to the university to read English and I enjoyed it so much that I really think it took me a long time to get over it.

(Jacket illustration "The Last of England" by Ford Madox Brown from *For Queen and Country* by Margaret Drabble.)

''I got married almost immediately after leaving the university. The week I finished, I got married and intended at that point to go on the stage but didn't because my husband was an actor and it just didn't work out somehow. I did do a year or two on the stage, but I also had a baby within the year. That rather cramped my style. So that was really how I began writing. I then wrote my first book during the year I was expecting my first baby. And now I have three.'' [Nancy S. Hardin, ''An Interview with Margaret Drabble,'' *Contemporary Literature,* Volume 14, number 4, Autumn, 1973.[1]]

Drabble's first novel was quickly followed with another. All of them have been very popular in England and in America. ''. . . Obviously the books are expressions of different aspects of me. I think that probably from book to book I've tended to have the same kind of slightly manic-depressive reaction that I have in my own self against myself. I tend to write a comic book, then a rather sad book, then a strong book, then a weak book. I think that they've alternated between strong and weak characters fairly consistently. The *Summer Bird-Cage* girl is rather confused; the *Garrick Year* woman is strong; the *Millstone* girl is pretty defective; the *Jerusalem the Golden* girl is go-ahead, lively, a grabber; the *Waterfall* woman is feeble; the *Needle's Eye* woman strong. I think there's something in me that is going between these two poles all the time. In the novels I tend to be tossed to and fro between these two aspects of myself.

(Jacket illustration by Muriel Nasser from *The Middle Ground* by Margaret Drabble.)

''. . . I can't deny that I've used an awful lot of incidents out of my own life. I think all novelists do. But I've also used

Margaret Drabble with her children.

again and again other people. Other people obviously see themselves as being specific and rigid or always being schizoid. I don't see myself as either. I see myself as being various."[1]

She prefers to write her books in the mornings, writing very fast and with very little rewriting. "I worry about it for about six months or so, and then when I get enough worry in my mind, enough anxieties, I then. . . . Well, I also need a first chapter, I have to have a beginning and then I can go and resolve it; and it's got to be a concrete beginning. . . . And so having got this very definite idea, a scene in my mind, I then start. As I write, the act of writing to me clarifies what happens next. I know the subject matter, I know the characters, but I don't know the events, and the events occur to me as I go on." ["Margaret Drabble," *The Writer's Place: Interviews on the Literary Situation in Contemporary Britain*, edited by Peter Firchow, University of Minnesota Press, 1974.[2]]

In 1985 the fifth edition to the *Oxford Companion to English Literature* was published. Drabble had revised and edited it—a task that took five years to complete. "In his introduction to the original *Oxford Companion to English Literature* (1932) Sir Paul Harvey stated that his volume would serve its purpose 'if it proves a useful companion to ordinary everyday readers of English literature,' and such remains my hope of this new version. While the revision inevitably reflects the increasing specialization and professionalism of English studies, the chief virtue of a one-volume reference book of this nature must be that it can quickly, easily, and clearly satisfy the immediate curiosity of the common reader, and direct that reader, where appropriate, to further sources of information. . . .

"The decision having been made to keep the one volume format, my first task was to decide what material to discard in order to make space for new entries and expansion of old ones. Ruthlessly, I resolved to drop most of Harvey's 'allusions commonly met with, or likely to be met with, in English literature,' a field which Harvey conceded was infinitely expandable and highly contentious. So dollars and pieces of eight have gone, the Cinque Ports have gone, and so has the Doge of Venice, and many more items that may be found in Brewer's *Dictionary of Phrase and Fable,* which Harvey credits as the authority for many of his own entries. I have retained most of the entries on British and Irish mythology, but I have not even attempted to cover classical allusions—not because I assume everyone is familiar with them, but rather because they are so numerous that they can only be properly covered in a dictionary of classical mythology. It must, however, be acknowledged that fewer readers have the benefit of a classical education; the entries on classical authors have therefore been thoroughly revised and their links with and influences on English literature have been more strongly emphasized.

". . . My sons Adam and Joseph and my daughter Rebecca responded nobly to my cries for help; they have worked as research assistants, chauffeurs, photocopy operators, and telephone answering machines, and I am very grateful to them all. I do not know how adequately to thank my husband Michael Holroyd, who married me and the *Companion* when it was half-way through its five-year-plan: the assistance he has given me has been invaluable, and I have made merciless use of his scholarship, his library, and his goodwill, all of which are remarkable." [Margaret Drabble, "Preface," *The Oxford Companion to English Literature,* fifth edition, Oxford University Press, 1985.[3]]

In 1980 Drabble was made a Commander of the British Empire. "You can't complain in the Western world about our

freedom to write; we can write whatever we like now. But we do perhaps seem to have lost some link with the people who don't write or read. I am looking for some way of revitalizing things that have dropped out of the novel a bit, and I think other people are looking for it, too: a sense of being rooted in day-to-day reality, social change, history. I think people are looking for a new way of relating the novel to history." [Miriam Berkley, "PW Interviews: Margaret Drabble," *Publishers Weekly,* May 31, 1985.[4]]

FOR MORE INFORMATION SEE: Margaret Drabble, "Money as a Subject for the Novelist," *Times Literary Supplement,* July 17, 1969; Bolivar Le Franc, "An Interest in Guilt: Margaret Drabble," *Books and Bookmen,* September, 1969; Nancy S. Hardin, "An Interview with Margaret Drabble," *Contemporary Literature,* summer, 1973; *Under Bow Bells: Dialogues with Joseph McCulloch,* Sheldon Press, 1974; Peter Firchow, editor, *The Writer's Place: Interviews on the Literary Situation in Contemporary Britain,* University of Minnesota Press, 1974; Nancy Poland, "Margaret Drabble: 'There Must Be a Lot of People Like Me,'" *Midwest Quarterly,* April, 1975; Mel Gussow, "Margaret Drabble; A Double Life," *New York Times Books Review,* October 9, 1977; Barbara Milton, "Margaret Drabble: The Art of Fiction LXX," *Paris Review,* fall, 1978; Dee Preussner, "Talking with Margaret Drabble," *Modern Fiction Studies,* winter, 1979-80; Fred Hauptfuhrer, "England's New Virginia Woolf: Some Say It's Maggie Drabble," *People Weekly,* October 13, 1980; Diana Cooper-Clark, "Margaret Drabble: Cautious Feminist," *Atlantic Monthly,* November, 1980; *Ms.,* November, 1982, April, 1983; Charles Moritz, editor, *Current Biography Yearbook 1981,* H. W. Wilson, 1982; Jay L. Halio, editor, *Dictionary of Literary Biography,* Volume 14, Gale, 1983; Clair Boylan, "Talking about Books: Margaret Drabble's Oxford Companion," *Vogue,* May, 1985; Miriam Berkley, "PW Interviews: Margaret Drabble," *Publishers Weekly,* May 31, 1985.

DUNCAN, Frances (Mary) 1942-

BRIEF ENTRY: Born January 24, 1942, in Vancouver, British Columbia, Canada. A writer since 1973, Duncan formerly worked for ten years as a child psychologist in British Columbia. Her first book, a historical novel for young adults entitled *Cariboo Runaway,* appeared in 1976. Since then she has completed novels for both adolescents and adults, as well as poems and short stories. Her works include *Kap-Sung Ferris* (Burns & MacEachern, 1976, Macmillan, 1980), a psychological novel that deals with the theme of young people searching for identity within themselves and in society; *The Toothpaste Genie* (Scholastic-TAB, 1981), a light fantasy for middle-grade readers; and *Dragonhunt* (Women's Educational Press, 1981), an adult novel based on the St. George myth which *Books in Canada* described as "experimental in form and content. . . . with passages of surreal, hallucinatory image and incident." In her young adult novel *Finding Home* (Avon, 1982), Duncan combines a flashback technique with alternating points of view from two different characters to reveal the story of fifteen-year-old Rondo, whose parents have died in a car crash. "Duncan's ability to juxtapose adult and adolescent perceptions is intriguing and provocative," noted *Kliatt,* while *School Library Journal* called the book "well-crafted. . . . stirring, thought-provoking." Duncan is currently working on two adult novels and a juvenile novel, along with a sequel to *The Toothpaste Genie. Office:* Writers Union of Canada, 24 Ryerson Ave., Toronto, Ontario, Canada M5R 1K5.

FOR MORE INFORMATION SEE: Irma McDonough, editor, *Profiles 2,* Canadian Library Association, 1982; *Contemporary Authors, New Revision Series,* Volume 17, Gale, 1986.

EVANS, Hubert Reginald   1892-1986

OBITUARY NOTICE: Born May 9, 1892, in Vankleek Hill, Ontario, Canada; died of pneumonia, June 17, 1986, in British Columbia, Canada. Journalist, novelist, poet, and author of juvenile fiction. A prolific writer, Evans celebrated life in the British Columbian wilderness in his works. Dog stories dominate his juvenile fiction, particularly the Derry series, including *Derry, Airedale of the Frontier* and *Derry of Totem Creek.* His prodigious output also includes three adult novels, among them *Mist on the River* and the autobiographical *O Time in Your Flight;* seven novels for teenagers; some two hundred stories; three books of poetry, including *Whittlings;* and numerous articles contributed to *Saturday Evening Post, Toronto Star Weekly, Maclean's,* and other periodicals. Evans also worked as a fisheries officer and as a reporter in Toronto, Ontario, and in British Columbia.

FOR MORE INFORMATION SEE: Contemporary Authors, Volume 103, Gale, 1982; Irma McDonough, editor, *Profiles 2,* Canadian Library Association, 1982; *Twentieth-Century Children's Writers,* 2nd edition, St. Martin's, 1983; *The Writers Directory: 1984-1986,* St. James Press, 1983. Obituaries: *Toronto Star,* June 18, 1986; *Facts on File,* June 20, 1986.

FLEMING, Elizabeth P.   1888-1985

OBITUARY NOTICE: Born in 1888 in Morioka, Japan; died December 16, 1985, in Elmwood Park, Ill.; buried in Acacia Park Cemetery, Chicago, Ill. Educator and author. Fleming wrote several children's books, including *A Gift from the Mikado,* a story based on a memory from her childhood in Japan. Fleming had lived with her missionary parents in Japan until she was five years old, when her family moved to New York. Educated in the United States, she taught school in Mt. Vernon, New York, until 1916 and in the 1930s wrote for the *New Yorker* magazine. Among her other writings are the children's books *Spell on the Stones, The Takula Tree, Robin Hood Harlan,* and *Red Cloud and Company.*

FOR MORE INFORMATION SEE: Authors of Books for Young People, 2nd edition, Scarecrow, 1971. Obituaries: *Chicago Sun Times,* December 18, 1985.

FORRESTER, Helen   1919-
(June Bhatia, June Edwards, J. Rana)

PERSONAL: Born June 6, 1919, in Hoylake, Cheshire, England; married Avadh Behari Bhatia (a professor), May 25, 1950 (deceased); children: Robert. *Education:* Privately educated in England; attended Liverpool Evening Institutes, 1933-40. *Address:* c/o The Writers' Union, 24 Ryerson St., Toronto, Ontario, Canada.

CAREER: Writer, 1953—. *Member:* Canadian Association of Children's Authors, Illustrators and Performers; Writer's Union of Canada; Society of Authors; Authors' Lending and Copyright Society. *Awards, honors:* Hudson's Bay Beaver Award

HELEN FORRESTER

for best unpublished manuscript, 1970, for *Liverpool Daisy,* and 1977, for *The Moneylenders of Shahpur;* literary excellence citation from city of Edmonton, 1977; Government of Alberta Achievement Award for literature, 1979; *Minerva's Stepchild* was chosen one of New York Public Library's Books for the Teen Age, 1982.

WRITINGS: (Under pseudonym J. Rana) *Alien There Is None,* Hodder and Stoughton, 1959, published under name Helen Forrester as *Thursday's Child,* Collins-Fontana, 1985; (under name June Bhatia) *The Latchkey Kid,* Longmans, 1970, published under name Helen Forrester, R. Hale, 1985; (under pseudonym June Edwards) *Most Precious Employee,* R. Hale, 1974; *Twopence to Cross the Mersey* (autobiography), J. Cape, 1974, new edition, Bodley Head, 1979, large print edition, F. A. Thorpe, 1984; *Minerva's Stepchild* (autobiography; sequel to *Twopence to Cross the Mersey*), Bodley Head, 1979, large print edition, F. A. Thorpe, 1979, new edition (also contains *Twopence to Cross the Mersey*), Beaufort Books, 1980, published as *Liverpool Miss,* Fontana, 1981; (under name June Bhatia) *Liverpool Daisy,* R. Hale, 1979, published under name H. Forrester, Fontana, 1984, large print edition, F. A. Thorpe, 1986.

(Fiction editor) *The Alberta Diamond Jubilee Anthology,* Hurtig, 1980; *By the Waters of Liverpool* (autobiography, sequel to *Minerva's Stepchild*), Merrimack, 1981, large print edition, F. A. Thorpe, 1984; *Three Women of Liverpool,* R. Hale, 1984, large print edition, F. A. Thorpe, 1985; *Lime Street at Two* (autobiography), Bodley Head, 1985; *The Moneylenders of Shahpur,* Collins-Fontana, 1987. Contributor to *Heritage Magazine;* contributor of book reviews to *Edmonton Journal* and *Canadian Authors.*

ADAPTATIONS: "Three Women of Liverpool" (cassette), Soundings, 1984; "The Latchkey Kid" (cassette), Chivers,

(Jacket illustration by Michael Garland from *Minerva's Stepchild* by Helen Forrester.)

1985; "Twopence to Cross the Mersey" (radio drama), B.B.C.-Radio, 1986.

WORK IN PROGRESS: A novel set in the nineteenth and early twentieth centuries about the shame of illegitimate birth, tentatively titled *Yes, Mama.*

SIDELIGHTS: At the commencement of *Twopence to Cross the Mersey,* the family of Forrester arrives in Liverpool to begin a new life. *Minerva's Stepchild* continues that story, one that began when Forrester's father had lost his job and his family's upper-middle-class status in England's depression of the 1930s. After fleeing his debtors he brought his family to Liverpool with hopes of finding work. His job-hunting efforts proved futile, however, and he, his wife, and his children were forced to live in a Liverpool slum.

Forrester, the eldest of the seven children, shouldered much of the family burden. Living and caring for her brothers and sisters in the cold and filth of an attic, she struggled against both poverty and her parents' neglect. The income of the little work her father could find was generally spent on liquor and cigarettes instead of food, soap, or fuel for the fireplace. Forrester's mother, outraged by her ignominious fall from society's heights, added to her family's problems by trying to keep Helen at home as housekeeper. Helen eventually found work, however, and was able to enroll in night school.

"I left school at the equivalent of grade five. I have been studying ever since. I study European and Indian history and languages (at which I am bad, but, nevertheless, enthusiastic).

I read a lot about financial matters and love a good, descriptive travel book.

"I write for adults, but am delighted that so many thousands of young people love my books. My novels, also have found additional readers amongst high school children. My growing up is described in my four books of autobiography. A great number of young people struggling to improve their education have told me that my books are an inspiration to them.

"I came to Canada as the wife of a scientist and could not stand the boredom of middle-class Canadian women's lives in the 1950s, so I shut myself up in our tiny flat and wrote a novel on the back of old copies of my husband's physics lecture notes. I have had a life full of troubles and travel—great experience for writers.

"I must have about 2,500,000 books in print, mostly in Britain. My ambition is to do as well in the United States."

Though now living comfortably as a writer in Edmonton, Forrester is still reminded daily of her impoverished past. "To this day, I can't bear to throw things away, and my store cupboards are always full. I just love starting a new bar of soap, and knowing I'll be able to use it all."

HOBBIES AND OTHER INTERESTS: Fan collecting, theater, people.

FOR MORE INFORMATION SEE: Toronto Daily Star, October 3, 1979; *Calgary Herald,* November 24, 1979; *Edmonton Journal,* August 25, 1979.

FRASCINO, Edward   1938-

PERSONAL: Surname is pronounced Fra-*shee*-no; born November 15, 1938, in Bronx, N.Y.; son of Mario (a couturier) and Rose (D'Agostino) Frascino. *Education:* Attended Parson's School of Design, 1951. *Residence:* Brooklyn, N.Y. *Office:* c/o *New Yorker,* 25 West 43rd St., New York, N.Y. 10036.

CAREER: Cartoonist, author and illustrator of books for children. Began career as a designer of greeting cards, worked as draftsman for Remington Rand, and in advertising; free-lance cartoonist, 1965—. *Military service:* U.S. Army, Korean War, 1951-53. *Awards, honors: Book World's* Spring Book Festival Award, 1970, for *The Trumpet of the Swan.*

WRITINGS—Self-illustrated: Eddie Spaghetti (juvenile fiction), Harper, 1978; *Eddie Spaghetti on the Home Front* (juvenile fiction), Harper, 1983; *Avocado Is Not Your Color: And Other Scenes of Married Bliss* (adult cartoons), Penguin, 1983; *My Cousin the King,* Prentice-Hall, 1985.

Illustrator; all fiction for children; all published by Harper, except as indicated: Mary Stolz, *Say Something,* 1968; M. Stolz, *The Dragons of the Queen,* 1969; M. Stolz, *The Story of a Singular Hen and Her Peculiar Children,* 1969; Marjorie W. Sharmat, *Gladys Told Me to Meet Her Here,* 1970; E. B. White, *The Trumpet of the Swan* (ALA Notable Book), 1970; Hans Christian Andersen, *The Little Mermaid,* translated by Eva Le Gallienne, 1971; Gladys Y. Cretan, *A Hole, a Box, and a Stick,* Lothrop, 1972; Carole Hart, *Delilah,* 1973; Robert E. Barry, *Snowman's Secret,* Macmillan, 1975; Shirley Gordon, *Crystal Is the New Girl,* 1976; S. Gordon, *Crystal Is*

My Friend, 1978; Nancy Robison, *UFO Kidnap!,* Lothrop, 1978; Nigel Gray, *It'll All Come Out in the Wash,* 1979; N. Robison, *Space Hijack!,* Lothrop, 1979.

S. Gordon, *Me and the Bad Guys,* 1980; N. Robison, *Izoo,* Lothrop, 1980; S. Gordon, *Happy Birthday, Crystal,* 1981; Charles Keller, compiler, *Oh, Brother: And Other Family Jokes,* Prentice-Hall, 1982; William Warren, *The Graveyard and Other Not-So-Scary Stories,* Prentice-Hall, 1984; W. Warren, *The Thing in the Swamp and More Not-So-Scary Stories,* Prentice-Hall, 1984; W. Warren, *Footsteps in the Fog: Still More Not-So-Scary Stories,* Prentice-Hall, 1985; Rudyard Kipling, *The Elephant's Child,* Prentice-Hall, 1987.

Contributor of cartoons to periodicals and newspapers, including *Punch, Saturday Review, New York Times,* and a regular series in *New Yorker.*

HOBBIES AND OTHER INTERESTS: Painting, sculpting, watching old movies, and the New York Mets.

SIDELIGHTS: Edward Frascino was born **November 15, 1938,** in Bronx, New York. "The part of Italy my family comes from was settled by Albanians in the twelfth century, following an invasion of Albania by the Turks. In the small area of Italy where they settled, the Albanians maintained their language and their culture. The language spoken by my parents' families is neither a dialect of Italian nor modern Albanian, but a language unto itself which was spoken in Albania during the Middle Ages. My father, who spoke high Italian as well as his native language, came to the United States as a young man, knowing not a word of English. In Italy he was a tailor; in this country he worked his way up through the Garment District to become a couturier. I've always been proud of my father. He loved his profession, worked hard and did well. Even during the Depression we suffered no hardship. In fact, we had an automobile and a maid.

"My mother was born in the states into an Albanian family from the same village as my father, and didn't learn English until she went to school. I think her early school years were traumatic for her. She wanted her children to be *American,* and made no effort to teach us Italian, let alone her regional dialect. Ancient Albanian was my parents' 'secret language'; they used it when they wanted to keep us in the dark.

"On Sundays the extended family gathered at my grandmother's, a sweet, gentle, submissive-seeming lady who, I eventually realized, ruled the family. We generally spent the afternoon in the living room—there were lots of jokes and banter, some of it quite clever. I didn't have the confidence to join in, but I soaked it up like a sponge. My grandmother always had a copy or two of *New Yorker,* and even as a kid I loved to look at the drawings and cartoons. In the evening, we all listened to the radio. I'm sure the wit I was exposed to at her house had a role in my becoming a cartoonist.

"Radio was very important to me. I listened every afternoon to shows like 'Jack Armstrong,' 'Captain Midnight,' and 'Little Orphan Annie.' You could send away one Ovaltine label in exchange for a Little Orphan Annie decoder ring, a cheap little piece of jewelry, a part of which turned to reveal a series

EDWARD FRASCINO

At length, he sat down, lifted his head, and began to howl. ■ (From *The Dragons of the Queen* by Mary Stolz. Illustration by Edward Frascino.)

of letters. At the end of each show, Annie would give us a message in code—numbers which corresponded to the letters in the decoder ring. By matching them, you had a hint as to what would happen in the next episode. In the evenings, my family listened to 'Jack Benny' and 'Fibber Magee and Molly', and at lunch my mother and I listened to soap operas. Radio exercised, as well as fed, one's imagination. You not only listened, but also envisioned the action and characters. And radio made one sensitive to the subtle nuances of sound and timing.

"Movies were also a favorite pastime. Disney's early animations just knocked me out. In those days, the artists painted every picture. It took many pictures to make just one scene— every gesture, each expression was done separately. Today a lot of animation is done by computer and though you can get some stunning effects, you don't get the painterly qualities and beautiful flow of movement you got in the forties, say. The animations I loved as a child were drawings *come to life.* Because my parents were film buffs, I also saw adult movies every weekend. My father would select a particular film because he wanted to see the cut of Joan Crawford's suit, for example, or a certain actor's lapels. Films in the forties were incredibly glamorous.

"Comic strips were a critical influence on me, not only as a visual artist, but as a storyteller, too. I spent a lot of time drawing and copying my favorite comics. As a kid I had a huge collection of comic books. In a certain way, cartoons were for us what television is today. They were the images we lived with day to day, the stories we thought about, the characters who were our heroes and villains, cut-ups and clowns. Personally, I loved the villains—the more moustache-twirling the better! In New York during the forties there were five dailies the size of *The New York Times,* four of which had comics. You can imagine what a bonanza the Sunday editions were! You would have pages and pages of wonderful art work. Comics were water colors then. Today the artist doesn't color his drawing; instead, he labels each area with a number which is 'read' by the printer who plugs in the color by computer.

My favorite comic strip artists were Alex Raymond, who did 'Flash Gordon,' and Milton Caniff who did 'Terry and the Pirates.' Caniff's use of black was sensational—his washes were thick, juicy, delicious. Soon I was drawing and writing my own adventure comic strips.

"I didn't read much as a child, but my parents (usually my mother) read to me, and those stories made a big impression, particularly Kipling's *The Jungle Book* and *Just-So Stories.*

"I was about eight years old when the U.S. entered World War II. The War was all you heard, all you saw. There were posters on every public, and many private, walls. Everybody was either in the service or doing something for the war effort. Only eight years old, I felt terribly frustrated that there was nothing significant I could do; no real way I could participate. In the face of the patriotic propaganda we were saturated with, collecting rubber bands seemed a pretty silly way to help beat the Germans and the Japanese.'' Frascino's novel, *Eddie Spaghetti on the Home Front,* is based in part on Frascino's growing-up years during the war.

"School was dreary. I can still look back and say, 'Nothing was worse than school.' I hated the regimentation, the routine. I had a couple of teachers who were inspiring, but the rest didn't seem to care whether or not we learned anything. I much preferred going to the movies, and played hooky every chance I got. They wouldn't sell you a ticket if they suspected you were supposed to be in school, so I would ask an adult to get my ticket and spent the afternoon watching Betty Grable. In those days, it was safe to ask a stranger to help sneak you into a movie house; today, however, it might not be such a good idea. I sometimes went to great lengths to get into the movies, and on occasion donned disguises to make myself look older.

"I was quite introverted in school, and didn't participate in many things at all. The extra-curricular activities seemed like kid-stuff. I'm not sure why, but I always wanted to be older, to hurry up and be an adult. In high school especially I felt like I was treading water. Even though I was majoring in art,

She didn't know how to read, and although she rather liked the looks of a young cob who had something hanging around his neck, she couldn't really get interested in a bird that was unable to *say* anything. ■ (From *The Trumpet of the Swan* by E. B. White. Illustrated by Edward Frascino.)

"Mice!" shrieked the farmer's wife. "Mice in my pantry. Mice in my parlor. Mice in my sewing basket. I need a cat!" ■ (From *My Cousin the King* by Edward Frascino. Illustrated by the author.)

She throws the dice again and says, "Come to Papa!" ■ (From *Crystal Is My Friend* by Shirley Gordon. Illustrated by Edward Frascino.)

I had no career plans and no concrete idea as to what place art would have in my adult life.

"I spent most of my time by myself. I had a few friends, but we weren't very close, and rarely if ever saw each other outside school. I'm sure there were kids who loved movies as much as I did, but I never wanted to go with anyone else. I loved, and still prefer, to go alone and escape into the world of fantasy. When the film is over, if you're with someone else, the fantasy comes to an end far too soon. If you're alone, you can prolong that dreamy feeling for hours and hours.

"By the time I graduated high school, I was quite sure that I wanted to be an illustrator. No art school then had a straight illustration major, but Parsons had fashion illustration, design, advertising and interior design. I enrolled in the fashion illustration course as a compromise and as an acknowledgement of my father's livelihood. But I found that I had no flair for fashion illustration. My talents were comedy and cartoons. Even my serious, high-fashion pictures had an inadvertent touch of the comic vignette—which was *not* an asset!

"Still, I learned basic technique in art school—how to mix colors, apply a wash, and control a paintbrush. After my second year, I went with a group of students and several teachers to Mexico. We traveled for over two months on a carefully planned itinerary, with lots of time to sit outside and draw or paint. This was a crucial experience for me. I began to feel that I was emerging as an artist. I suddenly had a confidence in my work that was totally new.

"Parsons was the first school environment in which I found people with whom I had a real rapport. I made friends during my three years there that I have to this day."

1951-1953. Drafted into the Army and sent to Korea. "The service was a good experience. It was the first opportunity I had to be in close contact with people from places and backgrounds vastly different from mine. Born and bred in New York City, I had no idea what the rest of the country was all about. There was a very special camaraderie—sort of like being shipwrecked together.

"My job in the Army was to draw maps. My unit never saw combat. Our colonel was a lunatic—career majors and sergeants quaked in his presence. For some unidentifiable reason

he wanted a topographical map of the area surrounding our encampment. He was planning his big defense strategy, even though the action was happening at least twenty miles from us. In any case, he took me out to the area and had me do a series of one-dimensional, black-and-white drawings. To make an accurate topographical map, you need surveyors and instruments. But he was so starved for some display of activity that I went ahead and made a map from my sketches. He thought it was sensational, even though I am certain it bore no resemblance to the land formations in which supposedly he was interested. If, as a result of this ridiculous map, he went to sleep feeling safer was anyone's guess. I certainly did not."

1954-1965. "My first job after the Army was as a draftsman for Remington Rand. I was part of a team of about six guys who made charts all day long. As you can imagine, this was not very interesting. In fact, it was a lot like typing—you had to be neat, correct, precise, but not creative. From there I went to an advertising agency where I did paste-ups and mechanicals. That, too, required neatness, accuracy, and little else. So I made a sort of contract with myself: each day I would complete one drawing. I also kept sketchbooks, as one keeps a diary. I showed some of my sketchbooks to a friend who knew someone at *New Yorker*. In those days, if they didn't want to buy the whole cartoon, they would purchase the idea and assign it to one of their regular artists. I was in my mid-twenties when they starting buying my ideas and passing them on to people like Charles Addams. Needless to say, I was thrilled. I started molding the cartoons I did in my off-hours to fit the *New Yorker* format. While working at the ad agency I did about ten cartoons a week which I'd send first to *New Yorker*, and then to other magazines if they were refused. For a long time, I sold only 'ideas' to *New Yorker*, but my cartoons began appearing in *New York Times Book Review*, *Punch*, *Look*, *Saturday Evening Post*."

Since 1965, Frascino has been a freelance cartoonist and has regularly contributed cartoons to *New Yorker*. He draws a parallel of similarity between cartoons and book illustrations. "Cartoons are similar in many ways to the illustrations in picture books. Both have to make an immediate effect, as they're intended to be taken in quickly. Everything in the drawing has to be clearly defined, so as not to get in the way of the message. I think my favorite cartoons—the purest cartoons—are without captions."

Soon she arrived at a small band shell, occupied by a small band. ■ (From *Delilah* by Carole Hart. Illustrated by Edward Frascino.)

Gladys hid me when Big Mitch came around. Then she said to him, "Irving went to Paris, France, forever." ■ (From *Gladys Told Me to Meet Her Here* by Marjorie Weinman Sharmat. Illustrated by Edward Frascino.)

In addition to art work for magazines and books, Frascino sculpts and, occasionally, paints. "In the late sixties, I rented a loft with a group of painters and sculptors. We each contributed a nominal amount to cover rent and models' fees. We were all on different schedules, but once a week or so, usually on a Saturday, we would all get together and work from the model. I showed my sculpture from time to time and had a big piece in a traveling show that started at Fairtree Gallery on Madison Avenue. The theme of the exhibit was the Bicentennial. My sculpture was a three-dimensional cartoon portraying the Statue of Liberty as a mere skeleton with a caricature of Richard Nixon standing in front of it making his two-armed 'V for Victory' sign. I had been particularly infuriated by the Watergate scandal, because generally I was not a political artist. Nixon was so dishonest, so scheming, that I had to do *something*.

"I had tried a few times to do some book illustrations, but was told by editors that my style was too cartoon-like. Then, in about 1967, I met someone who worked for Ursula Nordstrom, Harper & Row's renowned children's book editor. I showed Nordstrom my portfolio and she suggested I do a sketch on spec for a picture book by Mary Stolz. They had had a number of artists submit work, but Stolz had vetoed all of them. Much to my surprise, Stolz liked my drawing, and *Say Something* became the first of a number of books I have illustrated for her."

One of Frascino's favorite illustration projects was E. B. White's *The Trumpet of the Swan*, for which he won *Book World*'s Spring Book Festival Award. "Originally Harper & Row wanted Garth Williams, who illustrated *Charlotte's Web*, to do *Trumpet*. Williams was living in Mexico at the time and was unable to do it. So they hired another artist who quite late in the project refused to make certain changes they were requesting. 'Take it or leave it,' he said, and they asked him to leave. Needless to say, I was very happy to be asked to work on a book by E. B. White. Originally, they wanted me to work in pen and ink, so that there would be a visual tie-in with the line drawings Williams had done for *Charlotte's Web*. However, I've always worked best with wash and when I told Harper & Row I was uncomfortable with the line drawings I had made, they let me have my way. The final illustrations for *Trumpet* are all wash, even the lines are brush, rather than pen, lines.

"I worked very closely with White. By then he had moved to Maine and wasn't visiting New York, but we spoke often on the phone and he wrote me many letters. Because of the delays in getting *Trumpet* illustrated, we were under considerable time pressure. White relieved a lot of my tension. He was so gentle and encouraging. I also learned a great deal from him. Soon after we had finished the project, I made him a papier-mache swan with a golden trumpet around its neck. He wrote me a wonderful letter upon receiving it, and when he died, left it to a museum."

Frascino's close collaboration with E. B. White was an exceptional case. "Generally I don't work closely with the authors whose books I illustrate. The editor, in her relationship with author and illustrator, becomes crucial to the development of most books. Editing is a talent, a creative art. I have been extremely fortunate to have worked frequently with Nordstrom, the best editor around.

"I never thought I could be a writer, even though I have always loved to tell stories, 'You know, you really should write that down,' one of my editors told me. To my astonishment, once I got started, the words seemed to fall into place. In my head I was seeing the pictures, and used words to describe the image. The character is the most important element of a story. Characters don't have to accomplish enormous, dramatic feats. If he is well drawn and you really care about him, he can be tying his shoe and the reader will be engaged. I enjoyed writing *Eddie Spaghetti* more than I liked illustrating it. Because that story went through several drafts, I found it tedious to go through it again and again in search of fresh images. To avoid this feeling of boredom, I wrote and sketched simultaneously with *Eddie Spaghetti on the Home Front*. As soon as an image occurred to me, I dropped the writing and picked up a paintbrush. I must work spontaneously or I have trouble working at all. I can't even talk about work in progress. If I give voice to an idea, it's as if I've already realized it and the execution becomes a bore. I make so many exciting discoveries in the course of working. Sometimes ideas just explode. I never want to deny myself the joy of that by letting the energy seep out when it shouldn't."

For his most recent book, *My Cousin the King*, Frascino did the illustrations in full color. "Color work usually requires separations, a technique I don't favor because it makes for a hard edge. I prefer a washy effect. Water colors can be tricky, however. Unlike oil paints, or even acrylics, they dry fast, which leaves no time for revisions. The colors have a tendency to get muddy if you're not careful. I often do a number of drawings before I come up with one that I like. In a given draft, I may be concentrating on one small area, but I need to work on it in context of the entire drawing. Many artists I know cut and paste; I don't. It really doesn't work if you use any kind of wash. Patching gives you a definite line."

When asked if he has anything resembling a typical day, Frascino acknowledged that he likes to get up early and "get my household chores done so the rest of my day is free. I usually work from about ten until lunchtime; again from about two to five, and from about eight to eleven with interruptions to play with my five cats. The Park Slope section of Brooklyn, where I live now, is very conducive to my work. I'm near the park and the library; the streets are quiet and perfect for strolling.

"When I'm working, I can't listen to any kind of music. I like it to be as quiet as possible. However, when I'm doing color separations or something that's a bit tedious, I'll play the sound track to one of my favorite movies from the forties."

When he's not working, Frascino likes to read. "I just discovered Mark Twain's *The Mysterious Stranger*, the book he was working on when he died. It's very metaphysical. I also love mysteries and stories like *The Picture of Dorian Gray* and *Tarzan of the Apes*."

When asked if he had any advice to offer aspiring writers and artists, Frascino said, "Thomas Edison said that genius is one percent inspiration and ninety-nine percent perspiration, and I believe that's true. If you are going to do anything creative, you must really push yourself. Maybe only a tenth of what you produce will be at the standard to which you aspire, but it's the effort, concentration and growth in the other work that will eventually put you over the edge. Quantum leaps don't happen by themselves. You have to prepare for inspiration and have developed the skills to execute a great idea. I don't believe this can be done overnight. It takes a number of years to become an artist."

FOR MORE INFORMATION SEE: Martha E. Ward and Dorothy Marquardt, *Illustrators of Books for Young People*, 2nd edition, Scarecrow, 1975; Lee Kingman and others, compilers, *Illustrators of Children's Books: 1967-1976*, Horn Book, 1978; Sally Holmes Holtze, editor, *Fifth Book of Junior Authors and Illustrators*, H. W. Wilson, 1983.

FREEMAN, William Bradford 1938- (Bill Freeman)

BRIEF ENTRY: Born October 21, 1938, in London, Ontario, Canada. Author. Freeman's father was a mathematics teacher and politician prone to bringing home any number of political radicals who spent their time in constant debate. Consequently, Freeman learned very early in life how to effectively defend his opinions with words. Despite his strong home environment, Freeman dropped out of high school to wander across Canada and spend three carefree years in London, England. Growing tired of unskilled jobs, however, he returned to Canada and school, eventually earning a Ph.D. from McMaster University in 1979. Freeman's books reflect his upbringing and studies in sociology and political power. *Shantymen of Cache Lake* (Lorimer, 1975), a historical novel for young adults, centers around fourteen-year-old Meg and her younger brother Jamie in an Ottawa Valley lumber camp during the 1870s. The two are hired to work at the camp where their father died while organizing a trade union. While there, they learn to understand the benefits of cooperation and solidarity. The same pair appear in four additional novels, also published by Lorimer: *The Last Voyage of the Scotian* (1976), *First Spring on the Grand Banks* (1978), *Trouble at Lachine Mill* (1983), and *The Harbour Thieves* (1984).

In 1976 Freeman received a Canada Council Children's Literature Prizes award for *Shantymen of Cache Lake*. More recently, in 1984, he was the recipient of the Vicky Metcalf Award, presented by the Canadian Authors' Association to a Canadian writer who has produced at least four books of interest to readers age seven to seventeen. His works for adults include *Their Town: The Mafia, the Media, and the Party Machine* (Lorimer, 1979), an expose on the town of Hamilton, Ontario which he co-edited with his wife, Marsha Hewitt; and *1005: Political Life in a Union Local* (Lorimer, 1982), a history of Local 1005 of the United Steel Workers of America. *Residence:* Montreal, Quebec, Canada.

FOR MORE INFORMATION SEE: Who's Who in America, 41st edition, Marquis, 1980; Irma McDonough, editor, *Profiles 2,* Canadian Library Association, 1982.

GACKENBACH, Dick 1927-

PERSONAL: Born February 9, 1927, in Allentown, Pa.; son of William and Gertrude (Riechenbach) Gackenbach. *Education:* Attended Jameson Franklin School of Art, N.Y., and the Abbott School of Art, Washington, D.C. *Home and office:* Washington Depot, Conn. *Agent:* McIntosh & Otis, 475 Fifth Ave., New York, N.Y. 10017.

CAREER: J. C. Penney Company, New York, N.Y., began as paste-up artist, eventually became one of three creative directors, 1950-72; free-lance author and illustrator, 1972—. *Awards, honors:* Garden State Children's Book Award from New Jersey Library Association, 1979, for *Hattie Rabbit;*

McGoogan Moves the Mighty Rock was selected one of *New York Times* Outstanding Books, 1981; *Mag the Magnificent* was chosen one of Child Study Association of America's Children's Books of the Year, 1985.

WRITINGS—All for children; all self-illustrated: *Claude the Dog: A Christmas Story* (Junior Literary Guild selection), Seabury, 1974; *Do You Love Me?,* Seabury, 1975; *Claude and Pepper,* Seabury, 1976; *Hattie Rabbit,* Harper, 1976, large print edition, 1976; *Hound and Bear,* Seabury, 1976; *Harry and the Terrible Whatzit* (Junior Literary Guild selection), Seabury, 1977; *Hattie Be Quiet, Hattie Be Good,* Harper, 1977, large print edition, 1977; *The Leatherman* (Junior Literary Guild selection), Seabury, 1977; *Mother Rabbit's Son Tom,* Harper, 1977, large print edition, 1977; *Ida Fanfanny,* Harper, 1978; *Pepper and All the Legs,* Seabury, 1978; *The Pig Who Saw Everything,* Seabury, 1978; *Crackle Gluck and the Sleeping Toad,* Seabury, 1979; *More from Hound and Bear* (Junior Literary Guild selection), Seabury, 1979.

Hattie, Tom, and the Chicken Witch: A Play and a Story, Harper, 1980, large print edition, 1980; *A Bag Full of Pups,* Clarion Books, 1981; *Little Bug,* Clarion Books, 1981; *McGoogan Moves the Mighty Rock,* Harper, 1981; *Annie and the Mud Monster,* Lothrop, 1982; (reteller) *Arabella and Mr. Crack: An Old English Tale,* Macmillan, 1982; *Binky Gets a Car* (Junior Literary Guild selection), Clarion Books, 1983; *Mr. Wink and His Shadow, Ned,* Harper, 1983; (reteller) *The Princess and the Pea,* Macmillan, 1983; *What's Claude Doing?* (Junior Literary Guild selection), Clarion Books, 1984; *Poppy the Panda* (Junior Literary Guild selection), Clarion Books,

DICK GACKENBACH

Amanda lived in an old house with her parents and her cat Ferrari. ■ (From *Amanda and the Giggling Ghost* by Steven Kroll. Illustrated by Dick Gackenbach.)

1984; *The Dog and the Deep Dark Woods*, Harper, 1984; *King Wacky*, Crown, 1984; (reteller) *The Perfect Mouse*, Macmillan, 1984; *Mag the Magnificent*, Clarion Books, 1985; (adapter) *Timid Timothy's Tongue Twisters*, Holiday House, 1986; *Hurray for Hattie Rabbit!*, Harper, 1986; *Dog for a Day*, Clarion, 1987.

Illustrator: Gertrude Norman, *The First Book of Music*, F. Watts, 1954; Steven Kroll, *Is Milton Missing?* (Junior Literary Guild selection), Holiday House, 1975; Sally Cartwright, *What's in a Map?*, Coward, 1976; Miriam Anne Bourne, *What Is Papa Up to Now?*, Coward, 1977; Jim Murphy, *Rat's Christmas Party*, Prentice-Hall, 1979; S. Kroll, *Amanda and the Giggling Ghost*, Holiday House, 1980; Marjorie N. Allen, *One, Two, Three—Ah-Choo!* (Junior Literary Guild selection), Coward, 1980; S. Kroll, *Friday the 13th*, Holiday House, 1981; Janice L. Smith, *The Monster in the Third Dresser Drawer and Other Stories about Adam Joshua*, Harper, 1981; Barbara Isenberg and Susan Wolf, *The Adventures of Albert, the Run-*

ning Bear, Clarion Books, 1982; Crescent Dragonwagon, *Hate My Brother Harry*, Harper, 1983; J. L. Smith, *The Kid Next Door and Other Headaches: Stories about Adam Joshua* Harper, 1984; David A. Adler, *My Dog and the Green Sock Mystery*, Holiday House, 1986; Mary Calhoun, *Jack and the Whoopee Wind*, Morrow, 1987.

SIDELIGHTS: Born **February 9, 1927,** in Allentown, Pennsylvania. "Allentown was very small then, nothing like it is today. I grew up during the Depression, which was a hard time for all. Fried potatoes and oatmeal were often the only things we had to eat. Everyone was poor, but no one seemed to let it get the best of them. I was too young to understand what it was all about. My mother was a wonderful Pennsylvania Dutch housewife who scrubbed everything she could get her hands on, me included. My father, a kind man, worked, when there was work, as a house painter. We lived with my grandparents on a small farm, raising pigs, chickens, and vegetables.

I wrote him a letter and left it on his desk. ■ (From *I Hate My Brother Harry* by Crescent Dragonwagon. Illustrated by Dick Gackenbach.)

Himself, McGoogan, master guitar player and singer of songs. ■ (From *McGoogan Moves the Mighty Rock* by Dick Gackenbach. Illustrated by the author.)

"We didn't have books at home. As a matter of fact, my parents and grandparents worked too hard to find time to read. We listened to the radio instead. Radio was marvellous back then. 'The Shadow' was one of my favorite shows. The whole family gathered around to listen. Those are some of my fondest memories of growing up."

Gackenbach entertained himself by copying "funnies" from newspapers and by going to horror films at the local theater. "I would sit through double features of horror films, trembling

and munching Tootsie Rolls and Jujubes, loving every minute of it. Then the grand run home through dark tree-lined streets, terrified by every shadow. What wonderful glee!

"The family moved into town when it was time for me to go to high school. My grandparents remained on the farm. I enlisted in the Navy immediately after graduation in **1944** and was stationed just outside San Francisco. My first time away from home. A whole new world opened up for me. I must say, I had a terrific time, meeting interesting people, discovering museums, galleries, big city libraries, theaters, concerts. I saw my first Van Gogh and my first Impressionists in San Francisco on weekend leave. I read *Madame Bovary* and other classics. I was very fortunate to make a good friend whose guidance into the world of books and culture changed my life.

''I was determined to go to art school after the Navy and become a fashion illustrator for the *New York Times,* maybe. My sketches featured models dressed in high style, but barefoot. Why I thought barefoot was *de rigueur,* I don't recall.''

Attended Abbott School of Art in Washington, D.C. ''I realized that I wasn't a very good fashion illustrator after all. I had trouble with the special washes one must master. The rendering of texture was crucial. Velvet has to look like velvet and silk like silk. But art school exposed me to all kinds of art. I gravitated toward design and decided to go into advertising instead. I transferred to the Jameson Franklin School of Art in New York City and studied for two years. I would not have learned to render in classical style anywhere but in art school, but in many ways, the best art education I received was on the job.

''Paste-up artist, low man on the totem pole, at J. C. Penney's corporate headquarters in New York was my first professional job that would begin a twenty-five-year career in advertising.

(Detail of an illustration by Dick Gackenbach for *Claude and Pepper* by Dick Gackenbach.)

I ended as one of J. C. Penney's three creative directors. Coming up with ideas for slogans, the heart of any ad campaign, came easily to me.

"I lived in a number of different places in Greenwich Village. Those were exciting years. New York was safer then; you could walk anywhere downtown at just about any time of day without worry. I spent my time visiting galleries and museums, and did a good deal of traveling. I took several trips to Europe and visited Turkey. Turkey had too many flies, enormous flies!"

During the **1950s** Gackenbach began collecting children's books. "Maybe this had something to do with my never having had any books when I was a kid. When I started collecting, the art work was much more *avant-garde* than one generally sees in children's books today. There was also a lot more color work." A number of his books are antiquities from the late 1880s. A favorite is an early edition of *The Wizard of Oz*. Contemporary books by Maurice Sendak, Shel Silverstein, Irene Haas, Marilyn Hafner, and Gerald McDermott are also a part of his collection.

Also during the fifties, Gackenbach submitted his first children's book which was "almost published by *Parents Magazine*." But it would be another twenty-four years before he would be published.

"In **1962** I built myself a weekend house in Washington Depot, a small village in Connecticut. I spent weekends tending to my very large garden, a 'hangover' from my childhood. I planted everything we had on the farm in Allentown: lilacs, rhododendrons, azaleas, many other kinds of flowers, as well as tomatoes.

"By **1972,** I had to admit to myself that as a whole I found life much more pleasant in the country. It was an agonizing choice, for I'd had many good years in New York City at J. C. Penney. But I'd grown unhappy with my corporate executive life and wanted to write and illustrate children's books. So I pulled up stakes and moved to Washington Depot, a community of writers and artists, many of whom do children's books. Among other notables, sculptor Alexander Calder made his home here. What a wonderful man he was, and how sublime his work!"

Claude the Dog: A Christmas Story was published in 1974. A Junior Literary Guild selection, the book was inspired by a conversation between the author-artist and a neighbor's son, who told Gackenbach that his Christmas had been awful. "His answer made me think about my own Christmases. I loved to receive gifts, but I do remember a certain joy in giving some, too. I wanted my story to convey that great warm feeling you get when you give generously, when you make someone happy.

"When *Claude the Dog* was published, very few full color books were being done because of cost considerations. As a result, publishers rarely had in-house staff equipped or able to do separations. Anyone who works as an artist in advertising will tell you that separations are the first thing they teach you. When I stop to consider that advertising gave me precious training for what I really wanted to do, I feel a lot better about my long haul as corporate executive."

As both author and illustrator of his books, Gackenbach always "starts with the story. Sometimes I don't have a clear

And when I pulled its tail, it got even smaller. ■ (From *Harry and the Terrible Whatzit* by Dick Gackenbach. Illustrated by the author.)

I want my mother the way she is. Warm, soft, and furry. ■ (From *Hattie Rabbit* by Dick Gackenbach. Illustrated by the author.)

idea of what I want to do. I get out the typewriter and just see what comes. It comes easily; in that regard, I am a very, very lucky writer. I'll do an entire draft and then go back and revise and polish. A short story for a picture book generally takes five or six drafts which I do over a period of several days. As I'm writing I begin to visualize the pictures. Once the story is in shape, I begin work on the dummy. Most of my illustrations are essentially line drawings—my strongest asset. I then do the overlay of gray ink and water mix, followed by the wash, which may be in color. I have the reputation of sending very finished dummies to the publisher. It's easier for me this way to make changes later and gives the editor a much clearer idea of what I would like the book to look like. I usually do three books a year and take two months off to relax and 'recharge.'

"Doing research can be a lot of fun, particularly at a library as rich as the 42nd Street Branch of the New York Public Library. If you're doing a book set in the 1800s, you've got to make sure that the costumes, the architecture, the interiors, even the characters' posture is right for the time. Usually, though, I draw from memory or imagination. Having grown up in the country, birds, animals, trees, and flowers are a part of me. I can draw an animal or tree without any reference at all. I especially like to draw chickens—and there are lots of them in my books—maybe because we always had chickens on the farm in Allentown.''

Illustrating books for other authors is ''not quite as enjoyable. Strange as this may sound, I put even more effort into my drawing when they're for a story I didn't write. I guess I don't want to disappoint. When I'm working on someone else's book, the author and I don't confer at all. I believe it is better for the author and illustrator to work separately and to come together through their finished work. It is up to the editor to iron out disagreements, should any arise.''

In **1985**, Gackenbach sold his large house and moved into a condominium in Washington Depot. ''It's much easier to take care of. I don't have the ambitious garden I had before, but I do have a Japanese garden in the courtyard. The tranquility and coherence of the Japanese garden has long impressed and attracted me. I've never visited Japan, but have seen a number of Japanese gardens in this country and did a fair amount of research before making my plantings here. I miss the many flowers I had at the house, but buy a fresh bunch each week so my living space is nonetheless filled with blossoms.''

''Keep a notebook'' is Gackenbach's advice to young people interested in pursuing writing and illustrating. ''Whenever you get an idea, or something striking happens, jot it down. There may be a story there. The same goes for images. If you see something you want to sketch, just go ahead and *do* it. Don't be self-conscious. Not only is this a great way to learn and to 'keep track' of yourself, but it's an awful lot of fun.''

Gackenbach's works are included in the de Grummond Collection at the University of Southern Mississippi.

HOBBIES AND OTHER INTERESTS: Classical music, gourmet cooking, dogs.

FOR MORE INFORMATION SEE: Martha E. Ward and Dorothy A. Marquardt, *Authors of Books for Young People,* supplement to the second edition, Scarecrow, 1979; *New York Times Book Review,* December 9, 1979, February 22, 1981.

I put a piece of paper under my pillow, and when I could not sleep I wrote in the dark.

—Henry David Thoreau

GENTLE, Mary 1956-

PERSONAL: Born March 29, 1956, in Eastbourne, East Sussex, England; daughter of George William (a cinema manager) and Amy Mary (Champion) Gentle. *Education:* Attended high school in Hastings, East Sussex, England. *Politics:* ''Feminist.'' *Home:* Flat No. 1, 11 Alumhurst Rd., Westbourne, Bournemouth, Dorset, England.

CAREER: Author. Has worked as assistant movie projectionist, clerk for a wholesale bookseller, and civil servant. *Member:* Bournemouth Writers Circle (secretary, 1979-80).

WRITINGS: A Hawk in Silver (young adult novel), Gollancz, 1977, Lothrop, 1985; *Golden Witchbreed,* Morrow, 1984. Contributor of reviews and articles to *Vector.*

WORK IN PROGRESS: A science fiction novel for young adults, tentatively entitled *Star of Africa.*

SIDELIGHTS: ''I was writing for a good long while before I realized it was a serious occupation. Since then it has taken up progressively larger amounts of my time, though I am a lazy writer and should be chained forcibly to a typewriter. In short, I hate writing, but love having written. One of my avocational interests is gainful employment!''

GORDON, Shirley 1921-

PERSONAL: Born December 29, 1921, in Geneva, Ill.; daughter of Russell (a police officer) and Viola (a cashier; maiden name, LaVoy) Gordon; children: David Russell (adopted). *Education:* Pasadena City College, A.A., 1980. *Home:* 3039 Chadwick Dr., Los Angeles, Calif. 90032.

CAREER: TV-Radio Life (magazine), Hollywood, Calif., reporter, 1943-50; Columbia Broadcasting System, Inc. (CBS) Radio and Television, Hollywood, network publicist, 1951-55; writer, 1955—; Area H Alternative School, Los Angeles,

Don't you belong to anybody? ■ (From *The Boy Who Wanted a Family* by Shirley Gordon. Illustrated by Charles Robinson.)

Calif., teacher of creative writing and children's literature, 1973-76. Scriptwriter for network radio shows, including "Suspense," "The Whistler," "Hollywood Radio Mystery Theatre," and television shows, including "You Are There," "Climax," "Bob Cummings Show," "Courtship of Eddie's Father," and "Bewitched." Community mental health volunteer worker. *Member:* Writers Guild of America (West). *Awards, honors: Crystal Is the New Girl* was chosen one of Child Study Association's Children's Books of the Year, 1976.

WRITINGS—Juvenile: The Green Hornet Lunchbox, Houghton, 1970; *Crystal Is the New Girl* (illustrated by Edward Frascino), Harper, 1976; *Crystal Is My Friend* (illustrated by E. Frascino), Harper, 1978; *Grandma Zoo* (illustrated by Whitney Darrow, Jr.), Harper, 1978; *The Boy Who Wanted a Family* (illustrated by Charles Robinson), Harper, 1980; *Me and the Bad Guys* (illustrated by E. Frascino), Harper, 1980; *Happy Birthday, Crystal* (illustrated by E. Frascino), Harper, 1981; *Crystal's Christmas Carol,* Harper, in press.

WORK IN PROGRESS Books for children and young people.

SIDELIGHTS: "Writing has always appealed to the 'loner' in me. However, as a Hollywood scriptwriter, I found myself having to write in a crowded room of writers. When the air became blue with cigar smoke or off-color jokes I retreated to the ladies' room, where I spent a large part of my career as a television comedy writer.

"I think writing children's books is one of the world's happiest occupations. My favorite motto: 'Writing's fun—you can do it at home in your pajamas.'

"I like best to write with a pencil so that I can write outdoors, which is my favorite place to be. Before one submits a manu-

script to a publisher, however, it must be typed. So I frequently carry my typewriter outside, as well.

"Most of my stories start with something that actually happened to one of my young friends (*The Green Hornet Lunchbox, Crystal Is the New Girl*) or to my son as he was growing up (*Me and the Bad Guys*).

"*The Boy Who Wanted a Family,* of course, is the story of my son's adoption and the formation of our somewhat unusual family, with 'Miss Graham' (myself) as a single parent, unmarried, who actually *does* keep a Christmas tree up all year round.

"Also, as 'Michael' and his mom do in the story, my son David and I have gone on many 'Saturday adventures' to the mountains, beach, desert, and horse-and-farm country, all luckily within easy reach from our home in Los Angeles, California. In talking with young readers of this particular book, I find they always want to be assured that everything in it is true. It is."

Gordon's works are included in the de Grummond Collection at the University of Southern Mississippi.

HOBBIES AND OTHER INTERESTS: Walking in the out-of-doors, bird-watching, nature study, sketching, and reading.

HAGUE, Michael (Riley)   1948-

PERSONAL: Born September 8, 1948, in Los Angeles, Calif.; son of Riley H. (a truck driver) and Marie (King) Hague; married Susan Kathleen Burdick (an artist and author of children's books), December 5, 1970; children: Meghan, Brittany, Devon. *Education:* Art Center College of Design, BFA (with honors), 1972. *Residence:* Colorado Springs, Colo.

CAREER: Hallmark Cards, Kansas City, Kans., illustrator, 1973-75; Current, Inc., Colorado Springs, Colo., illustrator, 1975-77; author and illustrator of children's books, 1977—. *Awards, honors: Dream Weaver* was chosen for the American Institute of Graphic Arts Book Show (formerly known as Fifty Books of the Year), 1980; *The Man Who Kept House* was chosen one of International Reading Association's Children's Choices, 1982; *Aesop's Fables, The Legend of the Veery Bird,* and *Alice's Adventures in Wonderland* were all selected as Children's Books of the Year by the Child Study Association of America, 1985.

WRITINGS—For children; self-illustrated: (Reteller with wife, Kathleen Hague) *East of the Sun and West of the Moon,* Harcourt, 1980; (reteller with K. Hague) *The Man Who Kept House,* Harcourt, 1981; (selector) Hans Christian Andersen, *Michael Hague's Favourite Hans Christian Andersen Fairy Tales,* Holt, 1981; (selector) *Mother Goose: A Collection of Classic Nursery Rhymes,* Holt, 1984; (selector) *Aesop's Fables,* Holt, 1985; *A Child's Book of Prayers,* Holt, 1985; *Unicorn Pop-Up Book,* Holt, 1986; *World of Unicorns,* Holt, 1986.

Illustrator; for children: Ethel Marbach, *The Cabbage Moth and the Shamrock,* Star & Elephant Books, 1978; Beth Hilgartner, *A Necklace of Fallen Stars,* Little, Brown, 1979; Jane Yolen, *Dream Weaver,* Collins, 1979.

Deborah Apy, reteller, *Beauty and the Beast,* Green Tiger, 1980, reissued, Holt, 1983; Eve Bunting, *Demetrius and the Golden Goblet,* Harcourt, 1980; Julia Cunningham, *A Mouse*

MICHAEL HAGUE

Called Junction, Pantheon, 1980; Kenneth Grahame, *The Wind in the Willows,* Holt, 1980; Lee Bennett Hopkins, selector, *Moments: Poems about the Seasons,* Harcourt, 1980; Clement C. Moore, *The Night before Christmas,* Holt, 1981; Marianna Mayer, *The Unicorn and the Lake,* Dial, 1982; L. Frank Baum, *The Wizard of Oz,* Holt, 1982; Margery Williams, *The Velveteen Rabbit; or, How Toys Become Real,* Holt, 1983; K. Grahame, *The Reluctant Dragon,* Holt, 1983; C. S. Lewis, *The Lion, the Witch and the Wardrobe,* Macmillan, 1983; Nancy Luenn, *The Dragon Kite,* Harcourt, 1983; Jakob Grimm and Wilhelm Grimm, *Rapunzel,* Creative Education, 1984; K. Hague, *Alphabears: An ABC Book,* Holt, 1984; Elizabeth Isele, reteller, *The Frog Princess,* Crowell, 1984; J.R.R. Tolkien, *The Hobbit; or, There and Back Again,* Houghton, 1984.

Lewis Carroll (pseudonym of Charles Lutwidge Dodgson) *Alice's Adventures in Wonderland,* Holt, 1985; K. Hague, *The Legend of the Veery Bird,* Harcourt, 1985; K. Hague, *Numbears: A Counting Book,* Holt, 1986; K. Hague, *Out of the Nursery, Into the Night,* Holt, 1986; Frances Hodgson Burnett, *The Secret Garden,* Holt, 1987; J. M. Barrie, *Peter Pan,* Holt, 1987.

Also illustrator of several calendars, including a series based on C. S. Lewis's "Chronicles of Narnia" books.

WORK IN PROGRESS: Illustrations for *Rutabaga Story.*

SIDELIGHTS: Born **September 8, 1948,** in Los Angeles, California. Hague, the eldest of three children, has a younger brother and sister. His mother emigrated from London, England shortly after World War II. "I had a talent for drawing

as early as kindergarten. My mother had been to art school in England and encouraged me greatly by bringing home art books from which I could copy paintings and drawings. She never gave me lessons. I knew as a child that I wanted to illustrate books. I was always reading and rendering illustrations of my own creations for the King Arthur books as well as making portraits of such baseball heroes as Duke Snider of the Los Angeles Dodgers.

"There were lots of books in our house. I was one of those kids who believed everything in books and cartoons. I *still* have a hard time accepting that Prince Valiant is not a real character from English history. I loved comic books but had to sneak them into the house because my mother objected to them. The Disney books were my absolute favorite. My most cherished book of Disney animation showed how to draw and animate the studio's characters.

"I'm still a great Disney fan—I hold documents as one of the first Mickey Mouse Club members. To this day I remember an enormous man named Roy, a Disney animator often featured on the 'Mickey Mouse Club' television show. I used to think to myself, 'One day he'll retire, and then. . . .'

"I had lots of friends in Los Angeles where I grew up and was into baseball and all kinds of sports. I didn't take art classes in high school—too interested in baseball instead—but continued to draw nonetheless. I would have loved to have played professional baseball, but knew even then I didn't have the talent for it."

Attended junior college. "I majored in art and after two years transferred to the Art Center College of Design in Los Angeles where I spent four years. At first I majored in illustration—with a career in children's books in mind. But Art Center wasn't big on children's books, and tended to push its illustration students toward more lucrative careers in advertising and magazine illustration. I switched my major to painting so that I could take more life drawing courses and be in a less commercially-oriented environment. I had one art class a day, five days a week and an academic subject on Saturdays. I loved life drawing and had many wonderful teachers, including Harry Carmean and Lorser Feitelson.

"My wife, Kathleen, was a painting major at Art Center. We married while we were still students, and even held our reception at the school."

Following graduation, Hague worked as card designer for Hallmark Greeting Cards in Kansas. "Everyone told me I'd never make a living doing children's books, so I decided I'd teach to supplement my income. When that didn't work out, I applied to Hallmark Cards. For two years I worked in their Kansas City studio. It was great to get paid for drawing every day. I've done just about every kind of card from 'cutesy' greetings to wedding anniversaries. For the anniversary cards, they would show a couple on a beach from so far away you couldn't discern their ages, and in the foreground a close-up of a seashell. For each project Hallmark artists were given direction packs, called 'tickets.' After completing many 'ticketed' projects you were allowed to initiate ideas for card illustrations.

"Glad though I was to have my job, I was determined to eventually work in publishing. My first week at Hallmark, I worked at putting together a portfolio, which I sent around to publishers. Many of the comments I received early on were quite discouraging. Some editors said my work was 'too weird' for children. Many art directors sent back my portfolio with

(From *The Lion, the Witch and the Wardrobe* by C. S. Lewis. Illustrated by Michael Hague.)

no comment. Silence was the worst response, and alas, the most frequent. How did I keep my morale up? I just assumed they were idiots. Dr. Seuss went to twenty-nine publishers before he had his first book published. After five years, I finally was offered illustration work and then it all seemed to come at once.''

December 1978. "My first illustration job in publishing was a cover for *Cricket* magazine. Trina Hyman was then the art director there and she soon assigned me a cover and an inside story as well.

"My first published book illustration was *Gulliver's Travels,* a pop-up book brought out by Hallmark. I used myself as the model for Gulliver. It's not much fun to illustrate pop-up books, because they're pieced together. You are never working on a whole illustration, which makes it hard to visualize the final product. I made lots of mistakes."

Worked for Current, Inc. a greeting card company in Colorado Springs. "While I was working at Current I contacted Green Tiger Press. To my delight, they asked what *I* would like to illustrate. The first thing that came to mind was *Beauty and the Beast,* which they agreed to. My illustrations for the book were influenced by the Cocteau film.

"It took a long time before I had another opportunity to propose what *I* wanted to illustrate to a publisher. When you're getting started, it's the publishers who make suggestions, and illustrators tend to accept everything and anything. It still takes me a long time to say 'no' to a project that doesn't interest me. But after the publication and success of *The Wind in the Willows* in 1980, I was in a position to suggest books I like to illustrate.

Beauty rose at four in the morning to milk the cows, feed the chickens and geese. ▪ (From *Beauty and the Beast,* adapted by Deborah Apy Kohen. Illustrated by Michael R. Hague.)

So, carefully and gently, they lifted Dorothy in their arms and carried her swiftly through the air. ■ (From *The Wizard of Oz* by L. Frank Baum. Illustrated by Michael Hague.)

"Some books I'd love to do over again. *The Wizard of Oz,* which came out in 1982, is one of them. I wasn't using models at the time (*The Velveteen Rabbit; or, How Toys Become Real,* 1983, was the first book for which I used models). I've discovered that using child models is very helpful. I tend to draw children with adult features, a problem I've been trying to solve for the past few years. I work with both my own children and children from the neighborhood. For *Mother Goose: A Collection of Classic Nursery Rhymes* I used the children of the Colorado Springs School for models. When working with child models, I take photographs for reference, because kids can't sit still.

"I'm hard at work on my adult characters as well. Though I can draw adults fairly well I still have to be careful to be consistent. It's a challenge to maintain the look of a character. A face is so small on the canvas. The slightest movement of the nose, whether you draw it curved or straight, changes the entire face. I'd love to use models for everything, but I don't use them for adult characters, because I'm too timid to ask anyone to sit for me.

"I set up little technical problems to solve and correct myself as I go along. I've been working on backgrounds lately, trying to make them look more realistic and more colorful from book to book. Sometimes while I'm working on a book, it's difficult to spot the problems. It helps to finally see a project in book form. It gives me a new perspective. I like doing many books because it gives me a sense of progress. The only way for me to improve is to paint and draw all the time. But I haven't had a book yet which was close to my original painting in terms of sharp details or color—a limitation in the reproduction technology of book illustration.

"I try not to make a book monotonous. I work on finding a variety of different light sources, even if the light source is not described exactly in the story. Light is one of the elements which makes a painting real, especially when you are painting the fantastic. The more real a tree looks, or the light appears, the more believable the fantasy elements will be. One can't afford to be vague when illustrating fantasy. Ninety per cent of a fantasy book should be based on the real world; you don't need many strange elements to make a story work. In a good illustration of a knight riding on a horse, for example, the viewer will ride over the next hill with him, even though the artist hasn't illustrated what's over there.

"I don't like much science fiction because I can't relate to it. Some of the stories, aside from being poorly written, don't have any relationship to what we know."

Hague has illustrated a host of dragons. "Unlike people, dragons aren't hard to draw, although I tend to have a fuzzy image of a dragon at first. I have to concentrate on different angles of a dragon while I'm doodling until I come up with something that pleases me. Many of my dragons were dictated by their stories. I couldn't see the 'Reluctant Dragon' as an evil-looking or scary dragon. He was the kind of creature you'd like to get to know. Tolkien's dragon in *The Hobbit* was completely different: very menacing, very threatening.

"It's not hard to animate or give gesture to fantasy creatures once you have principles of drawing. I try to make movement and gesture look believable, and one way to do that is to be sure that the backgrounds are realistic. It adds emphasis. Once again, I build a concrete world—not a fuzzy, dream-like place—where kids can see real sky or walls or cities. Then a dragon can become believable.

"Animals, too, are much easier for me to draw than human beings. We don't see animals in the mirror every morning, so we're less critical about how they're portrayed in illustration.

"I don't have any magic answers or secret tricks. If something doesn't look right to me, I fiddle around until it does, often fudging perspective. Sometimes I'll have a bad day, when nothing seems to come easy. People ask me how long it takes to do a painting, and I can't really say because it changes from painting to painting from day to day. I've done some paintings in one day, others in two weeks. I couldn't say why that is."

About his method of working, Hague commented, "I try to infuse my illustrations with the same spirit that the author or the story produced in my imagination. I begin with character studies and try to capture on paper what I see in my mind's eye. Once I've chosen the subject for an illustration, I make some very small compositional sketches, which for me are most important. These small thumbnails are then enlarged to full-sized sketches, where I develop the details of the picture. From there I proceed to recreate these initial sketches in finished pencil illustrations. I always use 2H pencils because they don't smear when watercolor is applied. After the drawing is completed, I am ready to begin painting. The brushes, by the way, range from size 8 to 000. I put a neutral wash over the entire board with a wide brush, an ocher color for a warm painting and a bluish wash for a cool picture. When the wash dries I begin to paint the details. Only after coloring everything do I go in with my ink lines. This is a rather backward way of working, but I feel comfortable with it.

"I'm nervous about working closely with authors, partly because when I read a text I see images right away. However, I like the idea of meeting, getting to know and feeling comfortable with authors. Unfortunately, that is not always possible because I live outside of New York."

Hague feels that imagining and believing are "the only forms of magic left. When I was a kid, I thought that magicians actually did work magic—the power to cut a woman in two and put her back together again. As I got older I, of course, realized that these were optical illusions. After a while one draws a distinction between doing tricks and imagination. Our imagination is real magic. And while imagination may change in our increasingly technological world, it is still magic—it's what got us to the moon! Without it, we'd still be living in trees."

1980. Illustrated Kenneth Grahame's classic, *The Wind in the Willows,* for Holt. "My maternal grandmother was born in London in 1908, two years before the first publication of *The Wind in the Willows.* She can recall with delight her father reading aloud to her about the adventures of Mr. Toad and his friends. The book was her father's favorite, and indeed became hers as well. My grandmother passed on a love of 'Willows,' as she refers to it, to my mother; and so when the story reached me it had already claimed three generations and captivated its fourth generation in me. Very soon it will be my three children's turn to be caught in Toad's spell as well.

"Its principal characters—Ratty, Mole, Badger, and, of course, Mr. Toad—and their surroundings are cherished by countless readers. With such a loyal and affectionate following, from young children to their great-grandparents, I felt a great responsibility in illustrating the book. (What would my great-grandfather think?) I was also well aware that *The Wind in the Willows* had been earlier illustrated by two of my idols, Ernest Shepard and Arthur Rackham. Therefore, when I was first approached with the idea of my illustrating this classic, I was

Come with me and I'll show you what my life is like. ■ (From "The Town Mouse and the Country Mouse" in *Aesop's Fables*, selected and illustrated by Michael Hague.)

thrilled, honored, and a bit frightened. I love the book. I love the dependable Water Rat, the kindly Mole, the sturdy Badger, and especially Mr. Toad. And so it is, as when one is in love, one forgets all obstacles and fears. That is what happened to me.

"I've not tried to create a new visual style or interpretation of the story. I have instead tried to infuse my illustrations with the same spirit that Kenneth Grahame's magic words convey. There is, I think, a bit of Toad in all of us. Certainly there must have been some of Mr. Toad in me when I agreed to illustrate this book."

1981. *Michael Hague's Favourite Hans Christian Andersen Fairy Tales* published. "My love for Hans Christian Andersen goes back to my mom, who used to read to us. Andersen was one of her favorites. She felt we should know the classics, since they weren't taught to us at school. I never imagined Andersen as a real person. He seemed more like Mother Goose to me. I couldn't believe that someone had actually written all those stories. I like his work because it is strange and unpredictable. Some of his stories have sad endings—not just about living happily ever after. I think that's why his work still appeals to kids.

"I have mixed feelings about violence in the traditional fairy tales. I think the Grimm stories were in some way created to give real warnings to kids about real dangers of the time, such as getting lost in the forest. And while older kids do go through a phase of fascination about those scary tales, I know that younger children like my three-year-old son can be terrified by them and even have nightmares. If you don't have kids of your own, it is comparatively easy to say that kids *enjoy* being scared. It's another thing when you have kids and witness their fear. I tend to wait until the kids are older, that way they know that a fairy tale is imaginary, and that there is no need to be afraid. Because fairy tales are very real to younger children, I can see changing some elements of the original stories in a retelling. We should have *both* versions. I've noticed it's usually people who haven't children of their own who tend to say, 'We can't meddle with the original.'

"When I illustrate, I don't think about kids, or what age group the book is aimed toward. I don't like to generalize or second guess my audience. I try to please myself. I am still in touch with my childhood, with the child that still exists in me. I like to use nonsense to throw in elements which don't have anything to do with the story.''

1982. Illustrated *The Wizard of Oz* for Holt. "When I was a child, there were three places I would have given anything to visit. One was England in the days of King Arthur; another was the Wild West of Hopalong Cassidy; the third, quite different, was the Wonderful Land of Oz. Arthur's England and Hoppy's West were confined to earthly borders. The landscape of Oz was as large or as small as I wished it to be. And, like Alice's Wonderland, it was populated with such extraordinary creatures that I knew anything might happen there. It was a place where the laws of our universe seldom applied.

"My yearning to visit Oz has not diminished with the passing years. The idea of wandering among the Winkies and Munchkins remains as appealing as ever. So it was with great joy that I accepted the assignment to paint Oz.

"I count myself as one of the most fortunate of beings. For as an artist I have not only the pleasure but the duty to daydream. It is part of my work. I have been a contented daydreamer all of my life, often to the exasperation of those around me. While creating the illustrations for *The Wizard of Oz*, I would slip away. My hands went about their business while my mind walked among the Quadlings and the fierce Kalidahs.

"L. Frank Baum wrote *The Wizard of Oz* at the dawn of the twentieth century, and it is as bright and fresh now as it was the day it was written. I find it curious that the story of Oz is well known by so many Americans, and yet relatively few have read the book. Most have become familiar with Oz through the movie. But the movie and the book are quite different. It is my hope that with this new edition children and adults alike will journey down the yellow brick road and for the first time experience Oz as Baum created it.'' [Michael Hague, ''Afterword,'' *The Wizard of Oz*, Holt, 1982.]

1983. For *The Dragon Kite*, a Japanese tale by Nancy Luenn, Hague worked in association with the Japan Society in New York City. "The publisher sent all my sketches to the Japan Society. They went over the sketches and sent back critiques, sometimes xeroxing such reference material as the correct kind of sandal or building for the sixteenth-century in which the tale is set. It was interesting and very helpful, but I don't ordinarily pay much attention to historical detail.

"I often mix up centuries in my illustrations. In *The Reluctant Dragon* I have a twelfth-century knight with a Tudor house in the background. It doesn't bother me if it looks right. If it looks funny, I take it out. I wouldn't advise people to look for historical accuracy in my work. These are fairy tales, *not* historical books.

"Each book poses a different set of problems. For example, with the illustrations for Tolkien's *The Hobbit; or, There and Back Again*, I wanted to take a new approach to Bilbo. It seemed to me that earlier hobbits all looked the same. I didn't want my hobbits to have pointed ears, which, in fact, are not mentioned in the text. I felt if Tolkien had wanted readers to imagine his hobbits with pointed ears, he certainly would have said so. I decided to make the hobbits appear more like children, sort of like aged children, rather than dwarves. In his prologue to *Lord of the Rings* Tolkien did mention that the hobbits were childlike. I didn't use models, because I didn't want them to appear too childlike. I had so little time to do that book—fifty pieces of art in six months! And I was also involved in my *Mother Goose* book at the same time. I regret that some of the paintings aren't as finished as they would have been had I had a reasonable amount of time for the project.

"I know that some artists have said they solved problems in their work through their dreams. I'm the opposite. I don't get revelations. I dream I'm having problems—colors that won't come out right, or washes that bleed!''

Alphabears: An ABC Book was written by Hague's wife, Kathleen, published by Holt. "Kathleen and I had done some writings together, different versions of classics (such as *East of the Sun and West of the Moon*), but Holt wanted to do something more contemporary. Kathy told one of the editors that I collect teddy bears and suggested an ABC teddy bear book. I used my collection for reference. Although the book is dedicated to my old teddy bear, Potts, I didn't put him in the book because he's in pretty bad shape. I was still taking Potts to bed with me when I was eleven years old. My mom thought of taking me to a psychiatrist, until I finally told her that Potts was a kind of bodyguard. I used to tuck him under the covers, laying him on my chest, so that if a burglar came to stab me, they would stab Potts instead!

(From *The Velveteen Rabbit; or, How Toys Become Real* by Margery Williams. Illustrated by Michael Hague.)

The clerk stared at him and the rusty black bonnet a moment, and then laughed. . . ."Here, stand away from the window, please, madam; you're obstructing the other passengers!" ■ (From *The Wind in the Willows* by Kenneth Grahame. Illustrated by Michael Hague.)

(From *Alice's Adventures in Wonderland* by Lewis Carroll. Illustrated by Michael Hague.)

"I don't need your service, thank you," said Beorn, "but I expect you need mine." ■ (From *The Hobbit; or, There and Back Again* by J. R. R. Tolkien. Illustrated by Michael Hague.)

(From "The Ugly Duckling" in *Michael Hague's Favourite Hans Christian Andersen Fairy Tales*, selected and illustrated by Michael Hague.)

''I work all the time, but do not regiment myself because I work best without structure. Sometimes I work all through the week, including Saturday and Sunday, and have often worked through the night when I have been under the pressure of a deadline. I have a separate studio downstairs, but I get terribly lonely so far away from my family, that I bring everything, drawing board, brushes back up to the living room. I like to work with people around. Unlike some artists who absolutely cannot support distraction or noise, I'm driven crazy by silence and isolation. I often work with my three-year-old son crawling around under my table. I get helpful feedback and criticism from my wife and kids.

''We liked Colorado Springs so much that after I quit my job with Current to illustrate full time, we decided to stay. It's beautiful here. I love the stars, the pine trees. I'm sure that the light and the landscape have influenced my work—how could it be otherwise? Turner would have painted quite differently had he lived in Greece instead of London. We live in a fifty-year-old Tudor house, for which we are throwing a birthday party this year. To one side we have a lovely view of the mountains and to the other the city. It's very comfortable.''

Hague has been influenced by a wide variety of artistic styles, ''ranging from the work of the Disney Studios to the Japanese printmakers Hiroshige and Hokusai. I particularly love the work of turn-of-the-century illustrators Arthur Rackham, W. Heath Robinson, N. C. Wyeth and Howard Pyle. I am an avid collector of their books, as well as those of contemporary illustrators Sendak and Errol LeCain. I like the work of Arnold and Anita Lobel, the Provensens, the Dillons, and many others. It's difficult to put my finger on what makes an illustration a classic. I think it has to do with a universal quality of the work—a special something that strikes a chord in people. I wish I knew! I'd write a book on it—then we'd all write and illustrate classics!

''When I said that there is a little bit of Toad in all of us, I meant that one has to have a bit of confidence to go ahead and do the things one dreams of doing. Even when something doesn't work out, it is important to at least make the attempt. I know I haven't reached my potential as an artist. I'm hoping by the time I'm fifty I'll be in my stride. The next step for me is to illustrate and find publication for my own books. I seem to be running up against the same reactions I got years ago with my portfolio: 'your stories are too weird for children.' Rejections haven't seemed to dim my ardor. I still have hope and really love writing, though I write rather sporadically.

''People play down luck, but my advice to young artists would be to draw all the time and get lucky. Fill up notebooks with drawings. Once you learn to draw you can do anything, but drawing is not simply technique. Your work must have meaning, it must have something behind it, something beyond technical skill.''

For relaxation, Hague works on his illustration. ''Illustration is not taxing work—it's not like hauling things around. I enjoy it. I don't have to get away from it. We often take the kids on outings, to the zoo or even shopping. With three kids, that can be more tiring than work!''

Hague is presently working on illustrations for Carl Sandburg's *Rutabaga Story*. ''I usually get a new project right in the middle of something else. I get excited about the new book, put the old away and sometimes miss deadlines because of it. I get so inspired with the text, especially when it's a classic. I read it several times and then attempt to zero in on the sections I will illustrate. I get a feel for a book right away.''

FOR MORE INFORMATION SEE: Sally Holmes Holtze, editor, *Fifth Book of Junior Authors and Illustrators,* H. W. Wilson, 1983.

HAYNES, Betsy 1937-

PERSONAL: Born October 20, 1937, in Benton, Ill.; daughter of Paul DeWitte (a musician) and Marounah Lee (a secretary; maiden name, Phillips) Shadle; married James Monroe Haynes (a manager for General Telephone and Electronics Corp.), October 8, 1960; children: Craig Johansen, Stephanie Jo. *Education:* Attended University of Illinois, 1955-57; Southern Illinois University, B.J., 1962. *Home address:* 4009 Deepwood Rd., Colleyville, Tex. 76034.

CAREER: Author of books for young adults and young readers, 1967—. Has worked as clerk, switchboard operator, insurance claims examiner, classified advertising manager for a newspaper, and secretary. *Member:* Authors Guild, Authors League of America, Society of Children's Book Writers, Children's Reading Round Table. *Awards, honors:* Book for Brotherhood Award from the National Conference of Christians and Jews, 1974, for *Cowslip;* Journalism Alumnus Award from the School of Journalism, Southern Illinois University, 1978; finalist, Young Hoosier Award from Association for Indiana Media Educators, 1980, for *The Ghost of the Gravestone Hearth; Taffy Sinclair Strikes Again* was chosen as a Children's Choice by the Children's Book Council and the International Reading Association, 1985.

BETSY HAYNES

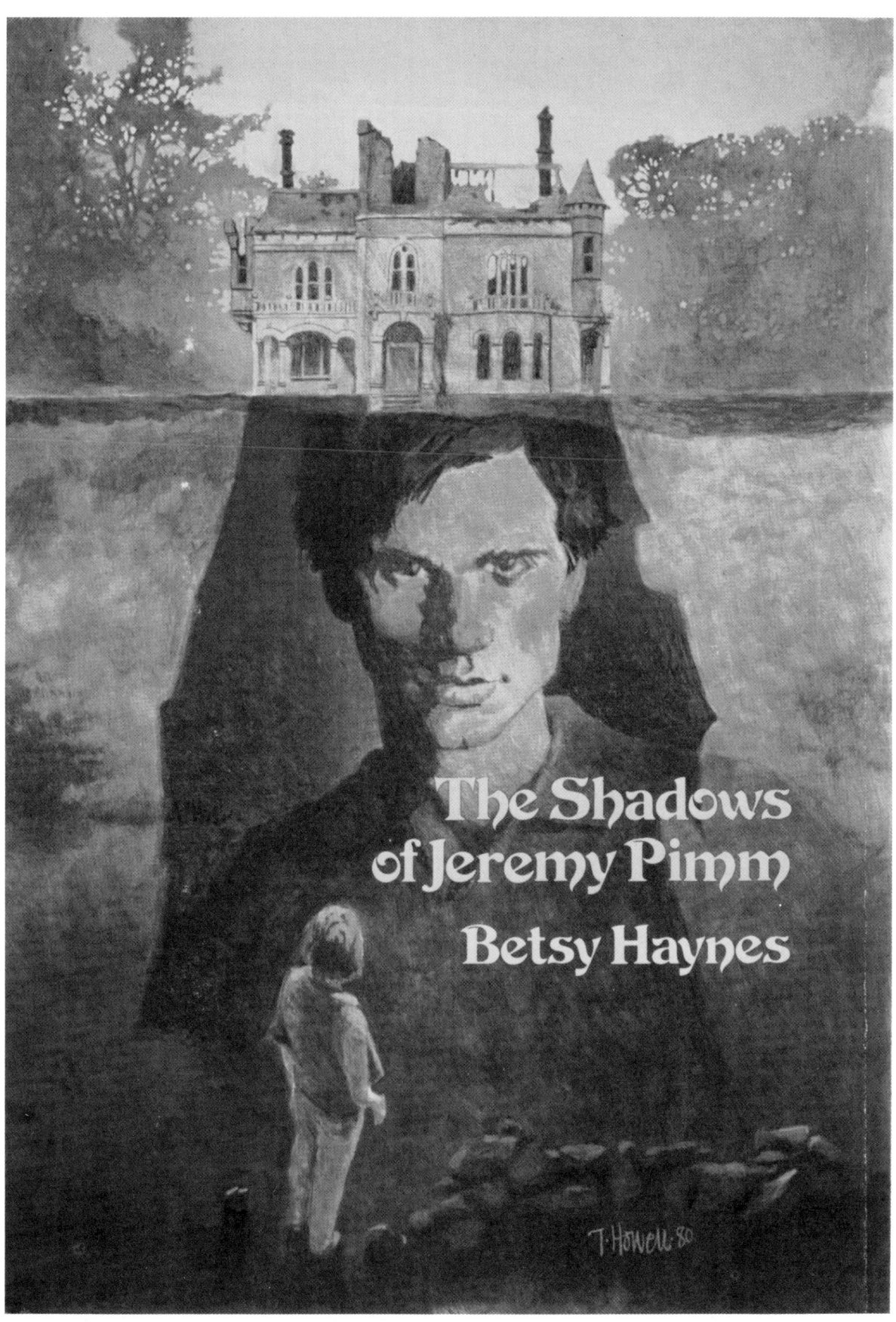

It was an L-shaped structure, two stories high, with tall dark-looking windows and all sorts of odd dormers and chimneys. ■ (Jacket illustration by Troy Howell from *The Shadows of Jeremy Pimm* by Betsy Haynes.)

WRITINGS: Cowslip (young adult), T. Nelson, 1973, published as *Slave Girl*, Scholastic Book Services, 1973; *Spies on the Devil's Belt* (young adult), T. Nelson, 1974; *The Against Taffy Sinclair Club* (juvenile), T. Nelson, 1976; *The Ghost of the Gravestone Hearth* (young adult), T. Nelson, 1977; *The Shadows of Jeremy Pimm* (young adult), Beaufort Books, 1981; *The Power* (young adult), Dell, 1982; *Taffy Sinclair Strikes Again* (juvenile), Bantam, 1984; *Taffy Sinclair, Queen of the Soaps* (juvenile), Bantam, 1985; *The Great Mom Swap* (juvenile), Bantam, 1986; *Faking It* (young adult), New American Library, 1986; *Taffy Sinclair and the Romance Machine Disaster*, Bantam, 1987.

Contributor of stories and articles to periodicals, including *Wee Wisdom, Weekly Reader, News Explorer, Five/Six, Junior Challenge, Ideals, Grit,* and *New York Times.*

WORK IN PROGRESS: Darlin' Ding-a-Ling, a sequel to *The Great Mom Swap; The Truth about Taffy Sinclair,* the fifth book in the "Taffy Sinclair" series.

SIDELIGHTS: "Although I wrote my first book, an epic novel entitled 'Peppy the Frog,' in the fourth grade, I look upon the fifth grade as the point when I began collecting the experiences of life which were later to become a part of my most popular books, the 'Taffy Sinclair' series. In fifth grade I had an enemy. Her name was Mary Beth, and she had long blond hair and big blue eyes and was the most beautiful girl in our school. Of course she had a rotten personality while I, on the other hand, had a fabulous personality. Mary Beth and I were rivals for everything, and our dislike for each other grew so intense that we actually had clubs against each other. Our relationship never really improved, but as we grew up and went on to live our separate lives, I forgot about Mary Beth. Following the dream of my childhood I became a writer, publishing short stories and two historical novels.

"Then one day my daughter, Stephanie, who just happened to be in fifth grade, began coming home with stories about her enemy, Laura. 'Mom, you should have seen Laura today,' she would begin and then launch into a story that, except for the date and setting, could have been one of my experiences with Mary Beth. It wasn't long until I began to realize that while times do change, we all must face many of the same growing up experiences, and that perhaps I had something to share with young readers about relationships, both good and bad. And so I wrote *The Against Taffy Sinclair Club.* I was asked to turn this book into a series by Bantam. The second book, *Taffy Sinclair Strikes Again,* was again based upon an incident from my childhood. My best friends and I had foolishly agreed that in the name of self-improvement we should level with each other and tell each other her worst fault. It had been a disaster in real life, and it became an even bigger disaster for my fictional characters. My series was off and running, and in 1985 *Taffy Sinclair, Queen of the Soaps* was published, followed by *Taffy Sinclair and the Romance Machine Disaster,* and *The Truth about Taffy Sinclair* is growing on a floppy disc.

"Through all this I have received many letters from readers telling me about the Taffy Sinclair in their lives. They have convinced me of the value of my original premise, that there is someone in each of our lives who dangles like the carrot in front of our nose, always prettier, always getting what we want, be it boyfriends or promotions, and that we must learn first to cope and then to deal with this person. If I could I would thank Mary Beth. I would thank her first for helping me to learn valuable things about life and relationships, and then I would thank her for being such a strong presence as to

keep the agonies and joys of that stage of childhood vivid enough in my mind so that I can translate them for my readers."

Cowslip has been translated into French and German; *Spies on the Devil's Belt* has been translated into French.

HOBBIES AND OTHER INTERESTS: "Meeting and getting to know new people. I also love animals. We've had horses, ducks, you name it, but we're down to two dogs and three cats at the moment."

HEYWOOD, Karen   1946-

PERSONAL: Born May 3, 1946, in Manchester, England; daughter of Walter (an architect) and Doreen (Grimshaw) Heywood; children: Daniel, Sam, Ben. *Education:* Stockport Art College, 1966; Leicester Art College, 1970. *Religion:* Spiritualist. *Home and office:* 273 Coppice Rd., Higher Poynton, Stockport, Cheshire SK12 1SP, England.

CAREER: CPV Advertising Agency, London, England, artist, 1970-71; Design Communications Ltd., London, graphic designer, 1971; Routledge & Kegan Paul, Publishers, London, graphic artist and illustrator, 1971-72; Geyer-Werker Film & Animation Co., Hamburg, Germany, animator, 1977; freelance illustrator, 1978—. *Member:* Royal Society of Arts, Association of Cinematic and Television Technicians. *Awards, honors:* Royal Society of Arts Bursary Award, 1970, for an advertising project.

ILLUSTRATOR: S. B. Cunningham, *Piccolo Book of Riddles,* Pan Books, 1973; Margaret Gossett, *Piccolo Book of Jokes,* Pan Books, 1973; Marguerite Pattern, *Sweetmaking for Children,* Pan Books, 1973; Anne Tibble, *Greenhorn,* Routledge & Kegan Paul, 1973; Gisela Kindt, *Der Chow-Chow,* Kosmos, 1976; Dagma Thies, *Katzenhaltung/Katzenpfege* (title means "Cat Keeping/Cat Care"), Kosmos, 1976; John Broughton, *The Wild Man of the Four Winds,* Hamish Hamilton, 1982, David & Charles, 1983; Robina Beckles Willson, *Square Bear,* Hamish Hamilton, 1983; Madeleine Edmond-

KAREN HEYWOOD

As he danced, the waters of the lake swelled into huge waves. ■ (From *The Wild Man of the Four Winds* by John Broughton. Illustrated by Karen Heywood.)

son, *Anna Witch,* Hamish Hamilton, 1983; Siân Lewis, *The Saddlebag Hero,* Hamish Hamilton, 1984; Mary Cockett, *Better than a Party,* Hamish Hamilton, 1984; (contributor) Wade, *Around the World* (folktales), Wheaton, 1986.

"Profile" series; all published by Hamish Hamilton: Mary Craig, *Pope John Paul II,* 1982; Alan Hamilton, *Queen Elizabeth II,* 1982, David & Charles, 1983; John Callaghan, *Geoffrey Boycott,* 1982; Craig Dodd, *Rudolf Nureyev,* 1982, David & Charles, 1983; Andrew Langley, *Ian Botham,* 1983, David & Charles, 1984; A. Hamilton, *Paul McCartney,* 1983; Rob Hunter, *Chris Bonington,* 1983, David & Charles, 1984; Kathryn Spink, *Gandhi,* 1984; Carolyn Sloan, *Helen Keller,* 1984, David & Charles, 1985; Angela Bull, *Florence Nightingale,* 1985; Tony Bradman, *John Lennon,* 1985; Josephine Ross, *The Princess of Wales,* 1986.

Television: "Die Astronauter," Berlin Television, 1977; "Rainbow," Thames Television, 1978, Jordanian Television, 1979; (animator) "The BFG" by Roald Dahl, Thames Television, 1986-87.

Contributor of illustrations to German magazines, including *Für Sie, Zu Hause,* and *Brigitte,* 1976-77.

WORK IN PROGRESS: Illustrating *The Alchemist's Tower* by John Broughton for Arnold Wheaton; illustrating another book by John Broughton.

SIDELIGHTS: "I began my career in advertising but I did not find this stimulating enough for my creativity so I steered my way into the publishing world. I have loved drawing ever since I can remember, and my sister (who is now an animator for television on 'The BFG' by Roald Dahl) and I spent hours illustrating stories we made up about our dolls. My father encouraged us and showed us the basic techniques of figure drawing—we were always drawing people. I won prizes for nearly all the competitions held at school and college, so it was obvious the direction I was going towards.

"I'd love to write books for very young children and illustrate them. Having small children of my own, it's amazing how many ideas come to me purely from observation and listening to their constant chatter, so maybe one day I'll achieve this ambition.

"I also enjoy illustrating fairy stories because this appeals to my love of the fantasy world. This is the direction I am aiming for at the moment, and I shall shortly be doing some drawings in this field for Arnold Wheaton Publishers.

"Animation has always fascinated me because the challenge is so exciting. Not only must you create the character and situation, but they actually move, which is very satisfying when the end result of the many hours of work materialize.

"My aim is to be self-sufficient with my own studio where I can do both book illustration and animated films without having to rely on other companies for their facilities.

"Sources of inspiration are Russian fairy story illustrations and the old masters. I find myself becoming more and more involved with detail and atmosphere with a surrealistic effect. Through meditation on symbols, colour and visions I have learnt a lot of what these mean to me personally. I do this with guidance from a medium in a development circle at the moment, but hope to do this alone eventually.

"I am never satisfied with my results, and want to go on, learning and finding out what I am capable of artistically."

HILLMAN, Priscilla 1940-

PERSONAL: Born July 24, 1940, in Newton, Mass.; daughter of Richard H. (an editor) and Alice (a homemaker; maiden name, Mattson) Hartford; married Norman Sherwood Hillman (an editor), June 25, 1965; children: Glenn Forrester. *Education:* University of Rhode Island, B.S., 1963. *Home:* 11 Allen Pl., Sloatsburg, N.Y. 10974.

CAREER: U.S. Oceanographic Office, Suitland, Md., oceanographer, 1963-65; author and illustrator of books for children.

WRITINGS—For children; self-illustrated; all published by Doubleday, except as noted: (With Adelaide Holl) *Minnikin,*

"This is my sister, Muffy, and it's her first day of school," Petunia said proudly to the teacher. ■
(From *The Merry-Mouse Schoolhouse* by Priscilla Hillman. Illustrated by the author.)

Midgie, and Moppet. Golden Press, 1977; *A Merry-Mouse Christmas ABC,* 1980; *The Merry-Mouse Book of Months,* 1980; *A Merry-Mouse Book of Nursery Rhymes,* 1981; *A Merry-Mouse Book of Favorite Poems,* 1981; *The Merry-Mouse Schoolhouse,* 1982; *The Merry-Mouse Book of Prayers and Graces,* 1983; *The Merry-Mouse Book of Opposites,* 1983; *The Merry-Mouse Counting and Colors Book,* 1983; *The Merry-Mouse Book of Toys,* 1983.

ADAPTATIONS—Filmstrips; all produced by Singer Society for Visual Education: "A Merry-Mouse Book of Months," 1982; "A Merry-Mouse Christmas ABC," 1982; "Merry-Mouse School Days" (contains *The Merry-Mouse Counting and Colors Book* and *The Merry-Mouse Book of Opposites*), 1986.

WORK IN PROGRESS: Priscilla Hillman's *Fairie Book,* a book about fairies and elves; *Precious Bears;* a Teddy Bear treasury.

SIDELIGHTS: "I was born in Newton, Massachusetts and have a twin sister, Greta and a younger brother, Richard. I spent the first eight years of my life in Portsmouth, New Hampshire and have happy memories of roaming the nearby fields picking berries and wildflowers in the spring and summer; in the fall, of walking through piles of colored leaves; and in winter, which seemed to last a long time, of sledding and building giant snow forts. My sister and I also spent a lot of time drawing especially on rainy days when we weren't exploring the attic. When I was eight we moved to Rhode Island. Gone were the nearby fields, but we lived rather close to Roger Williams Park, which I adored. My sister and I would walk through the park almost every Saturday morning instead of practicing with the violin. We both took violin lessons from the age of five till we entered college.

"I always wanted to be an artist or a marine biologist. At the advice of my high school art teacher, who said I had no creativity, I decided not to go to art school, but attend the University of Rhode Island instead. There I met my future husband, Norman, in an algae course. After graduation, my sister and I both got jobs in Suitland, Maryland at the U.S. Oceanographic Office. After working there two years, I married Norm and moved to New York where I resumed my interest in art and discovered that I also enjoyed writing children's verse.

"I was urged to write *The Merry-Mouse Schoolhouse* by Doubleday, but I much prefer to write children's verse. My very first efforts at writing any kind of verse were for my book *A Merry-Mouse Christmas ABC.* The inspiration for those verses was simply a strong desire to illustrate such a book. Since then, however, I've developed a strong love and desire to write children's verse, and hope someday that I may have a book of my poems for children published.

"I've always loved mice and rabbits and I guess I was just naturally led to paint them. For a short time, I had two field mice named 'Peanuts' and 'Popcorn' that my husband caught. They moved into our house one winter and after we caught them they had a cozy mouse house in our old fish tank."

We are now at the point where we must educate people in what nobody knew yesterday, and prepare in our schools for what no one knows yet but what some people must know tomorrow.

—Margaret Mead

HOFFMANN, Margaret Jones 1910- (Peggy Hoffmann)

PERSONAL: Born August 25, 1910, in Delaware, Ohio; daughter of Miles Hurst (a minister) and Renee (Roberts) Jones; married Arnold E. Hoffmann (a music educator), June 23, 1935; children: Theodore Charles, Rosemary Birky, Bruce Frederick. *Education:* Miami University, Oxford, Ohio, B.A., 1934; additional study, University of Chicago, 1934-35; occasional courses and private organ study, Colorado State Teachers' College (now University of Northern Colorado), University of Akron, and North Carolina State College (now University). *Religion:* United Church of Christ. *Home:* 1013 Gardner St., Raleigh, N.C. 27607.

CAREER: Free-lance writer. Church organist in Ravenna, Youngstown, and Oxford, Ohio, 1936—, and Raleigh, N.C., 1951-66, and 1979-82; music therapist, Umstead Hospital, Butner, N.C., 1964-68; teacher of creative writing, Continuing Education Division, Meredith College, 1977—. Consultant, Poetry-in-the-Schools, 1974—. *Member:* Mensa, Longview Writers. *Awards, honors:* Distinguished citation from Friends of American Writers, 1970, for *My Dear Cousin.*

WRITINGS: *Miss B's First Cookbook,* Bobbs-Merrill, 1950; *Sew Easy!,* Dutton, 1954; *Sew Far, Sew Good!* (Junior Literary Guild selection), Dutton, 1958; *The Wild Rocket,* Westminster, 1960; *Shift to High!* (Junior Literary Guild selection), Westminster, 1965; *A Forest of Feathers* (novel), Harcourt, 1966; *Grasshoppers Three* (rounds and canons), Harold Flammer, 1966; *Funeral Music for the Organ,* Harold Flammer,

MARGARET JONES HOFFMANN

1966; *The Cross Shines Forth,* Harold Flammer, 1966; *The Money Hat,* Westminster, 1969; *My Dear Cousin* (novel), Harcourt, 1970; (with Frank Watson) *Been There and Back,* Blair, 1977; (with Selve Maas) *The Sea Wedding,* Dillon, 1978; (with Gerald R. Hunter) *Bake a Snake: How to Survive by Your Own Cooking,* Meridional, 1981; *No Pedals* (collection of organ music), Art Masters Studios, 1986.

Also editor of fourteen collections of choral music, in simple arrangements for small choirs. Contributor of music reviews and book reviews to *Raleigh News and Observer.*

WORK IN PROGRESS: A collection of Estonian folk tales with Selve Maas; novel with Frank Watson, *No Sweet Bird Sings;* biographical novel, *Jellybean;* picture books; "Marlie and Charlie," a series for children; *First Men of Forestry.*

SIDELIGHTS: "When I was growing up we moved many times, so I have lived in nine states and can be at home anywhere. I have been in Raleigh, North Carolina for a long time and hope never to leave. Two of my novels: *A Forest of Feathers* and *Shift to High!* have a North Carolina setting."

Hoffman's children have inspired some of her books, including *Shift to High!.* "*Shift to High!* came about quite naturally

His head bowed over all his chins, waiting to know his punishment. ■ (From *The Sea Wedding and Other Stories from Estonia* by Selve Maas and Peggy Hoffman. Illustrated by Inese Jansons.)

because our older son, Ted, who is more or less the model for Tork, has been building hot rods—always in our front yard, of course—since he was about twelve or thirteen. I believe the sum total of completed creations was six, but there were seemingly hundreds of starts. My husband always wailed that the junk-yard atmosphere of our home made the neighborhood a blighted area; but the building and rebuilding went on relentlessly.

"Crate the Great was never actually built in its entirety, but Ted planned it with loving delight when I asked him what he would put into a car if he 'got lucky.' Research for the story was simple. I know the geographical area quite well, so that offered few problems. On matters of the car, I'd catch Ted at lunch, ask a question with pencil poised, and off we'd go."

Camping, an important part of *Shift to High!* is a family activity. "In a teacher's family it's about the only way extensive travel can be afforded. My husband was State Supervisor of Music in the North Carolina public schools. One summer we packed up sleeping bags, pup tent, etc., and went camping in Europe, using as our springboard the fact that my husband was asked to address an international music conference in Vienna.

"In the past ten years I've discovered that I have a talent and a love for teaching, although I do not have an education degree, only a B.A. My work with school children, hundreds of them all over the state in the Poetry-in-the-Schools program (one week each, four classes a day, third through sixth grades) and my classes in creative writing for adults in Continuing Education at Meredith College have been enormously stimulating. And the work must have been successful because they keep re-hiring me. My husband was a music educator, so that may have helped. It is exciting to explore other people's minds and try to bring out their greatest creativity. I like to do collaborative writing with other people when there can be a meeting of minds—but not when it involves the marketing end of it! I do not have an agent, so must find my own way. I have published three collaborative books.

"I *wish* I could draw. It is a frustration that I should solve by taking some classes through all the many opportunities here, but I don't seem to do it. I get my rewards by being an art-looker and am a senior docent at our prestigious North Carolina Museum of Art; this is a different form of teaching, I guess. One of the great challenges in an art museum is that there is always more to learn. And to share.

"For me travel is an incurable and delightful disease. I look at everything, not just cathedrals and vistas, but people and ways of life. I try to figure out the signs, read the newspapers, sample the food. And through my color slides can live the trip over and over again.

"To keep my hand in, I write music reviews and book reviews for the *Raleigh News and Observer,* often a challenge as late-night concerts must be written up first-draft and on the word processor in short order. This is a morning newspaper."

A Forest of Feathers has been translated into French.

HOBBIES AND OTHER INTERESTS: Travel, music, double crostics, knitting, sewing, and people.

FOR MORE INFORMATION SEE: Christian Science Monitor, July 10, 1958; *Picturebook of Tar Heel Authors,* State Department of Archives and History (Raleigh, N.C.), 1960, new edition, 1966; Martha E. Ward and Dorothy A. Marquardt, *Authors of Books for Young People,* 2nd edition, Scarecrow, 1971.

HOH, Diane   1937-

BRIEF ENTRY: Born April 28, 1937, in Warren, Pa. The mother of three children and a homemaker for twenty-six years, Hoh began writing for young adults in 1984. She chose this particular age group because, as she explained, "I never quite grew up, nor do I have any strong inclinations to do so." Hoh is the author of six novels in several romance series published by Scholastic. Her titles are _Loving That O'Connor Boy, Flirting, Betrayed, Staying Together, Brian's Girl,_ and _A Night to Forget._ Among her anticipated works for Scholastic are _Pulling Together, Prove It,_ and _Spring Break._ When she's not writing, Hoh spends her spare time gardening, reading, and with her family. _Home:_ 8400 Rockwood Lane, Austin, Tex. 78758.

HUBLEY, Faith (Elliot)   1924-

PERSONAL: Born September 16, 1924, in New York, N.Y.; daughter of Irving and Sally (Rosenblatt) Chestman; married John Hubley (a film producer), June 24, 1955 (died, 1977); children: Mark, Ray, Emily, Georgia, _Education:_ Attended Art Students' League, and Actor's Lab, California. _Home and studio:_ 355 E. 50th St., New York, N.Y. 10022.

CAREER: Worked as editor, script supervisor, and music editor of motion pictures in Hollywood, Calif., and New York City, 1944-55; animated motion picture producer, 1955—, writer and director, 1975—. Producer with husband, John Hubley, of animated motion pictures, including "Adventures of an *," 1956, "Moonbird," 1959, "The Hole," 1963, "The Hat," 1964, "Windy Day," 1968, "Of Men and Demons," 1969, "Voyage to Next," 1974, "People, People, People," 1975, and "A Doonesbury Special," 1977; producer of animated motion picture "Whither Weather," 1977. Founder with John Hubley of production company, Storyboard (now Hubley Studio, Inc.), New York, N.Y., 1955. Visiting lecturer at Yale University, 1972-85.

EXHIBITIONS: Paintings displayed in over twenty exhibitions in New York, California and Europe, including Theatre d'Annecy, France; Animator's Gallery, New York; Forum Gallery, New York; McKenzie Gallery, Los Angeles, Calif; "Faith Elliot Hubley: Painter and Cineaste" (one-woman exhibit of paintings, watercolors and films), Theatre d'Annecy. Retrospectives: "A Hubley Evening," Jerusalem Cinematheque, 1982; "A Tribute to John and Faith Hubley," University of California—Los Angeles, 1983; Yale University, New Haven, Conn., 1983; "An Homage to the Hubleys," Second Annual Santa Cruz Film Festival, 1983. _Member:_ International Animated Film Society, Motion Picture Editors, Art Students' League of New York (life member).

AWARDS, HONORS—All with husband, J. Hubley: Diploma Speciale, 1956, for "The Adventures of an *," honorable mention, 1957, for "Harlem Wednesday," Silver Lion Award 1958, for "Tender Game," Special Jury Prize, 1964, for "The Hat," and Golden Lion Award, 1968, for "Windy Day," all

FAITH AND JOHN HUBLEY

from Venice Film Festival; Academy Award from Academy of Motion Picture Arts and Sciences, 1960, for "Moonbird," 1963, for "The Hole," and 1966, for "Herb Alpert and the Tijuana Brass Double Feature," nomination for Academy Award, 1968, for "Windy Day," 1969, for "Men and Demons," and 1974, for "Voyage to Next"; First Prize Award from Venice Documentary Festival, 1960, for "Children of the Sun"; Prix Special du Jury from Annecy Film Festival, 1962, for "Of Stars and Men."

CINE (Council on International Nontheatrical Events) Golden Eagle Award, 1966, for "Urbanissimo,' 1970, for "Eggs," 1972, for "Dig," 1975, for "People, People, People," and 1978, for "A Doonesbury Special"; Blue Ribbon Award from American Film Festival, 1976, for "Everybody Rides the Carousel"; Special Jury Prize from Cannes Film Festival, 1978, for "A Doonesbury Special"; numerous other awards and prizes at international film festivals.

Sole winner: CINE Golden Eagle Award, 1975, for "WOW (Women of the World)," 1976, for "Second Chance: Sea," 1978, for "Whither Weather," 1979, for "Step by Step," 1980, for "Sky Dance," 1981, for "The Big Bang and Other Creation Myths," and 1985, for "Hello" and "Starlore"; Best Film Award from Dallas USA Film Festival, 1978, for "Whither Weather"; Best Children's Film Award from Annecy Film Festival, 1979, for "Step by Step"; Outstanding Achievement Award from San Francisco Film Festival, 1979, for "Step by Step"; Diploma of Merit from Tampere Film Festival, 1982,

for "Enter Life"; Special Jury Prize from Houston International Film Festival, and included in Best of Annecy 1983 Traveling Film Festival, both for "Starlore." Also won Silver Award from Houston International Film Festival, for "Hello."

WRITINGS—All adapted from screenplays: (With husband, John Hubley) *Dig: A Journey under the Earth's Crust,* Harcourt, 1973; (with J. Hubley) *The Hat,* Harcourt, 1974; (with J. Hubley and Garry Trudeau) *John and Faith Hubley's "A Doonesbury Special": A Director's Notebook,* Sheed, Andrews & McMeel, 1977; *Lullaby* (based on "Step by Step"), Harper, 1980; *Sky Dance,* Harper, 1981; (with Kenneth M. Towe) *Enter Life* (self-illustrated), Delacorte, 1982.

Illustrator: (with J. Hubley) Robert M. Hutchins, *Zuckerlandl!* (based on the cartoon film by J. Hubley and F. Hubley, from which illustrations are taken), Grove, 1968.

Animated films; all with husband, John Hubley; all produced by Films, Inc., except as noted: "The Adventures of an *," first produced for Solomon R. Guggenheim Foundation, 1956; "Harlem Wednesday," 1957; "Tender Game," 1958; "A Date with Dizzy," 1958; "Seven Lively Arts," 1959; (creator) "Moonbird," 1959.

"Children of the Sun," first produced for United Nations Children's Fund, 1960; "Of Stars and Men" (adapted from the book by Harlow Shapley), Museum of Modern Art, 1962; "The Hole," 1963; "The Hat," first produced for the World

(Still from the opening credit sequence of "A Doonesbury Special." From *A Doonesbury Special: A Director's Notebook* by Garry Trudeau.)

Law Fund, Institute for World Order, Films, Inc. in conjunction with the Museum of Modern Art, 1964; "Herb Alpert and the Tijuana Brass Double Feature," A & M Records, 1966; "Urbanissimo," 1966; "The Cruise," National Film Board of Canada, 1967; "Gulliver's Troubles," 1967; "Windy Day," 1968; "Zuckerlandl!," first produced for Center for the Study of Democratic Institutions, 1968; "Of Men and Demons," 1969.

"Eggs," 1970; "Dig," 1972; "Cockaboody," Pyramid Films in conjunction with the Museum of Modern Art, 1973; "Voyage to Next," first produced for Institute for World Order, Films, Inc. in conjunction with the Museum of Modern Art, 1974; "People, People, People," first produced for American Revolution Bicentennial Administration, Pyramid Films, 1975; (with the Child Development Center and Graphic Arts Department at Yale University) "In Quest of Cockaboody," 1975; "Everybody Rides the Carousel" (adapted from the works of Erik H. Erikson), first produced for CBS-TV, Pyramid Films, September 10, 1976; (with Garry Trudeau) "A Doonesbury Special," first produced for NBC-TV, Pyramid Films, November 27, 1977.

Other; all produced by Pyramid Films, except as noted: "WOW (Women of the World)," first produced for World Council of Churches, 1975; "Second Chance: Sea," first produced for Board of Global ministries of United Methodist Church, 1976; (and producer) "Whither Weather," 1977; "Step by Step," Pyramid Films in conjunction with the Museum of Modern

Art, 1978; "Sky Dance," Pyramid Films in conjunction with the Museum of Modern Art, 1979; "The Big Bang and Other Creation Myths," Pyramid Films in conjunction with the Museum of Modern Art, 1979; "Enter Life," 1981; "Starlore," first produced at the American Museum of Natural History, New York, 1982; "Hello," 1984; "The Cosmic Eye," 1985.

ADAPTATIONS—Videocassettes: "Academy Award Winners: Animated Short Films" (contains "The Hole" and "Moonbird"), Vestron Video, 1985; "The Ages of Humankind" (contains "Tender Game," "Dig," "WOW," "People, People, People," and "Cockaboody"), Disney, 1986; "Flights of Fancy" (contains "The Adventures of an *," "Moonbird," "Windy Day," and "Zuckerlandl!"), Disney, 1986.

SIDELIGHTS: **September 16, 1924.** Born in New York, New York. Hubley began her working career in the theater. She studied at the Art Students League and then moved to California where she worked as a film editor and script girl for live-action film.

Met husband, John Hubley, who was an animator for UPA animation company. "I was editing a film called 'Human Growth' on sex education (I think it was the first) produced by Eddie Albert, directed by Irving Lerner, and UPA [United Productions of America] did the animation. I started as a messenger at Columbia, in Hollywood, sound effect cutter, music cutter, a film editor, script supervisor (continuity), and an

associate producer. I worked on 'Twelve Angry Men' [1957] as script supervisor. So my background is in live action, editing, and production, and I studied painting at night. When John started to work on 'Finian's Rainbow'—an animated feature that never got made—I was hired as his assistant. We were married shortly after that and we continued working separately, some together. . . .'' [John D. Ford, ''An Interview with John and Faith Hubley,'' *The American Animated Cartoon: A Critical Anthology,* edited by Danny Peary and Gerald Peary, Dutton, 1980.[1]]

''People used to tell me I looked like Johnny, that we had the same smile.'' [Chris Chase, ''At the Movies,'' *New York Times,* November 4, 1983.[2]]

Returning to New York, Hubley continued to work in live-action films until she founded an animation studio with her husband. ''We made a compromise when we moved to New York: We would try to make one serious film a year and do whatever else we had to do to support that film. The first film that we made together was 'Adventures of an *.'

''If you're a painter, you don't presell your canvasses, you just feel you have to work. Sometimes you have commissions, sometimes you don't. The same is true in filmmaking. If you are going to grow, stay alive, remain sensitive, and valid, you have to keep working seriously.''[1]

The Hubleys' partnership represented a significant development in the animation field. Hubley explained how they worked on a project together: ''I think John makes the major aesthetic contribution. We both work on storyboard and concept. We both work on sound track. In most cases, John is the director, and I'll help in any way that I can. I'll be production organizer and see that the work gets finished on time. . . . 'Cockaboody,' was the most evenly divided. . . .

'''Adventures' was commissioned by the Guggenheim and financed jointly, but it was a big work of love. 'Tender Game' [1958], we started ourselves. 'The Hole' [1963] had no sponsor. 'The Hat' [1964] had a sponsor. 'Of Stars and Men' [1962] was absolutely ours. 'Tijuana Brass' [1966] was kind of a commercial. 'Urbanissimo' [1966] was commissioned by the Central Housing Mortgage of Canada, and it was a serious film on which we worked very hard and loved. 'Zuckerlandl' [1968]—half and half with the Center for the Study of Democratic Institutions. 'Windy Day' [1968] was ours with a little bit of help from Paramount. 'Harlem Wednesday' [1957], we did ourselves. 'Eggs' [1970], we did ourselves. 'Cockaboody' was made in partnership with Yale—a labor of love, again jointly financed.''[1]

Besides making films, the Hubleys raised a family of four— two boys and two girls. They worked on a project at home or in their nearby studio. ''It's given me a lot of freedom and has been gratifying in terms of expression and how I organize

Space kick Float. ■ (From *Skydance* by Elizabeth Swados. Illustrated by Faith Hubley.)

my life. And it's been terrific, being a woman, and being able to have a studio near home. Our kids have all worked here; they can draw, paint, and do voice. It's been like an atelier.

"... We try to keep the staff at half a dozen. This work is highly personal and it suffers terrifically if it gets farmed out to strangers."[1]

To the Hubleys, there was nothing in their family life that could not be used in their animated films. "We tend to be a very noisy family. We've learned that kids have a much better rapport with each other than adults do because they don't have our inhibitions. Kids can have a great time being in a room together for hours whereas it would drive most adults crazy. We don't have the creativity to carry on an enjoyable talk under those circumstances. I think that the only thing that really inhibits a child's expression is television." [Christopher Sharp, "Mr. Magoo's Creator Finds His Children's Hour," *Women's Wear Daily,* July 7, 1975.[3]]

The Hubleys' production company, Storyboard, was founded in 1955 and later changed to Hubley Studio, Inc. "An animator moves characters. It's a specific craft. In this sense my husband John and I are not animators. We create the characters, draw the positions, do the layout and direct the film or television special." [Kay Gardella, "CBS' 'Carousel' of Life Subject of Fall Special," *Daily News,* August 12, 1976.[4]]

1972. Visiting lecturer at Yale University in New Haven, Connecticut. "I say to my students, 'I'll share with you what I've learned, but you get out there and go to work like you're really making a movie.'"[2]

Although Hubley had drawn and painted all of her life, her husband knew far more about animation when they began to work together. "I'm musical, not verbal. I could play a Beethoven sonata before I could put a sentence together. But we live in a world where linear verbal thinking is preferred. Students are asked to verbalize, verbalize, write paper after paper. They come into my class and say they can't draw. I say: 'That's ridiculous. When you were in nursery school, didn't you draw? Does anybody tell you if you can't write like Proust, you can't write a sentence?'

"I have 14 students. . . . Half of them are art majors, the rest have never drawn before, and they're all designing films, one more interesting than another."[2]

(From the animated film "Children of the Sun," winner of a first prize from the Venice Documentary Festival. Music performed by Pablo Casals and the Budapest String Quartet. Produced by Hubley Studio, Inc., 1960.)

(From the animated film "A Doonesbury Special," presented on NBC-TV in 1977. Produced by Hubley Studio, Inc.)

February 21, 1977. Husband died during heart surgery at the Yale-New Haven Hospital. The Hubleys were working on "A Doonesbury Special" at the time of his death, and Hubley and Garry Trudeau finished the piece. "You have to work if you're not born rich, and I wasn't born rich. The working is not that hard. Living is hard. And staying open when you've had a big pain is hard. And mourning is very hard. I'm still not over it. I still wait for Johnny to walk in the door."[2]

November, 1983. A retrospective of animated films by the Hubleys was held at Yale University. About the event, Hubley remarked: "Johnny was a genius, so part of what I want to do at Yale is make sure that anybody who's interested in what he did can come there and find out about it."[2]

April 8, 1985. The Academy of Motion Picture Arts and Sciences honored Hubley and her husband with a special tribute. Between 1956 and 1975, the Hubleys completed twenty-two films, received three Oscars and were nominated for four more. From 1977, Hubley independently made ten films. "I like non-verbal communication. I think the function of animation and the original function of cinema is nonverbal. I think the word has set us back a great deal.

"If it didn't make sense musically, then you either were trying to say too much too fast or not enough." [Susan King, "Looking Toward the Future with Faith Hubley," *Los Angeles Herald Examiner*, April 8, 1985.[5]]

When asked what's wrong with animation today, Hubley criticized: "I think we need to have serious programming for children, and we don't. We would never consciously feed food of such low quality to children. We're putting food in their brains; and not to give them the best we have, it's absolutely wrong.

"I feel it's important for everyone on the planet to look to the things that are loving and inspiring and reinforcing."[5]

Hubley is inspired by the present day involvement of children in animation. "There are workshops. There's one in Vermont where an artist-in-residence has money from the state and teaches children to make animated films. They've just animated the Russian alphabet. There's a similar group in the Soviet Union who just animated the English alphabet. They're going to take these two films and put them together.

"The work is fresh and stimulating. These children are growing up with it (animation) demystified, so when they see junk, these kids will know it's junk. They'll know they can make good things. I think it's thrilling. I see a tremendous future."[5]

HOBBIES AND OTHER INTERESTS: Music, playing the cello.

FOR MORE INFORMATION SEE: New Yorker, August 5, 1961; *Park East,* April 2, 1970; Ralph Stephenson, *The Animated Film,* A. S. Barnes, 1973; *Women's Wear Daily,* July 7, 1975; *Daily News,* August 12, 1976; Mike Barrier, "John and Faith Hubley Transformed," *Millimeter,* February, 1977; *TV Guide,* November 26, 1977; Leonard Maltin, *Of Mice and Magic,* McGraw, 1980; Danny Peary and Gerald Peary, editors, *The American Animated Cartoon: A Critical Anthology,* Dutton, 1980; Maurice Horn, editor, *The World Encyclopedia of Cartoons,* Volume 1, Chelsea House, 1980; *New York Times,* November 4, 1983; *Los Angeles Herald Examiner,* April 8, 1985.

HUBLEY, John   1914-1977

PERSONAL: Born in 1914, in Marinette, Wis.; died during heart surgery, February 21, 1977, in New Haven, Conn.; married second wife, Faith Elliot Chestman (a writer, director, and producer of animated films), June 24, 1955; children: (first marriage) Ann Ricchioti, Susan Blakely, Mark Ross; (second marriage) Mark Daniel, Ray, Emily, Georgia. *Education:* Attended Art Center School of Los Angeles, 1933-35. *Residence:* Manhattan, N.Y. and Montauk, N.Y.

CAREER: Animator and producer of animated films. Walt Disney Studios, Burbank, Calif., 1936-41, began as background artist and became art director, worked on films "Snow White and the Seven Dwarfs," "Pinocchio," the "Rite of Spring" sequence in "Fantasia," "Dumbo," and "Bambi"; worked for Columbia Screen Gems Cartoon Studio, Burbank, 1942; United Productions of America (UPA), Burbank, 1945-54, began as supervising director and became vice-president and creative director, responsible for cartoon films "Robin Hoodlum," 1948, "The Magic Fluke," 1949, "Punchy de Leon," 1949, and "Rooty Toot Toot," 1952, also co-creator of cartoon character Mr. Magoo, introduced in "Ragtime Bear," 1949; Storyboard Inc. (production company; now Hubley Studio, Inc.), New York, N.Y., co-founder and producer of animated films with wife, Faith Hubley, 1955-77. Visiting lecturer, Yale University, beginning 1972.

EXHIBITIONS: American Cultural Center, Paris, France; Zagreb Film Festival; Tampere Film Festival; University of Cal-

John Hubley. Photograph courtesy of Faith Hubley.

ifornia—Los Angeles; Yale University Gallery of Art. Retrospectives: "A Hubley Evening," Jerusalem Cinematheque, 1982; "A Tribute to John and Faith Hubley," University of California—Los Angeles, 1983; Yale University, New Haven, Conn., 1983; "An Homage to the Hubleys," Second Annual Santa Cruz Film Festival, 1983. *Military service:* U.S. Air Force, 1942-44, producer of training films.

AWARDS, HONORS—All with wife, Faith Hubley: Diploma Speciale, 1956, for "The Adventures of an *," honorable mention, 1957, for "Harlem Wednesday," Silver Lion Award, 1958, for "Tender Game," Special Jury Prize, 1964, for "The Hat," and Golden Lion Award, 1968, for "Windy Day," all from Venice Film Festival; Academy Award from Academy of Motion Picture Arts and Sciences, 1960, for "Moonbird," 1963, for "The Hole," and 1966, for "Herb Alpert and the Tijuana Brass Double Feature," nomination for Academy Award, 1968, for "Windy Day," 1969, for "Men and Demons," and 1974, for "Voyage to Next"; First Prize Award from Venice Documentary Festival, 1960, for "Children of the Sun"; Prix Special du Jury from Annecy Film Festival, 1962, for "Of Stars and Men."

CINE (Council on International Nontheatrical Events) Golden Eagle Award, 1966, for "Urbanissimo," 1970, for "Eggs," 1972, for "Dig," 1975, for "People, People, People," and 1978, for "A Doonesbury Special"; Blue Ribbon Award from American Film Festival, 1976, for "Everybody Rides the Carousel"; Special Jury Prize from Cannes Film Festival, 1978, for "A Doonesbury Special"; and numerous other awards and prizes at international film festivals.

WRITINGS—Of interest to young readers; adapted from screenplays; written and illustrated with Faith Hubley: *Dig: A Journey under the Earth's Crust,* Harcourt, 1973; *The Hat,* Harcourt, 1974; (and Garry Trudeau) *John and Faith Hubley's "A Doonesbury Special": A Director's Notebook,* preface by F. Hubley, Sheed, Andrews & McMeel, 1977.

Illustrator: (With F. Hubley) Robert M. Hutchins, *Zuckerlandl!* (based on the cartoon film by J. Hubley and F. Hubley, from which the illustrations were taken), Grove, 1968.

Animated films; author of screenplays, all with F. Hubley; designer and producer; all produced by Films, Inc., except as noted: "The Adventures of an *," first produced for Solomon R. Guggenheim Foundation, 1956; "Harlem Wednesday," 1957; "Tender Game," 1958; "A Date with Dizzy," 1958; "Seven Lively Arts," 1959; "Moonbird," 1959.

"Children of the Sun," first produced for United Nations Children's Fund, 1960; "Of Stars and Men" (adapted from the book by Harlow Shapley), Museum of Modern Art, 1962; "The Hole," 1963; "The Hat," first produced for the World Law Fund, Institute for World Order, Films, Inc. in conjunction with the Museum of Modern Art, 1964; "Herb Alpert and the Tijuana Brass Double Feature," A & M Records, 1966; "Urbanissimo," 1966; "The Cruise," National Film Board of Canada, 1967; "Gulliver's Troubles," 1967; "Windy Day," 1968; "Zuckerlandl!," first produced for Center for the Study of Democratic Institutions, 1968; "Of Men and Demons," 1969.

"Eggs," 1970; "Dig," 1972; "Cockaboody," Pyramid Films in conjunction with the Museum of Modern Art, 1973; "Voyage to Next," first produced for Institute for World Order, Films, Inc. in conjunction with the Museum of Modern Art, 1974; "People, People, People," first produced for American Revolution Bicentennial Administration, Pyramid Films, 1975;

(with the Child Development Center and Graphic Arts Department at Yale University) "In Quest of Cockaboody," 1975; "Everybody Rides the Carousel" (adapted from the works of Erik H. Erikson), first produced for CBS-TV, Pyramid Films, September 10, 1976; (with Garry Trudeau) "A Doonesbury Special," first produced for NBC-TV, Pyramid Films, November 27, 1977.

Creator of animated film "Upkeep." Also producer of commercials and of movies for "Sesame Street" and "The Electric Company" segments and many organizations, including the National Film Board of Canada and the Bicentennial Commission.

ADAPTATIONS—Videocassettes: "Academy Award Winners: Animated Short Films" (contains "The Hole" and "Moonbird"), Vestron Video, 1985; "The Ages of Humankind" contains "Tender Game," "Dig," "People, People, People," and "Cockaboody"), Disney, 1986; "Flights of Fancy" (contains "The Adventures of an *," "Moonbird," "Windy Day," and "Zuckerlandl!"), Disney, 1986.

SIDELIGHTS: **1914.** Born in Marinette, Wisconsin. At the early age of three or four, Hubley became very interested in art. "I had a grandfather who was a painter. My mother went

to the Art Institute in Chicago, and we had a lot of paintings around our house. I used to watch my grandfather when I was a little kid; so I have that kind of studio background." [John D. Ford, "An Interview with John and Faith Hubley," *The American Animated Cartoon: A Critical Anthology*, edited by Danny Peary and Gerald Peary, Dutton, 1980.[1]]

1933-1935. Moved to Los Angeles to study at the Art Center School. "It was always ordained that I would go to art school. I went a couple of years to college in Los Angeles and then I went to the Art Center and studied painting. After three years I went to Disney. I was exactly twenty-two."[1]

"It was in the middle of the depression and I was attracted to animation because it combined graphics with movement and emotion. Also, my painting had gotten a little stale. I couldn't see much beyond Picasso; as far as I was concerned, he did it all." [Carolyn Dutton, "Magoo Character and Wife Eye Another Oscar," *Park East*, April 2, 1970.[2]]

1936-1941. Worked as an animator and art director for the Walt Disney Studios. "Disney's studio was like a marvelous Renaissance craft hall. Young people were given a chance to study drawing, composition, animation, action. We studied old movies, layout, art direction. All of us were encouraged

(From the animated film "Adventures of an *," winner of a Diploma Speciale. Produced by Hubley Studio, Inc. 1956.)

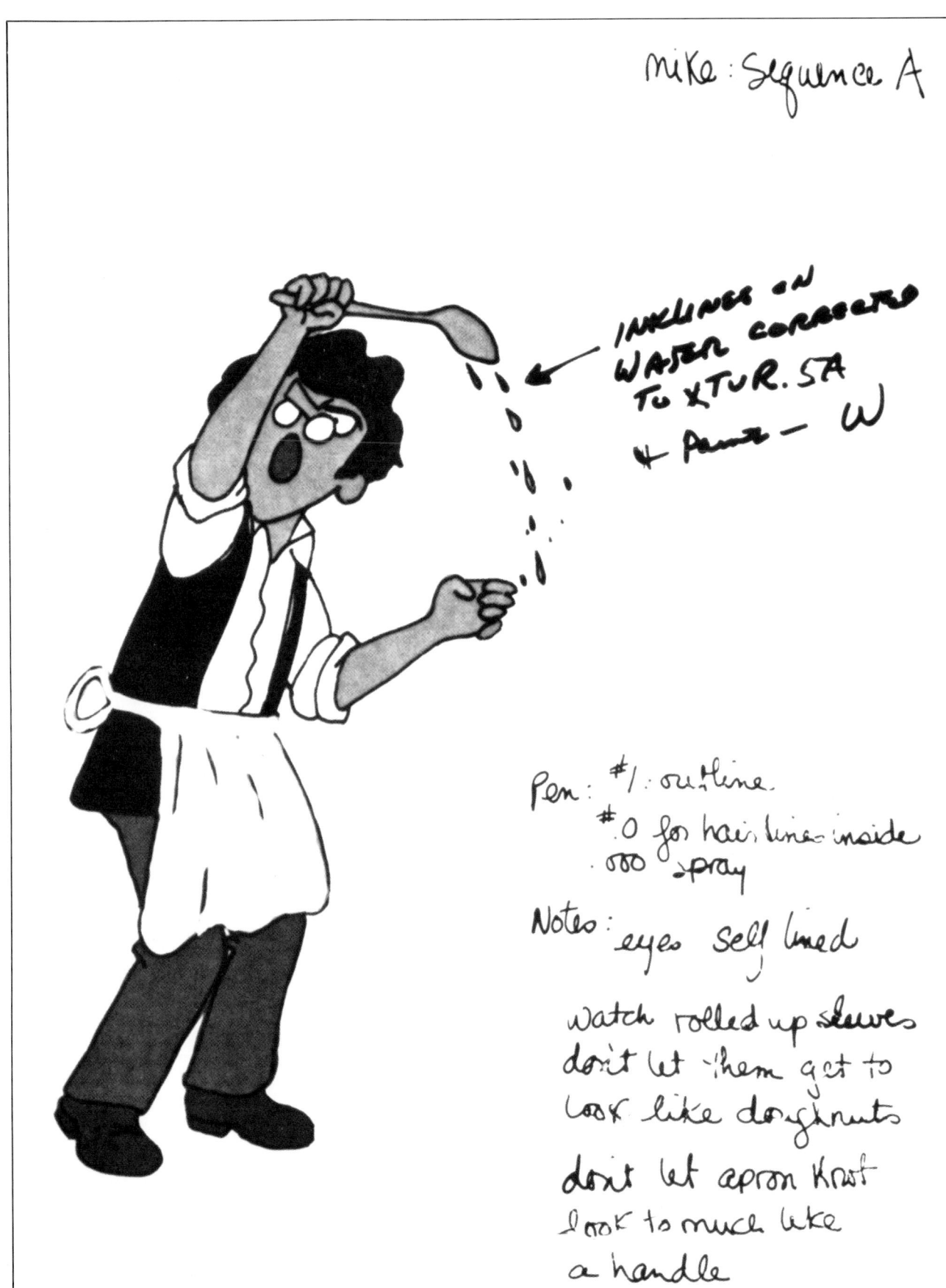

(Garry Trudeau's marginal notes provide rare insight into the process of animation. Illustration from *A Doonesbury Special: A Director's Notebook* by Garry Trudeau.)

to take these free courses. They were very anxious to find the exceptional people and move them up fast, because they were going through such a rapid expansion. When I got there, 'Snow White' [1937] had just gotten underway. I made background tracings and painted backgrounds and layouts for animators. On 'Pinocchio' [1940] I went from assistant art director to full art director; that is, to full layout man. I worked directly with the animation director on scene breakdowns. I did that also on 'Fantasia' [1940], 'Dumbo' [1941], and 'Bambi' [1942].'' [1]

He was also directly responsible for the fire in ''Bambi'' and for the volcanoes in ''Fantasia.''

1942. Worked for a brief time at Columbia Screen Gems Cartoon Studio before joining the Air Force. During World War II, Hubley created Air Force training films. While working on the Air Force films, he free-lanced for a new production company called United Productions of America. ''There was a year of working for Screen Gems. Columbia. Columbia had just hired Frank Tashlin, who replaced a man named Mintz. Tash was a Disney storyman, and when the Disney strike broke, he took on the job of refurbishing Screen Gems; so he hired a lot of Disney people. Under Tashlin we tried some very experimental things; none of them quite got off the ground, but there was a lot of ground broken. We were doing crazy things that were anti the classic Disney approach. That was in 1942. Tashlin was replaced by Dave Fleischer—the Out of the Inkwell, Popeye director. I left and went into the Air Force when an Air Force motion-picture unit was formed. About fifty of us

formed the animation branch. Frank Thomas was the unit director I worked with. He's still at Disney; one of the grand old men of animation. A nice guy. We worked on training films for three years. We also did a lot of experimental things like flat-area painting techniques and photocollage. We made about four films on aerial gunnery.

''We had developed a character called Trigger Joe, and Mel Blanc did the voice. We had a lot of fun with the obstinate side of this character, and he turned out to be a very good device for teaching. He kept progressing and growing as weapons developed. First it was a question of just how you aim a freewheeling 50-caliber gun. Then came an automatic sight that you put on the gun, which took care of all the calculations. The only thing you had to do was set it right. So we had to do a film on that with Trigger Joe. Then an automatic system came in, in which all the guns on the ship were run by a computer-automation firing system. The gunners didn't do anything but flip a couple of switches, and all the guns were automatically trained. By this time, Frank was discharged (honorably) and I got a chance to direct. This film put Joe in the B-29s. We had to unteach all the things we had taught him before and ask him to trust the system. The day this film was finished was the day the war was over, literally. I had been doing some moonlighting. It was permitted as long as it didn't interfere with Army duties. I had worked on a film called 'The Brotherhood of Man' [1946]—an early UPA picture—so I naturally drifted to UPA when I got out. That's where we did the Navy Flight Safety series, one of which was 'Flathatting' [1945]. At UPA I became a full-fledged producer/director.'' [1]

(Jimmy Thudpucker, in concert. Illustration from *A Doonesbury Special: A Director's Notebook* by Garry Trudeau.)

''The Brotherhood of Man'' was concerned with the theme of tolerance. Considered innovative in its day, it used stylized characters that were each an overall solid color rather than the conventional, rounded Disney characters. ''We went for very flat stylized characters, instead of the global three-dimensional Disney characters. It was greatly influenced by Saul Steinberg and that sharp-nosed character he was doing at the time. Bob Cannon did most of the animation; in fact, he was the director. I was a co-writer on it and did the layouts; if I recall correctly. Ring Lardner, Jr., and Phil Eastman shared writing credit. Paul Julian did the backgrounds very flat; he used areas of color that would be elided from the line. Very advanced graphics for that period. It was financed by the United Auto Workers. Victor Reuther, Walter Reuther, and Thomas had been having a lot of problems with racial tension during the war in the auto factories; so they embarked on a big education program on racial equality and antidiscrimination for their membership.

''I did the storyboards and some of the basic layouts and stylizations, but being in the Army I didn't get involved in the full production. It came out pretty well. I've got one print of it—they're hard to find!

''It didn't get much of a theatre distribution. It was a kind of controversial film at that time, because it dealt with racial equality. It was based on a pamphlet written by two anthropologists, Gene Weltfish and Ruth Benedict, from Columbia University. The pamphlet itself had a heavy distribution—the Army bought tons of them. At some point some Southern congressman started to squawk about this 'equality idea'; he didn't like the fact that the Army was spending money distributing this stuff. The film got involved too. The Army bought something like 300 prints to distribute through the whole overseas operations. When they buy something, they go all out! This congressman threw that in the fire with all the pamphlets, when he got sore about it. So it stopped the showing of the film for a while. The order went out that they couldn't use it. Anyway the film had a very wide circulation in libraries and schools. Then the distribution of it got a little muddy—a question of who really owned it and who had the rights to distribute it. It's still up for grabs; nobody really knows where that negative is. The auto union gave up on it, and are out of it. Brandon Films is reported to have made a lot of money on it.''[1]

1945-1954. Worked for United Productions of America (UPA), whose staff consisted largely of ex-Disney artists. ''I was hired originally as creative head of UPA, as the layout director. For about a year after I was there, we were doing the Navy films. There was an internal fight between the owners of the company. They got into a hassle about direction and policy and they split. Stephen Bosustow went out and raised the money to buy them out. As I understand it, he felt he could raise the money provided I stayed there as head of production. His money source said you can buy it if you keep the staff. I was the staff! The other two owners were both creative filmmakers, but they were leaving. So he came to me and made me a stock deal, and I stayed in. Part of the arrangement in my contract was to become head of production, to get a percentage of the stock, and to have a position on the board. That's when I really moved into a management position in the company. The other two guys moved to New York. We kept making industrial movies. Bob Cannon was there off and on; then he'd go to Warners and work some; then to Disney for a while. Different guys were floating in and out.

Then along came the Columbia Pictures deal, which was the old Screen Gems. We were able to sign a contract with them to produce six to eight shorts on a participating basis. They owned these old animal characters—the Fox and the Crow—and they wanted to keep the series going. By this time we were really feeling our oats. We had done the Navy films, 'The Brotherhood of Man,' and had the impetus of a new style and a new way of thinking about characters, stories, music, art, design, everything! That interested Columbia, too. They were ready to go with something new. So the first one with the Fox and the Crow was 'Robin Hoodlum' [1948]. The Fox

as Robin Hood, the Crow as the Sheriff of Nottingham. The Merry Men were a sanguine bunch of tea-drinking Englishmen. It was funny and very sophisticated. Columbia didn't like it—it wasn't a standard audience film. We made another one called 'The Magic Fluke' [1949], which was a more popular story. We were using very modern techniques even though we had to use the conventional characters of the Fox and the Crow. We were doing very modern backgrounds with flat patterns, opaque paint. After 'The Magic Fluke' we kept hitting Columbia with, 'We want to do original shorts and we're stuck with tired animals. Our strength and our vision is to do human characters. . . .'"[1]

1949. Developed a new cartoon character, a nearsighted little man named Mr. Magoo. "The character was based upon an uncle of mine, named Harry Woodruff, at least insofar as my relationship to Magoo was concerned. Jim Backus, who was introduced at an early stage, formulated a concept based upon his father, a Cleveland businessman and owner of a prosperous pump works. My Uncle Harry was a division head of a large national insurance company.

"Magoo, we decided, would always make an appraisal of a situation in one glance. . . . His stubborn rigidity was such that, having made a snap judgment, nothing could convince him he was wrong. Don't you know people like that? They become determined to act on the erroneous judgement, no matter what. This can lead to great comedy (or tragedy)." [Howard Rieder, "Memories of Mr. Magoo," *The American Animated Cartoon: A Critical Anthology*, edited by Danny Peary and Gerald Peary, Dutton, 1980.[3]]

Jerry Hausner, who helped develop the Magoo character, recalled how Jim Backus became the voice of Magoo: "Jim Backus had just come out from New York with the Alan Young Show. He was already fairly well-known as the voice of Hubert Updyke, the richest man in the world.

"We had been friends for over twenty years. I spoke to Hubley about Backus and he wanted to meet him. I arranged a luncheon at the Smoke House Restaurant, next door to the UPA studio in Burbank. Hubley spoke of this new character he was trying to find a voice for. He didn't want to have to ask Backus to audition for him because it might be an affront to an actor as well established as Backus.

"Hubley asked Backus if he could recommend someone to play the part. Backus asked what he was like, what he looked like. Hubley said, 'Well I haven't any pictures with me, but if we could wander over to UPA I will show you some sketches and a rough storyboard.'

"We walked over and looked at it. Backus studied the character, and when Hubley said he was nearsighted and lived in his own little world, Backus said he could do it. He said, 'My father lives in his own little world, never quite seeing things the way they really are. It isn't that he's nearsighted, but his whole attitude toward life is a kind of personal isolation toward the rest of the world.'

"Backus mentioned that he used to do a character called the Man in the Club Car. It was the character of the businessman, the tycoon, the loudmouth talker that you meet in a railroad train who offers all kinds of information on world events and who is filled with misinformation. He began to use this voice and it was the voice that ultimately became Mr. Magoo.'"[3]

The first Magoo cartoon was called "Ragtime Bear" and featured nearsighted Magoo and a bear who was mistaken as Magoo's nephew. Hubley recalled: "That was the beginning; the pressure was on to get into a series. We started making Magoos. I made (produced-directed) about four more. . . . The first three or four of those were really great. Developing the character was sort of a creative surge. But it got into a very rote style after a while. They just took very limited aspects of the character—mostly his nearsightedness—and hung onto it. His strength was the fact that he was so damn bullheaded. It wasn't just that he couldn't see very well; even if he had been able to see, he still would have made dumb mistakes.

(Zonker, shown in an animated sequence. Strip of drawings from *A Doonesbury Special: A Director's Notebook* by Garry Trudeau.)

(From the animated film "Of Stars and Men," adapted from the book by Harlow Shapley. Produced by Hubley Studio, Inc., 1962.)

"When they started cutting the budget, they used very simplistic animation and the gags became obvious. The simplified nature of the UPA style was due to the fact that we were working on lower budgets. We had to find ways of economizing and still get good results. So we cut down on animation and got into stylized ways of handling action. All of which became a basic pattern for the television daytime serial stuff. It was a natural development for lower budgets. There's no substitute for full animation. What the character can do if you make use of full drawings is really irreplaceable. You just can't fake it. Previously, we used to dream up a lot of subtleties and we ad-libbed a lot of the dialogue."[1]

Once the Magoo character was launched, Hubley went into other areas, developing UPA's design approach to other films. "... I was really getting spread too thin and was getting no creative work done; too busy being an executive. We arrived at a joint decision of a split between [Gerald] Cannon and me, making two units, each independent. So for several films we did our own thing. But 'Gerald McBoing-Boing' [1950] was one of the last of my supervisory period. Cannon was the actual animation director. He really did a great job on that—it was his own personal style. The first thing I did when I got back to directing was 'Rooty-Toot-Toot' [1952]—the Frankie and Johnny legend—the shooting of Johnny and trial of Frankie. This was pretty well made. It might be called sexist today.

A guy by the name of Phil Moore did the music on it. To my knowledge he was the first black composer to work directly on a theatrical cartoon and to get a screen credit for his work. And then I did a few more Magoos. Then a job called 'The Fourposter' [1953] came in, which was a series of interscenes in the Stanley Kramer movie with Rex Harrison and Lilli Palmer, a way of mixing animation with live action."[1]

1955. Formed his own television-commercial studio, Storyboard, Inc., and married film editor Faith Elliot Chestman, who had been hired as his assistant during the production of "Finian's Rainbow." The couple moved to New York City.

1956. Designed and produced with his wife the animated film "Adventures of an *," which was commissioned by the Guggenheim Foundation. Hubley believed in "the language of animation," and was one of the first to believe in the possibility of creating "a new visual language." "In animation, the artist and writer have at their command all the traditional means of graphic expression and the new means which grew out of moving symbols and sound. One of these is the concept of explanation through change from an object as it is to the thing it signifies. . . . Or, we might wish to give graphic expression to an emotional reaction. . . . These examples indicate the kind of picture solution that can be evolved from an idea no matter how abstract.

"We have found that the medium of animation has become a new language. It is no longer the vaudeville world of pigs and bunnies. Nor is it the mechanical diagram, the photographed charts of the old 'training film.' It has encompassed the whole field of visual images, including the photograph. We have found that line, shape, color, and symbols in movement can represent the essence of an idea, can express it humorously, with force, with clarity. The method is only dependent upon the idea to be expressed. And a suitable form can be found for any idea." [John Hubley and Zachary Schwartz, "Animation Learns a New Language," *Hollywood Quarterly*, Volume I, number 4, July, 1946.[4]]

1960. Animated film "Moonbird" won an Oscar. The film developed from a fantasy tale that Hubley's six- and three-year-old sons had created. Hubley and his wife continued to use the "ad lib" technique, taping conversations and then animating them, for other films.

"The Hole," their second Oscar-winning film, started with an improvised conversation between jazz musician Dizzy Gillespie and actor George Matthews. "Traditionally, the drawing of animated characters has been stylized and frequently insensitive and unrelated to actual life. Animation artists have too often been content with comic-strip simplicity in terms of drawing and, more important, in terms of characterization. Today's artists are exploring means of delineating rich and complex human capacities and 'character' in animation. Given a technological culture that often depersonalizes and dehumanizes, I think that this new vision of the reality of human beings seen as animation characters presents a most urgent and promising prospect. It demands purposeful extension. One might call it fourth-dimensional characterization. It would mean that the animator-artist would extend design beyond the simple limits of the past, find the means to form a collage, and, in a cubist sense, display multiple facets simultaneously.

"How to move toward this new concept? First, we need to reexamine some of the usual visual means that we have at hand when we design animation characters. We have the character's facial features and expressions, body shape, costume, personal effects, and affectations. We have also the fundamental character movements of his body, the manner in which he walks, sits, stands, and talks. We have, further, the specific gestures or idiosyncratic movements and reaction patterns—is he defensive or aggressive, fast or slow? These might be called the common outer visual aspects of the character.

"Now consider the more intriguing inner, nonvisual aspects of human character. Consider emotional patterns, ego struc-

(From the animated film "Cockaboody." Produced by Hubley Studio, Inc. 1973.)

ture, rational and unconscious drives, physical body systems (the many tracts), the nervous system, and so forth. Consider the Walter Mitty fantasy life that everyone leads. We have complexes and compulsions; we have religious and philosophical beliefs; repressed rages and anxieties exist with microcosmic physical systems operating and biochemical reactions going on; we have aggressive and passive reflexes.

"The same holds true for the environment in which a character exists. In addition to the ground plane and the horizon, we see the streets, walls, windows, doors, and whatever planes surround the character; we see buildings, trees, hills, objects, machines, abstract volumes, other characters; we see colors, surfaces, and atmosphere in variable states of motion. Some *non*visual, unseen aspects related to the environment might be air temperature, the molecular or atomic structures of surrounding objects; the processes of growth and decay, the influences of the ravages of past history. Educational film animators have been working for a long time on informative images of things that we know exist but that are not photographable. Here especially the legacies of the multiple-vision cubist approach to heighten the reality of the environment are apparent and invaluable.

"Now is the time to consider our 'stories' seriously. To deepen character delineation, to probe social meanings for today, to present material that approaches the scope of Swift or Carroll or Kafka, we must push the monodimensional graphic limits of the drawn image into a time-space multileveled realization. I can see the day when characters will be conceived and defined beyond the ordinary outer visual aspects as we presently know them. At any given moment we will see also a portrayal of two or three of the dramatically relevant inner facets of the character and, at the same moment, the nonvisual aspects of the environment." [John Hubley, "Beyond Pigs and Bunnies," *American Scholar*, spring, 1975.[5]]

1966. "Herb Alpert and the Tijuana Brass Double Feature," an animated film which included two of Herb Alpert's hit songs, "Tijuana Taxi" and "Spanish Flea," won Hubley his third Academy Award.

1968. Received the Golden Lion at the Venice Film Festival for "Windy Day," an animated film based on a conversation between the Hubley's two daughters, Emily and Georgia, as they played.

(From the animated film "People, People, People," winner of a CINE Golden Eagle Award. Produced by Hubley Studio, Inc., 1975.)

(From *A Doonesbury Special: A Director's Notebook* by Garry Trudeau.)

Despite the popularity of his animated films, Hubley believed that the movie cartoon was quickly becoming a dying art. "One of the reasons for the bad market in movie cartoons was the over abundance of canned cartoons in the '50s and '60s. The other problem is one of getting people in and out of the theater. The theater manager won't be able to get audiences in and out of the theater as easily when people either miss the cartoon or enjoy it so much that they want to see it a second time.

"Most distributors today will say that the short does nothing to add or detract from the box-office appeal of a show. It's true that a lot of things work against shorts in the movies. Unfortunately, there's no market either for shorts in television.

"The cartoon now has approximately the same status as does the short story. There's no way to market it and make a big profit. The result is that another unique art form dies." [Christopher Sharp, "Mr. Magoo's Creator Finds His Children's Hour," *Women's Wear Daily,* July 7, 1975.⁶]

Between 1956 and 1970, the Hubleys completed twenty-two films, received three Oscars, and were nominated for four others.

Besides owning their own production company, they also found time to pursue careers as painters and to teach a course at Yale University called "The Visualization of Abstract Themes." "As I see it, the animator is moving into an exciting period of change. From a vaudeville and comic-strip childhood, 'cartoons' seems to be struggling toward maturity. The films of Rene Leloux, Karel Zeman, Ralph Bakshi, and many others are forerunners of what may be a flowering of longer, more personal statements by film artists in this medium. But within the growing aggregate of animated film miles each year, I look for new ideas in certain aspects of the conceptual process. I am concerned with the move away from comic-strip generalities toward the development of individual, specialized, human character. I am also concerned with social criticism; by that I mean the presentation of scenes and problems and dilemmas from ordinary life, and narratives that both please and instruct an audience. These aims seem realizable; to increase awareness, to warn, to humanize, to elevate vision, to suggest goals, to deepen our understanding of ourselves and our relationships with each other."⁵

1974. "Voyage to Next" was produced for the Institute for World Order. "An example of an attempt to explore human problems in a way that is not dependent on verbal translation

(From the animated film "Moonbird," which won an Academy Award for Best Short Subject. Produced by Hubley Studio, Inc., 1949.)

is 'Voyage to Next,' a short film that Faith Hubley and I conceived and designed in a seminar at the Yale School of Art, collaborating with students there, as well as with scholars from the Institute for World Order. This film undertakes to put into visual images the current state of world interdependency. The attempt to solve global problems such as hunger, population, and war, without an effective global, legal structure is a dilemma that is difficult to present nonverbally.

"In the film, we see a broad stream upon which float hundreds of boxes filled with people. Human beings have cut themselves off from each other in a system of isolated nationalistic boxes. Each box floats aimlessly, bumping, swamping others, drifting toward some uncertain future collision. Later in the film, some hope is suggested when eyes appear looking out of the boxes to indicate a growing awareness of the others and a faith beginning toward imagining alternative possibilities. Dozens of films based on similar symbolic visual premises, and specifically conceived for instructional purposes, are being made from Calcutta to Zagreb. Animation artists around the world are breaking out of the limitations of the fairy tale to confront contemporary issues."[5]

1975. Produced and created, with the Yale Child Development Center and Graphic Arts department, a series of three half-hour film dramatizations of the eight stages of human development. "Our first problem is to show infants as they interact with their social environment, gaining inner strengths that become the core of their lifetime personalities. We begin, then, with an infant laughing and crying, feeding and sleeping. The figure is seen in silhouette, white against a background suggesting a nursery. We hear disconcerted whimpers. A nervous wavy pattern appears on the baby's stomach, representing a hunger pain. The baby reacts, winces, proceeds to cry in anguish. The background, the crib, the ceiling, simultaneously change focus; we see these objects from the point of view of the crying child, blurred and meaningless. The cry attracts the mother, who feeds the baby; the inner pain subsides and the lines of anguish animate into the benign smile of a kitten fleetingly moving from the stomach to the face of the now-contented infant.

"With musical support, the juxtaposition of the kitten symbol and the baby's emotional contentment expresses and affirms the concept of *trust,* a sense of confidence that the environment will somehow take care of one's basic needs, that it will be a safe place. Later, when the hunger pains return and the mother does not arrive immediately, a symbol of *mistrust* appears. This spurs further efforts for attention and becomes a necessary cautious polarity for trust.

"The multiple effect of these inner images, reacting and counteracting with the 'real' events of the baby's life, is an exploratory reach in the direction of joining so-called visual and nonvisual aspects of reality. Later in the film we must deal with the combined and increasingly complex interrelations of adult crises and growth through changes in perspective.

"In the sequence dealing with intimacy versus isolation, it becomes clear to a couple that their relationship is moving toward a deeper commitment to each other. Each must be prepared to share identity with the other. Each feels threatened, their faces turn inward, and masks appear. The masks continue a superficial relationship while the real faces, still turned inward, voice thoughts and feelings about the conflict. They drift apart, unable to remove the masks. When the two do away with their masks on a second try, and make real efforts at intimacy, they succeed in sharing. They reach maturity; the figures become abstract, Matisse-like. The enact-

ment is a ballet—a series of arms, legs, torsos, and heads flowing in a dance of love. A literal love scene at this point would be cartoon-like in the old sense, and would therefore present not realism but a flat and ineffective caricature.

"Another experimental element of the 'eight stages' film which is vital to the capturing of a sense of both outer and inner realities is the sound track. Instead of using a script of word-for-word dialogue, we are working with actors' improvisations. These are taped and edited to an effective statement of feeling and conflict. The visual images are then designed to fit the dialogue.

"To deal with the search for identity in the adolescent stage, we are visually transforming the characters (two teenage couples) into the roles they imagine for themselves as they test the environment of the adult world. A girl becomes a singer, a revolutionary, an executive, and a princess, at will—totally acceptable behavior as she walks down the street with her peers. A boy deprived of his identity and, assigned a number, explodes with rage and violence.

"Artists around the world are defying the old 'linear shape' order in graphics. Let's hope they also defy the limitations of the fairy tale and confront contemporary issues. May we be fortunate enough to see the development of visuals that are generated by dramatic and psychological imperatives—to continue to reveal human vulnerability and to increase the understanding of human relationships."[5]

September 10, 1976. "Everybody Rides the Carousel," an animated film narrated by Cicely Tyson, was shown on CBS-TV. The film was based on the "psycho-social crises" concept of psychoanalyst Erik Erikson.

February 21, 1977. Died during heart surgery at Yale-New Haven Hospital in New Haven, Connecticut.

November 27, 1977. "A Doonesbury Special," a film Hubley and his wife were working on when he died, was broadcast on NBC-TV. About Hubley's involvement in the television special, "Doonesbury" creator Garry Trudeau remarked: "Although John was not to survive the project, the momentum had been established before his death, and Faith Hubley ably finished the film we had set out to make. While some of what John must have envisioned was undoubtedly lost in the final product, 'A Doonesbury Special' stands as fitting testimony to the sane and compassionate sensibilities of one of animation's first true visionaries." [Garry Trudeau, "The Doonesbury Gang Comes Alive," *TV Guide,* November 26, 1977.[7]]

FOR MORE INFORMATION SEE: John Hubley and Zachary Schwartz, "Animation Learns a New Language," *Hollywood Quarterly,* July, 1946; D. Robinson, "Evolution of a Cartoonist," *Sights and Sound,* winter, 1961; *New Yorker,* August 5, 1961; *Park East,* April 2, 1970; John M. Smith and Tim Cawkwell, editors, *The World Encyclopedia of Film,* A. & W. Visual Library, 1972; John Hubley, "Beyond Pigs and Bunnies: The New Animators Art," *American Scholar,* spring, 1975; *Women's Wear Daily,* July 7, 1975; *Daily News,* August 12, 1976; *Oxford Companion to Film,* Oxford University Press, 1976; *Millimeter,* February, 1977; *Filmmakers Newsletter,* May, 1977; *TV Guide,* November 26, 1977; Maurice Horn, editor, *The World Encyclopedia of Cartoons,* Volume 1, Chelsea House, 1980; Danny Peary and Gerald Peary, editors, *The American Animated Cartoon: A Critical Anthology,* Dutton, 1980; *New York Times,* November 4, 1983.

Obituaries: *New York Times Biographical Service,* February, 1977; *New York Times,* February 23, 1977; *New York Post,*

February 23, 1977; *Variety,* February 23, 1977; *Broadcasting,* February 28, 1977; *Time,* March 7, 1977; Felice Levy, compiler, *Obituaries on File,* Facts on File, 1979.

JACKSON, Jesse   1908-1983

OBITUARY NOTICE—See sketch in *SATA* Volume 29: Born January 1, 1908, in Columbus, Ohio; died April 14, 1983, in Boone, N.C. A noted black author of children's books, Jackson worked as a journalist and probation officer for the juvenile court in Columbus, where he decided to write books for young people. His best-known book, *Call Me Charley,* first published in 1945, chronicles a black boy's experiences in an all-white school. Charley appears in two later books: *Anchor Man* and *Charley Starts from Scratch.* Jackson's other books include *Make a Joyful Noise Unto the Lord! The Life of Mahalia Jackson* and *Black in America: A Fight for Freedom,* both of which won Carter G. Woodson awards. He also wrote *The Sickest Don't Always Die the Quickest,* about Stonewall Jackson, and *Room for Randy.*

FOR MORE INFORMATION SEE: Contemporary Authors, Volumes 25-28, revised, Gale, 1977; *Twentieth-Century Children's Writers,* 2nd edition, St. Martin's, 1983. Obituaries: *Publishers Weekly,* June 3, 1983.

JOHNSON, Jane   1951-

PERSONAL: Born February 28, 1951, in London, England; daughter of Eric (an accountant) and Sheila (a painter; maiden name, Myer) Conrad; married Robin Johnson (divorced). *Education:* University of East Anglia, B.A. (with honors), 1973. *Politics:* Liberal. *Religion:* None. *Home:* 32 King Henry's

Rd., London NW3 3RP, England. *Agent:* Virgil Pomfret, 25 Sispara Gardens, London SW18, England.

CAREER: Medici Society (publisher), London, England, advertising assistant, 1973-74; Hodder & Stoughton (publisher), London, book designer, 1974-76; Jonathan Cape Ltd. (publisher), London, book designer, 1976-81; writer and illustrator, 1979—. Part-time teacher of illustration at art schools in London, 1983-85. *Member:* Association of Illustrators. *Awards, honors: Sybil and the Blue Rabbit* was named among the fifty best-designed books in the United Kingdom by the National Book League, and was runner-up for the Mother Goose Award from Books for Your Children Bookshop, both 1980.

WRITINGS—Juvenile; all self-illustrated: *Sybil and the Blue Rabbit,* Benn, 1979; *Bertie on the Beach,* Benn, 1981, Four Winds, 1982; (compiler) *A Book of Nursery Riddles,* A & C Black, 1984, Houghton, 1985; *Today I Thought I'd Run Away,* Dutton, 1985; *My Bedtime Rhyme,* Anderson Press, 1987.

Illustrator: Serghei Aksakov, *A Russian Gentleman,* Folio Society, 1977; David Lloyd, *Explorers* (juvenile), Walker Books, 1985; D. Lloyd, *Pirates!* (juvenile), Walker Books, 1985; D. Lloyd, *Dragon Catchers* (juvenile), Walker Books, 1985.

WORK IN PROGRESS: Pig George and *Duck Charlie,* self-illustrated picture books for the very young, to be published by Walker Books; illustrations for *From Me to You* by Paul Rogers to be published by Orchard Books.

SIDELIGHTS: ''I was very slow learning to read, so I looked at picture books for hours instead. A lonely childhood and sedentary habits led to my drawing to amuse myself. Because I have vivid memories of the sensations of being a child, I have no difficulty in returning to that world when I am starting a new book.

Sybil did not want to go to school, so she stayed in bed and was sick. ■ (From *Sybil and the Blue Rabbit* by Jane Johnson. Illustrated by the author.)

JANE JOHNSON

"My childhood was not happy, so it has remained very real to me. My books reflect the preoccupations I can remember, wanting to be the center of attention, feeling lonely, bored, uncomprehending, lost. Because I know how vulnerable a child can feel, the books are meant to comfort and encourage, to be fun rather than to seem dangerous and frightening."

KAHL, Virginia (Caroline) 1919-

PERSONAL: Born February 18, 1919, in Milwaukee, Wis.; daughter of Arthur H. and Frieda (Krause) Kahl. *Education:* Milwaukee-Downer College, B.A., 1940; University of Wisconsin, M.S.L.S., 1957. *Office:* Alexandria Public Library, Alexandria, Va.

CAREER: Milwaukee Public Library, Milwaukee, Wis., library assistant, 1942-48; U.S. Army, Special Services Section, librarian in Berlin, Germany, 1948-49, and Salzburg, Austria, 1949-55; Madison Public Schools, Madison, Wis., school librarian, 1958-61; Menomonee Falls Public Library, Menomonee Falls, Wis., library director, 1961-68; Alexandria Public Library, Alexandria, Va., branch librarian, 1971—, coordinator of public services, 1977—. Has taught courses in writing and illustrating children's books at George Washington University. *Member:* National League of American Pen Women, Children's Book Guild (Washington, D.C.). *Awards, honors:* New York Herald Tribune's Spring Book Festival Award Honor Book, 1954, for *Away Went Wolfgang!*; New York Herald

Tribune's Spring Book Festival Award Honor Book, 1955, and Lewis Carroll Shelf Award, 1972, both for *The Duchess Bakes a Cake*.

WRITINGS—All self-illustrated children's books; all published by Scribner: *Away Went Wolfgang!*, 1954; *The Duchess Bakes a Cake*, 1955; *Maxie*, 1956; *Plum Pudding for Christmas*, 1956; *The Habits of Rabbits*, 1957; *Droopsi*, 1958; (with Edith Vacheron) *Here Is Henri!* 1959, also published with French text as *Voici Henri!*, 1959; *The Perfect Pancake*, 1960; (with E. Vacheron) *More about Henri!*, 1961, also published with French text as *Encore Henri!*, 1961; *The Baron's Booty*, 1963; *How Do You Hide a Monster?*, 1971; *Gunhilde's Christmas Book*, 1972; *Giants, Indeed!*, 1974; *Gunhilde and the Halloween Spell*, 1975; *How Many Dragons Are Behind the Door?*, 1977; *Whose Cat Is That?*, 1979. Also author of *String Beans for Charlie*.

ADAPTATIONS: "The Duchess Bakes a Cake" (filmstrip with record or cassette), Miller-Brody.

SIDELIGHTS: After graduating from college, Kahl worked at the Milwaukee Public Library for six years. In 1948 she joined the Special Services Section of the U.S. Army and went to Europe. "My first assignment was in Berlin, and I spent eight months in that blockaded city. But it was during the next assignment, in Salzburg, Austria, where I remained for the next six years, that I began to think of writing and illustrating children's books. Everything about the country cried to be recorded—Salzburg in its romantic setting, the people in their colorful garb, the chalets that looked like illustrations torn from some book of fairy tales, and the gay and stylized designs that were evident not only in costume and architecture, but even in the landscape. The material was already there—it was not a matter of creating, but of interpreting. My style had been

(From the filmstrip "The Duchess Bakes a Cake." Produced by Random House/Miller-Brody Productions, Inc., 1984.)

One spring day, not so long ago, a small white cat wandered across a meadow, through a forest, and over a mountain. ▪ (From *Whose Cat Is That?* by Virginia Kahl. Illustrated by the author.)

influenced by my deep devotion to the art of the Middle Ages. In Austria, as well as in my travels about the rest of Europe, I sought out all the Romanesque and early Gothic churches, castles, and towns, trying to absorb their elements of color, line, and pattern. My ambition is to be able to spend another good chunk of my life in Europe, soaking up its charm, pursuing the medieval, and striving to produce some children's books that well reflect both." [Bertha M. Miller and others, compilers, *Illustrators of Children's Books: 1946-1956,* Horn Book, 1958.]

"I believe that everyone who writes for children finds his own level. For me, it is the picture book age group; and I've never been tempted to write for an older child. So, happily for me, the problems that have surfaced in the past couple of decades are of no concern. I plumb no murky depths, leave no story with [the] ending unresolved. Mine are simple books for simple folk, and I love to do them.

"Little children should enjoy their books. As long as possible, let them live in a world where characters are basically good, incidents are funny or exciting, and the story ultimately satisfying. I hope that the children who read my books have put them down with sighs of contentment, knowing that their expectations of cheerful uncomplicated tales with happy endings have been vindicated."

Kahl notes that she has always been a compulsive reader, especially of art history, cookbooks, mysteries, travel, and biography. Her second great interest is animals—she owns seven cats and would have other creatures, if possible. She "emphatically hates anyone who shoots, traps, poisons, hurts, or destroys wolves or eagles or prairie dogs or whales or seals, who lets oil spill onto beaches to destroy wildfowl, puts industrial wastes into streams and lakes, destroys forests, defaces mountains, or bulldozes his way across the landscape in the name of profit or progress."

FOR MORE INFORMATION SEE: Horn Book, February, 1955; Bertha Mahony Miller and others, compilers, *Illustrators of Children's Books, 1946-1956,* Horn Book, 1958; Muriel Fuller, editor, *More Junior Authors,* H. W. Wilson, 1963; Lee Kingman and others, compilers, *Illustrators of Children's Books: 1957-1966,* Horn Book, 1968; Lee B. Hopkins, *Books Are by People,* Citation Press, 1969.

VIRGINIA KAHL

KAHN, Joan 1914-

PERSONAL: Born April 13, 1914, in New York, N.Y.; daughter of Ely Jacques and Elsie Plaut (Mayer) Kahn. *Education:* Attended Barnard College. *Residence:* New York, N.Y. *Office:* St. Martin's Press, 175 Fifth Ave., New York, N.Y. 10010.

CAREER: Free-lance writer, 1935-45; Harper & Row Publishers, Inc., New York, N.Y., reader, 1945-46, editor, 1946-80. *Member:* International P.E.N., Authors Guild, Mystery Writers of America, National Arts Club, Art Students League of New York. *Awards, honors: Some Things Dark and Dan-*

gerous was chosen as a Children's Book of the Year by the Child Study Association, 1970, *Some Things Strange and Sinister* was chosen, 1973.

WRITINGS: Ladies and Gentlemen, Said the Ringmaster (self-illustrated; juvenile), Knopf, 1938; *To Meet Miss Long* (novel), Lippincott, 1943; *Open House* (novel), Lippincott, 1946; *Seesaw* (juvenile), Harper, 1964; *You Can't Catch Me* (juvenile; illustrated by Elizabeth Bridgman), Harper, 1976; *Hi, Jock, Run Around the Block* (juvenile; illustrated by Whitney Darrow, Jr.), Harper, 1978.

Editor; all collections of mystery and suspense stories: *The Edge of the Chair*, Harper, 1967; *Hanging by a Thread*, foreword by Ogden Nash, Houghton, 1969; *Some Things Dark and Dangerous* (juvenile), Harper, 1970; *Some Things Fierce and Fatal*, Harper, 1971; (and author of introduction) *Trial and Terror*, Houghton, 1973; *Some Things Strange and Sinister*, Harper, 1973; (and author of introduction) *Open at Your Own Risk*, Houghton, 1975; *Some Things Weird and Wicked: Twelve Stories to Chill Your Bones* (illustrated by Alan Cober), Pantheon, 1976; *Chilling and Killing*, Houghton, 1978; *Handle with Care: Frightening Stories*, Greenwillow, 1985.

Contributor to magazines, including *Writer*.

SIDELIGHTS: Joan Kahn wrote in *Writer* magazine: "Edgar Allan Poe started the mystery story proper about a hundred twenty years ago. . . . From Poe until about twenty years ago, the mystery novel enveloped its core of life-into-death with clues and with puzzles. . . . When the mystery novel shifted to the suspense novel, the game side became less important, and the people involved in the book's story became more important. . . . I do prefer people to puzzles. I get tired of games pretty quickly and doubt that I could have spent as many years in the business as I have, if the whodunit had not turned into the suspense novel when it did. . . . I'm certainly not keen about verbosity or padding for padding's sake . . . but I think a suspense novel has to be able to move freely in any manner that suits it best. All I ask of a book is that it's good reading, believable, and the best the author can do at the moment."

"Even after all the years I've been reading novels of suspense, I'm still excited by the new books coming along. . . . And though there are days when I wish no one was ever let near a typewriter again, I expect to go on reading suspense novels eagerly (and not just the ones I've published), because I think suspense novels are getting better all the time."

FOR MORE INFORMATION SEE: Writer, February, 1969.

JOAN KAHN

KLINE, Suzy   1943-

BRIEF ENTRY: Born August 27, 1943, in Berkeley, Calif. As an elementary schoolteacher, Kline finds her classroom to be the perfect source of inspiration for a children's book author. A teacher since 1968, Kline's first picture book, entitled *Shhhh!*, was published by Albert Whitman in 1984. She has since produced *Herbie Jones* (Putnam, 1985), a juvenile novel, and *Don't Touch* (Albert Whitman, 1985), a second picture book. Despite her success as an author, Kline has no intentions of relinquishing her job as second-grade teacher at Southwest School in Torrington, Connecticut. "I could never do one without the other," she explained in a *Waterbury Republican* article. "I get my ideas in the classroom; the children in the books aren't real, but the situations are."

Both of Kline's picture books are based on admonitions all too familiar to the very young. As *School Library Journal* observed, "Presenting a situation common to all children, *Shhhh!* will be fun for story hour sharing or for quiet reading in a parent's lap." Likewise, *Bulletin of the Center for Children's Books* noted that *Don't Touch* "should arouse a recognition reflex." Aimed at a slightly older reading audience, *Herbie Jones* reveals the dilemma of a third grader who finds himself placed in the lowest reading group of the class. "A funny and true-to-life story . . . ," said *Booklist*. "Kline has been teaching elementary school for twelve years, and it's obvious she's been paying close attention." *Herbie Jones* was selected a Children's Choice by the International Reading Association in 1986. That same year, a second novel featuring Herbie, titled *What's the Matter with Herbie Jones?* (Putnam, 1986), was a Junior Literary Guild selection. Kline is currently working a third Herbie Jones novel, *The Day Herbie Jones Cheated.* Her other anticipated works include a third picture book for Albert Whitman and several plays for *Instructor* magazine. *Home:* 124 Hoffman St., Torrington, Conn. 06790.

FOR MORE INFORMATION SEE: (Torrington and Winsted, Conn.) *Register Citizen*, September 18, 1984; *Waterbury Republican*, September 19, 1984.

KOHNER, Frederick   1905-1986

OBITUARY NOTICE—See sketch in *SATA* Volume 10: Born September 25, 1905, in Trnovany (one source cites Teplitz-Schoenau), Czechoslovakia; died July 6, 1986, in Brentwood, Calif. Educator and author of film scripts, stage plays, television series, and novels. Inspired by his daughter, Kohner created Gidget, a fictional California teenage girl whose adventures were detailed in his novels and eventually in films and a television series. He began his career as a journalist, reporting on the film industry in Hollywood and Paris. In the 1930s Kohner also worked as a studio writer, and in the early 1960s he taught in the film department at the University of Southern California. Among his writings are *Gidget, Gidget Goes Hawaiian, Affairs of Gidget, Gidget in Love,* and *Gidget Goes to New York.* Kohner also wrote plays screenplays, and scripts for television anthologies and the series "Gidget."

FOR MORE INFORMATION SEE: Contemporary Authors, New Revision Series, Volume 1, Gale, 1981; *International Motion Picture Almanac,* Quigley, 1986. Obituaries: *Hollywood Reporter Daily,* July 14, 1986; *Facts on File,* August 8, 1986.

It is good for a man that he bear the yoke in his youth.
—Lamentations 3:27

E. L. KONIGSBURG

KONIGSBURG, E(laine) L(obl)

PERSONAL: Born in New York, N.Y.; daughter of Adolph (a businessman) and Beulah (Klein) Lobl; married David Konigsburg (an industrial psychologist); children: Paul, Laurie, Ross. *Education:* Carnegie Institute of Technology (now Carnegie-Mellon University), B.S. (with honors), 1952; University of Pittsburgh, graduate study, 1952-54; also attended Art Students' League, 1962-66. *Address:* c/o Atheneum Publishers, 115 Fifth Ave., New York, N.Y. 10003.

CAREER: Shenago Valley Provision Co., Sharon, Pa., bookkeeper, 1947-48; Bartram School, Jacksonville, Fla., science teacher, 1954-55, 1960-62; writer, 1967—. *Awards, honors: Jennifer, Hecate, Macbeth, William McKinley, and Me, Elizabeth* was chosen as an honor book in *Book World*'s Children's Spring Book Festival, 1967, and as a Newbery honor book, 1968; Newbery Medal, and Lewis Carroll Shelf Award, both 1968, and William Allen White Award, 1970, all for *From the Mixed-Up Files of Mrs. Basil E. Frankweiler;* Carnegie-Mellon Merit Award, 1971; National Book Award finalist, 1974, for *A Proud Taste for Scarlet and Miniver;* American Library Association best book for young adults, 1975, for *The Second Mrs. Giaconda,* and 1976, for *Father's Arcane Daughter;* American Book Award finalist, 1980, for *Throwing Shadows; About the B'nai Bagels, Jennifer, Hecate, Macbeth, William McKinley, and Me, Elizabeth, Journey to an 800 Number,* and *A Proud Taste for Scarlet and Miniver* were all chosen as

Children's Books of the Year by the Child Study Association of America, 1986.

WRITINGS—Juvenile; self-illustrated: *Jennifer, Hecate, Macbeth, William McKinley, and Me, Elizabeth* (*Horn Book* honor list), Atheneum, 1967 (published in England as *Jennifer, Hecate, Macbeth and Me,* Macmillan, 1968); *From the Mixed-Up Files of Mrs. Basil E. Frankweiler* (*Horn Book* honor list; Junior Literary Guild selection), Atheneum, 1967; *About the B'nai Bagels,* Atheneum, 1969; *(George),* Atheneum, 1970 (published in England as *Benjamin Dickinson Carr and His (George),* Penguin, 1974); *A Proud Taste for Scarlet and Miniver* (ALA Notable Book; Junior Literary Guild selection), Atheneum, 1973; *The Dragon in the Ghetto Caper,* Atheneum, 1974.

Other juvenile works: *Altogether, One at a Time* (short stories; illustrated by Gail E. Haley, Mercer Meyer, Gary Parker, and Laurel Schindelman), Atheneum, 1971; *The Second Mrs. Giaconda* (illustrated with museum plates), Atheneum, 1975; *Father's Arcane Daughter,* Atheneum, 1976; *Throwing Shadows* (short stories; ALA Notable Book), Atheneum, 1979; *Journey to an 800 Number,* Atheneum, 1982 (published in England as *Journey by First Class Camel,* Hamish Hamilton, 1983); *Up from Jericho Tel,* Atheneum, 1986.

ADAPTATIONS: "From the Mixed-Up Files of Mrs. Basil E. Frankweiler" (record or cassette), Miller-Brody/Random House, 1969; "From the Mixed-Up Files of Mrs. Basil E. Frankweiler" (motion picture), starring Ingrid Bergman, Cinema 5, 1973, released under new title "The Hideaways," Bing Crosby Productions, 1974; "Jennifer and Me" (television movie; based on *Jennifer, Hecate, Macbeth, William McKinley, and Me, Elizabeth*), NBC-TV, 1973; "The Second Mrs. Giaconda" (play), first produced in Jacksonville, Fla., 1976; (contributor) *Expectations 1980* (braille anthology), Braille Institute, 1980.

SIDELIGHTS: Konigsburg was born in New York City and reared in mill towns in Pennsylvania. "Growing up in a small town gives you two things: a sense of your place and a feeling of self-consciousness—self-consciousness about one's education and exposure, both of which tend to be limited. On the other hand, limited possibilities also means creating your own options. A small town allows you to grow in your own direction, without a bombardment of outside stimulation. You can get a sense of yourself in relation to yourself not to a host of accomplished others. It is important to break out of small-town prejudices, however. It is easy to be arbitrary with little basis for comparison. Where I grew up, for instance, women over forty who dyed their hair or girls who wore black before the age of sixteen were considered immoral. All through high school, my father would not allow me to wear make-up. These 'rules' were established as principles of morality. Later I was to learn (as I had always suspected) that morality was concerned with larger issues.

"I read a lot as a child. There was no one to guide my reading, consequently I read a lot of trash along the *True Confessions* line. I have no objection to trash. I've read a lot of it and firmly believe it helped hone my taste. Besides, I had problems with a lot of the books I read. Nothing I picked up told me anything about the world in which *I* was living."

"[In] *Mary Poppins . . .* you get a good glimpse of upper-middle-class family life in England a quarter of a century ago, a family that had basis in fact. . . . Read *The Secret Garden,* and you find another world that I know about only in words. Here is a family living on a large estate staffed by servants who are devoted to the two generations living there. Here is a father who has no visible source of income. He neither reaps nor sows. . . . Families of this kind had a basis in fact, but fact remote from me.

"I have such faith in words that when I read about such families as a child, I thought that they were the norm and that the way I lived was subnormal, waiting for normal." [E. L. Konigsburg, "Newbery Award Acceptance," *Horn Book,* August 1968.[1]]

"I drew a lot as a child and was an excellent student for as long as I can remember. I graduated valedictorian from Farrell High School and wanted to go away to college. My high school had no guidance department and no one in my family had ever gone to university. I devised a plan whereby I would work for a year, earn enough for two semesters of tuition and board, go back to work to finance another academic year, and so on until I finished my degree. No one had ever told me about scholarships. Right after high school, I got a job as a bookkeeper in a wholesale meat plant.

"The following year I enrolled at Carnegie Institute of Technology in Pittsburgh as a chemistry major. If I had in mind eventually to be a writer and artist, the notion was so deeply submerged that I was unaware of it. Besides, if you were the first person in your family to go to college, you didn't say you were going away to become a writer. You said you were going away to become a *something*—a librarian, a teacher, a chemist, a *something*. I chose chemistry because I was good at it and there would be jobs waiting when I finished. In Farrell, I never met anyone who made his living from the arts. One day late in my freshman year as I was walking across campus, my English professor stopped me and inquired about my plans. When I told him that I would be returning to my job for another year, he said '*Miss* Lobl, I think that this school would not choose to lose students of your *ilk*.' Thanks to his intervention, I was able to get a scholarship. I had jobs all through school—

in the library, managing a laundry service in the dormitory— and I remained *enrolled.*

"An interesting thing about that time is that my closest friends and dormitory mates were women from other small towns in Pennsylvania—bright, ambitious, capable women, set on doing something with their education. We're still in touch with each other.

"College was a crucial 'opening up' for me. I worked hard and did well. However, the artistic side of me was essentially dormant. My close college friends never even knew that I could write and loved to draw. Chemistry majors spend long hours in the lab; some of our courses were full-day labs, and there was not a lot of time for much besides work and school work."

Graduating with honors, she then married David Konigsburg, an industrial psychologist, and continued her education at graduate school at the University of Pittsburgh. After two years there, "I had passed all those courses with flying colors; unfortunately, that is also the way I passed the lab courses. There the colors flew because of a few explosions in the lab sink." [Doris de Montreville and Donna Hill, editors, *Third Book of Junior Authors,* H. W. Wilson, 1972[2]]

Konigsburg moved with her husband to Jacksonville, Florida, where she taught science at a private girls' school. "I began to suspect that chemistry was not my field. Not only did I always ask my students to light my Bunsen burner, having become match-shy, but I became more interested in what was going on inside them than what was going on inside the test tubes."[2]

"I had the mind for chemistry, but not the temperament. There were rumblings of this in my head much earlier, I believe, but I wasn't listening."

I needed an excuse to not play musical chairs, so I invented a sore leg. ■ (From *Jennifer, Hecate, Macbeth, William McKinley, and Me, Elizabeth* by E. L. Konigsburg. Illustrated by the author.)

Konigsburg left teaching shortly before the birth of son Paul. Soon after her second child, Laurie, was born, she took up painting in local adult education classes. "I had good luck in that I won the first art competition I entered. There were mostly Jacksonville artists in the show, but the judge had some renown. Not long afterward, we moved to New York. I was so ready! Just as getting an education was critical exposure for me, New York was a kind of graduate school. I took Saturdays 'off': in the morning I attended drawing classes at the Art Students' League; in the afternoon I explored the galleries, museums and streets of Manhattan."

Her writing began when her youngest child went to school. "I learned that no one respects the housewife's time. I had waited in every pediatrician's office, every dentist's office, and even at the shoe store for my boys to be fitted for orthopedic shoes. Once when I telephoned a supermarket and asked to speak to the butcher, I was not allowed. They would give him my message and I could call back to find out what he said. His time, too, was more valuable than mine. I realized that no one would value my time except me. So I decided that I would take the mornings—not make a bed, not do the dishes—and write. This turned out to be easier than I expected. We had just moved to Port Chester, New York, where I knew no one, so I was spared the endless round of telephone calls from friends, neighbors and acquaintances. I kept my writing a secret except from my family. When my kids came home for lunch, I would often read them what I'd written and watch their reactions."

"[I wanted to] tell how it is normal to be very comfortable on the outside but very uncomfortable on the inside. Tell how funny it all is. But tell a little something else, too. . . . about how you can be a nonconformist and about how you can be an outsider. And tell how you are entitled to a little privacy."'

Konigsburg made children's book history in 1968 when her second book, *From the Mixed-Up Files of Mrs. Basil E. Frankweiler* won the Newbery Medal and her first, *Jennifer, Hecate, Macbeth, William McKinley, and Me, Elizabeth*, was the Newbery runner-up. She illustrated both novels, using her children as models. "The illustrations probably come from the kindergartner who lives . . . somewhere inside me, who says, 'Silly, don't you know that it is called *show* and tell?' . . . Besides, I like to draw, and I like to complete things, and doing the illustrations answers these simple needs."'

Her overriding feeling is that she owes kids a good story. "[I try to] let the telling be like fudge-ripple ice cream. You keep licking the vanilla, but every now and then you come to something darker and deeper and with a stronger flavor."'

About the B'nai Bagels is a good example of "fudge-ripple" style of storytelling. In this book, The Bagels, a baseball team sponsored by a suburban Jewish Community Center, has lost its coach. The mother of one of the boys steps in—an unprecedented move, as the coaches had always been men—and fields a championship team. "I was trying to write a story about a mother invading her child's 'alone' time. I was having trouble,

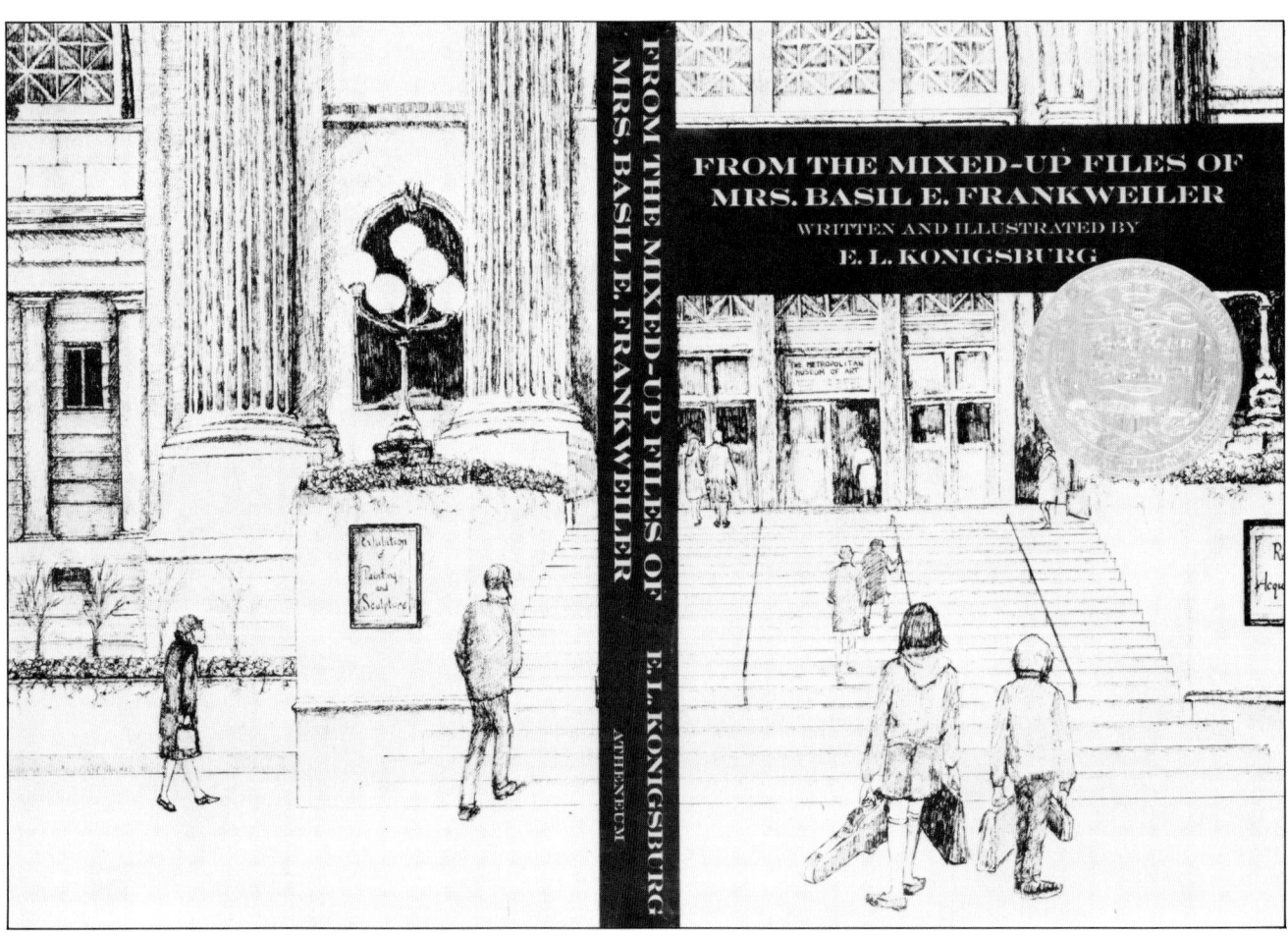

Her violin case kept bumping him, and he began to walk a few steps ahead of her. ■ (Jacket illustration by E. L. Konigsburg from *From the Mixed-Up Files of Mrs. Basil E. Frankweiler* by E. L. Konigsburg.)

If you think of doing something in New York City, you can be certain that at least two thousand other people have the same thought. And of the two thousand who do, about one thousand will be standing in line waiting to do it. ■ (From *From the Mixed-Up Files of Mrs. Basil E. Frankweiler* by E. L. Konigsburg. Photograph from the movie adaptation. Produced by Cinema 5, 1973.)

couldn't get a handle on it. Then one day, we went to a JCC basketball game (my son was on the Port Chester team). One of the players was dribbling in, but couldn't make his shot because his older brother, who was on the opposing team, was guarding him very closely. Their mother stood up in the stands and yelled, '*Peetuh, leave your brother alone!*' Well, this woman unlocked the story for me, and set the tone for Bessy, the mother in my book. I love this character—she's so full of life and so funny—still, the underlying theme of *The B'nai Bagels* is a kid's need for privacy.''

Rich in details of Jewish secular culture, this book has been called by reviewers a ''Jewish Diaspora story.'' Another underlying theme is anti-Semitism. ''My kids were living that. Gentile children would line up across the sidewalk, blocking them, taunting them, as they tried to get to Hebrew School.'' When asked about the novel's emphasis on the secular over the non-secular (even though the protagonist is preparing his Bar Mitzvah), and the characters' generally unorthodox handling of the non-secular, Konigsburg replied, ''Being Jewish is very important to me. As with many things, however, one must find one's own way within a larger context.'' With characteristic humor, she added, ''I love being Jewish, but I have some trouble with the synagogue.''

Konigsburg is routinely praised for the depth, wit, and sophistication of her novels. Her protagonists exhibit an extraordinary capacity for growth, even when that growth cannot be

achieved without pain. Her books tend to be classed by librarians, teachers, and the press as ''young adult'' novels. ''I have serious reservations about the young adult genre. I think there's too much trash being published under that label, too much of the sort of thing I used to read in *True Confessions*—though, as I've said, I'm not against reading trash, but I do object to trash masquerading as literature. You might say I like my trash pure and simple. What bothers me most is that too many young adult novels are not extensions of a personal history or imagination but are 'novelizations' of television. They display sit-com humor, deal with the disease of the month or a current social disorder. I feel more at home in the category of 'children's books,' which is an older, more literary tradition.

''When [editor] Jean Karl sent me the first great letter of acceptance, she told me that my book would be part of Atheneum's spring list of novels for the middle-aged child. That was the first I had ever heard the term, middle-aged child, and I thought that it was ridiculous. I couldn't think of a more contradictory set of words than 'middle-aged' and 'child.' However, I have since moved from disdain to acceptance of the phrase.

''To the publishing world the middle-aged child is the child from ages eight through twelve. A child whose reading habits are post-Dr. Seuss but pre-*The Sensuous Woman*. The child rated 'G' through 'PG.' But my acceptance of the term has come about as a result of establishing a relationship between the child, aged eight through twelve, and the Middle Ages—the Middle Ages of Western Civilization, that is. Those dark centuries of history from the time of the collapse of the Roman Empire until the great rebirth of the Renaissance. Those so-called one thousand years without a bath.

"I started drawing my parallel when we lived in the suburbs of New York, and I took my children to the Cloisters, the branch of the Metropolitan Museum of Art that is devoted exclusively to medieval art. One of the works of art that fascinated my son was a rosary bead, a giant as far as rosary beads go—about the size of a golf ball. It is hinged, and is displayed opened up. There, within that tiny realm, is carved

(From *A Proud Taste for Scarlet and Miniver* by E. L. Konigsburg. Illustrated by the author.)

a three-dimensional scene of Christ's crucifixion, complete with Mary and Joseph of Arimathea and troops of Roman soldiers. The whole carving is so exquisite that one can read the expressions on the faces of the people, faces no bigger than a quarter-grain saccharine tablet.

"My son was so impressed with this bead that he decided to carve one for his Hebrew teacher, his favorite teacher of the moment. He knew that she would appreciate Moses on Mt. Sinai more than she would appreciate Christ on Calvary. So that was the scene he decided upon. He borrowed a paring knife from me and stole a small piece of pine from some construction site and went to work. There you have the mind of a middle-aged child—he was eight at the time. He wanted to carve a rosary bead for a teacher of Hebrew. He wanted to make something beautiful, and he stole to do it. His thinking was truly Middle Aged or medieval."

Konigsburg's fascination with the relation between *child* and *Middle Ages* led her to immerse herself in the history, culture, and art of the period. She was bothered by the depiction of Henry II's wife, Eleanor of Aquitaine, in Jean Anouilh's play *Becket* as "a whiny, no talent nag. I have observed a lot of executives in my time—and what is a medieval king but an executive in drag?—and I've known a lot of executive wives. And I have noticed that executive wives are strong ladies. To stay with a man of vitality and ego requires a woman of character." After researching Eleanor of Aquitaine, Konigsburg found that she "was in essence everything that women's liberation is in slogans." She resolved to write about Eleanor, and did so in *A Proud Taste for Scarlet and Miniver*, which she also illustrated.

"Eleanor of Aquitaine was the lady who was wife not to one king, but to two. She divorced Louis VII of France and married Henry of England. She was thirty at the time, and he was eighteen, and you can't tell me that's not doing your own thing. She was the mother, not of one king but two—Richard the Lion Heart and King John, who signed The Magna Carta at Runnymede in 1215. Eleanor of Aquitaine was the lady who was responsible for lifting a minor Saxon king by the name of Arthur from the dusty pages of a history book and handed him over to her troubadours who in turn imbued him with grace and chivalry, bedecked him with honor, and seated him at a round table with a bunch of noble, if sometimes lecherous, knights. She established the rules of courtly love. Rules that caused a gentleman to rise when a lady entered the room; rules that took a Woodstock and a sexual revolution to change.

"I wanted to write about this queen, this women's libber, for children. I wanted to do it accurately, but I didn't want to invent a small child character and plop him into the twelfth century. I felt I didn't need to do that. Eleanor of Aquitaine already had an age in common with children: The Middle Ages. . . . Everyone who inhabits [the book] has lived. But I [chose] to have [them] live both then and in the 1970s. They speak in phrases that are historically documented as well as others blatantly invented. But there is throughout this mixture of historical fact and fiction a truth—a true portrait of Eleanor of Aquitaine, a portrait of a liberated woman."

Eleanor of Aquitaine is only one of Konigsburg's many brainy, feisty, and witty female characters. Her girls don't have it easy. They deal with and surmount complex conflict. Yet Konigsburg holds that the creation of her characters doesn't start from an overtly feminist agenda. "I didn't realize how consistently feminist my female characters were until I read it in a review. Not that I object! I'm not a very brave person in social situations. I always think of brilliant rejoinders *after* the party. Perhaps my witty female characters are a form of 're-venge.'"

Konigsburg is vehemently outspoken against censorship of any form in reading materials. Her ire derives not only from an intellectual stance protective of civil liberties but from personal experience as well. Certain textbook editors and publishers have attempted to expurgate her novels to make excerpts "suit-able" for inclusion in sixth-grade readers. School librarians have removed her books from the shelves. Administrators have requested Konigsburg to change certain words and after her refusal, forbade teachers and librarians from ordering her books. An incident particularly grating to her involved a textbook company's wanting to print a chapter from *From the Mixed-Up Files of Mrs. Basil E. Frankweiler*. The chapter deals with a brother and sister running away from home to live in New York's Metropolitan Museum of Art. Each evening just after the Museum closes, they must hide from the guards making their daily rounds. Their scheme is to take refuge in the bath-rooms and remain undetected by standing on the toilet seats. The publisher relinquished the chapter when Konigsburg re-fused to delete mention of the toilets.

Another instance involved her story, "Momma at the Pearly Gates," from a collection entitled *Altogether, One at a Time*. A school system deemed the story "inappropriate" for its li-braries because it contained the word "nigger." "[The story] takes place in the 1940s, a time when the term *black* was unknown to the blacks as well as to the whites of eastern Ohio [where the characters live].... I have read 'Momma at the Pearly Gates' to audiences of children of mixed races, and they have never had any doubt about how cleverly Momma picks up Roseann's weapon, the word *nigger* and cudgels her with it.... I predict that black Americans will feel patron-ized ... and cheated. Cheated of a black heroine who triumphs over being called nigger to become the heroine of her own story.... What [censors] are showing ... readers is con-tempt.... I say that anyone who looks at the word 'nigger' in 'Momma at the Pearly Gates,' like anyone who looks at the word 'nigger' in *Huckleberry Finn* and who does not see be-yond that word, who refuses to see where the author's senti-ments lie, is showing contempt for that author. And anyone who properly sees where that author's sentiments lie and does not trust others to do so is showing contempt for them...." [E. L. Konigsburg, "Excerpts from My Bouboulina File," *Library Quarterly,* Volume 51, number 1, 1981.[3]]

Konigsburg generally spends a year to a year and a half writing a book, unless a lot of research is involved, in which case the work takes considerably longer. "I'm very hard on myself, revising and rewriting as I go along. By the time I send in a manuscript, I've been over it a number of times with a fine-toothed comb. Several of my books have gone directly from manuscript to galleys."

To young people who aspire to be writers and/or artists, Kon-igsburg advises, "*Finish*. The difference between being a writer and being a person of talent is the discipline it takes to apply the seat of your pants to the seat of your chair and finish. Don't talk about doing it. Do it. Finish."

Her contemplation of the creative process has had its fullest expression in her novel about Leonardo Da Vinci, *The Second Mrs. Giaconda*. Central to the book is Leonardo's relationship with Salai, a fetching young thief who was the artist's lover, assistant, and companion of more than twenty years. "In his notebooks Leonardo complains of Salai as a *glutton, thief, mule-head, liar*. Every great work of art, every work of gen-

ius, has a wild element. Some artists carry that wild element within them. Michelangelo did; Rembrandt did; Beethoven did; but Leonardo did not.

"Leonardo, the bastard son, the uneducated, defensive, self-conscious, inhibited genius, needed Salai to supply that irrev-erence, that wild element, that all-important something awful that great works of art have. Salai gave Leonardo a necessary sense of unimportance. We all need a child to do that; Salai was in many ways a perpetual child....

"... Writing for children demands a certain kind of excel-lence: ... the quality that young readers demand, as Renais-sance viewers demanded it—that works of art must have weight and knowing beneath them, that works of art must have all the techniques and all the skills; they must never be sloppy but must never show the gears. Make it nonchalant, easy. The men of the Renaissance called that kind of excellence *sprez-zatura*.

"And because Salai appreciated this quality, Leonardo kept him with him. And because children demand it subliminally and appreciate it loudly, and because I do, too, I write for children." [E. L. Konigsburg, "Sprezzatura: A Kind of Ex-cellence," *Horn Book,* June, 1976.[4]]

Up until October of last year my mother had two hobbies: major league baseball and my brother, Spencer. ■ (From *About the B'nai Bagels* by E. L. Konigsburg. Illustrated by the author.)

When I at last turned around, I did so abruptly and asked directly, "Are you the children who have been missing from Greenwich for a week?"... I have a finely developed sense of theatrics. ▪ (From *From the Mixed-Up Files of Mrs. Basil E. Frankweiler* by E. L. Konigsburg. Photograph from the movie adaptation, starring Ingrid Bergman. Produced by Cinema 5, 1973.)

HOBBIES AND OTHER INTERESTS: Painting, reading, gardening (in fair weather), taking long walks, chocolate.

FOR MORE INFORMATION SEE—Books: Martha E. Ward and Dorothy A. Marquardt, *Authors of Books for Young People,* 2nd edition, Scarecrow, 1971; Miriam Hoffman and Eva Samuels, *Authors and Illustrators of Children's Books: Writings on Their Lives and Works,* Bowker, 1972; Doris de Montreville and Donna Hill, editors, *Third Book of Junior Authors,* H. W. Wilson, 1972; Lee Bennett Hopkins, *More Books by More People,* Citation Press, 1974; Lee Kingman, editor, *Newbery and Caldecott Medal Books: 1966-1975,* Horn Book, 1975; Ann Block and Carolyn Riley, editors, *Children's Literature Review,* Volume I, Gale, 1976; D. L. Kirkpatrick, *Twentieth-Century Children's Writers,* St. Martin's, 1978, 2nd edition, 1983; E. L. Konigsburg, *Throwing Shadows,* Atheneum, 1979; John Rowe Townsend, *A Sounding of Storytellers: Essays on Contemporary Writers for Children,* Penguin Books, 1979.

Periodicals: *Library Journal,* October 15, 1967, March 15, 1968; *New York Times Book Review,* November 5, 1967, February 25, 1968, March 30, 1969, November 8, 1970, May 30, 1971, October 14, 1973, November 4, 1973, October 5, 1975, November 7, 1976, December 9, 1979, May 30, 1982; *Publishers Weekly,* February 26, 1968; *School Library Journal,* March, 1968, February, 1970; *Top of the News,* April, 1968; *Horn Book,* August, 1968, December, 1970, August, 1971, April, 1973, June, 1976, February, 1978, ·April, 1980; *Times Literary Supplement,* October 3, 1968, April 3, 1969, July 2, 1971, April 4, 1975, March 25, 1977, June 16, 1983; *Saturday Review,* November 9, 1968, November 14, 1970; *Chicago Tribune Children's Book World,* November 8, 1970; E. L. Konigsburg, "The Genesis of *A Proud Taste for Scarlet and Miniver*" (pamphlet), Atheneum, 1973; E. L. Konigsburg, "Forty Percent More Than Everything You Want to Know about E. L. Konigsburg" (pamphlet), Atheneum, 1974; *Christian Science Monitor,* May 1, 1974; E. L. Konigsburg, "Excerpts from My Bouboulina File," *Library Quarterly,* Volume 51, number 1, 1981; *Learning Today,* fall, 1981; *Washington Post Book World,* April 11, 1982; *Times* (London), June 16, 1983.

Other: "E. L. Konigsburg" (videocassette), Profiles in Literature, Temple University, 1983.

KOOYKER-ROMIJN, Johanna Maria 1927-
(Leonie Kooiker)

PERSONAL: Born October 20, 1927, in Markelo, Netherlands; daughter of Jan C. (a doctor) and Johanna (Gorter) Romijn; married Gerard Kooyker (a doctor), August 26, 1946; children: Albert, Robert Jan, Huibert, Annelie *Home:* Kerkbuurt 4, 3354 XK Papendrecht, Netherlands.

CAREER: Writer. *Member:* Vereinging van Letterkundigen. *Awards, honors:* Gold Pencil Award from Commissie voor de propaganda van het Nederlandse boek (best children's book of the year), 1971, for *Het malle ding van bobbistiek.*

WRITINGS—Under pseudonym Leonie Kooiker: *De heksensteen,* Ploegsma, 1974, translation from the Dutch by Richard Winston and Clara Winston published as *The Magic Stone* (illustrated by Carl Hollander), Morrow, 1978; *Het oerlanderboek,* Ploegsma, 1979, translation by Patricia Crampton

published as *Legacy of Magic* (illustrated by C. Hollander), Morrow, 1981.

In Dutch: *Het malle ding van bobbistiek* (title means "The Queer Thing of Bobbistic"), Ploegsma, 1970; *De boevenvangers* (title means "The Villain Catchers"), Ploegsma, 1972; *De diamant van de piraat* (title means "The Pirate's Diamond"), Ploegsma, 1972; *Het laantje met de lindeboom* (title means "The Lane with the Lindentree"), Lemniscaat, 1972; *De dochter van de schilder op de berg* (title means "The Daughter of the Painter on the Hills"), Ploegsma, 1973; *Je hart of je heerlijkheid* (title means "Your Heart or Your Happy Home"), Bigot en van Rossum, 1974; *Het levende beeld in de tempel* (title means "The Living Sculpture in the Temple"), Ploegsma, 1976.

Tante Mien (title means "Aunt Mina"), Leopold, 1981; *Ga niet te ver, je valt eraf* (title means "Don't Go Too Far, You'll Fall"), Zwijsen, 1982; *Je mag een poosje los* (title means "Release for a While"), Zwijsen, 1982; *Dan liever de lucht in* (title means "I Prefer to Go by Air"), Leopold, 1982; *Met de grote vogel mee* (poems and illustrations; title means "Along with the Big Bird"), Terra, 1982; *De zwarte bende* (title means "The Bandits"), Zwijsen, 1983; *Het woekerkoraal* (title means "The Growing Coral"), Leopold, 1983; *Je kunt het niet meenemmen* (title means "You Can't Take It with You"), Leopold, 1983; *De maanlandexpres* (title means "Express to Moonland"), Leopold, 1984; *De Kleine dief* (title means "Little Thief"), Ploegsma, 1984; *Oplossing, losgeld, verlost* (title means "Solution, Ransom, Released"), Leopold, 1985.

SIDELIGHTS: "I was born in the small village of Markelo in the East of the Netherlands, where I used to spend as much time as possible in the woods and heatherlands. My father was taken away by the Germans and subsequently died in a concentration camp.

"I married a young doctor. He had to go to fight in Indonesia and after he left our first son was born. After two years we moved near Rotterdam. During the first years of our marriage I was an assistant in the practice and made the medicines, as we had our own dispensary. The house we lived in was at the riverside where all the ships pass going from Rotterdam to France and Germany. Here I developed a great love for the water. We had a boat and sailed all over Holland.

"I think the best education for children is to teach them as early as possible to live with earth, water, fire and living animals and plants. So my books are full of these things.

"I have been writing for many years, but I never sit at my desk for long periods of time. I am not good at sitting quietly. I am better at work in the garden, building, and cooking. It is difficult to leave the house and my friends for the world of fantasy. I try to include in my books all the ingredients of real life, fun, sorrow, love, adventure, stupidity and so on with an extra something that is only possible in a book. I try not to influence my readers with my beliefs or opinions.

"Apart from Europe I have traveled in Africa, South America, Mexico and Indonesia. France and Ireland are my favourite countries except for South America, but it is a bit too far away.

"My eldest son, Albert, is a goldsmith; Bobbie studied biology; and Huibert photography, though now he is a navigation officer. My daughter studied agriculture at the university. My husband, Gerard, and I have three grandchildren."

HOBBIES AND OTHER INTERESTS: Painting, philosophy, psychology.

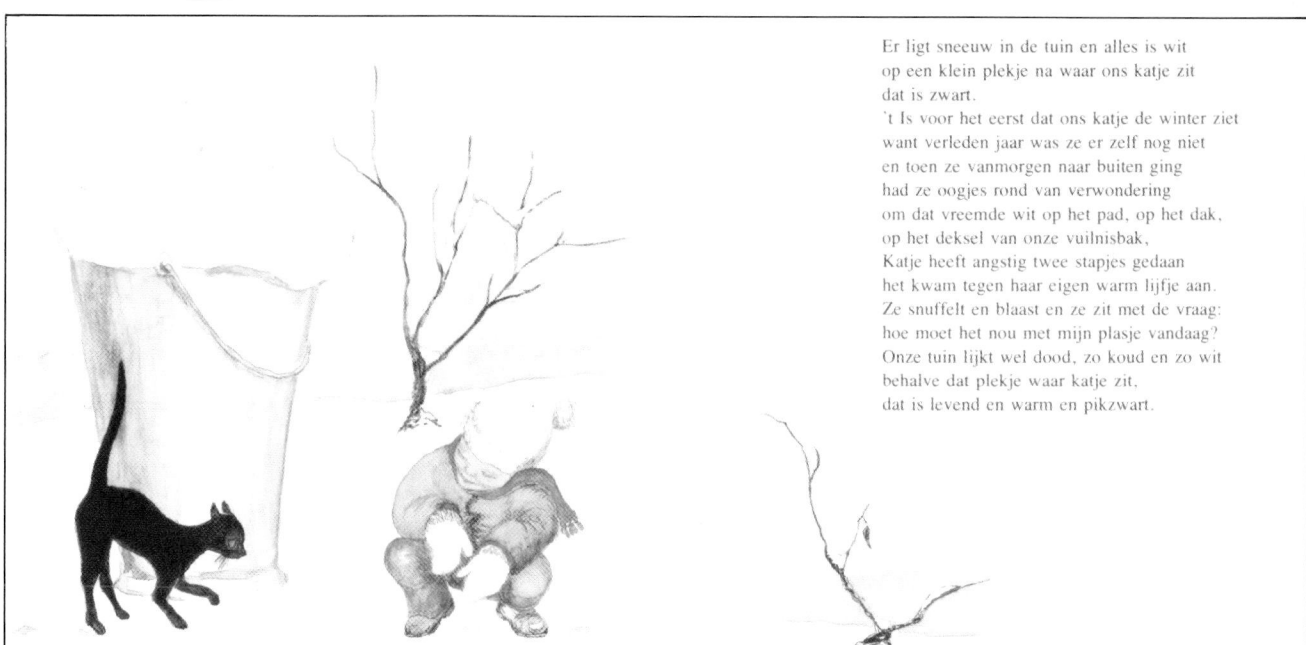

Er ligt sneeuw in de tuin en alles is wit
op een klein plekje na waar ons katje zit
dat is zwart.
't Is voor het eerst dat ons katje de winter ziet
want verleden jaar was ze er zelf nog niet
en toen ze vanmorgen naar buiten ging
had ze oogjes rond van verwondering
om dat vreemde wit op het pad, op het dak,
op het deksel van onze vuilnisbak,
Katje heeft angstig twee stapjes gedaan
het kwam tegen haar eigen warm lijfje aan.
Ze snuffelt en blaast en ze zit met de vraag:
hoe moet het nou met mijn plasje vandaag?
Onze tuin lijkt wel dood, zo koud en zo wit
behalve dat plekje waar katje zit,
dat is levend en warm en pikzwart.

(From *Met de grote vogel mee* by Leonie Kooiker. Illustrated by the author.)

JOHANNA MARIA KOOYKER-ROMIJN

JOSEPH KRUMGOLD

KRUMGOLD, Joseph (Quincy) 1908-1980

PERSONAL: Born April 9, 1908, in Jersey City, N.J.; died of a stroke July 10, 1980, in Hope, N.J.; son of Henry (a film exhibitor) and Lena (Gross) Krumgold; married Helen Litwin, January 10, 1947; children: Adam. *Education:* New York University, B.A., 1928. *Politics:* Democrat. *Religion:* Jewish. *Home:* Shiloh Farm, Hope, N.J. 07844.

CAREER: Novelist and author of children's books. Publicity writer, Metro-Goldwyn-Mayer, New York, N.Y., 1928; screenwriter and producer for film companies, including Paramount, RKO, Columbia, and Republic, in Hollywood, Calif., and Paris, France, 1929-40; producer and director, Film Associates, New York City, and Office of War Information, 1940-46; president in charge of production, Palestine Films, New York City and Jerusalem, Israel, 1946-52; Joseph Krumgold Productions (producer of motion pictures and television films), Hope, N.J., proprietor, 1952-60; writer, director, and producer for Columbia Broadcasting System, Inc., National Broadcasting Company, Inc., National Educational Television, and Westinghouse Television, 1960-70. Press agent. Member, Freling Huysen Township (N.J.) school board. *Member:* Screenwriters Guild, Authors League of America, Jewish Center (Newton, N.J.), Players (New York), Pi Lambda Phi.

AWARDS, HONORS: Newbery Medal, American Library Association, 1954, for *. . . And Now Miguel,* and 1960, for *Onion John;* Boys' Club Junior Book Award from Boys' Club of America, 1954, and Freedoms Foundation Award, 1973, both for *. . . And Now Miguel;* Robert Flaherty Award honorable mention, 1954, for movie *". . . And Now Miguel";* Lewis Carroll Shelf Award, 1960, for *Onion John; The Most Terrible Turk* was chosen as one of Child Study Association's Children's Books of the Year, 1969; first prizes for films and documentaries at Venice, Edinburgh, and Prague film festivals.

WRITINGS: Thanks to Murder (adult), Vanguard Press, 1935; *Sweeney's Adventure* (based on the film "Sweeney Steps Out"; illustrated by Tibor Gergely), Random House, 1942; *. . . And Now Miguel* (based on screenplay; ALA Notable Book; illustrated by Jean Charlot), Crowell, 1953, reissued, Harper, 1984; *Onion John* (ALA Notable Book; illustrated by Symeon Shimin), Crowell, 1959, reissued, Harper, 1984; *Henry 3* (ALA Notable Book; illustrated by Alvin Smith), Atheneum, 1967; *The Most Terrible Turk: A Story of Turkey* (illustrated by Michael Hampshire), Crowell, 1969; (editor) *The Oxford Furnace, 1741-1925* (history), Warren County Historical Society, 1976.

Screenplays: (With Fred Niblo, Jr., Arthur Strawn, and Ben G. Kohn) "Lady from Nowhere," Columbia, 1936; (with Lee Loeb and Harold Buchman) "The Blackmailer," Columbia, 1936; (with others) "Adventure in Manhattan," Columbia, 1936; (with Bruce Manning and Lionel Houser) "Lone Wolf Returns," Columbia, 1936; (with Olive Cooper and Karl Brown) "Join the Marines," Republic, 1937; (with O. Cooper and Octavus Roy Cohn; also associate producer) "Jim Hanvey—Detective," Republic, 1937; (with O. Cooper) "Lady Behave," Republic, 1938; (contributor) "Speed to Burn," Twentieth Century-Fox Film Corp., 1938; "Main Street Lawyer" (based on a story by Harry Hamilton), Republic, 1939; "The Phantom Submarine" (based on a short story by Augustus Muir), Columbia, 1940; (with Garnett Weston, E. E. Paramore, and Richard Blake) "The Crooked Road," Repub-

We stood on the drenched sidewalk of 33rd Street in New York City and we looked up, Fletch and I, to the top of where the Empire State Building ought to be. ■
(From *Henry 3* by Joseph Krumgold. Illustrated by Alvin Smith.)

lic, 1940; "Seven Miles from Alcatraz" (based on a novel by John D. Klorer), RKO, 1942; (with Robert Riskin) "Magic Town," RKO, 1947; (also author and director) "Dream No More," produced in Israel, 1950.

Also author of screenplays; all documentaries: (With Henwar Rodakiewicz) "One Tenth of a Nation," 1940; "Mr. Trull Finds Out," 1941; (with H. Rodakiewicz; also director and original author) "Hidden Hunger," 1942; "Israel Speaks," Twentieth Century-Fox; "The Autobiography of a Jeep," 1943; (also director) ". . . And Now Miguel," United World Films, 1953, Universal, 1966; "The House in the Desert"; "Adventure in the Bronx"; "The Promise"; and others. Author of television scripts. Contributor to numerous periodicals.

ADAPTATIONS: "And Now Miguel" (filmstrip with record or cassette), Miller-Brody, 1978; "Onion John" (record or cassette), Miller-Brody, 1978; "Onion John" (filmstrip with record or cassette), Miller-Brody, 1978.

SIDELIGHTS: **April 9, 1908.** Born in Jersey City, New Jersey into a family that was associated with the early motion picture industry. Krumgold's father was an exhibitor who owned and operated movie houses, and his older brother accompanied the silent films on the organ. Consequently, by the time he was twelve years old, Krumgold had decided on a career in the motion picture industry.

Attended Dickinson High School in Jersey City. Krumgold once remarked that during his school days he looked for things that would help him when he went to work. "I think we learned how things grow, most of us, back in our high school biology class. We found out that to grow did not mean simply to get larger, to expand, to take on increasing size. If this kind of ballooning were all there were to the process, the end in every case would be—explosion.

"We learned, as I remember, that what got larger had also to stay together—if real growth were to be achieved. That it had to keep on being what it started out as. We learned there were two factors essential and complementary to the process of growth. Along with expansion there had to be cohesion. The first alone ends in a Big Bang. To cohere alone ends in the contraction of rigor mortis. To grow—both are needed." [Joseph Krumgold, "Acceptance Paper," *Newbery Medal Books: 1922-1955,* edited by Bertha Mahony Miller and Elinor Whitney Field, Horn Book, 1955.[1]]

1928. Received a bachelor's degree from New York University, where he had majored in English and history.

1929. Went to Hollywood where the first "talkies" were being made by the film companies. There he began an eleven-year association with several major movie companies as a press agent, producer, and writer of screen plays.

1940. During World War II, worked for the Office of War Information. Krumgold became more interested in real people in real places, and so began making documentary films. ". . . This way of making a movie seemed more exciting, working with facts—the real thing—instead of actors and fake scenery. Part of the excitement, anyway, is that you have to go where the story is happening. And that involves a lot of travel. I've made pictures all over the United States and in Europe and in the Middle East." [Muriel Fuller, editor, "Joseph Krumgold," *More Junior Authors,* H. W. Wilson, 1963.[2]]

January 10, 1947. Married Helen Litwin.

1947-1951. Lived in Israel where he was associated with Palestine Films. He made fifteen films during his four years in Israel, and one of them, "The House in the Desert," won a prize at the Venice Film Festival.

1952. Began an eight-year enterprise as owner and operator of his own production company. Lived with his wife and son, Adam, on the 120-acre Shiloh Farm, in Hope, New Jersey.

Next day when he came home from school his Uncle Mustafa was gone. ■ (From *The Most Terrible Turk* by Joseph Krumgold. Illustrated by Michael Hampshire.)

Onion John was a lot different from anyone I ever hung out with before. Like his age. ■ (From *Onion John* by Joseph Krumgold. Illustrated by Symeon Shimin.)

1953. Made a documentary film under the auspices of the U.S. State Department about the life of southwestern sheep raisers. The film required Krumgold and his wife to live with the Chavez family in Taos, New Mexico and to record their lives.

Thomas Y. Crowell Company commissioned Krumgold to adapt his film, "*. . . And Now Miguel*" into a children's book. Although the screenwriter had written two books before this project (*Adventures in the Bronx* and *Thanks to Murder*), he found the story of Miguel Chavez, that of a boy with a wish, to be a challenge. "In examining again this old story of the wish, in chapter after chapter, I came up against many surprises. Each classic turn of the oft told tale provided me, if no one else, with a revelation. I was obliged to rummage around and inspect once again, for the truth that may be hidden, all the old toys and tales which once served us for our playthings. In speculating on what was familiar through working on the book, I finished richer than when I started. I knew better who I was." [Elizabeth Riley, "Newbery to Krumgold," *Library Journal*, March 15, 1954.[3]]

1954. Received his first Newbery Medal from the American Library Association for his book, *. . . And Now Miguel*. "During the time I spent with Miguel, he introduced me I guess to more than a hundred people. A good many of them had inter-

ests that were peculiar, and habits that Miguel regarded with critical distaste. But his bond with these people did not depend on any such tenuous reference as a common interest or curiosity. All of them appeared to be *primos* of Miguel, if my bewildered impression is accurate. They were all his cousins. All of them *belonged* to each other—for life.

"If we set out to find, in simple language that we can understand, what benefit there might be in talking over the problem with someone of another species, some other animal, we have either to read a children's book—or to write one. And the same goes for finding what it takes to face around to the hobgoblins, the ogres and the giants that live in our subconscious.

"If you want to burrow back into the earth to take another new look at who we are, along with Alice; if you want to learn the precise danger of dealing with a genie in the bottle, along with Sinbad, you'll have to go off to the children's section, please, two counters to the right.

"When I was impelled to study the mechanics of the wish, I had to cross over those two counters and confer with the godmothers and magicians established there—or I had to write . . . *And Now Miguel*.

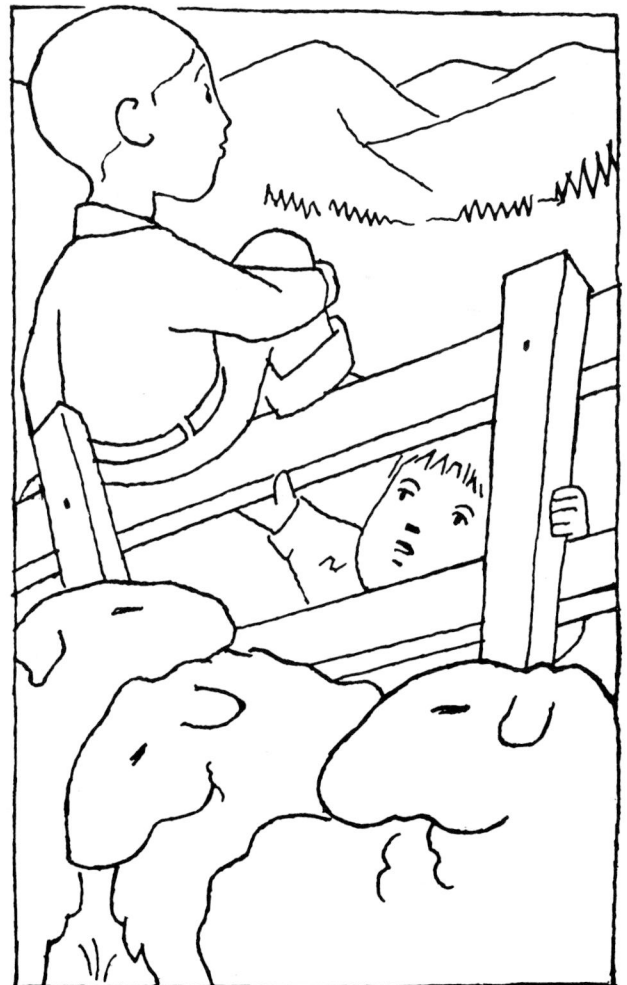

"It is better to be sitting here on the fence," said Pedro, "just watching and doing nothing else." ■ (From *. . . And Now Miguel* by Joseph Krumgold. Illustrated by Jean Charlot.)

"It would be good to know that we've sold at least one copy in Los Alamos. So that this particular mechanism, intricate as it is, might be studied up there on The Hill as well. For Los Alamos is as much an answer to a wish as any gilded coach that was turned from a pumpkin. To be sure, no one specifically wished for the town and the atom bomb to appear. All that was wanted—the wish—was for a more efficient steam engine, and a practical incandescent light, and such like conveniences. The bomb, as Gabriel observes, 'that part was the surprise.'

"If only one person up there on The Hill joins the adventure that my hero has with his ego, from the thundering affirmation, *I am Miguel*, to the only conclusion that permits one to grow,—that *Thy wish not mine be done*,—then I shall have been beyond all measure rewarded.

"As it is, I've been rewarded enough. It's enough that the book has helped me along my own way to the ideal place that I've spotted.... What a profound satisfaction it is for me to get my only literary honor—this Newbery Medal, for the writing of a children's book.''[1]

... *And Now Miguel* was translated into thirty-one languages. It won prizes both as a film and as a book, and the Newbery

(From the movie "And Now Miguel," starring Pat Cardi. Released by Universal Pictures, 1966.)

Medal gave Krumgold a new focus. "The medal gave me a new ambition, the first new one I have had since I was twelve years old. And that is to become a full-fledged author of children's books." [Norah Smaridge, "Joseph Krumgold," *Famous Modern Storytellers for Young People,* Dodd, 1969.[4]]

1958. The second book in a trilogy that explored the values by which a modern child comes of age was written at his New Jersey farm.

In July, Krumgold wrote his editor at Crowell: "I'm 30 pages from the end of *Onion John*. I'd hoped to be finished by now and well into the rewrite. But I ran into trouble with the end. I found the runaway sequence to Philadelphia very much off key with the rest of the book, far too melodramatic unless handled at greater length than the book can afford. I recall you had a similar fear about this episode, but I had to write my way into it unfortunately before I found out for myself.

"And so the delay. I'm very pleased with the new ending and with the entire book. And I look forward to the rewrite as a happy time. This will take about a month, of cutting down from about 300 pages and of sharpening the story I tell. I'll get started on this new draft immediately I'm finished, in about a week's time, and that should put a manuscript in your hands come September." [Elizabeth M. Riley, "Second Newbery to Krumgold," *Library Journal,* March 15, 1960.[5]]

1960. Awarded his second Newbery Medal, for *Onion John,* which made him the first person to receive two Newbery Medals. "Whatever literature might be... it isn't achieved by finishing your last breakfast cup of coffee and going into your room to light a cigarette and rip some of the stuff off. You can't put in a day's work at it.

"And if you try, you can't put in a day's work at much else. The normal dialogue between a writer and a reader is delicate enough to keep going. Once the question is asked whether all the talk has any cultural value, the whole thing stutters to a stop. The sentence gets pencilled, the paragraph shifted, and again and again—to meet this new abstract requirement of literature—the chapter gets revised. And replotted, and redrafted and rewritten. The problem can get desperate.

"Until you begin to wonder about the Newbery Medal, and the worth of it, as a piece of equipment up there on the shelf in your workroom. At least, that's the way it happened to me.

"And I'm glad to report that I, personally, was lucky. Simply because the book I was working on, *Onion John,* had to deal with this very problem. Curiously, I was writing about two characters who found themselves overwhelmed, as I was, by a substantial gift. We were all three of us concerned with our role as a recipient. Andy was being given an abstract future he didn't know anything about. Onion John was being dragged out of a meaningful past into a mechanical present he didn't know anything about. And I had the honor of carrying on a literature that, the more I rewrote and revised, I got to know less and less about.

"We considered the matter, the three of us. And we came to a common conclusion. Each one of us rejected our gifts. Onion John ran away. Andy finally spoke his mind to his father. And I, well I took the Newbery Medal away from the quiet—now grown desperate—of the room where I work. I put it outside my working day. I got rid of it. And when this was done, I was indeed able to go to work.

"Only then, did the familiar dialogue return—between me and my reader. And soon even my reader was forgotten and the

(From the animated filmstrip "Onion John." Produced by Random House/Miller Brody Productions, 1978.)

only presences in that room were Andy Rusch, Jr., and Onion John and myself—the three of us working our way to an end.

"And curiously, again, we came to a common end. We three discovered that whoever presents us with a gift must wholly accept in return whatever it is we have to offer. Andy gave his father—not the rational cooperation that was expected— but the only small present a child can make to a human being, his own deep love, his devotion and the admiration he feels.

"It was accepted.

"And once this was done, Onion John could come back. It was safe for him again. The boy had no need any longer to misuse him as a refuge. Nor had the father, to use him as a tool. And Onion John could again send back over the town of Serenity the smoke of his oak fire—and along with it the mystery and the wonder that this oversized image of a child brought to the people of the town.

"I'm sure it was accepted. For what town can get along without these gifts that our children bring us?

"And I—well, I did get the book done. And with the whole esoteric concern with literature placed to one side, I find that it too, to my astonishment, is accepted." [Joseph Krumgold, "Newbery Award Acceptance," *Newbery and Caldecott Medal Books: 1956-1965*, Horn Book, 1965.°]

1967. Completed his trilogy on the theme of a boy's progress to maturity with the publication of *Henry 3*. The trilogy included his three most widely read books, . . . *And Now Miguel, Onion John* and *Henry 3*. ". . . Running into fairy tales is a familiar professional predicament of mine. It happened with each of the three books that make up the trilogy I've written on how we grow up. In each case, I started out to write a thoroughly realistic story of how a child turns adult in one of three different areas of our society. In each case, I found I was writing, by the time I got halfway through the book, simply a new variation of a well-known fairy tale.

"Always this came as a surprise, one that I vaguely resented. After all, a basic vanity of authorship is that you have a new story to tell. It's belittling to come up against the fact that what you're actually doing is no more than an intricate piece of plagiarism. But once I got over this resentment, invariably the fairy tale that appeared offered me an advantage, the glimpse of a deeper meaning in the story under way than any I had suspected.

"In the book . . . *And Now Miguel* the fairy tale was the story of the Three Wishes, totally appropriate to a boy who grows up in a tradition-bound religious society. He must learn that the rewards of maturity come through believing in a wisdom far more universal than his own. And the third wish in this old story is always an acceptance of this belief, always some form of the Lord's Prayer, that 'thy will be done (again) on earth as it is in Heaven.' Like King Midas and all the other heroes of this tale, Miguel is obliged to make this wish in order to grow up.

"In *Onion John* the fairy tale proved to be the one about the Hero Who Learns the Language of the Animals. We're told that this story may preserve the dim memory of a prehistoric knack we had of communicating with our fellow beasts at a time when we domesticated some of them. It sets up the problem of identity—whether one is indeed a man or an animal—and ends with the hero trying to exploit, and being repudiated by, the creature whose language he's come to know. The boy in *Onion John* follows this pattern. Confused as he is by changing values of an American small town, his search is for his identity. The magic and adventure of speaking an unknown language doesn't help in the end. He finds out who he is and turns adult only when he forces a new acknowledgement of kinship with his own kind, with his own father.

"After this second experience, I found I was grateful for the fairy tale. It seemed to offer a guide, as reliable as a slide rule to a mathematician, for anyone who writes a book for children. But I had no premonition that I'd run into anything so archaic and so useful when it came to writing *Henry 3*.

"For this book took me into the suburbs, with none of Miguel's saints around and none of Onion John's rainmaking or stewing up a pot of gold. Here I dealt with the straightforward, the bedroom annex to the corporation acting as administrator of the very power I have been talking about, the science and technology that shapes and threatens our lives. This was completely new. How a boy grows up here had nothing to do, I thought, with any folklore.

"I was wrong. Henry's suburb turns out to be a community far more antique, in one respect, than either the small town of Onion John or the church town of Miguel. This suburb is a woman's town. Unlike the earlier two boys, Henry has no father to grow up with—not after the 8:02 leaves every morning. He lives in a matriarchy. And it is an unusual experience for a young fellow—for any young fellow, that is, since the dawn of recorded history.

"By happy coincidence, it happened that while working on *Henry 3* I found myself in the exact place where recorded history did dawn—in the Mediterranean. I was living in Rome and making films in Turkey and Italy and Spain, with frequent stopovers in Greece. The southern parts of all these countries are much more closely related to each other than they are to the rest of the states they belong to. . . .

"And one of the common ties binding these seaboard people together is the heritage of the Goddess, and her worship. In the south of Italy this adoration continues in the Catholic Church today as the Marianna cult, the devotion to the Virgin Mary as the Mother. In the Muslim faith of southern Turkey, Fatimah seems almost as important as Mohammed.

"What all this goes back to is the garden civilization that immediately preceded the writing of history, the culture of crop and cattle in which the woman had taken the place of the hunter as chief provider. The history of these unrecorded times, this matriarchy, comes to us as myth, made clearer each year by the improved skill of our archaeologists. . . .

"For anyone writing about a kid who grows up in a Long Island suburb outside New York City, what he thought was a brand-new kind of community, all this was pretty interesting. At least it was interesting to compare Ma, the early Hittite Goddess of Anatolia, with Ma, the suburban matron of our supermarket." [Joseph Krumgold, "Archetypes of the Twentieth Century," *School Library Journal*, October, 1968.[7]]

Of the overall theme in his children's trilogy, Krumgold remarked: ". . . They are a trilogy devoted to the drama of confirmation, that turn of life when a child is acknowledged to be grown-up. Whether this happens through ritual or less formal, it's a two-way process. The child is examined by the adult for his maturity and understanding. And—less obviously—the community is examined, its wisdom and values are measured with all innocence by the child. It is this fresh insight, the test we're put to by our young, that determines the shape of these stories." [D. L. Kirkpatrick, editor, "Joseph Krumgold," *Twentieth-Century Children's Writers*, St. Martin's, 1978.[8]]

Although Krumgold turned to writing children's books in mid life, he regarded his second profession as important as his first. "Of several possible reasons, the most complete answer to why I write books for children is that I find it therapeutic. Adults generally have lost their potential for growth, their ability to believe in countless possibilities for achievement. The only way we can get back to a life of choice, of personal change that will at least match the irresistible evolution of our technology, must certainly be to learn to grow again. . . . My own way of going back is through the . . . children's books that I've written." [A. H. Horowitz, "Joseph Krumgold," *Wilson Library Bulletin*, March, 1961.[9]]

July 10, 1980. Died at the age of seventy-two at his home in Hope, New Jersey. "The stories the old man tell of how we grew out of this earth and how we can continue to grow, the legends that recount for us the history of our own humanity—if ever these get into print at all, it's in the books that we make for our children."[1]

HOBBIES AND OTHER INTERESTS: Farming, fishing, swimming, skating.

FOR MORE INFORMATION SEE: Saturday Review, November 14, 1953, September 16, 1967, July 19, 1969; *New York Times Book Review*, November 15, 1953, October 8, 1967; *Horn Book*, December, 1953, February, 1968; *Library Journal*, March 15, 1954, March 15, 1960; *Publishers Weekly*, March 20, 1954; Bertha Mahony Miller and Elinor Whitney Field, editors, *Newbery Medal Books: 1922-1955*, Horn Book, 1955; A. H. Horowitz, "*Wilson Library Bulletin* Biography: Joseph Krumgold," *Wilson Library Bulletin*, March, 1961; Muriel Fuller, editor, *More Junior Authors*, H. W. Wilson, 1963; *Junior Bookshelf*, July, 1964.

Lee Kingman, editor, *Newbery and Caldecott Medal Books: 1956-1965*, Horn Book, 1965; *Christian Science Monitor*, November 2, 1967; *Book World*, November 5, 1967, September 7, 1969; *School Library Journal*, October, 1968, January, 1971; *Children's Literature in the Elementary School*, 2nd edition, Holt, 1968; Cornelia Meigs, editor, *A Critical History of Children's Literature*, revised edition, Macmillan, 1969; Norah Smaridge, *Famous Modern Storytellers for Young People*, Dodd, 1969; Martha E. Ward and Dorothy A. Marquardt, *Authors of Books for Young People*, 2nd edition, Scarecrow, 1971; Jacqueline S. Weiss, "Joseph Krumgold" (videocassette), Temple University, 1971; *Children and Books*, 4th edition, Scott, Foresman, 1972; D. L. Kirkpatrick, editor, *Twentieth-Century*

Children's Writers, St. Martin's, 1978, new edition, 1983; *Contemporary Literary Criticism*, Volume XII, Gale, 1981.

Obituaries: *New York Times*, July 16, 1980; *Variety*, July 23, 1980; *Publishers Weekly*, August 1, 1980; *AB Bookman's Weekly*, September 1, 1980.

KURLAND, Michael (Joseph) 1938- (Jennifer Plum)

PERSONAL: Born March 1, 1938, in New York, N.Y.; son of Jack (a manufacturer) and Stephanie (a dress designer; maiden name, Yacht) Kurland. *Education:* Attended Hiram College, 1955-56, University of Maryland, 1959-60, foreign study in Germany, 1960-61, and Columbia University, 1963-64. *Politics:* Whig. *Religion:* Secular Humanist. *Residence:* New York, N.Y. *Agent:* Sharon Jarvis, 260 Willard Ave., Staten Island, N.Y. 10314.

CAREER: Full-time writer, 1963—. High school English teacher in Ojai, Calif., 1968; managing editor, *Crawdaddy* magazine, 1969. Occasional director of plays for Squirrel Hill Theatre, 1972—. *Military service:* U.S. Army, Intelligence, 1958-61.

MEMBER: Authors Guild, Authors League of America, Mystery Writers of America, Science Fiction Writers of America, Institute for Twenty-first Century Studies, Computer Press Association. *Awards, honors:* Edgar Scroll from Mystery Writers of America, 1971, for *A Plague of Spies,* and 1979, for *The Infernal Device;* American Book Award nomination, 1979, for *The Infernal Device.*

MICHAEL KURLAND

WRITINGS—All fiction: (Under pseudonym Jennifer Plum) *The Secret of Benjamin Square*, Lancer Books, 1972; *The Whenabouts of Burr*, DAW Books, 1975; *Pluribus*, Doubleday, 1975; *Tomorrow Knight*, DAW Books, 1976; *The Princes of Earth*, T. Nelson, 1978; *The Infernal Device*, New American Library, 1978; (with S. W. Barton) *The Last President*, Morrow, 1980; *Death by Gaslight*, New American Library, 1982; (editor with H. Beam Piper) *First Cycle*, Ace Books, 1982; *Gashopper*, Doubleday, 1987; *Ten Little Wizards*, Berkley, 1987.

Fiction; published by Pyramid Publications: (With Chester Anderson) *Ten Years to Doomsday*, 1964; *Mission: Third Force*, 1967; *Mission: Tank War*, 1968; *A Plague of Spies*, 1969; *The Unicorn Girl*, 1969; *Transmission Error*, 1971.

Author of editorials for *National Examiner*, 1966, and of "Impropa-Ganda" column in *Berkeley Barb*, 1967. Contributor of articles to periodicals, including *Worlds of Tomorrow*.

WORK IN PROGRESS: A science-fantasy trilogy; a fact book about spies.

SIDELIGHTS: "*The Unicorn Girl* is part of a unique trilogy, the middlework of a linked three-book opus with three different authors. The first [is] *The Butterfly Kid* by Chester Anderson, and the third [is] *The Probability Pad* by T. A. Waters. The *Ten Little Wizards* is a continuation of the 'Lord Darly' novels of Randall Garrett.''

HOBBIES AND OTHER INTERESTS: Politics, bear baiting, barn storming, lighter-than-air craft, carnivals, vaudeville, juggling, book collecting, history, and "Apples and Pears."

LAIKEN, Deirdre S(usan) 1948-

PERSONAL: Born January 21, 1948, in New York, N.Y.; daughter of David and Shirley (Lewis) Laiken; married Alan J. Schneider (a psychotherapist), June 21, 1978. *Education:* State University of New York College at Buffalo, B.S.Ed., 1969, M.S.Ed., 1970. *Religion:* Jewish. *Agent:* Berenice Hoffman Literary Agency, 215 West 75th St., New York, N.Y. 10023.

CAREER: Buffalo Public Schools, Buffalo, N.Y., teacher of English, 1970-74; *Scholastic* (magazine), editor, 1974—; writer, 1976—. Part-time creative writing teacher. *Awards, honors: Listen to Me, I'm Angry* was selected one of New York Public Library's Books for the Teen Age, 1981 and 1982.

WRITINGS: Mind/Body/Spirit (young adult nonfiction), Messner, 1978; *Beautiful Body Building*, New American Library, 1979; (with husband, Alan J. Schneider) *Listen to Me, I'm Angry* (young adult nonfiction; illustrated by Bernice Myers), Lothrop, 1980; (with Lilian Rowen) *Speedwalking*, Putnam, 1981; *Daughters of Divorce* (adult nonfiction), Morrow, 1981; (with A. J. Schneider) *The Sweet Dreams Love Book: Understanding Your Feelings* (young adult), Bantam, 1983; (with Dorothy Greenburm) *Lovestrong: A Woman Doctor's True Story of Marriage and Medicine* (adult), Times Books, 1984.

SIDELIGHTS: "*Daughters of Divorce* is a result of five years of research and interviews. It is a study of how parental divorce affects women's attitudes, expectations, and perceptions. To write *Daughters of Divorce*, I spent many hours researching, interviewing women whose parents had divorced, and talking with psychoanalysts. I also included in the book many personal moments in my own life and insights I developed about my own parents' divorce and how that event shaped my attitudes.

"I am interested in writing on psychological topics for both children and adults."

HOBBIES AND OTHER INTERESTS: Travel (including residence in Portugal), athletics.

LATTIMORE, Eleanor Frances 1904-1986

OBITUARY NOTICE—See sketch in *SATA* Volume 7: American citizen born abroad; born June 30, 1904, in Shanghai, China; died after a brief illness, May 12, 1986, in Raleigh, N.C. Artist, illustrator, and author. Lattimore began her career as an artist but became best known as the illustrator and author of books for children, often creating stories based on her experiences growing up in China. Many of Lattimore's more than fifty books were translated into foreign languages and transcribed into braille. Her writings include the popular *Little Pear: The Story of a Little Chinese Boy; Little Pear and His Friends; Wu, the Gatekeeper's Son; The Monkey of Crofton; Laurie and Company;* and *The Taming of Tiger.*

FOR MORE INFORMATION SEE: Martha E. Ward and Dorothy A. Marquardt, *Authors of Books for Young People,* 2nd edition, Scarecrow, 1971; *Contemporary Authors, New Revision Series,* Volume 6, Gale, 1982; *Twentieth-Century Children's Writers,* 2nd edition, St. Martin's, 1983. Obituaries: *Raleigh News and Observer,* May 13, 1986.

LEDERER, Muriel 1929-

PERSONAL: Born May 31, 1929, in Chicago, Ill.; daughter of Arnold Philip (in manufacturing) and Stella (in real estate; maiden name, Franklin) Natenberg; married Frederick E. Lederer (a manufacturer's sales representative), February 16, 1952; children: Jill, William, Margaret. *Education:* Attended Vassar College, 1947-50; Lake Forest College, B.A., 1951. *Politics:* Republican. *Religion:* Jewish. *Home:* 756 Lincoln Ave., Winnetka, Ill. 60093. *Agent:* Anita Diamant, 310 Madison Ave., New York, N.Y. 10017.

CAREER: Free-lance writer, 1953-79; Arthur Andersen & Co., Chicago, Ill., marketing manager, 1979—. Lecturer; public relations and marketing consultant. *Member:* American Society of Journalists and Authors (director-at-large, 1976-78). *Awards, honors: Blue-Collar Jobs for Women* was chosen one of New York Public Library's Books for the Teen Age, 1980, 1981, and 1982.

WRITINGS: Guide to Career Education, Quadrangle, 1974; *New Job Opportunities for Women,* Publications International, 1975; *Blue-Collar Jobs for Women,* Dutton, 1979.

Author of nationally syndicated weekly newspaper column, "Memo to a Working Woman." Contributor to magazines and newspapers, including *Seventeen, McCall's, Viva, Woman's Day,* and *Science and Mechanics.*

The man who does not read good books has no advantage over the man who can't read them.
—Mark Twain
(pseudonym of Samuel L. Clemens)

LENS, Sidney 1912-1986

OBITUARY NOTICE—See sketch in *SATA* Volume 13: Surname originally Okun; name changed in 1930s; born January 28, 1912, in Newark, N.J.; died of cancer, June 18, 1986, in Chicago, Ill. Political activist, educator, advertising copywriter, journalist, editor, and author. Lens was known for his activities as a union organizer and political spokesman. He became involved with unions while working as a copywriter for the Hecht Brothers advertising agency in New York City. After organizing workers' activities in Detroit and Chicago, Lens began writing for *Progressive,* and in 1978 he became its senior editor. In his academic lectures at various universities and in his writings he was critical of American policies toward Communist Cuba and Vietnam, and he also opposed the development and use of nuclear weapons. In 1980 Lens made an unsuccessful bid for the U.S. Senate on the Citizens party ticket. He wrote such books as *The Counterfeit Revolution, A World in Revolution, The Futile Crusade, The Forging of the American Empire, The Day before Doomsday: An Anatomy of the Nuclear Arms Race,* the autobiography *Unrepentant Radical: An American Activist's Account of His Five Turbulent Decades,* and, for young adults, *The Bomb* and *Strikemakers and Strikebreakers.*

FOR MORE INFORMATION SEE: Martha E. Ward and Dorothy A. Marquardt, *Authors of Books for Young People,* 2nd edition, Scarecrow, 1971; *Contemporary Authors, New Revision Series,* Volume 17, Gale, 1986. Obituaries: *New York Times,* June 20, 1986; *Chicago Tribune,* June 22, 1986; *Facts on File,* June 27, 1986; *AB Bookman's Weekly,* July 7, 1986.

MARR, John S(tuart) 1940-

PERSONAL: Born April 22, 1940, in New York, N.Y.; son of James Pratt and Anne (Johnson) Marr; married; children: Jessica. *Education:* Yale University, B.A., 1962; New York Medical College, M.D., 1967; Harvard University, M.P.H., 1972. *Home:* 108 Valley Rd., Cos Cob, Conn. 06807. *Office:* Medicine and Environmental Health Dept., Exxon Corp., 1251 Avenue of the Americas, New York, N.Y. 10020.

CAREER: Metropolitan Hospital, New York City, resident in internal medicine, 1968-71; Bureau of Preventable Diseases, New York City, director, 1974-80, assistant commissioner, 1979-80; Exxon Corp., Medicine and Environmental Health Dept., New York City, assistant medical director, 1980—. *Military service:* U.S. Army, Health Environment Division.

John S. Marr and co-author Gwyneth Cravens.

1972-74, became major; U.S. Army Reserve, became Lieutenant Colonel. *Member:* American College of Preventive Medicine (fellow), American Society of Tropical Medicine and Hygiene, American College of Physicians (fellow), American Public Health Association, New York City Academy of Medicine, New York City Tropical Medicine Society, American College of Epidemiology (fellow), Alpha Omega Alpha, Explorers Club (New York City).

WRITINGS: The Good Drug and the Bad Drug (illustrated by Lynn Sweat; with teacher's manual), M. Evans, 1970; *A Breath of Air and a Breath of Smoke* (juvenile; illustrated by L. Sweat), M. Evans, 1971; *The Food You Eat* (juvenile; illustrated by L. Sweat), M. Evans, 1973; (with Gwyneth Cravens) *The Black Death* (novel), Dutton, 1976. Contributor of articles on infectious and tropical diseases to medical journals.

WORK IN PROGRESS: Research on a factual account of "Typhoid Mary."

SIDELIGHTS: "I am presently working for the Exxon Corporation and travel extensively to Latin America, where I am able to utilize my background in tropical medicine, preventive medicine and occupational medicine. My more recent writings, which periodically appear in Exxon's in-house publications, are devoted to wellness topics.

"I am happily married and live in Connecticut with my wife and young daughter, Jessica, who is already an avid reader."

FOR MORE INFORMATION SEE: New York Times, February 13, 1971; *Publishers Weekly,* November 1, 1976; *Newsweek,* January 10, 1977; *New York Times Book Review,* January 30, 1977; *Times Literary Supplement,* May 6, 1977.

MARTIN, Patricia Miles   1899-1986
(Patricia A. Miles; Jerry Lane, Miska Miles, pseudonyms)

OBITUARY NOTICE—See sketch in *SATA* Volume 43: Born November 14, 1899, in Cherokee, Kan.; died January 2, 1986, in San Mateo, Calif.; cremated; ashes scattered at sea. Author of children's books. Martin has earned many awards for her more than eighty books. Among her best-known writings are several works published under the name Miska Miles. They include *Annie and the Old One,* for which she received the Newbery Honor Book Award, *Wharf Rat,* for which she received a citation from the New York Academy of Sciences, and *Swim, Little Duck,* which was one of her many books honored as selections of the Junior Literary Guild. Martin also wrote such children's books as *In the Zoo* and *Run!* under the pseudonym Jerry Lane.

FOR MORE INFORMATION SEE: Contemporary Authors, New Revision Series, Volume 2, Gale, 1981; *Fifth Book of Junior Authors and Illustrators,* H. W. Wilson, 1983; *Twentieth-Century Children's Writers,* 2nd edition, St. Martin's, 1983; *The Writers Directory: 1984-1986,* St. James Press, 1983. Obituaries: *Times* (San Mateo), January 4, 1986.

McMULLAN, Kate (Hall)   1947-
(Katy Hall)

BRIEF ENTRY: Born January 16, 1947, in St. Louis, Mo. Author of books for children. After earning her B.A. from the University of Tulsa in 1969, McMullan taught at schools in Los Angeles, California, and Hahn, Germany. From 1976 to 1978 she was employed as an editor at Harcourt, Brace, Jovanovich in New York City. She has also served as a consultant to *Let's Find Out* magazine and as editor of *Early Bird.* McMullan is the author of over a dozen children's books, a number of them written under the name Katy Hall. These include her very first book entitled *Nothing but Soup* (Follett, 1976), featuring one Q. Leonard Faroop, a passionate lover of soup. While *Booklist* described the "energetic rhymes" in this story as "reminiscent of Dr. Seuss," *School Library Journal* praised the text that "slurps and sloshes along and rolls readily off the tongue."

Also under the name Katy Hall, McMullan has produced several joke-and-riddle books written with Lisa Eisenberg, among them *Chicken Jokes and Puzzles* (Scholastic, 1977), *A Gallery of Monsters* (Random House, 1980), *Fishy Riddles* (Dial, 1983), and *Buggy Riddles* (Dial, 1986). She also teamed up with author Jane O'Connor to write *Magic in the Movies: The Story of Special Effects* (Doubleday, 1980), which received honorable mention in the tenth annual Children's Science Book awards presentation by the New York Academy of Sciences. As Kate McMullan, her works include *The Mystery of the Missing Mummy* (Scholastic, 1984) and *The Great Ideas of Lila Fenwick* (Dial, 1986). Currently, she is working on another riddle book in collaboration with Eisenberg as well as *Be Prepared, Lila,* a sequel to her first Lila Fenwick book. *Home and office:* 88 Levington Ave., Apt. 12E, New York, N.Y. 10016.

McQUEEN, Lucinda

BRIEF ENTRY: A graduate of the Rhode Island School of Design, McQueen is the illustrator of more than a dozen picture books for children. Her work has been represented at several Society of Illustrators shows; she was the recipient of the Judges' Gold Seal Award at the first annual show sponsored by the society's Boston branch. As an illustrator, McQueen has displayed an ability to aptly interpret whatever message the author is conveying through the text. In a review of Graham Tether's *Skunk and Possum* (Houghton, 1979), for example, *Publishers Weekly* observed: "Tether's gentle humor and McQueen's soft watercolor scenes of a peaceful woodland harmonize in an effective collection of short stories." In the same manner, according to *Booklist, The Water of Life* (Four Winds, 1980) contains "[Jay] Williams' thoughtful message . . . evocatively wrapped in a gentle folkloric telling that McQueen deftly interprets with delicate yet full-bodied colors." *Publishers Weekly* again noted that "McQueen's colorful, artless drawings illustrate a momentous day for the kitten" in Dorothy M. Kunhardt's *Kitty's New Doll* (Golden Press, 1984), while in *Cheltenham's Party* (Golden Press, 1985) "the merriment in [Jan] Wahl's new tale is visible in . . . action-packed, full-color pictures." Among the other books McQueen has illustrated are Patty Wolcott's *The Cake Story* (Addison-Wesley, 1974) and *Beware of a Very Hungry Fox* (Addison-Wesley, 1975); Irene Herz's *Hey! Don't Do That!* (Prentice-Hall, 1978); Michaela Muntean's *Theodore Mouse Goes to Sea* (Golden Press, 1983); and Linda Hayward's *Snowy Day Bear, Windy Day Puppy* (both Putnam, 1985), *Rainy Day Kitten,* and *Sunny Day Bunny* (both Putnam, 1986).

'What is the use of a book,' thought Alice, 'without pictures or conversation?'

—Lewis Carroll
(pseudonym of Charles L. Dodgson)
(From *Alice's Adventures in Wonderland*)

MESSICK, Dale 1906-

BRIEF ENTRY: Original name, Dalia Messick; name changed in 1927; born in 1906 in South Bend, Ind. Creator of the comic strip "Brenda Starr, Reporter." Messick grew up in Hobart, Indiana, where she became interested in drawing. Not a good student, she finally graduated from high school at the age of twenty and studied one summer at the Art Institute of Chicago. She worked as an engraver, sign painter, commercial artist, and card designer in Chicago before moving to New York City, where she again worked at designing cards. Messick's ultimate goal, however, was to find work as a professional cartoonist. Because of the prejudice that existed against women in the field, she changed her name to Dale; even so, she was virtually ignored. After a disappointing interview with Joseph Medill Patterson, publisher of the *New York Daily News* and head of the Chicago Tribune-New York News Syndicate, in which Patterson admitted he would not hire a female cartoonist, Messick's work came to the attention of his assistant, Mollie Slott. Together, Messick and Slott worked out the plot for a feature strip featuring a red-headed female reporter. Although Patterson refused to run the strip in the *Daily News,* he did allow Slott to sell it to other newspapers.

On June 30, 1940, "Brenda Starr, Reporter" began running in Sunday editions; a daily strip was added in 1945. Messick later supervised a staff of assistants in the production of the strip. One drew backgrounds, the male characters, and did the lettering; another drew buildings and automobiles. Messick blocked the stories, did comic panel roughs, and drew the figure of Brenda Starr. The strip, popular despite its oftentimes improbable storyline and uncertain artwork, was carried by about 100 newspapers in the United States and five foreign countries by 1960. It eventually appeared in the *Daily News,* after Patterson's death. Messick wrote and illustrated one book based on the comic strip, *Brenda Starr, Girl Reporter* (Whitman Publishing, 1943), and a motion picture serial was produced in 1945. *Residence:* Chicago, Ill.

FOR MORE INFORMATION SEE: Current Biography Yearbook, H. W. Wilson, 1961; Judith O'Sullivan, *The Art of the Comic Strip,* University of Maryland Department of Art, 1971; *The World Encyclopedia of Comics,* Chelsea House, 1976; *Liberty's Women,* G. & C. Merriam, 1980; *Who's Who of American Women,* 13th edition, 1983; *Who's Who in America,* 43rd edition, Marquis, 1984; *Who's Who in American Art,* 16th edition, Bowker, 1984.

MOMADAY, N(avarre) Scott 1934-

PERSONAL: Surname is pronounced *Ma*-ma-day; born February 27, 1934, in Lawton, Okla.; son of Alfred Morris (a painter and teacher of art) and Mayme Natachee (a teacher and writer; maiden name, Scott) Momaday; married first wife, Gaye Mangold, September 5, 1959; married Regina Heitzer, July 21, 1978; children: (first marriage) Cael, Jill, Brit (all daughters); (second marriage) Lore (daughter). *Education:* University of New Mexico, A.B., 1958; Stanford University, M.A., 1960, Ph.D., 1963. *Home:* 1041 West Roller Coaster Rd., Tucson, Ariz. 85704. *Office:* Department of English, University of Arizona, Tucson, Ariz. 85721.

CAREER: University of California, Santa Barbara, assistant professor, 1963-65, associate professor of English, 1968-69; University of California, Berkeley, professor of English and comparative literature, 1969-73; Stanford University, Stanford, Calif., professor of English, 1973-82; University of Ar-

N. SCOTT MOMADAY

izona, Tucson, professor of English, 1982—. Artist; has exhibited his drawings and paintings in galleries. Trustee, Museum of American Indian, Heye Foundation, New York City, 1978—. Consultant, National Endowment for the Humanities, National Endowment for the Arts, 1970—.

MEMBER: Modern Language Association of America, American Studies Association, Gourd Dance Society of the Kiowa Tribe. *Awards, honors:* Academy of American Poets Prize, 1962, for poem "The Bear"; Guggenheim fellowship, 1966-67; Pulitzer Prize for fiction, 1969, for *House Made of Dawn;* National Institute of Arts and Letters grant, 1970; shared Western Heritage Award with David Muench, 1974, for nonfiction book *Colorado, Summer/Fall/Winter/Spring;* Premio Letterario Internazionale Mondello (International Literary Prize, Mondello, Sicily, Italy), 1979, for *House Made of Dawn.*

WRITINGS: (Editor) *The Complete Poems of Frederick Goddard Tuckerman,* Oxford University Press, 1965; *The Journey of Tai-me* (retold Kiowa Indian folktales; original etchings by Bruce S. McCurdy), limited edition, University of California, Santa Barbara, 1967, enlarged edition published as *The Way to Rainy Mountain* (illustrated by his father, Alfred Momaday), University of New Mexico Press, 1969; *House Made of Dawn* (novel), Harper, 1968, limited edition, Franklin Library, 1977; (editor) *American Indian Authors,* Houghton, 1971; *Colorado, Summer/Fall/Winter/Spring* (nonfiction; illustrated with photographs by David Muench), Rand McNally, 1973; *Angle of Geese and Other Poems,* David Godine, 1974; *The Gourd Dancer* (self-illustrated), Harper, 1976; *The Names: A Memoir,* Harper, 1976.

Also author of film script of Frank Water's novel, *The Man Who Killed the Deer*. Contributor of articles and poems to periodicals; frequent contributor to *New York Times*.

M. H____" (record; poems from
louse Made of Dawn),

nerican poetry, tenta-
Science and Literature
iversity Press; a novel
day; a book on story-

Lawton, Oklahoma in
the Kiowa Indians on
her, Mayme Natachee
n early American pi-
ived from a Cherokee
was a Kiowa Indian.
father's name—at that
was the name that was
the only name that he
maries came in, and the
of the surname and the
er was given the name
Mammedaty, and Mam-
his family. It was passed
noma still use that spell-
omaday."

where his parents worked
in the state's canyon and

You may wish to discuss your decision.

should choose the higher study skills and probably
level course would offer a good
the borderline in terms of
will need to decide which
one of your scores is at a
of the span of scores, or

res primarily and the

tion of English sounds,
dents with severe

pending upon courses

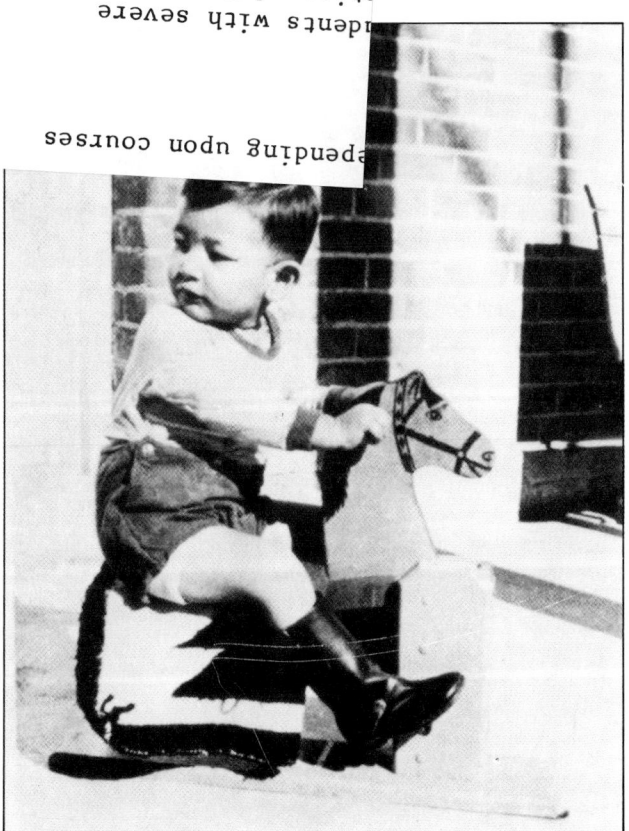

The horse is Tony. I am being pursued. ■ (From *The Names: A Memoir* by N. Scott Momaday. Photograph reproduction by Jim Kalett.)

(From *The Gourd Dancer* by N. Scott Momaday. Illustrated by the author.)

mountain country. "When my parents and I moved to Jemez I was 12 years old. I could not have imagined a more beautiful or exotic place. The village and the valley, the canyons and the mountains had been there from the beginning of time, waiting for me, so it seemed; they were my discovery. Marco Polo in the court of Kublai Khan had nothing on me. I was embarked upon the greatest adventure of all; I had come to the place of my growing up.

"The landscape was full of mystery and of life. The autumn was in full bloom. The sun cast a golden light upon the adobe walls and the cornfields; it set fire to the leaves of willows and cottonwoods along the river; and a fresh, cold wind ran down from the canyons and carried the good scents of pine and cedar smoke, of bread baking in the beehive ovens and of rain in the mountains. There were horses in the plain and angles of geese in the sky.

"Gradually and without effort I entered into the motion of life there. In the winter dusk I heard coyotes barking by the river, the sound of drums in the kiva and the voice of the village crier, ringing at the rooftops. And on summer nights of the full moon I saw old men in their ceremonial dress, running after witches.

"I had a horse named Pecos, a fleet-footed roan gelding, which was my great glory for a time. I did a lot of riding in those days, and I got to be very good at it; my Kiowa ancestors, who were centaurs, would have been proud of me. I came to know the land by going out upon it in all seasons, getting into it until it became the very element in which I lived my daily life.

Five generations. Kau-au-ointy, Keah-dine Keah, Mammecaty, Clara, and Marland. ■ (From *The Names: A Memoir* by N. Scott Momaday. Photograph reproduction by Jim Kalett.)

"This was discovery, crucial, once and for all. And it was, I see now, a matter of some moment and intricacy. For not only did I discover an incomparable landscape in all of its colors and moods, but I discovered myself within it. From that time I have known that the sense of place is a dominant factor in my blood. It happens that I have traveled far and wide, and I have made my home elsewhere. But some elemental part of me remains in the hold of northern New Mexico. . . .

"When I was a boy I climbed into the great octagonal bell tower of the church—the view commands the whole of the village of Jemez Springs and indeed the whole of the canyon to its mouth. It is a breathtaking sight. The walls of the canyon rise hundreds of feet directly above the village, and the hours of daylight are relatively few, but the consequent early morning and later afternoon light is extraordinary. It exists for a time as a diaphanous aura on the high skyline, then it touches fire to the western vertical face of the cliff; and in the afternoon the shadow of the west wall rises slowly on the east wall until the great rock face, above timber, half red and half white, blazes above the dark canyon floor. Snow comes down from the north with the big logging trucks, hauling their tons of pine. In summer the canyon is lime green with aspens and willows and cottonwoods, and yellow with paintbrush and

chamisa." [N. Scott Momaday, "Discovering the Land of Light," *New York Times Magazine,* March 17, 1985.[1]]

Momaday inherited his artistic skill and writing ability from his father who was an artist and from his mother who was a writer. He began writing seriously in college while an undergraduate student at the University of New Mexico. "I think I had wanted to be a writer, as so many young people do, but I didn't know what that meant until I was an undergraduate. Then I started writing poems and kept up the writing of poetry pretty much through graduate school. Then I turned to prose."

Following graduation, Momaday was awarded a creative writing fellowship at Stanford University. His first published book, *The Complete Poems of Frederick Goddard Tuckerman,* was originally his doctoral dissertation. "When I got to Stanford I didn't really know much about American literature. In fact, when I went there it was as a fellow in creative writing, and I did not intend to take an advanced degree at first. I thought, well, I'll go, and this is a good opportunity to write, since they're paying my way for a year. But when I got to Stanford, Yvor Winters, who became my close friend and advisor, talked me into staying on through graduate school. I think it was he who really got me interested in Tuckerman. I didn't know

My parents about the time of their marriage. ■ (From *The Names: A Memoir* by N. Scott Momaday. Photograph reproduction by Jim Kalett.)

Tuckerman when I went to Stanford, but Winters had taught some of Tuckerman's poems in one of his courses. I got particularly interested in that period, I think, mainly because of my deep admiration of the poems of Emily Dickinson. But then when I was thinking about a dissertation I boiled it down to a couple of choices, and Tuckerman turned out to be the most feasible—I had discovered that his manuscripts were collected in one place and it would not be difficult to work with them. So I selected Tuckerman on that basis. And he is, besides, a great poet, after all.''

Momaday's second book, *The Way to Rainy Mountain,* told the story of the Kiowas' journey 300 years ago from Yellowstone down to the plains where they domesticated horses and became a sophisticated society. ''The Indian writer has the advantage of a very rich spiritual experience. As much can be said, certainly, of some non-Indian writers. But the non-Indian writers of today are culturally deprived. I think, in the sense that they don't have the same sense of heritage that the Indian has. I'm told this time and time again by my students, who say, 'Oh, I wish I knew more about my grandparents; I wish I knew more about my ancestors and where they came from and what they did.' I've come to believe them. It seems to me that the Indian writer ought to make use of that advantage. One of his subjects ought certainly to be his cultural investment in the world. It is a unique and complete experience, and it is a great subject in itself.''

The Way to Rainy Mountain was originally a collection of Kiowa Indian folktales that was published as *The Journey of Tai-me,* with etchings by Bruce S. McCurdy. In 1969 it appeared as an enlarged edition, retitled *The Way to Rainy Mountain* and illustrated by the author's father, Alfred Momaday.

During that same year, Momaday was the recipient of the Pulitzer Prize for fiction for his novel *House Made of Dawn.* The selection of a relatively unknown author for such a distinguished prize came as a shock to the publishing community as well as to Momaday. ''I had started writing *House Made of Dawn* when I left Stanford in 1963 as a graduate student. When I graduated I went to Santa Barbara, which was my first teaching post, and there I started writing *House Made of Dawn.* I had a letter one day from Frances McCullough, who had been the editor of the literary magazine at Stanford, called *Sequoia.* She had published some of my poems there when I was a student and she was a student (she was an undergraduate student at that time), and when we both left Stanford, she went to New York and entered a publishing house—I've forgotten which one. But anyway, she moved over to Harper & Row after a time, and she wrote to me and asked me if I had a sufficient number of poems for a book that I might be willing to submit. I didn't have enough and I told her that, but I said, 'I happen to be working on a novel. Why don't I send you some of that?' So I sent her what I had; it must have been, oh, two chapters, say. Harper & Row accepted the novel, and that's how it all happened. It was all quite a fluke, really. I was very fortunate, and believe me, it's not lost upon me. I'm grateful.''

Besides writing prose and poetry, the author has taught English literature in several universities and is an accomplished artist. He also maintains a rigid daily writing schedule. ''Writing, I find, goes on in the mind for a long time before you really put anything down on paper. . . . When I'm really writing I do it in the morning. I find that I can write about six hours and that's all. But I try to do it every day and get an early start when I think my energies are at their very best.

''I want to keep painting and writing. And I want to write a book on storytelling eventually. I haven't really begun that,

but I have thought about it a good deal and I've signed a contract with Oxford for it, though I don't have a deadline yet.

''I'm interested in the origin of storytelling and the function of the storyteller and what his relationship is to his listener. There is a great deal to be learned about that. I will, of course, focus on American Indian storytelling, but I also want to be able to make references to other ancient forms of storytelling. That's something in the future, and it may be the next thing I turn to. . . .''

FOR MORE INFORMATION SEE: New York Times Book Review, June 9, 1968, June 16, 1974, March 6, 1977; *Best Sellers,* June 15, 1968, April, 1977; *Nation,* August 5, 1968; *Commonweal,* September 20, 1968; *Listener,* May 15, 1969; *New Yorker,* May 17, 1969; *Times Literary Supplement,* May 22, 1969; *Spectator,* May 23, 1969; *Observer,* May 25, 1969; *Saturday Review,* June 21, 1969; *Southwest Review,* summer, 1969, spring, 1978; *Washington Post,* November 21, 1969; N. Scott Momaday, *The Way to Rainy Mountain,* University of New Mexico Press, 1969.

New York Times, June 3, 1970; *Southern Review,* winter, 1970, January, 1978, April, 1978; Marion E. Gridley, editor, *Indians of Today,* I.C.F.P., 1971; M. E. Gridley, *Contemporary American Indian Leaders,* Dodd, 1972; *Contemporary Literary Criticism,* Gale, Volume II, 1974, Volume XIX, 1981; *South Dakota Review,* winter, 1975-76; N. S. Momaday, *The Names: A Memoir,* Harper, 1976; *Contemporary Novelists,* 2nd edition, St. Martin's, 1976; *Atlantic,* January, 1977; *New York Review of Books,* February 3, 1977; *Harper's,* February, 1977; *Sewanee Review,* summer, 1977; *World Literature Today,* summer, 1977; *American Indian Quarterly,* May, 1978; *American Literature,* January, 1979; *American Poetry Review,* July/August, 1984; *New York Times Magazine,* March 17, 1985.

MOONEY, Elizabeth C(omstock) 1918-1986

OBITUARY NOTICE: Born February 8, 1918, in Rome, N.Y.; died of cancer, May 20, 1986, in Washington, D.C. Journalist and author. A free-lance writer since 1946, Mooney had previously served the *Utica Press* and *Observer-Dispatch* as a reporter and bureau chief. She wrote her first three books, *Jane Addams, The Mystery of the Narrow Land,* and *The Sandy Shoes Mystery,* for young adults, but she turned to writing nonfiction for adults in the 1970s. Mooney's books *In the Shadow of the White Plague,* a memoir of her mother's battle with tuberculosis, and *Not My Daughter: Facing Up to Adolescent Pregnancy,* were both published in 1979. Additional titles include *Alone: Surviving as a Widow* and *Men and Marriage: The Changing Role of Husbands.* During the late 1970s and early 1980s Mooney wrote the column ''The Weekend Traveller'' for the *Washington Post,* and she contributed travel articles to women's magazines and to such newspapers as the *Boston Globe* and *Newsday.* A collection of these pieces was published as *Country Adventures.*

FOR MORE INFORMATION SEE: Elizabeth C. Mooney, *Alone: Surviving as a Widow,* Putnam, 1981; *Contemporary Authors, New Revision Series,* Volume 9, Gale, 1983. Obituaries: *Washington Post,* May 22, 1986.

To read without reflecting is like eating without digesting.

—Edmund Burke

MOORE, Don W.   1905(?)-1986

OBITUARY NOTICE: Born about 1905; died April 7, 1986, in Venice, Fla. Screenwriter, journalist, and author of comic strips. Moore was best known as the author of the popular syndicated comic strip "Flash Gordon," which appeared weekly in newspapers throughout the United States. He began his journalism career in the 1920s, working for newspapers in Miami, Florida. Later he moved to the Bahamas where he worked simultaneously—although surreptitiously—for the competing United Press and Associated Press news services and founded the Nassau News Bureau. In the 1930s Moore returned to the United States and, while working in New York City as an editor of *Argosy All-Story Weekly,* an adventure and mystery magazine, he began to write "Flash Gordon" for King Features. The strip was drawn by Alex Raymond. Moore also wrote the "Jungle Jim" comic strip and worked as a film writer for Warner Brothers and RKO Studios before turning to television in 1949. His first television script was "Captain Video." Later he also wrote scripts for such popular shows as "Rawhide," "Sea Hunt," and "Death Valley Days." Obituaries: *New York Times,* April 10, 1986; *Facts on File,* April 18, 1986; *New York Times Biographical Service,* April, 1986.

MOORES, Richard (Arnold)   1909-1986 (Dick Moores)

OBITUARY NOTICE: Born December 12, 1909, in Lincoln, Neb.; died April 22 (one source cites April 23), 1986, in Asheville, N.C. Television producer and cartoonist. Moores was best known as the author and illustrator of the syndicated comic strip "Gasoline Alley," which appeared in 180 daily newspapers and 125 Sunday editions. In 1950 he co-produced national television's first daily cartoon shows for NBC Comics, and in 1956 he began working for Frank King, the creator of "Gasoline Alley." When King died four years later, Moores took over as chief artist and writer for the comic strip.

Moores began his career in 1931 as an assistant to Chester Gould, creator of "Dick Tracy" comics and later worked for United Features Syndicate as the writer and illustrator of "Jim Hardy," a detective strip which became a western titled "Windy and Paddles." In 1942 Moores joined Walt Disney Studios as a newspaper-comic artist, co-developing the "Scamp" strip in 1955. He also illustrated a number of Disney books and record albums. Collections of his comics were published as *The Smoke from Gasoline Alley, Gasoline Alley,* and *Jim Hardy: An Original Compilation of First Year 1936-1937.* Moores won two Reuben Awards from the National Cartoonist Society, one in 1974 for best story strip and the other in 1975 as that year's outstanding cartoonist.

FOR MORE INFORMATION SEE: Judith O'Sullivan, *The Art of the Comic Strip,* University of Maryland Department of Art, 1971; *Contemporary Authors,* Volumes 69-72, Gale, 1978; *The World Encyclopedia of Cartoons,* Gale, 1980; *Who's Who in America,* 44th edition, Marquis, 1985. Obituaries: *Daily Variety,* April 23, 1986; *Chicago Tribune,* April 24, 1986; *International Herald Tribune,* April 24, 1986; *New York Times Biographical Service,* April, 1986.

Do you believe in fairies? Say quick that you believe.
If you believe, clap your hands!
—Sir James Matthew Barrie
(From *Peter Pan*)

MORRILL, Leslie H(olt)   1934-

PERSONAL: Born February 10, 1934, in Hudson, N.H.; son of Edwin Arthur (a laborer) and Leona (a housewife; maiden name, Stone) Morrill; married Judith Garziano (a landscape designer), December 27, 1965; children: Melissa. *Education:* School of the Boston Museum of Fine Arts, certificate, 1960; Tufts University, B.S., 1960; Cranbrook Academy of Art, M.F.A., 1965. *Home:* 161 Bishop Lane, Madison, Conn. 06443. *Agent:* Dilys Evan, 40 Park Ave., New York, N.Y. 10016.

CAREER: Artist and illustrator of books for children. Groton Public Schools, Groton, Conn., art supervisor, 1961-65; Slippery Rock State College, Slippery Rock, Penn., assistant professor, 1967-69. Also worked as a school art teacher in Webster, Mass. *Exhibitions:* Ball State University, Muncie, Ind., 1965; Dulin Gallery, Knoxville, Tenn., 1967; *Cricket* magazine travelling shows, 1978, 1979; has also exhibited in New York City, 1983, 1984, 1985. *Military service:* U.S. Air Force, 1953-57. *Member:* Graphic Artists Guild (member of governing board).

AWARDS, HONORS: Purchase Prize from Dulin Gallery, 1967, for portrait of Susie Katz; *Book World's* Spring Book Festival Award middle honor book, 1971, for *Beaver Valley; Life Battles Cold* was chosen one of Child Study Association of America's Children's Books of the Year, 1974, and *Guess What Rocks Do,* 1975; *The Captain of Battery Park* was chosen for the American Institute of Graphic Arts Book Show, 1979; *Mouse Six and the Happy Birthday* was chosen one of the

LESLIE H. MORRILL

International Reading Association's Children's Choices, 1979, and for the American Institute of Graphic Arts Book Show, 1979; *Biological Clocks* was chosen as an Outstanding Science and Trade Book by the National Science Teachers Association and the Children's Book Council, 1983.

ILLUSTRATOR—Juvenile: Anne Eliot Crompton, *The Sorcerer*, Little, Brown, 1971; Walter D. Edmonds, *Beaver Valley*, Little, Brown, 1971; Mary Wesley, *Speaking Terms*, Gambit, 1971; Mildred Teal and John Teal, *Pigeons and People*, Little, Brown, 1972; Pearl S. Buck, *Mrs. Starling's Problem*, John Day, 1973; Matt Christopher, *Desperate Search*, Little, Brown, 1973; Harold Coy, *Man Comes to America*, Little, Brown, 1973; Lucy Kavaler, *Life Battles Cold*, John Day, 1973; Eve Bunting, *Box, Fox, Ox, and the Peacock*, Ginn, 1974; David McCord, *Away and Ago: Rhymes of the Never Was and Always Is*, Little, Brown, 1974.

Russell Freedman, *Growing Up Wild: How Young Animals Survive*, Holiday House, 1975; John Teal and Mildred Teal, *The Sargasso Sea*, Little, Brown, 1975; Barbara Rinkoff, *Guess What Rocks Do*, Lothrop, 1975; Delia Goetz, *Valleys*, Morrow, 1976; Margery Sharp, *Bernard the Brave: A Miss Bianca Story*, Little, Brown, 1977; Laurence Pringle, *Animals and Their Niches: How Species Share Resources*, Morrow, 1977; Miska Miles (pseudonym of Patricia Miles Martin), *Mouse Six and the Happy Birthday*, Dutton, 1978; M. Miles, *Noisy Gander*, Dutton, 1978; Eugene Pool, *The Captain of Battery Park*, Addison-Wesley, 1978; M. Sharp, *Bernard into Battle: A Miss Bianca Story*, Little, Brown, 1978; Gladys Conklin, *Black*

I have a very elegant figure—for what I am. ■ (From *The Wind in the Willows* by Kenneth Grahame. Illustrated by Leslie Morrill.)

Widow Spider—Danger!, Holiday House, 1979; Sheila Dolan, *The Wishing Bottle*, Houghton, 1979; Patricia Reilly Giff, *Fourth-Grade Celebrity*, Delacorte, 1979; P. R. Giff, *The Girl Who Knew It All*, Delacorte, 1979; Beth Hilgartner, *Great Gorilla Grins: An Abundance of Animal Alliterations*, Little, Brown, 1979.

P. R. Giff, *Left-Handed Shortstop*, Delacorte, 1980; M. Miles, *This Little Pig*, Dutton, 1980; Larry Callen, *Dashiel and the Night*, Dutton, 1981; Vicki Cobb, *How to Really Fool Yourself: Illusions for All Your Senses*, Lippincott, 1981; Elizabeth Parsons, *The Upside-Down Cat*, Atheneum, 1981; P. R. Giff, *The Winter Worm Business*, Delacorte, 1981; Margaret Laurence, *Jason's Quest*, Seal Books, 1981; Mary Caldwell, *Morning Rabbit Morning*, Harper, 1981; Phyllis Reynolds Naylor, *All Because I'm Older*, Atheneum, 1981; Mary Calhoun, *The Night the Monster Came*, Morrow, 1982; Ted Clymer and M. Miles, *Horse and the Bad Morning*, Dutton, 1982; Kenneth Grahame, *The Wind in the Willows*, Bantam, 1982; Kathryn Jackson and Byron Jackson, *Katie the Kitten*, Golden Press, 1982; Judith Whitelock McInerney, *Judge Benjamin: Superdog*, Holiday House, 1982; Sarah R. Riedman, *Biological Clocks*, Crowell, 1982; George Selden, *Irma and Jerry*,

Mitchell looked as if he were freezing. ■ (From *The Winter Worm Business* by Patricia Reilly Giff. Illustrated by Leslie Morrill.)

Kangaroo rats and pocket mice collect food in their fur-lined cheek pouches. ■ (From *Animals and Their Niches: How Species Share Resources* by Laurence Pringle. Illustrated by Leslie Morrill.)

Avon, 1982; Judy Delton, *Back Yard Angel,* Houghton, 1983; R. Freedman, *Dinosaurs and Their Young,* Holiday House, 1983; James Howe, *The Celery Stalks at Midnight,* Atheneum, 1983; J. W. McInerney, *Judge Benjamin: The Superdog Secret,* Holiday House, 1983; Sharon Sigmond Shebar and Judith Schoder, *The Bell Witch,* Messner, 1983; Margarete Sigl Corbo and Diane Marie Barras, *Arnie the Darling Starling,* Houghton, 1983.

Clifton Fadiman, compiler and author of commentary, *The World Treasury of Children's Literature,* Little, Brown, Volumes 1-2, 1984, Volume 3, 1985; P. R. Giff, *Rat Teeth,* Delacorte, 1984; J. Howe, *Morgan's Zoo,* Atheneum, 1984; (with Ted Enik) Lois McCoy and Floyd McCoy, *The Bytes Brothers GOTO a Getaway: A Solve-It-Yourself Computer Mystery,* Bantam, 1984; L. McCoy and F. McCoy, *The Bytes Brothers Input an Investigation: A Solve-It-Yourself Computer Mystery,* Bantam, 1984; L. McCoy and F. McCoy, *The Bytes Brothers Program a Problem: A Solve-It-Yourself Computer Mystery,* Bantam, 1984; J. W. McInerney, *Judge Benjamin: The Superdog Rescue,* Holiday House, 1984; Walter Dean Myers, *Mr. Monkey and the Gotcha Bird: An Original Tale,* Delacorte, 1984; Willo Davis Roberts, *Eddie and the Fairy Godpuppy,* Atheneum, 1984; Marileta Robinson, *The Big Bicycle Race* (cassette available), Parker Brothers, 1984; Pat Ruane and Jane Hyman, *LOGO Activities for the Computer: A Beginner's Guide,* Wanderer Books, 1984; J. Delton, *Angel in Charge,* Houghton, 1985; J. W. McInerney, *Judge Benjamin: The Superdog Surprise,* Holiday House, 1985; Lillian Stokes and Donald Stokes, *Mammals of North America,* Little, Brown, 1985; Gary Gygax and Flint Dille, *Sagard the Barbarian: The Ice Dragon,* Archway, 1985; Walter R. Brooks, *Freddy the Politician,* Knopf, 1986; J. W. McInerney, *Judge Benjamin: The Superdog Gift,* Holiday House, 1986; (with Kurt Wiese) W. R. Brooks, *Freddy and the Perilous Adventure,* Knopf, 1986; (with K. Wiese) W. R. Brooks, *Freddy Goes Camping,* Knopf, 1986; (with K. Wiese) W. R. Brooks, *Freddy the Pilot,* Knopf, 1986; G. Gygax and F. Dille, *Sagard the Barbarian: The Green Hydra,* Archway, in press; G. Gygax and F. Dille, *The Crimson Sea,* Archway, in press.

"Hardy Boys Mystery Stories" series; written by Franklin W. Dixon (house pseudonym); published by Wanderer Books: *Mystery of the Samurai Sword,* 1979; *Night of the Werewolf,* 1979; *The Apeman's Secret,* 1980; *The Mummy Case,* 1980; *Mystery of Smuggler's Cove,* 1980; *The Pentagon Spy,* 1980; *The Hardy Boys Handbook: Seven Stories of Survival,* 1980; *The Four-Headed Dragon,* 1981; *The Infinity Clue,* 1981; *The Outlaw's Silver,* 1981; *The Stone Idol,* 1981; *The Submarine Caper,* 1981; *The Vanishing Thieves,* 1981; *The Billion Dollar Ransom,* 1982; *Tic-Tac-Terror,* 1982; *Track of the Zombie,* 1982; *The Voodoo Plot,* 1982 (Morrill was not associated with other books in the series).

"Choose Your Own Adventure" series; all published by Bantam: *Indian Trail,* 1983; R. A. Montgomery, *Lost on the Amazon,* 1984; Edward Packard, *Mountain Survival,* 1984; Fred Graver, *Journey to Stonehenge,* 1984; Shannon Gilligan, *Mona Is Missing,* 1985; Louise M. Foley, *Danger at Anchor Mine,* 1985; Susan Saunders, *Attack of the Monster Plants,* 1986; Raymond Montgomery, *The Owl Tree,* 1986.

Also illustrator of films and filmstrips, including "Animals, Animals: Song of the Turtle" for ABC-TV, 1980. Contributor of illustrations to magazines, including *Cricket.*

WORK IN PROGRESS: Illustrations for another of McInerney's "Judge Benjamin" books; *Fang,* concerned with a child's growth, a book about a child who projects his fears onto his dog, and than teaches the dog to negotiate these fears. "As usual, I'm working on a number of things. I think my favorite work in progress is *The Lost Notebooks of Loren Eisley* for Little Brown; a Pinocchio coloring book I've developed from the conceptual stage and hope to fully design for Random House."

SIDELIGHTS: "I grew up in Hudson, a small town in New Hampshire. You may remember the song Frank Sinatra sang, 'It Was a Very Good Year,' with the description of the village green. Well, Hudson was like the town in the song. We had a village green complete with a Civil War cannon and beautiful trees.

"What set Hudson apart from other small towns was Benson's Wild Animal Farm. Originally, the farm was used as a quarantine station for animals brought into the U.S. At that time, New York and New Orleans were the two approved points of entry for animals, and many were shipped directly to Hudson where they stayed until they passed health requirements. The keeper of the station realized that people wanted to see the animals and began to charge admission. He eventually started making trips to Africa and Asia to buy animals for what became one of the first outdoor zoos in the United States. It was quite odd to live in a small New England town—with all that that implies—which was regarded as one of the major international centers for wild animals.

"I worked at Benson's all through my later childhood and adolescence. By then, the farm had trainers from all over the world. In fact, the first two American women to become big cat trainers worked there. My time was spent primarily with the horse act, periodically with the lions and other cats and a stint with one of the smaller animal acts. The acts went on at two-hour intervals all day long. I am sure that this was the start of my work as an illustrator. One of my strengths is drawing animals. It's not that I had time to sketch on the job, but I was observing and learning all the time, without ever realizing it.

"I began to draw long before I can remember. My mother liked to paint, and did paintings as gifts and for church bazaars. One year, unbeknownst to us children, our parents spent months creating in wood an entire barn and yard of birds and animals. It was the most marvelous Christmas gift we had ever received, and looking back, there was a special poignancy, because it was in a particularly hard year in the none-too-prosperous late 1930s.

"My father was a laborer, my mother a housewife who had aspired to become a dancer until she discovered she had a heart condition. My three brothers and I were very independent as kids, not competitive, but not all that close. The one thing that drew us together was our intense involvement with the arts, particularly dance. My older brother took ballroom dancing and, in fact, competed; another did interpretive dance; I tapped. In addition, we all studied ballet. As you can imagine, this was highly unusual in a small town and certainly wasn't considered the most masculine activity in the world! It made for a certain feistiness on our part.

"I can remember the first time I was taken to the Boston Opera House at the age of thirteen. The physical reality of the place was something I'll never forget. The building itself was sumptuous and as this was a Saturday performance, many audience members were wearing evening clothes. I was all eyes! We went to see the Ballet Russes de Monte Carlo, and saw legendary dancers Maria Tallchief, Danilova, and Leonid Massine.

The horse laid her hay on the ground. ■ (From *Mouse Six and the Happy Birthday* by Miska Miles. Illustrated by Leslie Morrill.)

Dear Tracy, I received your letter. ■ (From *Fourth-Grade Celebrity* by Patricia Reilly Giff. Illustrated by Leslie Morrill.)

Dear Cassandra Eleanor.... ■ (From *Fourth-Grade Celebrity* by Patricia Reilly Giff. Illustrated by Leslie Morrill.)

"Very early on I knew I was at home in that large body we call 'art.' Books were very important in our house. We had some illustrated books, of which my favorite was *Mary Murphy,* about an Irish potato, much anthropomorphized. My mother wrote poetry, as did all of her sons. I took myself very seriously at the time, although I never considered becoming a writer. In third and fourth grade, I was mad about 'Pogo' and the work of Hal Foster. I was impressed with the authenticity of Foster's work and concluded that there was little to equal it. Even the costume films done in the U.S. at the time, romantic and swashbuckling, were unreal. Looking back, Foster's work reminds me of the contemporary costume movies done in England which are so careful to capture an era with such accuracy you believe you are there.

"At seventeen I had to decide whether or not I was going to pursue a career in dance. Dancers have a comparatively short 'performing' life, and the self-sacrifice necessary to dance well for such a limited time was something to which I couldn't commit myself.

"So after high school I went directly to the Boston Museum School. I lived at home and commuted about forty miles to Boston. It was excellent training in the fundamentals, and very classical when compared with what's taught in most art schools today. Life drawing, for example, was a requirement every year. I stayed in school for one year and then joined the Air Force.

When the taxi driver glanced into his rearview mirror, his cigar almost fell out of his mouth. ■ (From *Morgan's Zoo* by James Howe. Illustrated by Leslie Morrill.)

"I suppose I could have gotten my service deferred, but I never considered it seriously. In those days, one didn't question serving in the military. Also, after a year at school, I was just about broke. For someone in my financial position, education on the GI Bill was a real boon, and the prospect of travel was an enticement, to say the least."

1953-1957. "My four years in the Air Force were as atypical of military service as they could have been. I was able to choose my posting and picked Germany, where I served in a special security/intelligence outfit. When we were finished with our day's work, we were free to go into town. Twice weekly I took painting classes in Darmstaadt, a university city in which I made a lot of artist friends. I also studied ballet. In the basement of our installation—originally a World War I cavalry headquarters—I had a studio with excellent lighting."

Morrill's tour of duty brought him to Spain as well. "The time I spent in Spain, however, was the most artistically important to me. For the most part, I stayed in the south, in the region of Andalucia. Spain got 'under my skin' in a way that no other foreign country has. In the south, one feels particularly close to Africa and the Moorish influence—architecture, music, language, cooking—which is still very strong. There were such sharp contrasts between the wealth of the church and the poverty of the people, between the vibrant colors of the festivals and the ever-present women in black. And, of course, with Franco in power there were heavily armed police all over. In Barcelona I fell in with a group of gypsy musicians and dancers. When I left, I gave them the many drawings I had made of them.

"I believe that artists should be given international passports. The camaraderie among them should not be constricted by borders, politics, or accidents of birth."

1957-1965. Morrill enrolled in the Boston Museum School once again after his discharge from the Air Force. "I graduated three years later with a certificate in fine arts and a college degree in art education from Tufts, which was affiliated with the Museum School. My first job in Webster, Massachusetts was as an art teacher. From there, I went on to Groton, Connecticut, to serve as one of two art supervisors for the entire elementary school system. I tried to integrate art with the other subjects. For example, if the kids were studying history, I would get them involved in mapmaking; for English class, if they were studying Carl Sandburg, I would use a scene from one of his poems as a point of departure for painting and drawing. I utilized musical compositions in the same way. I always tried to maintain a feeling of play and encouraged experimentation. We developed a series of teaching aid booklets for the classes from kindergarten through the sixth grade.

"In 1965, I had an experience that was to prove terribly important. I had gone to a performance of the Detroit Symphony at which Claudio Arrau was the guest soloist. The concert hall was filled. Out of thousands of faces, I became transfixed by that of a young woman. Dressed rather incongruously, she was alone and obviously very much out of place. She got my head going in so many directions at once, I couldn't stand it. I stayed up most of that night drawing her. The final portrait won a purchase prize in a national drawing competition and hangs in the museum at Dulin Gallery in Knoxville, Tenn. I cannot put my finger on why she impressed me so deeply, but she unleashed something in my work that lay dormant.

"In Groton, my own art work consisted mostly of wire sculptures, much like Calder's. But I was still on the periphery of my own work. I worked all the time, but without a clear direction. This worried me, so I left my job for graduate school at Cranbrook Academy in Bloomfield Hills, Michigan. The Academy was located on an estate owned by the Booth family of the Scripps-Booth newspaper chain. The Booths went to Italy and brought back scores of artisans from small towns in Tuscany to build their estate, erect a church on it, and landscape the grounds. All this accomplished, they decided to found a center for pastoral studies with a small museum and observatory, rock collections, lapidary courses, and an exclusive girls' and boys' school (Kingswood and Cranbrook, respectively), modeled after the English public school system. The art school was based on the *atelier* system wherein students worked in the studio and foundry with master artists brought over from Europe. I concentrated on painting and drawing, but dabbled as well in printmaking and ceramics. It was an absolutely marvellous place. I worked uninterruptedly amid beautiful gardens and lakes with swans.''

1967-1969. Taught at Slippery Rock State College. "When I arrived, there were only four people in the art department. By the time I left, there were thirteen. These were the tough years of Kent State, the Vietnam War and general student unrest. There was so much infighting among the faculty that it interfered with education. When the department chairman retired and I was offered the post, I knew I had arrived at a crossroads. The life of a tenured academician was so secure it scared me to death. I had to admit that I had never challenged myself with putting bread on my table via my art, and so decided to move back with wife and child to the Boston area and began illustrating books.

"Somehow I knew that illustration would be a natural thing for me, liking, as I always have, Rembrandt, Daumier, Goya, and Brueghel. I didn't know, however, in which direction my interest in illustration might manifest. At the time I saw illustration and fine art as separate categories. Having arrived at the age of fifty-two, I realize that true art overspills all the categories. Fine cooking may well be fine art, as may fine flower arranging. Fine illustration is fine art.

"I know artists who see form in terms of volume, color relationships, etc. I see form in terms of line. Perhaps this comes from so many years of working with a stylus, a pencil-type tool, or it comes from dance. I think of line as gesture, and gesture is to me very important.''

Morrill, who produces from eight to twelve books a year, is a most eclectic artist. His work is by turn realistic, expressionistic, and fantastic. "Of course, what I consider realistic, someone else may consider fantastical and vice versa. After all, we all operate according to our individual perceptions of reality. I know there is a dark side to my work, and if I don't watch it, I'm apt to lean toward things that are a little grotesque. Often, what others find ugly I find fascinating, even alluring. I don't separate the beautiful from the ugly. They are different sides of the same coin as far as I am concerned. This has sometimes interfered with my children's book illustration. I would prefer to show kids wearing rumpled clothes and a little dirty from a good day of playing, but most book publishers see children differently.

"I keep an extensive clipping file, but it seems that I never have what I really need for a given illustration. Generally, I'll use a face, a pose, or a set-up from my file as a jumping-off point and improvise from there.

"I try to spend the morning doing my own art work and devote the afternoon and part of the evening to book illustrations. The two activities complement each other nicely.'' Generally, Morrill

has little if any contact with the author whose book he is illustrating. "The publishing houses seem to prefer it that way, and I agree. Particularly with less experienced writers and/or artists who may be somewhat insecure, problems could easily arise. And I must say that I rather like working independently. Generally when artists are given freedom, the work deepens. Of course I'm delighted when an author is pleased with my illustrations. One thing I never do is work against the text. My point of departure is invariably what I found most compelling in the story or poem.

"I would love to illustrate the classics. I feel that the classics need to periodically be reinterpreted, as they are in the theatre, giving them a fresh relevance for contemporary culture. I would love, for example, to set a fairy tale—Grimm or Andersen, for instance—in another solar system and people it with characters from another universe.''

In **1984,** Morrill moved with his family to Madison, Connecticut. "We bought this particular house because it has an enormous master bedroom, which I immediately converted into my studio.'' In his spare time, Morrill enjoys long walks in the woods. He also spends a lot of time near water. "Water is traditionally a symbol of the unconscious and creativity. I know many artists who are extremely sensitive to the special energies of water.

"I was recently walking by the sea with an artist friend who felt that we should take up a hobby. 'I'll take up sculpture,' was my reply. And I have. I work entirely from found objects,

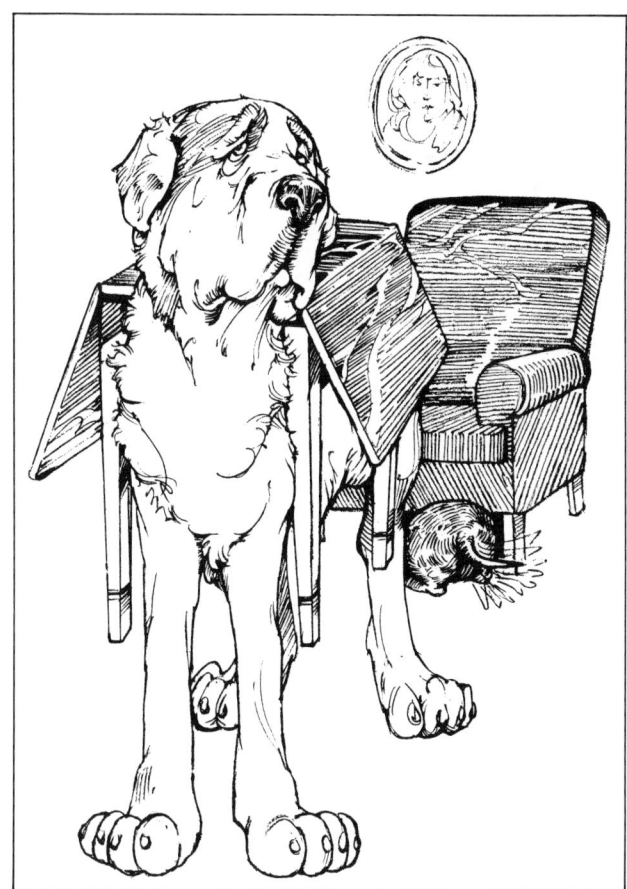

Once I got tired of the usual spots and tried to curl up under the drop-leaf coffee table. Dumb. ■ (From *Judge Benjamin: Superdog* by Judith Whitelock McInerney. Illustrated by Leslie Morrill.)

anything that catches my eye—pebbles, shells, feathers from the dead hawk my cat brought home. For the most part, I have been making masks of the type which would fit over the head of a shaman.''

Morrill has also begun to work in video and film. He did an animated segment on turtles for a series on animals for ABC and is currently working on a fundraising video for a local arts organization, of which he is a board member. ''The Alliance of the Arts is a seven-community umbrella organization dealing with music, drama, photography, art, and dance. We give scholarships; sponsor music competitions, the prize for one is a concert at New York's Carnegie Hall; underwrite master classes with dancer Pearl Primus; offer classes in talking drums, an ancient African tradition; and fund the Nutmeg Players, a small theatre company.

''You're defining yourself every time you draw or paint,'' Morrill tells young people interested in art. ''For all of us, the sooner we get in touch with whatever it is that makes it *necessary* for us to make art, the better. We must rely on our own vision, honesty and discipline. It may well be that you won't find out what you're about until you're fifty. In a way, I feel I've returned to the stage I was at when I first attended Museum School. I feel again as though I'm at the beginning, but the difference is that I now have decades of accumulated experience and the tools. I'm finally at the point where I'm using those tools intuitively and my mind is freer in a way that it never was before.

''This whole business of living takes a long time—and you should give yourself that time. When he reached eighty, Hokusai, probably the most celebrated of Japanese printmakers, said, 'Now I think I understand animals and birds; maybe if I have another hundred years, I will understand figures.' The purpose of living, as I'm finding out, is in the action itself, in the process. The person who races up a mountain doesn't know where he's been because he hasn't seen anything. The person who takes his time to look around knows the ground he's covered, and will keep ascending long after he's reached the summit, and if he is truly listening, the mountain will speak to him.''

FOR MORE INFORMATION SEE: Martha E. Ward and Dorothy A. Marquardt, *Illustrators of Books for Young People,* Scarecrow, 1975.

MOST, Bernard   1937-

PERSONAL: Born September 2, 1937, in New York; son of Max (a painter) and Bertha (Moskowitz) Most; married Amy Beth Pollack, February 12, 1967; children: Glenn Evan, Eric David. *Education:* Pratt Institute, B.F.A. (with honors), 1959. *Politics:* Independent. *Home:* 3 Ridgecrest E., Scarsdale, N.Y. 10583. *Office:* MCA Advertising, 405 Lexington, New York, N.Y. 10017.

CAREER: McCann-Erickson, Inc. (advertising agency), New York City, art director, 1959-65; Benton & Bowles, Inc. (advertising agency) New York City, associate creative director, 1965-68; MCA Advertising, Inc., New York City, senior vice-president and creative director, 1978—; Bernie & Walter, Inc., creative consulting company, 1986—. Author and illustrator of children's books, 1965—. *Awards, honors:* Awards from Art Directors Club, Type Directors Club, and American Institute of Graphic Arts; Clio Award; Andy Award; *If the Dinosaurs Came Back, My Very Own Octopus, Boo!,* and *There's*

an Ant in Anthony were each selected as a Children's Choice by the International Reading Association and Children's Book Council.

WRITINGS—Self-illustrated children's books: *If the Dinosaurs Came Back,* Harcourt, 1978; *There's an Ant in Anthony* (ALA Notable Book), Morrow, 1980; *Turn Over,* Prentice-Hall, 1980; *My Very Own Octopus,* Harcourt, 1980; *Boo!,* Prentice-Hall, 1980; *There's an Ape Behind the Drape,* Morrow, 1981; *Whatever Happened to the Dinosaurs?,* Harcourt, 1984. Contributor of illustrations to national magazines.

WORK IN PROGRESS: Dinosaur Cousins? for Harcourt.

SIDELIGHTS: ''I was interested in becoming an artist since I was four or five years old. I was fascinated with the idea of drawing. In school, I was always drawing or painting. I was lucky enough to be accepted by the High School of Art & Design in New York City, and eventually to win a scholarship to Pratt Institute in Brooklyn, New York.

''My favorite theme when I appear at schools and libraries is: 'Desire and believing in yourself is more important than ''natural'' talent.' You must love what you do and work very hard to make your own 'luck' happen. Too many children, as well as grown-ups, get discouraged easily and give up on their goals and dreams. I like to point out to children that some of my books were published after many, many rejections. It is important not to give up.

''My books are 'concept books' in that they get children to participate in the ideas of the books beyond the actual reading of them.''

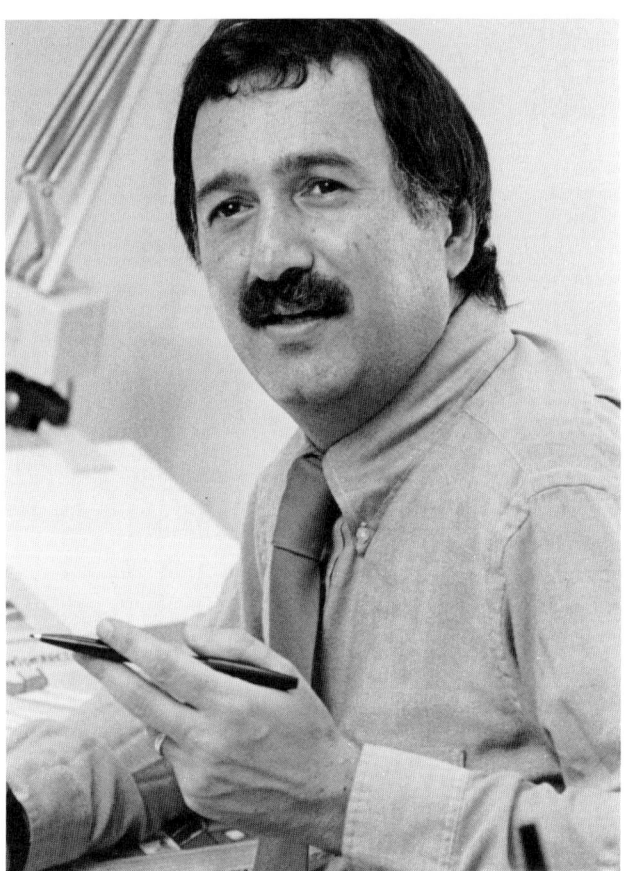

BERNARD MOST

We love to visit the library and read all about the dinosaurs. ■ (From *Whatever Happened to the Dinosaurs?* by Bernard Most. Illustrated by the author.)

MUNSCH, Robert N. 1945-

BRIEF ENTRY: Born June 11, 1945, in Pittsburg, Pa. A storyteller and author of children's books, Munsch estimates that he has made up and told more than 700 different stories, nearly a dozen of which he has put into writing. Born and raised the fourth of nine children in Pittsburg, Pennsylvania, Munsch became a Jesuit novice at age eighteen and began studying philosophy. While studying for a master's degree in anthropology at Boston University, Munsch visited an orphanage where be began telling stories. He later gave up the Jesuit ministry and anthropology—"I liked the kids better"—worked in day care centers and nursery schools, and earned a master's degree in early childhood education from Tufts University. Munsch worked part time as professor of family studies and head teacher at Family Studies Laboratory Preschool for eight years and, since 1984, has been a writer and househusband. Now living in Guelph, Ontario, Canada, Munsch and his wife, Ann, an instructor at the Family Studies Laboratory Preschool, have a daughter, Julie, and a son, Andrew.

Munsch's books begin as oral stories. Using details children add in "group composition," Munsch continually amends a story each time he tells it. According to Munsch, it takes at least three years for a good oral story to evolve. He then puts it in writing. Humorous and contemporary, the stories are written in read-aloud language and portray situations where children have power and often turn the tables on adults. In *Jonathan Cleaned Up, Then He Heard a Sound; or, Blackberry Subway Jam* (Annick, 1981), young Jonathan takes on city hall to change the location of a subway stop that has appeared in the middle of his apartment. In *Mud Puddle* (Annick, 1979; revised edition, 1982), Jule Ann is attacked three times by a mud puddle which leaves her "completely all over muddy." Following three baths and changes of clothes, Jule Ann takes matters into her own hands and frightens away the puddle by throwing a bar of soap into it. Munsch's other published stories include *The Dark* (1979), *The Paper Bag Princess* (1980), *Murmel, Murmel, Murmel* (1982), *Mortimer* (1983), and *Millicent and the Wind* (1984), all published by Annick. *Office:* c/o Writers Union of Canada, 24 Ryerson Ave., Toronto, Ontario, Canada M5T 2P3.

FOR MORE INFORMATION SEE: Books in Canada, December, 1981; Irma McDonough, editor, *Profiles 2,* Canadian Library Association, 1982; "The Weird and Wonderful Whimsy of Robert Munsch," *Quill & Quire,* May, 1982; *Twentieth-Century Children's Writers,* St. Martin's, 1983; *Canadian Children's Literature,* no. 43, 1986.

NATHAN, Adele (Gutman) 1900(?)-1986

OBITUARY NOTICE: Born about 1900 in Baltimore, Md.; died July 24, 1986, in New York, N.Y. Director of stage productions, scriptwriter, and author of children's books. Beginning in 1931 Nathan wrote more than fourteen books, mainly on historical subjects for children. In her early career she was involved with the theater, and in 1916 she founded and directed the Vagabond Players in Baltimore, Maryland. Nathan later directed plays in New York and in several other Eastern states and directed short subjects for both Paramount and Grand National studios. In 1941 she was chief scriptwriter for the U.S. Department of Education.

Active in historical associations, Nathan organized and staged numerous commemorative events for communities and corporations. She also installed the historical museum at Niagara Falls, New York, and wrote *How to Plan and Conduct a Bicentennial Celebration.* Among her books for children are *The Farmer Sows His Wheat, When Lincoln Went to Gettysburg, Churchill's England,* and *Major John Andre: Gentleman Spy.* In addition, Nathan was feature editor for *St. Nicholas* magazine and contributed to such periodicals as *Vogue* and *Atlantic Monthly.* She received a Freedoms Foundation Award in 1953.

FOR MORE INFORMATION SEE: Who's Who of American Women, 8th edition, Marquis, 1974; *Contemporary Authors,* Volumes 73-76, Gale, 1978. Obituaries: *New York Times,* July 26, 1986; *AB Bookman's Weekly,* September 8, 1986.

NOLAN, Paul T(homas) 1919-

PERSONAL: Born April 4, 1919, in Rochester, N.Y.; son of John J. (in investments) and Anna (Sweeney) Nolan; married Peggy Hime (an elementary school librarian), June 1, 1947; children: John, Peter, Elizabeth Anne. *Education:* Arkansas State Teachers College (now University of Central Arkansas), B.A., 1947; Tulane University, M.A., 1949, Ph.D., 1953. *Politics:* Democrat (liberal). *Religion:* Presbyterian. *Home:* 219 Renee Ave., Lafayette, La. *Address:* Box 40552, USL Station, Lafayette, La. 70504. *Office:* English Department, University of Southwestern Louisiana, P.O. Drawer 44691, Lafayette, La. 70504.

PAUL T. NOLAN

CAREER: Arkansas State Teachers College, Conway, instructor in English, 1947-48; Centenary College of Louisiana, Shreveport, assistant professor of English, speech, and journalism and director of publicity, 1949-54; Tulane University, New Orleans, La., instructor in English, 1951-53; Arkansas State College (now University), Jonesboro, Ford Foundation lecturer in humanities, 1954-55; University of Southwestern Louisiana, Lafayette, La., professor of English, 1955—, Dupré Professor of the Humanities, 1967—. Board member and college coordinator, Deep-South Writers Conference, 1960-63. *Military service:* U.S. Army Air Forces, 1942-45. *Member:* South-Central Modern Language Association, Modern Language Association, Missouri Historical Association, Phi Kappa Phi, Alpha Chi, Phi Alpha Theta, Sigma Tau Delta. *Awards, honors:* Player's Workshop Award in Drama, 1964, for "There's Death for the Lonely"; Best Published Play for Young People from Plays, Inc., 1974, for "Cinderfellow."

WRITINGS: Round-the-World Plays for Young People, Plays, 1961; (editor and author of introduction) *The One-Act Plays of Lee Arthur,* Pioneer Drama Service, 1962; *Chaucer for Children: An Evening's Entertainment from the Canterbury Tales,* Little Red Schoolhouse Press, 1963; (author of dramatization) Stephen Crane, *The Bride Comes to Yellow Sky,* Pioneer Drama Service, 1963; *Writing the One-Act Play for the Amateur Stage,* Pioneer Drama Service, 1964; *Buffalo Bill's Life on the Border,* Pioneer Drama Service, 1965; (editor) *Three Plays by J. W. Crawford: An Experiment in Myth-Making,* Mouton, 1966; *The Other Great Plays,* National Thespian Society, 1967; *Provincial Drama in America,* Scarecrow, 1968.

Drama Workshop Plays (juvenile), Plays, 1970; *Describing People* (textbook), Heath, 1970; *Marc Connelly,* Twayne, 1971; *A Groom for the Loveliest Mouse,* Edgemoor, 1971; (with James Burke) *Between Hisses,* Pioneer Drama Service, 1976; (with J. Burke) *The Highwayman,* Pioneer Drama Service, 1976; *Hedda Gabler South,* Edgemoor, 1977; *The Eavesdrop Theatre,* Edgemoor, 1976; *The Monsters Ride Again,* Eldridge Publishing, 1979.

John Wallace Crawford, Twayne, 1981; *Folk Tale Plays Round the World: A Collection of Royalty-Free, One-Act Plays about Lands Far and Near* (juvenile), Plays, 1982; *Directing for the Amateur Stage,* Pioneer, 1985.

Two-act adaptations of Shakespeare's plays; "Globe Theatre" series, all published by Pioneer, 1977-82: *Romeo and Juliet, The Taming of the Shrew, A Midsummer-Night's Dream, Much Ado about Nothing,* and *Love's Labours Lost.*

Also author of "Squeak to Me of Love" (musical; based on play "A Groom for the Loveliest Mouse"), first produced at Theater Wagon of Virginia, Staunton, December, 1979. Contributor of plays to anthologies, including *Louisiana Stories for Boys and Girls,* edited by Marguerite Bourgere, Louisiana State University Press, 1966; *Diversity,* edited by William K. Durr and others, Houghton, 1974; *New Voices 3,* edited by Jay Cline and others, Ginn, 1978; *First Watch,* edited by Louise Matteoni, Economy, 1981; *Banners,* edited by W. K. Durr, Houghton, 1981. Contributor of children's plays to *Plays: The Drama Magazine for Young People, Grade Teacher, Instructor,* and other periodicals. Contributor of articles to drama, historical, and educational journals, including *Dramatics, Journal of Southern Speech, Louisiana Studies, Alabama Review, Georgia Review, Journal of the Mississippi Historical Society, Chronicles of Oklahoma, New Mexico Schools, Louisiana Schools,* and *Scholastic.*

WORK IN PROGRESS: A crime thriller; academic articles on drama.

SIDELIGHTS: "When I was growing up in Rochester, on the shores of Lake Ontario, I went to many movies, a few plays, and to the ice-skating rink near my home. One February, I had a choice between a play and going skating. I went skating. The temperature dropped to thirty-five degrees below zero, and as I walked home, I vowed I was going to move to a warmer climate and take theatre over skating whenever I had a choice.

"By the time I was in college, I knew I wanted to live on a college campus and work with community theatre. I wrote my first play in 1940 and it was produced on campus at the University of the Ozarks.

"World War II postponed some of my plays and plans, but not my determination to live in a warm climate and write plays. After the war I went to Arkansas to study with two 'great teachers'—Roberta Clay and J. B. Wilson, both of whom encouraged me to write plays and become a college professor.

"Until 1956, I taught and wrote plays for the campuses on which I lived. When I came to what is now my home, Lafayette, Louisiana, there was little theatre. I wrote a play for *Plays: The Drama Magazine* and developed an association with one of my all-time heroes, the late A. S. Burack, editor of *Plays* and the *Writer*. With his advice and suggestions, I have been writing for *Plays* for thirty years, a total of over seventy-five plays for his journal and an equal number for other journals and play-publishing houses.

"In 1975, a group in Lafayette started a playwrights' theatre, The Eavesdrop; and for the past ten years I have been writing plays for this one-act theatre and for another dinner theatre, The Playwrights' Theatre of Louisiana.

"Although at least half of my plays are labeled 'for young people,' I don't really write for any age group. Some of the plays I've written have been done by adults as old as seventy and performed by young people as young as eight. All my plays are intended for a community theatre of some sort—the academic community, the town or neighborhood, or the off-off Broadway theatre, in which (at the Quaigh Theatre on West 43rd Street in New York), many plays from the Eavesdrop Theatre are produced every May.

"Teaching at the University of Southwestern Louisiana is my profession, but since I teach dramatic literature in the English department, writing plays and about plays has been a perfectly natural activity. Theatre—live and on the screen—is still my favorite activity, but with in-door skating rinks, I may try skating again.

"I am married to an elementary school librarian and have three children, two sons and one daughter. Largely I would 'credit' them with giving me an interest in writing for young people."

FOR MORE INFORMATION SEE: Louisiana Schools, May, 1961; *Rectangle,* spring, 1962; Katherine Finley, *Sherif,* Kent University, 1966; James M. Salem, *The Teacher as Writer: Paul T. Nolan, Example,* Scarecrow, 1970.

I wish our clever young poets would remember my homely definitions of prose and poetry; that is, prose = words in their best order;—poetry = the best words in the best order.

—Samuel Taylor Coleridge
(From *Table Talk, 12 July 1827*)

NOURSE, Alan E(dward) 1928-
(Dr. X, Al Edwards)

PERSONAL: Born August 11, 1928, in Des Moines, Iowa; son of Benjamin Chamberlain (an electrical engineer) and Grace (Ogg) Nourse; married Ann Jane Morton, June 11, 1952; children: Benjamin, Rebecca, Jonathan, Christopher. *Education:* Rutgers University, B.S., 1952; University of Pennsylvania, M.D., 1955. *Religion:* Episcopalian. *Home address:* Route 1, Box 173, Thorp, Wash. 98946. *Agent:* Brandt & Brandt Literary Agents, Inc., 1501 Broadway, New York, N.Y. 10036.

CAREER: Virginia Mason Hospital, Seattle, Wash., intern, 1955-56; free-lance writer 1956-58, and 1964—; North Bend Medical Clinic, North Bend, general practitioner and partner, 1958-64. *Military service:* U.S. Navy, Hospital Corps, 1946-48. *Member:* American Medical Association, Science Fiction Writers of America (president, 1968-69), Washington State Medical Society, King County Medical Society, Alpha Kappa Kappa. *Awards, honors:* Junior Book Award from the Boys' Clubs of America, 1963, for *Raiders from the Rings;* Washington State Governor's Award, Governor's Festival of the Arts, 1966, and 1974; Russell L. Cecil Award, magazine category, from the Arthritis Foundation, 1979, for medical journalism; American Academy of Family Physicians Journalism Award, 1983.

WRITINGS—Juvenile; published by F. Watts, except as indicated: *Junior Intern,* Harper, 1957; *Venus and Mercury: A First Book,* 1972; *The Backyard Astronomer,* 1973; *The Giant Planets: A First Book,* 1974, revised edition, 1982; *The Asteroids: A First Book,* 1975; *Viruses: A First Book,* 1976,

ALAN E. NOURSE

revised edition, 1983; *Lumps, Bumps and Rashes, A Look at Kids' Diseases: A First Book*, 1976; *Clear Skin, Healthy Skin: A Concise Guide* (illustrated by Ric Estrada), 1976; *Fractures, Dislocations and Sprains: A First Book*, 1978; *Menstruation, Just Plain Talk: A First Book*, 1980, revised edition, 1987; *Your Immune System: A First Book*, 1982; *Herpes*, 1985; *AIDS*, 1986.

Novels; published by McKay, except as indicated: *Trouble on Titan* (Junior Literary Guild selection), Holt, 1954; *A Man Obsessed*, Ace Books, 1954, revised edition published as *The Mercy Men* (Junior Literary Guild selection), 1968; *Rocket to Limbo* (Junior Literary Guild selection), 1957; *Scavengers in Space* (Junior Literary Guild selection), 1959; (with J. A. Meyer) *The Invaders Are Coming*, Ace Books, 1959; *Star Surgeon* (Junior Literary Guild selection), 1960; *Raiders from the Rings* (Junior Literary Guild selection), 1962; *The Universe Between* (Junior Literary Guild selection), 1965; *The Bladerunner*, 1974; *The Practice*, Harper, 1978; *The Fourth Horseman*, Harper, 1983.

Nonfiction; published by Harper, except as indicated: *So You Want to Be a Doctor*, 1957, revised edition, 1963; (with brother, William B. Nourse) *So You Want to Be a Lawyer*, 1958; *So You Want to Be a Scientist*, 1960; *Nine Planets*, 1960, revised

edition, 1970; (with E. Halliday) *So You Want to Be a Nurse*, 1961; (with J. Webbert) *So You Want to Be an Engineer*, 1962; (with Geoffrey Marks) *The Management of a Medical Practice*, Lippincott, 1962; *So You Want to Be a Physicist*, 1964; (with the editors of *Life*) *The Body*, Time, Inc., 1964, revised edition, 1980; (with J. Webbert) *So You Want to Be a Chemist*, 1964; (under pseudonym Dr. X) *Intern*, 1965; *So You Want to Be a Surgeon*, 1966; (with C. Meinhardt) *So You Want to Be an Architect*, 1969; *Universe, Earth and Atom: The Story of Physics*, 1969; *Ladies' Home Journal Family Medical Guide*, 1973; *The Outdoorsman's Medical Guide: Common Sense Advice and Essential Health Care for Campers, Hikers, and Backpackers*, 1974; *Vitamins: A Concise Guide*, F. Watts, 1977; *The Tooth Book*, McKay, 1977; *Hormones: An Impact Book*, F. Watts, 1979; *Inside the Mayo Clinic*, McGraw, 1979; (with Janice K. Phelps) *The Hidden Addiction and How to Get Free*, Little, Brown, 1986; *The Elk Hunt*, Macmillan, 1986.

Short story collections: *Tiger by the Tail and Other Science Fiction Stories*, McKay, 1960; *The Counterfeit Man: More Science Fiction Stories*, McKay, 1965; *Psi High and Others* (Junior Literary Guild selection), McKay, 1967; *Rx for Tomorrow: Tales of Science Fiction, Fantasy and Medicine*, McKay, 1971.

Author of column, "Family Doctor," and contributing editor, *Good Housekeeping*, 1976—. Contributor of articles and short stories to numerous periodicals, including *Saturday Evening Post, Argosy, Playboy, Astounding Science Fiction, Magazine of Science Fiction and Fantasy. Woman's Day, Better Homes and Gardens*, and *Boys' Life;* contributor to medical journals.

WORK IN PROGRESS: Birth Control and *Radioastronomy: A First Book*, both for F. Watts.

SIDELIGHTS: "*The Universe Between* has a rather strange history. The original idea for the book arose in my mind many years ago, and was actually the basis of the first story I ever had published, a science fiction short story called 'High Threshold' which appeared in Street and Smith's *Astounding Science Fiction* magazine in 1951. A somewhat longer sequel, 'The Universe Between,' was published in *Astounding* later the same year. It was only after this second story came out that I realized I had not really solved the problems of communication with the Threshold world at all, and began exploring a third story, to be of novel length, to finish the one I had already started.

"Unfortunately, this proved harder to accomplish than to think about. I actually started the novel about five times over a period of ten years but never could find exactly the approach that I wanted. Then . . . I found the piece that had been missing, and started to plan the whole book over again from the beginning. Some of the two original stories have survived in this now-final one, but only after complete rewriting. So instead of three incomplete fragments we now have one complete tale. It might be interesting for readers to see if they can guess the 'missing link' that held up completion of *The Universe Between* so long, but telling would be giving away trade secrets!

"*The Elk Hunt* is a personal account of my four-year recovery from a severe heart attack in 1980. In the book I used my personal experiences as a starting place for explaining all aspects of coronary artery disease—symptoms, course, the variety of modern treatments and, especially, means of prevention—in terms understandable to any layman reader."

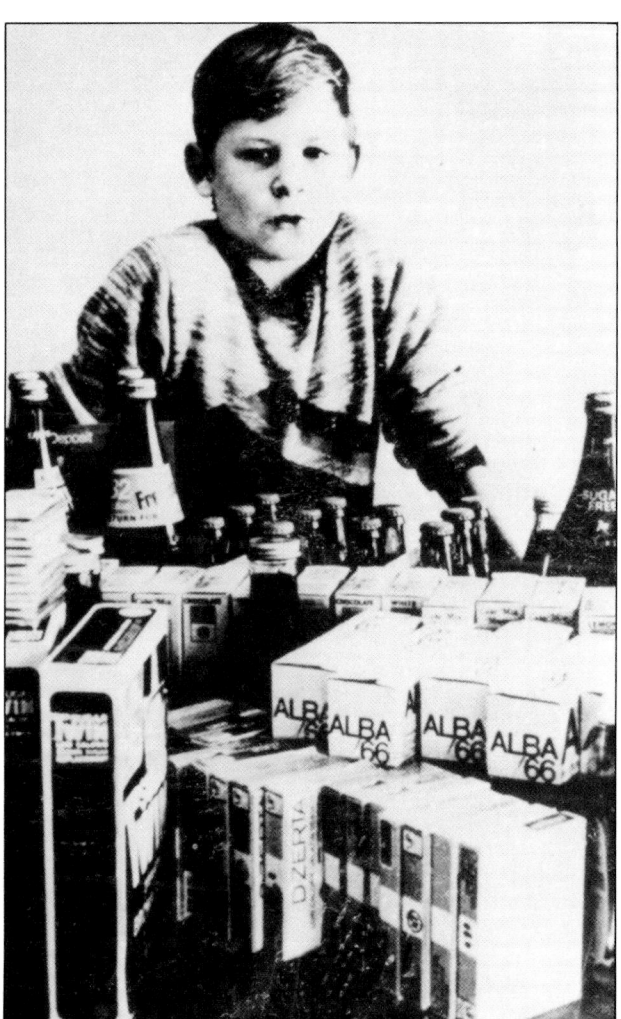

In keeping with the proper diabetic diet, this boy uses products that do not contain real sugar. ■ (From *Hormones* by Alan E. Nourse. Photograph courtesy of United Press International.)

HOBBIES AND OTHER INTERESTS: Hunting, fishing, climbing, backpacking.

FOR MORE INFORMATION SEE: Martha E. Ward and Dorothy A. Marquardt, *Authors of Books for Young People*, Scarecrow, 1971; *New York Times Book Review*, June 25, 1978; *Los Angeles Times Book Review*, October 7, 1979.

O'BRIEN, Anne Sibley 1952-

BRIEF ENTRY: Born July 10, 1952. Author and illustrator of children's books. The daughter of medical missionaries, O'Brien grew up in South Korea and later graduated cum laude from Mount Holyoke College in Massachusetts. As a result of the years she spent in the Far East, O'Brien found herself "bilingual and bicultural. . . . caught between cultures. My illustrations and stories always reflect a multiracial perspective." She has written and illustrated eight board books, each of which focuses on a situation or problem of concern to the preschooler. All published by Holt, the titles are *Come Play with Us, I Want That!, I'm Not Tired, Where's My Truck?* (all 1985), *I Don't Want to Go, It's Hard to Wait, It Hurts!,* and *Don't Say No!* (all 1986). As *Booklist* observed in a review of the first series, "The episodes are right on target for the intended age group. Simply composed, realistic watercolors have a strong presence. . . ." O'Brien is the illustrator of Juanita Havill's *Jamaica's Find* and Judy Delton's *The Mystery of the Haunted Cabin* (both Houghton, 1986). Among her anticipated works are several picture books and a young adult novel, *Finding Home*, about the relationship between a Hmong refugee child and an American schoolgirl. *Home:* Maple St., Peaks Island, Me.

OLSON, Helen Kronberg

PERSONAL: Born in Mt. Angel, Ore.; daughter of Paul (a farmer) and Christine (a homemaker; maiden name, Faulhaber) Kronberg; married Anthony Perillo (deceased); married John Harold Olson (a representative for an electronics company), July 23, 1955; children: (first marriage) Paul Anthony. *Education:* Mt. Angel College, B.S., 1952, also graduate study. *Politics:* Democrat. *Home:* 20739 Hazelnut Ridge Rd. N.E., Scotts Mills, Ore. 97375.

CAREER: Marion County Welfare, Salem, Ore., child welfare caseworker, 1960-63; Oregon State Hospital, Salem, social worker, 1964-65; art and elementary school teacher in Marion County, Ore., for eighteen years; full-time writer and tree farmer. *Awards, honors:* Surrey School Book of the Year Award and nominated for the Hoosier Award, both 1984, both for *The Secret of Spirit Mountain*.

WRITINGS—Children's books: *Stupid Peter and Other Tales: New Stories to Read Together* (original children's folk tales; illustrated by Jack Delano and Irene Delano), Random House, 1970; *The Secret of Spirit Mountain* (wilderness suspense novel; illustrated by Hameel Benjamin), Dodd, 1980; *The Strange Thing That Happened to Oliver Wendell Iscovitch* (humorous novel; illustrated by Betsy Lewin), Dodd, 1983.

Contributor to anthologies, including *The Real Book of First Stories*, edited by Dorothy Haas, Rand McNally, 1974, *The Princess Book*, edited by D. Haas, Rand McNally, 1975, and *The Witch Book*, edited by D. Haas, Rand McNally, 1976. Contributor of short stories to numerous publications, includ-

The baby birds screamed for their father and mother to come and save them from the strange-looking bird in a cowboy suit. ■ (From *The Strange Thing That Happened to Oliver Wendell Iscovitch* by Helen Kronberg Olson. Illustrated by Betsy Lewin.)

ing *Humpty Dumpty, Children's Playmate, Encyclopaedia Britannica, Scholastic,* and *Adventure.*

WORK IN PROGRESS: A children's mystery novel; several stories.

SIDELIGHTS: "As soon as I learned to read I became an insatiable reader—and a literary critic. There were many good children's books, and the satisfaction I received from them I still treasure today. But, then there were the books that didn't make it. I skipped whole passages and fumed at disappointing endings. Now, as a children's author, I only write what both the child and adult in me fully enjoy reading.

"It was while I was working as a social worker for Oregon State Hospital that I, with my husband, Harold, and son, Paul, moved from Salem to the wooded Cascade foothills into a cedar home we had built ourselves. Here I handled my husband's business calls. Finding myself with free time I began writing. As I had worked extensively with children my creative product was children's stories. The stories sold almost immediately—to children's magazines—to educational markets.

"A sale of one of the stories to a mass market picture book publisher motivated me to submit stories to hard cover publishers. In 1970 Random House published a collection of my original folk tales under the title, *Stupid Peter and Other Tales.* Rand McNally commissioned and bought stories for their hard cover anthologies.

"In the late seventies I decided it was time I wrote a children's novel. *The Secret of Spirit Mountain* was the result.

"At the present time I am working on another children's mystery novel and several stories.

HELEN KRONBERG OLSON

"My advice to would-be authors: Read—read—read, and then write what you, yourself, like to read."

HOBBIES AND OTHER INTERESTS: Reading, travelling.

FOR MORE INFORMATION SEE: Silverton Appeal Tribune, November 26, 1970; *Statesman* (Salem, Ore.), December 13, 1970; *The Oregonian,* December 19, 1970.

ORMAI, Stella

BRIEF ENTRY: An illustrator of children's books, Ormai graduated from the Rhode Island School of Design with a B.F.A. in illustration. She also studied her craft at Uri Shulevitz's workshop, the Bread Loaf Writer's Conference, and the illustrators' workshop at Marymount College. As a child, Ormai developed an abiding love of nature during the many summers she spent exploring the countryside near her grandfather's farm in Pennsylvania. This appreciation, along with an affinity for children's fantasy, can be seen in her illustrations for stories like Norma Q. Hare's *Mystery at Mouse House* (Garrard, 1980) and Jacqueline Briggs Martin's *Bizzy Bones and Uncle Ezra* (Lothrop, 1984), as well as *Creatures: Poems* (Harcourt, 1985), selected by Lee Bennett Hopkins. Ormai has also provided illustrations for a number of science-and-technology books, including *Kids' Computer Capers* (Lothrop, 1983) and *The Programmer's Guide to the Galaxy* (Lothrop, 1984) by Sandra Markle; *Bet You Can! Science Possibilities to Fool You* (Avon, 1983) by Vicki Cobb and Kathy Darling; and *Soap Bubble Magic* (Lothrop, 1985) by Seymour Simon. Ormai enjoys collecting children's books as well as illustrating them.

PELLOWSKI, Michael J(oseph) 1949-(Ski Michaels)

BRIEF ENTRY: Born January 24, 1949, in New Brunswick, N.J. Author of books for children, television producer, and stand-up comedian. After graduating from Rutgers University in 1971, Pellowski was affiliated with the New England Patriots as a professional football player until 1973. His career in football was followed by one as teacher of philosophy, art, and physical education at Gibbons School in New Brunswick. In 1975 Pellowski again changed fields, becoming a free-lance writer. Since 1979 he has written more than two dozen children's books, several of which reflect his interest in the world of sports, such as *The Great Sports Question and Answer Book* (Waldman Publishing, 1979), *Great Baseball Quiz Book, Great Football Quiz Book,* and *Amazing but True Sports Stories* (all published by Moby Books, 1982).

Pellowski is also the creator of "Fun Stop," a children's series that airs weekly on cable television. Using the stage name Ski Michaels, he acts as the show's writer, host, and producer. In 1982 "Fun Stop" was nominated for the Ace Award by the Academy for Cable Excellence. Along with his sports books, Pellowski has written a number of picture books, beginning with *Clara Joins the Circus* (Parents Magazine Press, 1981). In 1986 Troll Associates published nearly twenty of his stories (many under the Michaels pseudonym). These include *The Duck Who Loved Puddles; Felix, the Funny Fox; Wake Up, Sam!; Mystery of the Windy Meadow; No Fleas, Please!; Who Can't Follow an Ant?;* and *Something New to Do.* In addition to writing children's books, Pellowski produces comedy material for stand-up comedians. As Ski Michaels, he also performs as a comedian himself. *Office address:* P.O. Box 726, Bound Brook, N.J. 08805.

FOR MORE INFORMATION SEE: Contemporary Authors, Volume 110, Gale, 1984.

PERKINS, (Richard) Marlin   1905-1986

OBITUARY NOTICE—See sketch in *SATA* Volume 21: Born March 28, 1905, in Carthage, Mo.; died of lymph cancer, June 14, 1986, in St. Louis (one source cites Clayton), Mo. Zoologist, television personality, and author. For twenty-three years, Perkins was co-host of "Wild Kingdom," the television series that pioneered the filming of animals in their natural habitats. Perkins began his career in 1926 as a curator of reptiles at the St. Louis Zoo, and he subsequently served as curator of the City Zoo in Buffalo, New York, and then as director of the Lincoln Park Zoo in Chicago, Illinois, before returning to the St. Louis Zoo as director in 1962. While in Chicago he developed the idea of putting wild animals on television; as host of NBC's "Zoo Parade," which began its twelve-year run in 1949, he presented animals from the Lincoln Park Zoo.

NBC began broadcasting "Wild Kingdom" in 1963, with Perkins as co-host, and in 1972 the series was purchased and syndicated by Mutual of Omaha. Aired over two hundred television stations in more than forty countries, the series ran for twenty-four uninterrupted seasons (the last without Perkins) and won four Emmy Awards. During the filming of "Wild Kingdom," Perkins sustained several near-fatal injuries, and he was one of the first known survivors of a bite from the West African gaboon viper. In 1960 he participated in Sir Edmund Hilary's expedition on Yeti investigation in the Himalayas. Perkins' books include *Animal Faces,* for which he supplied the photographs, *One Magic Night: A Story From the Zoo, Zoo Parade, "I Saw You From Afar": A Visit to the Bushmen of the Kalahari Desert,* written with his wife, Carol, and the autobiography, *My Wild Kingdom.* In addition, he wrote the introductions to various books on wildlife subjects and contributed to such magazines as *Copeia* and *Parks and Recreation.*

FOR MORE INFORMATION SEE: Current Biography, H. W. Wilson, 1951; *Contemporary Authors,* Volume 103, Gale, 1982; Marlin Perkins, *My Wild Kingdom: An Autobiography,* edited by William Doerflinger, Dutton, 1983. Obituaries: *Detroit Free Press,* June 15, 1986; *Los Angeles Times,* June 15, 1986; *Washington Post,* June 15, 1986; *Chicago Tribune,* June 16, 1986; *New York Times,* June 16, 1986; *Facts on File,* June 20, 1986; *Time,* June 30, 1986; *People,* August 9, 1982.

PETERSEN, P(eter) J(ames)   1941-

PERSONAL: Born October 23, 1941, in Santa Rosa, Calif.; son of Carl Eric (a farmer) and Alice (a farmer; maiden name, Winters) Petersen; married Marian Braun (a nurse), July 6, 1963; children: Karen, Carla. *Education:* Stanford University, A.B., 1962; San Francisco State College (now University), M.A., 1964; University of New Mexico, Ph.D., 1972. *Home:* 1243 Pueblo Court, Redding, Calif. 96001. *Agent:* Ellen Levine Literary Agency, Inc., 432 Park Ave. S., Suite 1205, New York, N.Y. 10016. *Office:* Department of English, Shasta College, Box 6006, Redding, Calif. 96099.

CAREER: Shasta College, Redding, Calif., instructor in English, 1964—. *Member:* Society of Children's Book Writers.

P. J. PETERSEN

Awards, honors: National Endowment for the Humanities fellowship, 1976-77; American Library Association's list of best books for young adults, 1981, for *Would You Settle for Improbable?,* and 1982, for *Nobody Else Can Walk It for You;* nominated for the Dorothy Canfield Fisher Award, 1981, for *Would You Settle for Improbable?*

WRITINGS—Young adult novels: *Would You Settle for Improbable?,* Delacorte, 1981; *Nobody Else Can Walk It for You,* Delacorte, 1982; *The Boll Weevil Express,* Delacorte, 1983; *Here's to the Sophomores* (Junior Literary Guild selection), Delacorte, 1984; *Corky and the Brothers Cool,* Delacorte, 1985; *Going for the Big One* (Junior Literary Guild selection), Delacorte, 1986; *Good-bye to Good Ol' Charlie,* Delacorte, 1987.

WORK IN PROGRESS: A book for younger children; *The Freshman Detective Blues,* a mystery for Delacorte; an adventure novel, *How Can You Hijack a Cave?*

SIDELIGHTS: "I grew up on a farm in Northern California, six miles from the town of Geyserville. My main source of books was the tiny branch library. Because the children's books were only replaced every two or three months, I generally read every volume on the shelves.

"I read everyone from Zane Grey to Carolyn Keene. My favorite book was *Tom Sawyer,* which I read at least once a year. (The picture of Injun Joe trapped in the cave still sends chills through me.) In early high school I discovered John Steinbeck and Tennessee Williams, whose treatments of rural life amazed me. William Saroyan was a later favorite, along

(Jacket illustration by Paul Bachem from *Here's to the Sophomores* by P. J. Petersen.)

with Willa Cather and James Thurber. I also read Agatha Christie, Superman comic books, and *Mad* magazine, however. The habit of indiscriminate reading dies slowly.

"Making up stories was a natural outgrowth of my reading. I can't remember when I didn't want to be a writer, although I had occasional fleeting desires to perform brain surgery or play center field for the Giants.

"I began writing seriously when I was still in high school and earned my first rejection slips at sixteen. In my early twenties I finished my first novel and sent it off with great hopes. It was rejected by five publishers before I gave up and stuffed it into a drawer. After that painful experience, I avoided similar disappointments by never finishing anything. I spent years writing the first halves of novels.

"Writing words that nobody read seemed as pointless as delivering a speech to an empty room. I gradually wrote less and less, although I could never quite give up the habit.

"In the summer of 1978, after returning from my twenty-year high school reunion, I decided to make one final effort at writing. I set up a rigorous schedule and followed it faithfully. Just when I was casting about for a project, my daughter Karen, an eighth grader then, began sharing her books with me. Seeing how excited she was about reading, I decided to write a book for her. If I couldn't interest a publisher (and I was under-

standably pessimistic), I intended to give her the manuscript—a present from a loving father.

"As I worked on that novel, which came to be called *Would You Settle for Improbable?*, I felt a quiet satisfaction growing inside me. By luck, I had stumbled into the kind of writing that was right for me.

"Although most of my novels are set in and around small towns in California, only one of my books (*The Boll Weevil Express*) is set in a real place. It's based on an experience I *didn't* have. When I was a sophomore in high school, a boy from the local youth home wanted me to run away with him. I didn't go, but the idea always stayed with me. I should add, though, that only the idea came from my experience. My character Doug Walker bears no resemblance to the fellow I knew, and Lars isn't much like me.

"I prefer imaginary settings, so that I can put the river anywhere I like. At the same time, I work hard to make my imaginary places seem real. I compulsively collect details. (My family calls me a detail kleptomaniac.) I am always on the lookout for a small touch—the shape of a boot or the squawk of a bluejay—that will make my work ring true.

"On good days when I write, a play is going on in my head, and I take all the roles. I usually talk out loud as I type, my voice changing with each character. Because I play all the parts, experiencing each emotion, I suppose there are aspects of me in all the characters.

"This kind of dramatization has its drawbacks. When I have a character sprawled on the ground, I often get out of my chair and assume the position to see where the arms and legs would be. If people happen by and see me lying on the floor with my legs in the air, mumbling to myself, they are convinced that I've finally gone over the edge.

"My novels deal with the difficult ethical problems that young people face. *Would You Settle for Improbable?* involves the difficulty of changing destructive behavior patterns. *Nobody Else Can Walk It for You* concerns responses to violence. In *The Boll Weevil Express,* a runaway has to decide between two unsatisfactory ways to live. Although I try to avoid preaching, my own preferences can be seen in the approach to life taken by my central characters—the ones who keep trusting and hoping and caring, even though they're often hurt and disappointed.

"*Here's to the Sophomores,* my fourth novel for young adults, involves the characters who appeared in [my] first book. I had left them at their junior high school graduation. What, I wondered, would have happened to them in high school? How would the change of surroundings affect each of those people? I finally decided to write about their first two weeks of high school. By stopping at that point I could leave it up to the readers to decide how things would go after that.

"As a child I loved listening to the dramatic programs on the radio: 'The Whistler,' 'Suspense,' 'The Fat Man.' Naturally, much of my elementary school writing was in the form of radio plays. As I look over my novels, I can see the influence of this background: My books are primarily told through dialogue, with very little description or analysis.

"I am not a 'natural' writer. For every hour I spend writing, I probably spend ten hours rewriting. Before beginning a novel, I usually have a story in my head, complete with characters and scenes. However, it takes me many, many drafts to trans-

(Jacket illustration by Robert Tannenbaum from *Corky and the Brothers Cool* by P. J. Petersen.)

fer the vision from my mind onto paper. I find description especially difficult. It is far easier to imagine a face or a tree than it is to conjure up the words that will allow a reader to share those pictures. And, regardless of how many revisions I make, the story in my head is always more powerful than what I manage to get on paper.

"When a person has two demanding jobs, there's always the problem of finding time for both. There is a less obvious problem, though. English teachers turn into compulsive correctors. We go into a restaurant, pick up a menu, and want to add a comma. That's why we're often frustrated writers. It's hard (maybe impossible) to create and correct at the same time.

"At my worst, I was two people when I sat down to write—the 'writer' and the 'teacher.' As soon as the writer put down a sentence, the teacher examined it, made several suggestions for improvement, then shook his head sadly at the poor quality. I finished these sessions with a case of writer's block and a stomachache.

"I have learned to lock up the English teacher in me before approaching the typewriter. Critical editing is necessary, of course, especially with writing like mine that tends to repeat words and sentence patterns, but self editing has to be separate from the act of creation.

"Because my writing and teaching keep me inside and inactive, I spend much of my leisure time outdoors. I especially

enjoy hiking and bicycling, which give me exercise and a chance to think. Mt. Lassen National Park is an hour's drive from my house. When I need a change of pace and a new perspective, I drive there and spend a few hours tramping along through the pines and lava rocks."

PETROSKI, Catherine (Ann Groom)　1939-

PERSONAL: Born September 7, 1939, in St. Louis, Mo.; daughter of Robert John (an engineer and businessman) and Mary Louise (a businesswoman; maiden name, Sterling) Groom; married Henry Petroski (an engineer and writer), July 15, 1966; children: Karen Beth, Stephen James. *Education:* MacMurray College, B.A., 1961; graduate study at Bread Loaf School of English, Middlebury College, 1961; University of Illinois, M.A., 1962, further graduate study, 1965-67. *Home and office:* 2501 Perkins Rd., Durham, N.C. 27706. *Agent:* Ellen Levine, Suite 1205, 432 Park Ave. S., New York, N.Y. 10016.

CAREER: Belleville Township High School, Belleville, Ill., teacher of English, 1962-65; Belleville Area College, Belleville, Ill., teacher of English, 1963-65; University of Illinois, Urbana, teacher of English, 1965-67; National Council of Teachers of English, Champaign, Ill., staff writer and editor, 1967-68; writer and book critic, 1968—; University of North Carolina, Chapel Hill, teacher of literature, 1982; Duke University, Durham, N.C., teacher of writing, 1983—. Writer-in-residence, Illinois Arts Council, 1976-78; Duke University Writers Conference, workshop leader, 1983—. *Awards, hon-*

CATHERINE PETROSKI

I am building a house under the loquat tree. ■ (From *Beautiful My Mane in the Wind* by Catherine Petroski. Illustrated by Robert Andrew Parker.)

ors: John Crowe Ransom Fiction Prize from *Sou'wester,* 1974, for "You and Me, Claude"; Bread Loaf Writers Conference, Bridgman scholar, 1974, and Collins fellow, 1982; short story prize from Texas Institute of Letters, 1976, for *Beautiful My Mane in the Wind;* National Endowment for the Arts writing fellow for fiction, 1977-78 and 1983-84; Yaddo fellow, 1980 and 1984; D.Lit. from MacMurray College, 1984.

WRITINGS: Gravity and Other Stories, Fiction International, 1981; *Lady's Day,* Night Eye Press, 1982; *Beautiful My Mane in the Wind* (juvenile; illustrated by Robert A. Parker), Houghton, 1983; *The Summer That Lasted Forever,* Houghton, 1984.

Works represented in anthologies, including *Having Been There,* edited by Allan Luks, Scribner, 1979, and *Stories for Free Children,* McGraw, 1982; and in magazines, including *Ms., North American Review, Virginia Quarterly Review, Prairie Schooner,* and *New Directions.*

WORK IN PROGRESS: A novel for adults; a new collection of short stories; a young adult novel.

SIDELIGHTS: "My two children are a direct stream of inspiration for the writing I have done for young readers. Though the stories I write are not *about* them, they are stories I could not have written without seeing Karen and Stephen in everyday situations, reacting to friends, to family members, to the 'big events' that have touched their lives.

"Both of my children provide me with a second, indirect kind of inspiration: through them, I gain a more direct access to the stored memories of my own childhood which was very different from theirs. Their words will key me back to a vividly remembered scene or some important person in my past. My picture book *Beautiful My Mane in the Wind* has as its basic idea the shared inclinations and feelings between a girl and her mother, even feelings that a daughter may be surprised to discover in her mother. My daughter's passion for books and for riding sends me back to the afternoons I spent hiding with *Wuthering Heights* or with my Welsh pony; my son's passion for sports sends me back to 'field days' and swimming and long summer nights listening to Harry Carray doing the St. Louis Cardinals' play by plays.

"In my own reading, I've often felt that the books I read (or that were read to me) before I was ten or twelve are the books that have formed me. I feel that writing for young readers is very important work and try to write about situations that will engage the reader's imagination, yet be a source of strength to him. In *The Summer That Lasted Forever,* Molly is a specific girl, not every girl, but one whose situation can be translated into almost everyone's life: she learns to rely on herself, basically, and not linger in the past or make excuses.

"*The Summer That Lasted Forever* is not an autobiographical novel in its outline—my real mother is an energetic, very-much-alive lady, unlike Molly's in the book; the father, too, is different from my own. But Molly's grandfather is almost literally one of mine, as are many details of setting and family—their occupations, the relatives, etc. Even the novel's opening scene is built on an actual event, but the conflicting characters of Melissa and Dr. Tyde are completely made-up. In my books fiction is an adjustment of the facts, to find a more real truth. I may often use real people and things to get started, but then imagination takes over, and the actual people and events recede, while the imaginary ones become (I hope) 'real.'"

HOBBIES AND OTHER INTERESTS: Photography and almost every form of needlework.

PHILLIPS, Elizabeth Louise (Betty Lou Phillips)

BRIEF ENTRY: Born in Cleveland, Ohio. A teacher in Shaker Heights, Ohio, for six years, Phillips turned to sportswriting for the Cleveland Press in 1976. She also worked as a special features editor of *Pro Quarterback* magazine in New York City for three years and, since 1976, has been a free-lance writer and children's book author. Phillips's juvenile works consist of informational books and biographies of sports figures. The first category includes an introductory handbook, *The American Quarter Horse* (McKay, 1979), which describes the history and standards of the quarter horse as well as how to buy and care for one; *Go! Fight! Win! The National Cheerleaders Association Guide for Cheerleaders* (Delacorte, 1981), shows all the glamour and nitty-gritty of cheerleading explained in photographs and easy-to-read text, along with chapters on the rules of football and basketball and a sample constitution for a cheerleading squad; *Something for Nothing: Give-Aways and Near Give-Aways for Teenage Girls* (Ace, 1981); and *Brush Up on Hair Care* (Messner, 1982).

Among the people Phillips has profiled in her biographies are Chris Evert, Dorothy Hamill, Earl Campbell, and Nancy Lopez. Like the others, *The Picture Story of Dorothy Hamill* (Messner, 1978), realistically treats some of the problems in amateur sports with, according to *Booklist,* "an acceptable amount of fictionalization." In a review of *Earl Campbell, Houston Oiler Superstar* (McKay, 1979), *School Library Journal* noted that reconstructed dialogue, action photographs, and clear writing put this work "head and shoulders above most sports biographies." Phillips also contributes articles to young adult and sports magazines. *Home:* 1923 Olympia Dr., Houston, Tex. 77019.

FOR MORE INFORMATION SEE: Who's Who of American Women, 14th edition, Marquis, 1984.

PIERCE, Meredith Ann   1958-

BRIEF ENTRY: Born July 5, 1958, in Seattle, Wash. An author of fantasy novels for young adults, Pierce writes "with plenty of skill and elfish craft," according to *New York Times Book Review.* She conceived the idea for her first book, *The Darkangel* (Little, Brown, 1982), from a dream recounted in Carl Jung's autobiography, *Memories, Dreams, Reflections.* First in a projected trilogy, *The Darkangel* centers around the graceful servant girl, Aeriel, who, after a series of adventures with strange and magical creatures, overcomes the vampire-like Darkangel, thereby freeing him from his enchantment and revealing him to be a young prince. "While the narrative suggests the inspiration of writers like Andersen, Lewis, and Tolkien, the author has her own personal vision, creating a sense of place through powerful images in a haunting, provocative novel," *Horn Book* observed. *The Darkangel* received the International Reading Association Children's Book Award in 1983, and was chosen both a New York Times Outstanding Book and Parents' Choice in 1982.

In its sequel, *A Gathering of Gargoyles* (Little, Brown, 1984), Aeriel is married to the Darkangel, now called Irrylath; however, he remains under the power of the White Witch, and Aeriel embarks on an adventurous journey to gather the gargoyles which will help fight the witch and set her husband free. "The author's imagination seems boundless," noted *Publishers Weekly,* "and she writes with such assurance that readers believe in every magic being and occurrence controlling the destiny of Aeriel and Irrylath.'' Pierce is also the author of *The Woman Who Loved Reindeer* (Atlantic, 1985), the tale of a young girl who raises and falls in love with a ''trangl''—a being who can take the form of deer or man. ''Readers of the author's *Darkangel* will revel in her flair for odd romance and the sometimes striking descriptions of a barren northland,'' commented *Bulletin of the Center for Children's Books.* Pierce's *Birth of the Firebringer* (Macmillan, 1985), involving anthropomorphic unicorns, is the first of another projected trilogy. *Home:* 703 Northwest 19th St., Gainesville, Fla. 32603.

FOR MORE INFORMATION SEE: Contemporary Authors, Volume 108, Gale, 1983.

PRICE, Willard   1887-1983

PERSONAL: Born July 28, 1887, in Peterborough, Ontario, Canada; came to United States in 1901; died October 14, 1983; son of Albert Melancthon and Stella (Martin) Price; married Jean Reeve, August 4, 1914 (died, 1929); married Mary Virginia Selden, May 28, 1932; children: (first marriage) Robert. *Education:* Western Reserve University (now Case Western Reserve University), B.A., 1909; graduate study at New York University, Columbia University, M.A., 1914, Litt.D., 1930. *Residence:* Laguna Hills, Calif. 92653.

CAREER: Explorer, naturalist, writer. Member of editorial staff, *Survey,* 1912-13; Methodist Episcopal Church, editorial secretary, Board of Foreign Missions, 1915-19, editor of *World Outlook,* 1915-20; worked as foreign affairs correspondent, 1933-37; director of periodicals department, Interchurch World Movement; supervising editor of various travel publications.

WRITINGS—Published by John Day, except as indicated: *Ancient Peoples at New Tasks,* Interchurch, 1918; *The Negro around the World,* Doran, 1925; *Pacific Adventure,* 1936; *Children of the Rising Sun,* 1938; *Barbarian,* 1941; *Japan Rides the Tiger,* 1942; *Japan's Islands of Mystery,* 1944; *Japan and the Son of Heaven,* Duell, Sloan & Pearce, 1945; *Key to Japan,* 1946; *Roving South,* 1948; *I Cannot Rest from Travel,* 1951; *The Amazing Amazon,* 1952; *Journey by Junk,* 1953; *Adventures in Paradise,* 1955; *Roaming Britain,* 1958; *Incredible Africa,* 1962; *The Amazing Mississippi,* Heinemann, 1962, John Day, 1963; *Rivers I Have Known,* 1965; *America's Paradise Lost,* 1965.

Juvenile; all published by John Day, except as noted: *Amazon Adventure,* 1949, reissued, Merrimack, 1983; *South Sea Adventure,* 1954, reissued (illustrated by Pat Marriott), Merrimack, 1980; *Underwater Adventure,* 1954, reissued, Merrimack, 1983; *Volcano Adventure,* 1956, reissued, Merrimack, 1983; *Whale Adventure,* 1960, reissued, Merrimack, 1983; *African Adventure,* 1963; *Elephant Adventure,* 1964, reissued, Merrimack, 1983; *Safari Adventure,* 1966, reissued (illustrated by P. Marriott), Merrimack, 1980; *Lion Adventure,* 1967, reissued (illustrated by P. Marriott), Merrimack, 1980; *Gorilla Adventure,* 1968, reissued (illustrated by P. Marriott), Merrimack, 1980; *Diving Adventure,* 1969, reissued (illustrated by P. Marriott), Merrimack, 1980; *Cannibal Adventure,* 1970, reissued, Merrimack, 1983; *Tiger Adventure* (illustrated by P. Marriott), J. Cape, 1980; *Arctic Adventure,* J. Cape, 1980; *My Own Life of Adventure: Travels in 148 Lands,* J. Cape, 1982.

Contributor to *Encyclopaedia Britannica* and national periodicals.

SIDELIGHTS: ''I was born in the Canadian town of Peterborough, where canoes are made. The year was **1887.**

Stratford by the tranquil Avon. ■ (From *Roaming Britain* by Willard Price. Photograph by the author.)

''At the age of four I had my first great adventure. My father took me to Stony Lake, a few miles north of town.

''He rented a canoe. He did not place me in the bow where I would have nothing to do. He didn't believe in making things too easy for his son.

''He placed me in the stern and put a paddle in my hands. I paddled and the canoe went round in a circle.

'' 'This boat is no good,' I complained. 'It doesn't go straight.'

'' 'You can make it go straight,' Dad said. 'Now, slowly, draw the paddle back through the water.'

''I did.

'' 'Stop. Don't take the paddle out. Turn it like this.' I turned it flat against the canoe. 'Now push out.'

''I pushed out and the canoe went straight.

''In two minutes he had taught me what many canoeists never learn. They keep flipping the paddle from side to side to stop the turning. The wet paddle showers anyone in front. After being soaked, the person or persons in front decide that canoeing is just not for them. Then they lose one of the greatest pleasures a lake or river can offer.

"Later on I was rude to our maid. She was ugly. I said, 'You look like an old crow.' She told Father what I had said.

"Father got a stick and took me far from the house so my howls could not be heard. There he stopped. I braced myself. I was not going to yell, no matter how much it hurt. I would take it out on the maid later.

"Dad looked at me sadly, tears in his eyes.

"He handed me the stick. 'Whip *me*,' he said.

"That took all the hate out of me. I was so surprised that I could not speak.

"I dropped the stick and we walked back to the house. His action did more for me than the stick could ever have done." [Willard Price, *My Own Life of Adventure*, Jonathan Cape, 1982.[1]]

From the age of four, Price had decided to become an explorer. "My adventures began in my boyhood on a home pond in Canada. I pretended it was the ocean. I sailed across it on my homemade raft to Hong Kong, Shanghai, and Manila and got back home in time for supper. It was a great day when I first saw a river and was allowed to row a boat on it. During my teens I made many canoe trips down wild Canadian rivers, shooting the rapids." [Willard Price, "I Began My Adventures on a Pond," *Young Wings*, June, 1952.[2]]

1901. Father moved the family to Cleveland for business reasons.

1905. "In Cleveland I submitted to the grind of education in Western Reserve University, supplemented later by a spell in Columbia for an M.A. and doctorate.

"The best time of the year was the summer vacation. With a passion for exploration I walked three hundred miles from Cleveland to Detroit and back. My journey was relieved now and then by a ride on a farmer's wagon. I slept in barns, always with the farmer's permission. Sometimes I was invited in to eat with the family. One night there was no barn, but there was a haystack. I bored a hole in it, inserted myself and slept well.

"One summer I jumped at the chance to earn one dollar a day for only ten hours' work daily as deck-hand on the coal boat, *Socapa*, sailing the Great Lakes from Cleveland to Duluth. I scrubbed decks, painted bulkheads, polished brass. I was hose supporter for Winnie the Watchman. He handled the nozzle: I came fifty feet behind lugging the weight of the four-inch hose."[1]

1909. "Graduating from Western Reserve University . . . I was faced with the necessity of getting a job. There would be more chance of this in New York than in Cleveland.

"On a raw December morning I stepped off the train in New York, without a friend in the city, with only a few dollars in my pocket, and had to find a job at once. I was going to find out for myself just what it was to be a stranger in a vast city, to search for work, to live in a cheap boardinghouse, and to withstand temptations. I think I vaguely hoped that there would be a few temptations.

"During the day I applied for positions as agent for a credit firm, driver of a butcher's wagon, salesman in a department store, member of the mounted police, conductor on a street car, and valet.

"The job I finally landed, about four o'clock in the afternoon, was as a printer's devil at six dollars a week. The Red Diamond Press had advertised for 'a boy to learn the business.' The shop was on Twenty-third Street opposite the Metropolitan Life Insurance Building and the owner was John Whiting. He was a clergyman on the side; or perhaps he was a clergyman first, and a printer on the side—I never quite learned which. I apologized for not being a 'boy,' but declared myself eager to learn printing.

"Within half an hour I was launched upon the typical work of the printer's devil—running errands, toting enormous bundles of stock about town, taking orders from the office girls, compositors and press men, sweeping floors, making fires, cleaning presses and distributing type.

"Within a few weeks I was trying my hand at feeding presses, setting up type, pulling proofs, and making estimates. I received my cheque for six dollars every week with my title 'printer's devil' actually written in after my name—that was Mr Whiting's little joke—and how proud I was one week when I saw that the amount on the cheque had been boosted to four times its old size, and that the title had been changed to 'assistant manager.'

"Even while my wages stood at six dollars I saved money, for I was curious to see how little a fellow could live on in a great city. Besides, I was already dreaming of a trip to London.

The young Willard Price, deckhand on the coal boat, *Socapa*.

"Things I used to think I had to have, I got along without. I read other people's newspapers. I walked a mile and a half morning and night to and from work. I did without candy, ice-cream sodas, motion pictures, new clothes. During one week I spent not a single penny outside of the four dollars for board and room. I got what free entertainment I could from libraries, lectures, boarding-house life and churches."[1]

After four months of work in New York, Price had saved enough money to buy a one-way, third-class ticket on a ship bound for Scotland. From Glasgow he traveled by train to London. "I arrived in London with thirty dollars in my pocket. But what of that? I had got myself a job on my first day in New York. I would do the same in London. Anyone could get a job if he went after it with enough determination. I had no

patience with lazy youths who complained that they could not find work. They didn't really try. They waited for work to come to them on a silver platter.

"I set out to find a job before nightfall. Night fell and I had no job.

"At the end of five weeks, jobless as ever, I had three shillings. Then the doors of opportunity rolled open with this advertisement: 'Wanted—an experienced press reviser to pass for press the varied work of a good commercial jobbing printer; 44s. 53 hours per week.'

"'What experience? asked young, spectacled Harry Wilkes in the big plant of the Wilkes Brothers south of the Thames.

Vic looked utterly defeated. ■ (From *Tiger Adventure* by Willard Price. Illustrated by Pat Marriott.)

"I told him of my four months in the Red Diamond Press.

"He smiled, 'Normally, it takes three years of experience to qualify for this work. But, somehow, I think you can do it. Start on Monday.'

"I went out walking on air. I was sobered when my fingers encountered the few shillings and pence in my pocket. I could not ask for an advance on my salary. There would be no bus fares and other expenses, not to mention food. But nothing seemed difficult now.

"No one knew during the first wonderful week in the press room that the new press reviser was fasting. Not fasting completely, to be sure, but limiting himself to penny meals. My total expense for food that week was one shilling and sixpence. . . .

"On Saturday I drew my pay, forty-four shillings. As if this were not enough good fortune, Mr Lambert, foreman of the press room, invited me to go home with him to dinner. He suggested that we walk. Weak from lack of food I could hardly keep up with him. I broke into a sweat. The blue veins stood out so prominently on my temples and forehead that he remarked on them.

"The meal was a very plain one of beef, potatoes and a sweet. But my stomach could not hold it. As soon as I left the house I retired into an alley and threw it up.

"I went to the pawn-shop where I had deposited my watch, and redeemed it. I paid my rent and spent sixteen shillings on a pair of shoes. It is wonderful what a good feeling thick, new soles and heels give to a person.

"I saved most of my princely salary for a trip through Europe. . . ."[1]

1911. Set out on a 2,000 mile bicycle trip through Europe that included visits to seven nations. "I cycled on into Belgium, visiting Antwerp and Brussels, and the field of Waterloo, made vivid to me by my own school oration on the fall of Napoleon. I dipped into France. Then to Germany, to be transported into olden times by the ruins of castles crowning the heights along the Rhine. I cycled through Heidelberg, Ulm, Munich, and to Oberammergau.

"I made my way into Austria, through Innsbruck and up the valley of the swift-flowing Inn, cooking my own dinner over a camp-fire by the turbulent stream.

"Up to the roof of Europe where a sign marks the divide between waters flowing to the North Sea and those to the Black.

"Down and across Switzerland, to gaze upon the peak-reflecting mirrors of Lakes Constance, Zurich, Zug, Lucerne, Brienz, and to explore the blue grottoes in the heart of Grindewald glacier. From Geneva I circled up through the French province of Savoy to the vale of Chamonix, then again entered Switzerland and dropped down to Martigny by a dizzy road that made my arms stiff and numb from gripping the brake.

"The palaces of Genoa and the leaning tower of Pisa made slight impression upon me compared with the art treasures of Florence. How wonderful were the Italian people, who could create a 'Last Supper' or carry off a locked bicycle with equal ease. I filled a note-book with detailed descriptions of the great paintings in the Uffizi and Pitti Galleries.

"Then to Rome, where I marvelled again. And to Naples, where I promptly climbed Vesuvius, then began to look for a passage to America.

"The bicycle trip had covered 2,180 miles. I had enjoyed it, but I was saddle-sore, and did not care particularly if I never saw a bicycle again as long as I lived. After I sold my bicycle I had seven pounds."[1]

Returned to the United States as a steerage passenger on a ship carrying immigrants.

1912. Began writing for journals and newspapers. ". . . If I was going to write, I might as well begin. I had no false notion that it would bring much—but I could live on little. I went to the editor of *Leslie's Weekly* and told him about my steerage experience. 'Write it,' he said. I wrote and he published.

"I worked evenings in the Neighbourhood House in Newark; made a survey of Newark's slums and published it; investi-

Meet the most beautiful monkey in all Africa. . . .This is the colobus. ■ (From *Safari Adventure* by Willard Price. Illustrated by Pat Marriott.)

He suddenly learned something about tigers. Tigers *love* water. ■ (From *Tiger Adventure* by Willard Price. Illustrated by Pat Marriott.)

gated with my friend, Herschel Jones, child labour conditions in a Pittsburgh steel plant, wrote articles about it, and had the satisfaction of seeing conditions improved; was appointed editor of three magazines, *World Outlook, Everyland,* and, later, *Journey's Beautiful.* Since all three were on world affairs, I had to travel the world to get material.

"There was also a ready market in *National Geographic, Saturday Evening Post, Harper's* and many other magazines and newspapers in America, Britain, France, Germany and Japan.

"In Cuba I wrote about sugar and in Jamaica about black and white; in Guatemala I made a 150-mile donkey-back ride through Indian villages, eating Indian food, sleeping in Indian homes; in British Honduras I saw how readily Englishmen take to the tropics; in Honduras I had a look at the dollar diplomacy of the United Fruit Company; I went on to Costa Rica to ride horseback through that lovely land. . . ."[1]

". . . I could not edit a magazine on foreign lands without going to foreign lands, could I? So off I went—to Japan, China, Korea; to Panama, Guatemala, Costa Rica; a year later, to most of the countries of South America; the next year, to England, France, Italy; and then to Morocco, Algeria, Tunisia."[2]

1914. Married Jean Reeve, who died in 1929. One son, Robert, was born to the marriage.

1930. Went on a round-the-world journey which included a visit to the island of Sumatra where he studied and wrote about the customs of the Bataks, a tribe of cannibals.

". . . The brain of the father or the heart of the mother was eaten by their children to acquire their virtues. The aged looked forward to being eaten upon death. It was a mark of great honour. When an old man felt that he had about completed his life and should now distribute his knowledge among his fellowmen, he would, if he had the courage and strength, climb a tree and fall to his death from the branches as ripe fruit falls. The villagers would then feast upon his wise old flesh.

"I filled a note-book with data about these remarkable people."[1]

1932. Married Mary Virginia Selden, who often accompanied him on his many expeditions. Throughout his writing career, he traveled to over 140 countries, working as an author, explorer, and naturalist for the National Geographic Society and the American Museum of Natural History. "Of all the curious expeditions I was asked to make by geographic societies perhaps the most absorbing was a year's journey of 23,000 miles through twenty-seven countries of Latin America.

"Of primitive arts, one of the most remarkable was the shrinking of a human head to the size of an orange and treating it so that it would last.

"Locked away from the world behind the Andes, in the little-explored jungle about the headwaters of the Amazon, the Jivaro Indians had developed this peculiar talent.

"And they were making it pay. To be sure, the traffic in heads is forbidden by the laws of Ecuador and Peru, and any person caught selling or buying a head is fined. But a bootleg business thrives. Few tourists can spend a day in Quito without being offered one or more such trophies, at about $60 each."[1]

1933. "We went to Japan intending to stay there a year. We stayed five.

"There was plenty to write about. A stream of articles went back to the U.S. and U.K.

"We had rented a house in Hayama, a fishing village on the coast of Sagami Bay. We were the only foreigners in the village. It gave us an opportunity to study the real Japan; and yet it was only an hour's train journey from Tokyo.

"In Hayama one must speak Japanese or nothing. Houses were of wood and paper, floors were meant to be slept on, baths were four feet deep.

"We had a view of Mt. Fuji across Sagami Bay and of smoking Mihara Volcano out to sea.

He kept waving the meat in the air so that the sight of it and the smell of it would attract the shark. ■ (From *Cannibal Adventure* by Willard Price. Illustrated by Pat Marriott.)

"... When we arrived in 1933 the Japanese did not feel too unkindly towards foreigners. Before we left in 1938 the Japanese army had succeeded in whipping up a bitter anti-foreign sentiment, and any Japanese seen in conversation with foreigners were called to police headquarters for questioning. Visits to our neighbours' houses or their visits to ours had to be secret. But even those who carefully avoided close friendship with us always showed a courtesy hardly to be expected in a rough fishing village.

"Our fellow-villagers were as honest as they were thoughtful. We never locked our doors. In fact we left the sliding doors open at night to admit air. . . .

"During the day we were likely to be in Tokyo. Occasionally we left the Hayama house for months at a time, travelling in Japan, Korea, Manchuria, Mongolia, China and the Philippines. Besides a roving commission with the *New York Herald Tribune* and London *Daily Telegraph,* I had assignments from

Price playfully trying out a cannibal stewpot.

They sank rapidly through shoals of brightly coloured angelfish. . . . They began to see the roofs of Undersea City. ■ (From *Diving Adventure* by Willard Price. Illustrated by Pat Marriott.)

American and British magazines. Now, for the first time, I thought of myself as being really a writer.

"My son, Robert, was well along in his schooling and would clear Cornell and Harvard Law School without much more help.

"Considerable dabbling in natural history had led to a pleasant relationship with the American Museum of Natural History, the Explorers' Club, the National Geographic Society, the American Geographical Society, of which I became a Fellow, and the Royal Geographical Society, with which I had no connection except as an occasional reporter. Watching for material of interest to such groups, we had an excuse to make expeditions that otherwise would have been foolish, if not foolhardy. . . .

"Bitterness against America because she objected to Japan's ambitions to gobble up Asia had reached such intensity that lovely Japan was no longer lovely for Americans. We left in 1938.

"On **December 7, 1941,** it happened—the attack on Pearl Harbor.

"I happened to be scheduled to lecture on Japan the next day in the Ambassador Hotel, Los Angeles.

"After the talk a woman rose and asked, 'How long do you think this war will last?'

"'How can we tell? But if I must guess I would say that it may last five years.'

"I was wrong by one year. The war lasted four years.

It was enough to discourage most hunters—but not the young pygmy. ■ (From *Elephant Adventure* by Willard Price. Illustrated by Pat Marriott.)

"Why so long? Because to get to Japan our main fleet must battle its way from Australian waters through the incredible barricade of 2,100 Micronesian islands.

"My son fought in that war. I did not—too old. But, as it happened, I had a small share in it. My book, *Japan's Islands of Mystery,* was the only book in English about the islands. It was no guide book, but it did describe the islands, therefore it was better than nothing. A member of Admiral Nimitz's staff informed him of its existence and the Admiral placed three hundred copies in the hands of his officers. He wrote me a warm letter of appreciation. The book was reprinted nine times."[1]

1946. A trip through the Amazon jungle resulted in two books, *The Amazing Amazon,* for adults, and *Amazon Adventure,* for children. "It took ten months . . . to visit every Central American country, coffee-rich Colombia, lofty Ecuador, Peru with its modern Lima and ancient Cuzco, Bolivia, breathlessly high, and beautiful Lake Titicaca, Chile with its copper mines, Argentina with its overbearing Peron and even more evil Eva, Patagonia near the south end of the world, progressive Uruguay, sleepy Paraguay, Brazil with its bustling Sao Paolo and charming Rio, and *the world's greatest river.*

"We flew a thousand miles up the Amazon to Manaus.

"From childhood we have been taught that the Amazon is a river. That seems plain enough. We know what a river is. A river is a stream of water flowing between banks. Therefore in our mind's eye we see the Amazon as a great stream flowing between walls of jungle.

"The Amazon is not like that. It might better be described as a moving sea. It resembles the Mediterranean more than the Mississippi. It has in fact been called the Mediterranean of South America. Early explorers named it Mar Dulce, Sweet Sea, or Freshwater Sea. Brazilians call it the Sea River.

"Place the mouth of the Amazon at New York and its arms would reach up into Canada and down into Mexico and almost to California. Straighten out the kinks, and the small end would stretch twelve hundred miles out into the Pacific. All Europe could be placed within the Amazon basin and have room left for a dozen Japans."[1]

1949. First book for boys published. Price's books, filled with action and intrigue, included a series of adventure stories featuring two teenage boys and their zoologist father. "The best way to write adventure is to live adventure—and that is what led me into many strange experiences: hunting tigers, sharks, and wild boars; climbing volcanoes; riding a runaway elephant; seeing the Sahara Desert from the hump of a camel; sailing the Nile River in a small boat; traveling in seventy lands. Out of such experiences I have written [over] fifteen books. My most interesting adventures were in the Amazon jungle and the South Seas, and it is upon these experiences that I have drawn in writing my two books for boys: *Amazon Adventure* and . . . *South Sea Adventure.*"[2]

1958. Met Albert Schweitzer in Africa and visited with him at his hospital. "Albert Schweitzer was the most interesting man we found in Africa.

"He had lived very comfortably in Germany, respected by everyone, a fine organist, a philosopher, winner of the Nobel Prize for Peace.

In a convulsive struggle the manta flailed out with arms, wing ends, and tail. ■ (From *South Sea Adventure* by Willard Price. Illustrated by Pat Marriott.)

"But he left all this fame and fortune to go to Africa and do what he could for the sick and suffering natives of the Gabon forest.

"He selected a spot on the Ogooué River in dense jungle, and there he built a hospital.

"There was no road to his hospital. . . . A python dropped from an overhanging branch into the water barely missing the boat. The snouts of waiting crocodiles nudged up on to the beach. Cranes strutted on the sandbars.

"Around the cape, and 'There it is,'—a group of red-roofed buildings were seen on a climbing shore among the palms and Dr. Schweitzer fairly ran to meet us, beaming as if we were the only visitors he had seen in a year. Perhaps we were.''[1]

1961. Returned to Africa. "The Nile was great—but the greatest thing in Africa was the wildlife.

There were more wild animals in East Africa then the total in all the rest of the world!

". . . On the second journey we chose the long way around. Our ticket strips this time were twelve feet in length.

"They would take us to every important country down the west coast of Africa, allow us to stop as long as we pleased in each, then up the east coast with stops, to Kenya.

Price with the first Thames bridge.

"I filled note-books with solid facts, commercial, industrial, political, for a new book, but in this book I am expected to stick to adventures.

"Flying south across the Sahara Desert we nearly crashed into dunes six hundred to a thousand feet high.

"These hills of sand were constantly on the move. The prevailing wind kept them going. If there was an oasis in the way, it was buried.

"There are few places in the world where hills walk. Desert tribes must be constantly anxious for fear that they might wake up some morning gasping for breath under a walking hill.

"We flew to Casablanca, where stores are closed three days a week—because you are not supposed to do business on the Sabbath. And Casablanca has three Sabbaths—Friday for the Muslims, Saturday for the Jews, Sunday for the Christians!

"Next, Dakar, on a point closer to South America than any other part of Africa.

"Then the countries under the bulge, Ivory Coast, Ghana, Dahomey, Nigeria and Cameroon, all of which were forced in the past to ship black people to slavery in so-called civilized lands.

"To Namibia whose beaches are sprinkled with diamonds. To the Cape of Good Hope in South Africa where I feel there is little good hope for millions of black people.

"And so we travelled up the east coast, stopping in every country, and arriving at last in Nairobi, heart of the greatest multitude of wild animals on the face of the earth.''[1]

1964. Visited New Zealand and Australia.

1982. At the age of ninety-five the author-explorer wrote about his many adventures in 148 countries in a book entitled *My Own Life of Adventure*. On his trips to remote areas he traveled by bicycle, camel, canoe, elephant, boat, train and plane. "Since our last round-the-world trip we have visited Switzerland, Hawaii, Alaska, Greece, Austria, Mexico, New Zealand and Australia. But the only notable adventure was a misadventure—a crash on the highway causing twenty-six injuries. That took the travel bug out of my system. Now, 95 years old, I am content to rest on my oars, or, rather, my paddle, and let the world go by.''[1]

October 14, 1983. Died at the age of ninety-six.

FOR MORE INFORMATION SEE: Martha E. Ward and Dorothy A. Marquardt, *Authors of Books for Young People*, 2nd edition, Scarecrow, 1971; Willard Price, *My Own Life of Adventure: Travels in 148 Lands*, J. Cape, 1982.

PRIMAVERA, Elise 1954-

BRIEF ENTRY: Born May 19, 1954, in West Long Branch, N.J. A children's book illustrator, Primavera originally intended to be a professional equestrian. Torn between riding and art, she eventually decided on art, majoring in fashion illustration at Moore College of Art and later studying at the Arts Students League in New York City. She worked as a free-lance fashion illustrator for three years before turning to full-time book illustration in 1979. Horses are still a part of her life; she raises them as a hobby, and the first book she wrote as well as illustrated, *Basil and Maggie* (Lippincott, 1983), is about a pony. In the humorous story, Maggie's aunt sends her best pony, Basil, from England. Maggie expects to win a horseshow astride Basil, but compared to the other horses in the show, he is shaggy and clumsy, laughed at by the other riders, and terrible in all the events. Saved by pouring rain and a muddy track, on which the England-bred pony is used to running, Basil wins the last event. According to *Booklist*, Primavera's illustrations depict "gawky, ungainly creatures with outrageously personified faces that reflect and exaggerate the story's events." Primavera has illustrated Art Buchwald's *The Bollo Caper: A Furry Tail for All Days* (Putnam, 1983), Natalie Savage Carlson's *Surprise in the Mountains* (Harper, 1983), Jean Fritz's *Make Way for Sam Houston* (Putnam, 1986), Delia Ephron's *Santa and Alex* (Little, Brown, 1983), and others. *Residence:* New Jersey.

FOR MORE INFORMATION SEE: Jim Roginski, *Behind the Covers: Interviews with Authors and Illustrators of Books for Children and Young Adults*, Libraries Unlimited, 1985.

RICHARDS, Norman 1932-

PERSONAL: Born March 14, 1932, in Winchendon, Mass.; son of Burton W. (in business) and Berthalene (a nurse; maiden name, Webster) Richards; children: Gary, Gayle, Gregory. *Education:* Boston University, B.S., 1958; graduate study at Harvard University, 1959. *Home:* 905 Fox Run Road, Findlay, Ohio 45840. *Office:* Publications Dept., Marathon Oil Co., 539 South Main St., Findlay, Ohio 45840.

Lumbermen brought the finest planks of live oak and red cedar. ■ (From *The Story of Old Ironsides* by Norman Richards. Illustrated by Tom Dunnington.)

CAREER: United Airlines, Chicago, Ill., managing editor of monthly travel magazine, *Mainliner*, 1962-68; *Chicago* (magazine), Chicago, editor, 1968-69; *Patient Care* (medical magazine), Greenwich, Conn., 1969-71; Exxon Corp., New York, N.Y., managing editor of magazine, *The Lamp*, 1971-79; Marathon Oil Co., Findlay, Ohio, manager of publications, 1979—. *Military service:* U.S. Navy, served as aircraft crew member and control tower operator during Korean War.

WRITINGS—All for young people, except as noted; all published by Childrens Press, except as noted: *Douglas MacArthur*, 1967; *Giants in the Sky* (Junior Literary Guild selection; illustrated by Robert Borja and Corinne Borja), 1967; (with John P. Reidy) *John F. Kennedy*, 1967; *The Story of Old Ironsides* (Junior Literary Guild selection; illustrated by Tom Dunnington), 1967; *The Story of the Mayflower Compact* (illustrated by Darrell Wiskur), 1967; *Ernest Hemingway*, 1968; *Helen Keller*, 1968; *Robert Frost*, 1968; *The Story of the Declaration of Independence* (illustrated by T. Dunnington), 1968; *Dag Hammarskjöld*, 1969; *Pope John XXIII*, 1969; *The Story of the Bonhomme Richard* (illustrated by T. Dunnington), 1969; *The Story of Monticello* (illustrated by Chuck Mitchell), 1970; *The Story of the Alamo* (illustrated by T. Dunnington), 1970; *Jetport*, Doubleday, 1973; *The Complete Beginner's Guide to Soaring and Hang Gliding*, Doubleday, 1976; *Tractors, Plows, and Harvesters: A Book about Farm Machines*, Doubleday, 1978; (with Pat Richards) *Trucks and Supertrucks*, Doubleday, 1980; *Dreamers and Doers: Inventors Who Changed the World*, Atheneum, 1984; *Cowboy Movies* (adult nonfiction), Bison Books, 1984.

Contributor of articles to periodicals, including *Gentlemen's Quarterly, Reader's Digest,* and a variety of travel magazines.

WORK IN PROGRESS: In conjunction with Cleveland Clinic, a book on open-heart surgery for patients and patients' families.

ROOT, Phyllis

BRIEF ENTRY: Born in Fort Wayne, Ind. A graduate of Valparaiso University, Root is a free-lance writer and author of children's books. In *Moon Tiger* (Holt, 1985), young Jessica refuses to read her little brother a story and is sent to bed. Once in her room, she indulges in several flights of fancy. *Bulletin of the Center for Children's Books* described *Moon Tiger* as "lyrical in both illustration and narrative . . . the stuff of which dreams are made," while *Booklist* called it "a satisfying story that deals with emotions familiar to all children." *Soup for Supper* (Harper, 1986) tells the story of a wee small woman and the giant who invades her vegetable garden in search of soup ingredients. After a fuss, the woman cooks up a pot of soup for both of them, and the two learn to live in harmony as neighbors. According to *School Library Journal*, this book contains "ideal material for storytelling or for reading aloud." Among Root's other picture books are *Hidden Places* (Raintree, 1983), *Joshua Holly's Big Family Blues* (Raintree, 1985), and *My Cousin Charlie* (Raintree, 1985). She has also collaborated with author Carol A. Marron on several additional children's books, including *Gretchen's Grandma* (Raintree, 1983), *Just One of the Family* (Raintree, 1984), and *No Place for a Pig* (Raintree, 1984). *Residence:* Minneapolis, Minn.

Education is the ability to listen to almost anything without losing your temper or your self-confidence.

—Robert Frost

ROSEN, Michael (Wayne) 1946-

PERSONAL: Born May 7, 1946, in Harrow, Middlesex, England; son of Harold (a professor) and Connie Ruby (a college lecturer; maiden name, Isakovsky) Rosen. *Education:* Attended Middlesex Hospital Medical School, 1964-65, Wadham College, Oxford, 1965-69, and National Film School, 1973-76. *Politics:* Socialist. *Religion:* Atheist. *Home:* 49 Parkholme Rd., London E8 3AQ, England. *Agent:* Sara Drake, A. D. Peters, 10 Buckingham St., London WC2, England.

CAREER: Writer, poet, playwright, and broadcaster. *Awards, honors: Sunday Times* National Union of Students Drama Festival Award for best original full-length play, 1968, for *Backbone;* Signal Poetry Award, 1982, for *You Can't Catch Me!;* Other Award from *Children's Book Bulletin,* 1983, for *Everybody Here!.*

WRITINGS—Juvenile; published by Deutsch, except as indicated: *Mind Your Own Business* (verse; illustrated by Quentin Blake), 1974; *Once There Was a King Who Promised He Would Never Chop Anyone's Head Off* (fiction; illustrated by Kathy Henderson), 1976; *Wouldn't You Like to Know* (verse; illustrated by Q. Blake), 1977, revised edition, Penguin (London), 1981; *The Bakerloo Flea* (fiction; illustrated by Q. Blake), Longmans, 1979; (with Roger McGough) *You Tell Me* (verse; illustrated by Sara Midda), Kestrel, 1979.

I See a Voice, Hutchinson, 1981; *You Can't Catch Me!* (illustrated by Q. Blake), 1981; *Nasty!* (fiction; illustrated by Amanda Macphail), Longmans, 1982, revised edition, Puffin, 1984; (editor) *Everybody Here!,* Bodley Head, 1982; (editor with Susanna Steele) *Inky Pinky Ponky: Collected Playground Rhymes* (illustrated by Dan Jones), Granada, 1982; *A Cat and Mouse Story* (fiction; illustrated by William Rushton), 1983; *Quick, Let's Get Out of Here* (illustrated by Q. Blake), 1983; *How to Get Out of the Bath and Other Problems,* Scholastic, 1984; *Bloody L.I.A.R.S.* (adult), privately published, 1984; *Hairy Tales and Nursery Crimes* (poems and stories), 1985; *Kingfisher Book of Children's Poetry,* Kingfisher, 1985; *Don't Put Mustard in the Custard* (poems; illustrated by Q. Blake), 1985; *Under the Bed* (poems and jokes; illustated by Q. Blake), Walker, 1986; *Smelly Jelly, Smelly Fish* (poems and jokes; illustrated by Q. Blake), Walker, 1986; *When Did You Last Wash Your Feet* (illustrated by Tony Pinchuk), Deutsch, 1986; *You're Thinking about Doughnuts* (illustrated by T. Pinchuk), 1987; *The Hypnotiser* (illustrated by T. Pinchuk), 1987.

Television: "You Tell Me" (series), Thames TV, 1981; "The Juice Job" (series), Thames TV, 1981, 1984; "Everybody Here" (multicultural children's series), Channel 4, (England), 1982; "Black and White and Read All Over" (series), Channel 4, (England), 1984; "Talk Write Read," Central TV, 1986.

Plays; for adults: "Stewed Figs," first produced in Edinburgh at University of Durham, 1968; *Backbone* (first produced at Oxford University, 1967; produced on the West End at Royal Court Theatre, February, 1968), Faber, 1968; "Regis Debray" (radio play), first produced on BBC-Radio 4, 1971.

(From *Smelly Jelly, Smelly Fish* by Michael Rosen. Illustrated by Quentin Blake.)

MICHAEL ROSEN

Also author of *Speaking to You,* with David Jackson, Macmillan, and *That'd Be Telling,* with Joan Griffiths, Cambridge University Press.

Contributor of drama features for radio and articles to *New Statesman.*

WORK IN PROGRESS: The Amazing Adventures of Till Owlyglass for Walker; *We're Going on a Bear Hunt* for Walker; six scrapbooks for Walker; *Aziz,* a picture book, for Deutsch; a series called "Solly the Sulk."

SIDELIGHTS: "I used to write in school. I was very interested in all that, and I got a lot of encouragement from home. But the first time I actually started writing out of school was when I was about sixteen or seventeen. That was mostly under the influence of having read *Portrait of the Artist as a Young Man.* That book really came home to me. It was really quite extraordinary, because for the first time I realised that you could write in different voices to suit different characters or different purposes. It was the first time I realised you could actually play around with different ways of saying something. So, for example, you could do a stream of consciousness or you could write about things that happened to you when you were six, and you could do it in the voice of a child of six. So I became absolutely fascinated by this idea and I started to write a few things of that sort.

"At the same time . . . I was writing a lot of adolescent stuff. That was greatly influenced by having to study Gerard Manley Hopkins. I got into a thing about the ways in which you could use imagery, compress ideas, that sort of thing. I got quite fascinated by all that, and I spent quite a lot of time—probably the next four or five years—writing like that.

". . . When I went to university, I did quite a lot of fooling around in 'revue' and that sort of thing. Later, I wrote a play

which was actually put on at the Royal Court. . . . I was very interested in performance, in drama, and mucking around in comedy on the stage.

"It was round about then that I realised I could write about my own childhood. At the time my mum, Connie, was doing some programmes for 'Living Language' [a BBC-Radio program]. Home from university, and, seeing her preparing the programmes and the wonderful poems she was choosing, I thought, 'I wouldn't mind having a bash at writing poems like that.' I realised, you see, that you could write about your own childhood in a serious way and yet still be appreciated by children. That is, rather than write about it from an adult point of view, you could look back on your childhood and write about it from within. So I started to write some poems in that sort of area. Connie used one or two in her programmes, and I began to build up a pile of these. Then various producers at the BBC, people like Joan Griffiths and Paddy Becheley, started using my poems in their programmes, so, after I'd got about sixty or seventy odd, I sent them around to publishers. They turned them down, saying that 'Children don't like poems written from the child's point of view.' Then Pam Royds, from Andre Deutsch, saw them and they said 'What lovely fun!,' 'Tremendous!' and so they married me to [illustrator] Quentin Blake, and that's how *Mind Your Own Business* came about.

". . . What pleased me about what I do is that I've built up a style, a performance for young children that is my own and that I've drawn from things like that." ["An Interview with Michael Rosen," *Language Matters,* Centre for Language in Primary Education, 1983.[1]]

Rosen has earned a reputation as a children's poet who writes nonsense verse and humor in dialogue form. In his poems he deals with everyday situations—sharing a bedroom, having your hair cut, tying your shoes—from a child's viewpoint. "There is a strand of poetry that tells the child to look at the world in a certain way. That is as though a poem is saying, 'Look here, and you'll see autumn or trees or a lamb. Isn't it nice? . . . 'Although plenty of people have written about their childhood, they haven't written about it in the kind of speaking voice that is totally accessible to child, so that they can read it out loud. What I try to do in my mind is to go back and write about my feelings when I was ten. . . . I write about my experience using the voice of a ten year old. I write in that voice, using what I know as a performer will work, knowing, that is, what children can take off a page.

". . . I think Robert Louis Stevenson was doing it in the *Child's Garden of Verses.* . . . I was brought up on some of these by the way. But it's not just writing from the child's point of view—another one was A. A. Milne—it's which aspects of your childhood you look at. For example, many of these people haven't looked at the slanging matches, the kind of banter that goes on inside the home; whereas, for me, that's the very stuff of life."[1]

Rosen has contributed to a children's series on poetry for Thames Television in London, and for Central Television two programs for the series "Talk Write and Read." ". . . All the nitty-gritty of everyday life for children has never been written about, but they can do it. They can do it, and they do. They do it with their everyday experience and with their own language. . . ."[1]

Besides writing poetry, Rosen has written children's stories and three plays for adults. "Mostly I write about myself. This is potentially very boring, but I try to make sure it isn't by meeting children in schools and libraries, and informally. I try to discover where my experiences overlap with theirs. Some people are worried about whether what I write is 'poetry.' If they are worried, let them call it something else, for example, 'stuff.'"

HOBBIES AND OTHER INTERESTS: Popular culture, folk culture, oral tradition.

FOR MORE INFORMATION SEE: Christian Science Monitor, February 21, 1968; *Punch,* May 15, 1968; *Prompt,* number 12, 1968; *Times Literary Supplement,* March 29, 1974, October 28, 1977, November 25, 1983, March 8, 1985; *Times Educational Supplement,* January 1, 1982; Daniel Kirkpatrick, editor, *Twentieth-Century Children's Writers,* 2nd edition, St. Martin's, 1983.

ROSS, Clare (Romano)   1922-
   (Clare Romano)

PERSONAL: Born August 24, 1922, in Palisade, N.J.; daughter of Antonio (a furniture refinisher) and Louisa (Cafora) Romano; married John Ross (an artist, painter, and professor), November 23, 1943; children: Christopher, Timothy. *Education:* Attended Cooper Union School of Art, 1939-43, Ecole des Beaux Arts, Fontainebleau, France, 1949, and Instituto Statale d'Arte, Florence, Italy, 1959. *Home:* 110 Davison Pl., Englewood, N.J. 07631. *Office:* Pratt Graphic Art Center, New York, N.Y.

CAREER: Artist. Art Center of Northern New Jersey, Tenafly, instructor in painting and design, 1961-65; New School for Social Research, New York City, instructor in printmaking, 1960—; Pratt Graphic Art Center, New York City, instructor in printmaking, 1963—; Manhattanville College, Purchase, N.Y., instructor in printmaking, 1964-65; Pratt Institute, Brooklyn, N.Y., 1964—, began as assistant professor, currently associate professor in printmaking. Lecturer for television, colleges, and universities. U.S. Information Agency, artist-in-residence at "Graphic Arts U.S.A.," an exhibition. *Exhibitions:* Has had about forty one-person shows, including Associated American Artists Gallery, 1967, and Boston Museum of Fine Arts, 1968, and group exhibitions. Work is included in many permanent collections, including Metropolitan Museum of Art, Library of Congress, Smithsonian Institution, National Collection of Fine Arts, more than a dozen U.S. embassies abroad, and private galleries. Art work has been commissioned by Jewish Museum, Hilton Hotel, International Graphic Arts Society, Philadelphia Print Club, and Manufacturers Hanover Trust.

MEMBER: Society of American Graphic Artists (president, 1970-72), American Color Print Society, National Academy (associate member), Federation of Modern Painters and Sculptors, Print Club of Philadelphia, Boston Printmakers. *Awards, honors:* Purchase awards from Brooklyn Museum, 1951, Library of Congress, 1951, 1966, New Jersey State Museum, 1967, 1970, Boston Printmakers, 1967, eighth national print exhibit of Silvermine Guild, 1970; Louis Comfort Tiffany grant for printmaking, 1952; awards from Society of American

CLARE ROSS

Graphic Artists, 1953, 1962, 1967, 1968, 1971; Fulbright grant for printmaking in Florence, Italy, 1958-59; awards from Philadelphia Print Club, 1960, 1971, Montclair Museum, 1962; citation for professional achievement from Cooper Union School of Art, 1966; John Taylor Arms Memorial Prize from National Academy, 1967; presentation artist award from Boston Printmakers, 1967; *God Wash the World and Start Again* was selected one of Child Study Association of America's Children's Books of the Year, 1971, and *Conjure Tales,* 1974.

WRITINGS—Under name Clare Romano: (Author of introduction) Burton Wasserman, *Bridges of Vision,* New Jersey State Museum, 1969; (contributor of article and collagraph) Pat Gilmour, *Modern Prints,* Dutton, 1970; (with husband, John Ross) *The Complete Printmaker,* Free Press, 1972; (with J. Ross) *The Complete Intaglio Print,* Free Press, 1974; (with J. Ross) *The Complete New Techniques in Printmaking,* Free Press, 1974; (with J. Ross) *The Complete Relief Print,* Free Press, 1974; (with J. Ross) *The Complete Screen Print and the Lithograph,* Free Press, 1974; *The Complete Collagraph: The Art and Technique of Printmaking from Collage Plates,* Free Press, 1980. Contributor to *Artist's Proof,* 1966, and to *Encyclopedia Americana,* 1971.

Illustrator; all with husband John Ross, except as indicated: May Garelick, *Manhattan Island,* Crowell, 1957; Gerald Doan

McDonald, compiler, *A Way of Knowing: A Collection of Poems for Boys,* Crowell, 1959; Sophia Cedarbaum, *Chanukah, the Festival of Lights,* Union of American Hebrew Congregations, 1960; S. Cedarbaum, *Passover, the Festival of Freedom,* Union of American Hebrew Congregations, 1960; S. Cedarbaum, *Purim, a Joyous Holiday,* Union of American Hebrew Congregations, 1960; S. Cedarbaum, *Sabbath, a Day of Delight,* Union of American Hebrew Congregations, 1960; Clyde R. Bulla, *The Ring and the Fire: Stories from Wagner's Nibelung Operas,* Crowell, 1962; (contributor of woodcuts) Edgar Lee Masters, *Spoon River Anthology,* Macmillan, 1963; Walt Whitman, *Poems of Walt Whitman,* Crowell, 1964; (contributor of woodcuts) W. Whitman, *Leaves of Grass* (poems), selected by Lawrence C. Powell, Crowell, 1964.

Lillian Morrison, editor, *Sprints and Distances: Sports in Poetry and the Poetry in Sport* (ALA Notable Book), Crowell, 1965; (under name Clare Romano) James Marnell, *Labor Day,* Crowell, 1966; (contributor of collagraphs) Edmund Fuller, editor, *Poems of Henry Wadsworth Longfellow,* Crowell, 1967; Mira Brichto, *God around Us,* Union of American Hebrew Congregations, 1969; (sole illustrator) Lorenz Graham, *God Wash the World and Start Again,* Crowell, 1971; Molly Cone, *About God,* edited by Jack D. Spiro, Union of American Hebrew Congregations, 1973; (under name Clare Romano) Charles W. Chesnutt, *Conjure Tales,* retold by Ray A. Shepard, Dut-

They set to bring the living things
That walk and crawl and fly

■ (From *God Wash the World and Start Again* by Lorenz Graham. Illustrated by Clare Romano Ross.)

ton, 1973; Helen Hill and Agnes Perkins, compilers, _New Coasts and Strange Harbors: Discovering Poems,_ Crowell, 1974.

SIDELIGHTS: Romano commented on her collaboration with her artist husband, John Ross: "We collaborate on our books doing separate illustrations by each of us, yet establishing a direction immediately, so that there is a cohesive, unifying quality in the work. Because we are each fine artists on our own, working in print and painting with separate identities, we feel we can collaborate on books and submerge identities more easily. Since we are printmakers, our relation to the book is very close. We both feel very strongly about a commitment the artist can have to the interpretation of literature." [Lee Kingman and others, compilers, _Illustrators of Children's Books: 1957-1966,_ Horn Book, 1968.[1]]

A collaborative effort with her husband, _Poems of Henry Wadsworth Longfellow,_ was the first book to be published that was illustrated with collagraphs. "The collagraph, as we know it, developed initially in the United States, because time and conditions were ripe. The post-World War II years were richly creative for all artists and for printmakers in particular. . . .

"Our . . . work with the collagraph developed in 1964 out of cardboard relief prints we both had been making since the mid-1950s.

"How one begins a collagraph depends on so many personal forces that it is almost impossible to list all the methods feasible. . . . Imaginative, individual, expressive work may come from the source material of sketches, photographs, found objects, and other things. It can also come out of the 'feel' and stimulation of the material itself without any preconceived notion of pre-felt imagery.

". . . Making a collection of materials and surfaces that are of interest might be a selective way to begin. . . . Choose with an eye to the gluing and platemaking processes. With experience, the artist will develop an ability to know which materials will work best. . . .

"The best procedure we have found in almost every method is to assemble an experimental plate with a wide variety of papers, cloth, and cardboard that is as shallow as possible. Cut and glue the materials carefully onto a base plate. Use fairly thick gesso or polymer as the adhesive. Keep in mind that all the surfaces and textures must hold ink and be able to produce a printed image in desired tonalities." [Clare Romano, "The Complete Clare Romano and John Ross," _American Artist,_ August 16, 1981.[2]]

FOR MORE INFORMATION SEE: Art in America, fall, 1960, April, 1965; _Artist's Proof,_ Volume V, Pratt Graphic Art Center, 1964; _At Cooper Union,_ summer, 1964; _New York Times,_ October 24, 1965; _Christian Science Monitor,_ November 24, 1967; _Art News,_ May, 1967; _Pratt Alumnus,_ spring, 1967; Lee Kingman and others, compilers, _Illustrators of Children's Books: 1957-1966,_ Horn Book, 1968; Ray Faulkner and Edwin Ziegfeld, _Art Today,_ Holt, 1969; Jules Heller, _Printmaking Today,_ Holt, 1972; L. Kingman and others, compilers, _Illustrators of Children's Books: 1967-1976,_ Horn Book, 1978; Clare Romano, "The Complete Clare Romano and John Ross," _American Artist,_ August 16, 1981.

Books, like proverbs, receive their chief value from the stamp and esteem of ages through which they have passed.

—Sir William Temple

ROSS, Pat 1943-

BRIEF ENTRY: Born February 4, 1943, in Baltimore, Md. Editor and author. After graduating from Hood College in 1965, Ross began her publishing career as assistant editor of _Humpty Dumpty's Magazine_ and quickly moved to the position of managing editor. Three years later she began working in children's books at David White and eventually became vice president and editor in chief of Knopf and Pantheon. Inspired by her daughter, Ross's beginning-to-read series of books features two best friends named Mandy and Mimi. In _Meet M and M_ (Pantheon, 1980), the girls do everything together until "one crabby day" they quarrel and spend the next few days snubbing each other. "The author is clearly a keen observer of the nuances of close friendships—their making and breaking," observed _Horn Book._ All published by Pantheon, the further adventures of Mandy and Mimi include _M and M and the Haunted House_ (1980), _M and M and the Big Bag_ (1981), _M and M and the Bad News Babies_ (1983), _M and M and the Mummy Mess_ (1985), and _M and M and the Santa Secrets_ (1985). For the same age group, Ross has written _What Ever Happened to the Baxter Place?_ (Pantheon, 1976), a picture book depicting the decline of a farm in the face of modern development; _Molly and the Slow Teeth_ (Lothrop, 1980), _Your First Airplane Trip_ (Lothrop, 1981); and _Gloria and the Super Soaper_ (Little, Brown, 1982).

During the 1970s, Ross was one of the founding members of Feminists on Children's Media, a group dedicated to improving the portrayal of girls and women in books. Her feminist concerns are evident in a young adult book entitled _Young and Female: Turning Points in the Lives of Eight American Women_ (Random House, 1972), which contains excerpts from the autobiographies of Shirley MacLaine, Dorothy Day, Shirley Chisholm, Althea Gibson, and four other women who fought against female stereotyping. Although she continues to write for children, Ross is no longer involved in editorial work. In 1985 she left the publishing field to open a "country" store called Sweet Nellie on Madison Avenue in Manhattan, New York.

FOR MORE INFORMATION SEE: Jim Roginski, _Behind the Covers: Interviews with Authors and Illustrators of Books for Children and Young Adults,_ Libraries Unlimited, 1985.

SACHS, Elizabeth-Ann 1946-

PERSONAL: Born June 25, 1946, in New York, N.Y.; daughter of Carl Raymond (a film editor) and Amelia (Romano) Sachs. _Education:_ Pace University, B.A., 1968; State University of New York at Albany, M.L.S., 1969. _Home:_ 75 Nashville Rd., Bethel, Conn. 06801. _Agent:_ Anne Borchardt, Georges Borchardt, Inc., 136 East 57th St., New York, N.Y. 10022.

CAREER: Lincoln Center, Library and Museum of the Performing Arts, New York City, librarian, 1969-70; Schenectady County Public Library, Schenectady, N.Y., librarian, 1970-77; St. Rose College, Albany, N.Y., adjunct lecturer, 1977-81; Union College, Schenectady, N.Y., adjunct lecturer in creative writing and publishing children's books, 1977-81; State University of New York, Albany, adjunct lecturer, 1978-81; Thornton Communications, Schenectady, lecturer, 1980—; Schalmont School System, Rotterdam, N.Y., writer-in-residence, 1981; Western Connecticut State University, Danbury, adjunct lecturer in freshman and advanced composition, 1982—. _Member:_ Authors Guild, Associated Writing Programs, Society of Children's Book Writers, Poets and Writers. *Awards, honors:* Bread Loaf Writers' Conference, staff scholarships, 1979, 1980, and 1986, Braughton fellowship, 1981; grants from Poets and Writers, 1980, 1981; Wesleyan University Writers' Conference, Xerox scholarship, 1983.

WRITINGS: Just Like Always (juvenile), Atheneum, 1981; *Where are You, Cow Patty?* (juvenile), Atheneum, 1984; *Lord of the Flies: Book Notes,* Barron's, 1984; *Shyster* (juvenile; illustrated by Judith Gwyn Brown), Atheneum, 1985; *Our Town: Book Notes,* Barron's, 1985. Contributor of articles to local periodicals, including *Fairfield County Women* and *Litchfield County Times.*

WORK IN PROGRESS: Tales from Greno (working title); *Concerto for Cows.*

SIDELIGHTS: ''I spent my college and early career years saying I wanted to be a writer. I worked in a children's library and spent much of my free time reading and reviewing children's books. I think that was the foundation of my writing career. But I didn't begin to write until a woman came into the library and asked for a copy of a book about children coping with a hospital stay. She wanted a story, not information. I had been in a hospital as a child and I thought, 'that's my book.' I think all those years of reading and procrastinating were a search for a story that was truly mine.

''Out of that encounter came *Just Like Always.* However, it wasn't that easy. I'd been telling myself I could do better than what I'd been reading. Writing children's books looks simple but it's deceptively simple. A juvenile reader is unlike an adult

Becky, our apartment is just too small for an animal, especially one who is used to running free—. ■ (From *Shyster* by Elizabeth-Ann Sachs. Illustrated by Judith Gwyn Brown.)

one. A child demands that a book be entertaining. He or she will not tolerate a story that wanders or characters who condescend. If the reader happens to be educated about something on his or her way through the story that's all right, as long as that's not the point of the story.

''I realized very quickly that it was difficult to reach young readers and that the only way was to rediscover the youngster within myself. I began to entertain the twelve year old me, and I discovered—after the publication of the first book when children began to write to me—that their questions were the same as I once had. I believe, as many writers do, that writing for the child within is the most honest way to address young readers.

''Currently I am working on the story of Greno. I am translating the lost legends of the Grens and the Shell Masters, two tribes who once lived in a peaceful gift-giving culture. I discovered the existence of the Grens when I was working on my first book but did not have time to begin studying them until recently. I have, however, amassed a wealth of information about them. There are bits and pieces of the Grens culture left all over our modern society. I have been saving what I found and I hope to retell their story.

''My stories are a collection of ideas, memories and dreams. Once I have the core of a story, I wait for the characters to reveal themselves. It takes a long time for a book to gather itself together. As I write I feel as though I stumble along,

ELIZABETH-ANN SACHS

feeling my way. Sometimes I come to a dead end, but I think that is part of the process of creativity. I don't think you can start out knowing everything ahead of time. The story would become too mechanical and besides it wouldn't be any fun that way. Part of the reason I enjoy writing is that I can't and don't try to figure it all out ahead of time. Then I am kept involved. It's as though I'm writing the book I'd most like to find in the library.''

SENN, Steve 1950-

BRIEF ENTRY: Born August 4, 1950, in Americus, Ga. "All I want to do is tell good stories that bring new feelings, fears, loves, ideas, and insights to the reader," Senn said about his writing. Illustrated by the author, *Spacebread* (Atheneum, 1981) and its sequel, *Born of Flame: A Spacebread Story* (Atheneum, 1982), take place in outer space. In the first, the white feline Spacebread sets out to avenge a friend's murder, meeting up with an intelligent flying fig, a black cat spy, and a blind woman who can see the future. Together they help Spacebread defeat the evil VolVarnix, freeing the planet Ralph from his power. In the second book, Spacebread helps a priestly ruling insect escape from Quan, a religious enemy. "Touches of humor lighten the battles and violence," noted *Booklist,* "and an underlying message about the power of love will intrigue readers looking for more than just action."

A Circle in the Sea (Atheneum, 1981) is a science-fiction fantasy in which a girl turns into a dolphin, becoming the link between humans and sea creatures. According to *Science Fiction and Fantasy Book Review,* Senn "skillfully blends fantasy elements such as the fire crystals and the shape-shifting ring and mythic songs of the whales with modern themes of ecological pollution, dolphin communication and undersea exploration." Senn has also written *The Double Disappearance of Walter Fozbek* (Hastings, 1980), in which Walter finds himself in a world of dinosaurs; *In the Castle of the Bear* (Atheneum, 1985), featuring Jason, who believes his stepmother is a witch; and *Ralph Fozbek and the Amazing Black Hole Patrol* (Avon, 1986). Senn plans to use his childhood experiences in small-town Georgia in future books. Previously an editorial artist for two Florida newspapers, he works as an advertising staff writer.

FOR MORE INFORMATION SEE: Contemporary Authors, Volume 105, Gale, 1982.

SHERMAN, D(enis) R(onald) 1934-

PERSONAL: Born December 20, 1934, in Calcutta, India; son of Denis Basil (a printer) and Marjorie (Clayton) Sherman; married Sylvaine Dingwall, November 6, 1961. *Education:* British School of Wireless Telegraphy, London, P.M.G. certificate, 1952. *Residence:* Praslin Island, Seychelles. *Agent:* A. M. Heath & Co. Ltd., 40-42 William IV St., London WC2N 4DD, England.

CAREER: Marconi Marine, Chelmsford, Essex, England, radio officer, 1952-54; Rhodesia Railways, Africa, station foreman, beginning 1956. *Military service:* Royal Navy, 1954-56.

WRITINGS: Old Mali and the Boy (novel), Little, Brown, 1964; *Into the Noonday Sun* (novel) Little, Brown, 1966; *Brothers of the Sea,* Little, Brown, 1966; *The Sinners,* Cassel, 1970; *Ryan,* Ace Books, 1973; *The Boat,* Cassel, 1973; *The Lion's Paw,* Doubleday, 1974. Occasional contributor of short stories to magazines.

SIDELIGHTS: "[I] hope to be able to write well enough one day to earn my living at it. I really like to write, but most days it's an effort to make the start, and usually after two thousand words or so I get tired and begin to lose interest." Sherman adds that he has not written anything at all since 1978, but "maybe the fire will come back. I don't know, but in any case, I've learned to live without it."

HOBBIES AND OTHER INTERESTS: Horseback riding, hunting, drinking.

FOR MORE INFORMATION SEE: New York Times Book Review, September 25, 1966; *Times Literary Supplement,* October 6, 1966; *Publishers Weekly,* April 9, 1973; *Kirkus Reviews,* May 1, 1975.

SINGER, Marilyn 1948-

PERSONAL: Born October 3, 1948, in Manhattan, N.Y.; daughter of Abraham (a photoengraver) and Shirley (Lax) Singer; married Steven Aronson (a financial manager), July 31, 1971. *Education:* Attended University of Reading, 1967-68; Queens College of the City University of New York, B.A. (cum laude),

Then, while you're awake, they take a knife and open up your leg and shove a tube this long.... ■ (From *It Can't Hurt Forever* by Marilyn Singer. Illustrated by Leigh Grant.)

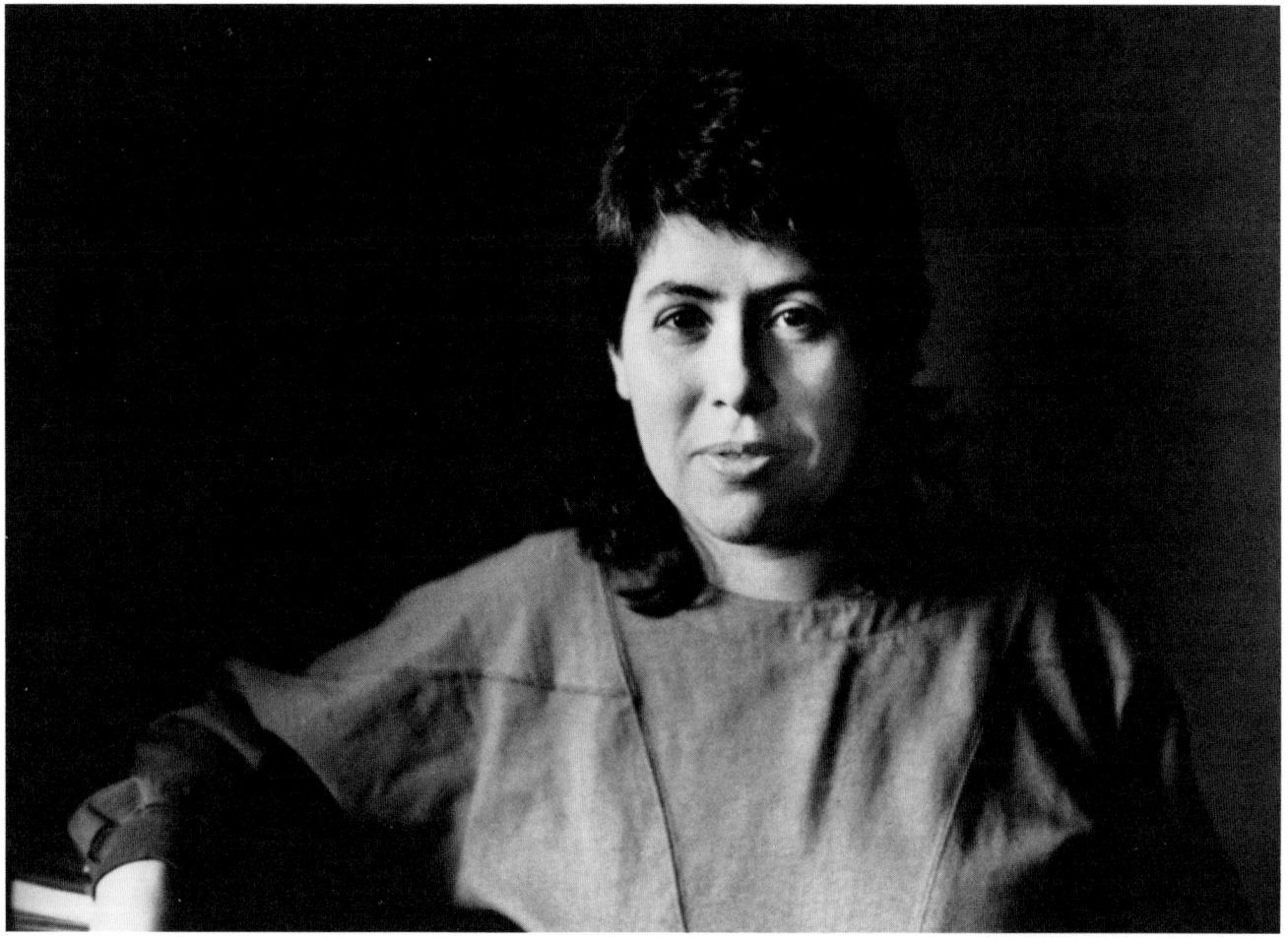

MARILYN SINGER

1969; New York University, M.A., 1979. *Home and office:* 42 Berkeley Pl., Brooklyn, N.Y. 11217.

CAREER: Daniel S. Mead Literary Agency, New York City, editor, 1967; *Where* (magazine), New York City, assistant editor, 1969; New York City Public High Schools, teacher of English and speech, 1969-74; writer, 1974—. *Member:* Society of Children's Book Writers, American Civil Liberties Union, Audubon Society, Phi Beta Kappa. *Awards, honors:* Children's Choice of the International Reading Association, 1977, for *The Dog Who Insisted He Wasn't;* Children's Choice of the International Reading Association, 1979, Maud Hart Lovelace Award from the Friends of the Minnesota Valley Regional Library (Mankato), 1983, both for *It Can't Hurt Forever; The Course of True Love Never Did Run Smooth* was chosen one of American Library Association's Best Young Adult Books, 1983; Parents' Choice Award from the Parents' Choice Foundation, 1983, for *The Fido Frame-Up.*

WRITINGS: The Dog Who Insisted He Wasn't (juvenile; illustrated by Kelly Oechsli), Dutton, 1976; (editor and author of introduction) *A History of Avant-Garde Cinema,* American Federation of Arts, 1976; (editor and contributor) *New American Filmmakers,* American Federation of Arts, 1976; *No Applause, Please* (juvenile), Dutton, 1977; *The Pickle Plan* (juvenile; illustrated by Steven Kellogg), Dutton, 1978; *It Can't Hurt Forever* (juvenile; illustrated by Leigh Grant), Harper, 1978.

The First Few Friends (young adult novel), Harper, 1981; *Will You Take Me to Town on Strawberry Day?* (picture book;

illustrated by Trinka Hakes Noble), Harper, 1981; *The Fanatic's Ecstatic, Aromatic Guide to Onions, Garlic, Shallots and Leeks* (nonfiction; illustrated by Marian Perry), Prentice-Hall, 1981; *Tarantulas on the Brain* (juvenile; illustrated by L. Grant), Harper, 1982; *The Course of True Love Never Did Run Smooth* (young adult novel), Harper, 1983; *The Fido Frame-Up* (juvenile; illustrated by Andrew Glass), Warne, 1983; *Leroy Is Missing* (juvenile; illustrated by Judy Glasser), Harper, 1984; *The Case of the Sabotaged School Play* (juvenile; illustrated by J, Glasser), Harper, 1984.

A Clue in Code (juvenile; illustrated by J. Glasser), Harper, 1985; *The Case of the Cackling Car* (illustrated by J. Glasser), Harper, 1985; *Archer Armadillo's Secret Room* (picture book; Junior Literary Guild selection; illustrated by Beth L. Weiner), Macmillan, 1985; *Horsemaster* (young adult fantasy), Atheneum, 1985; *A Nose for Trouble* (juvenile; illustrated by A. Glass), Holt, 1985; *Lizzie Silver of Sherwood Forest* (juvenile), Harper, 1986; *Where There's a Will, There's a Wag* (juvenile), Holt, 1986; *The Lightey Club,* Four Winds Press, 1987; *Ghost Host,* Harper, 1987; *Mitzi Meyer, Fearless Warrior Queen,* Scholastic, 1987.

Author of scripts for television series "The Electric Company" and for "Video and Film Review" and of teacher's guides. Contributor of poems to magazines, including *Yes, Encore, Corduroy, Tamesis,* and *Gyre.*

WORK IN PROGRESS: Charmed, a fantasy; two more Sam and Dave mysteries; a young adult novel about loss and emotional release.

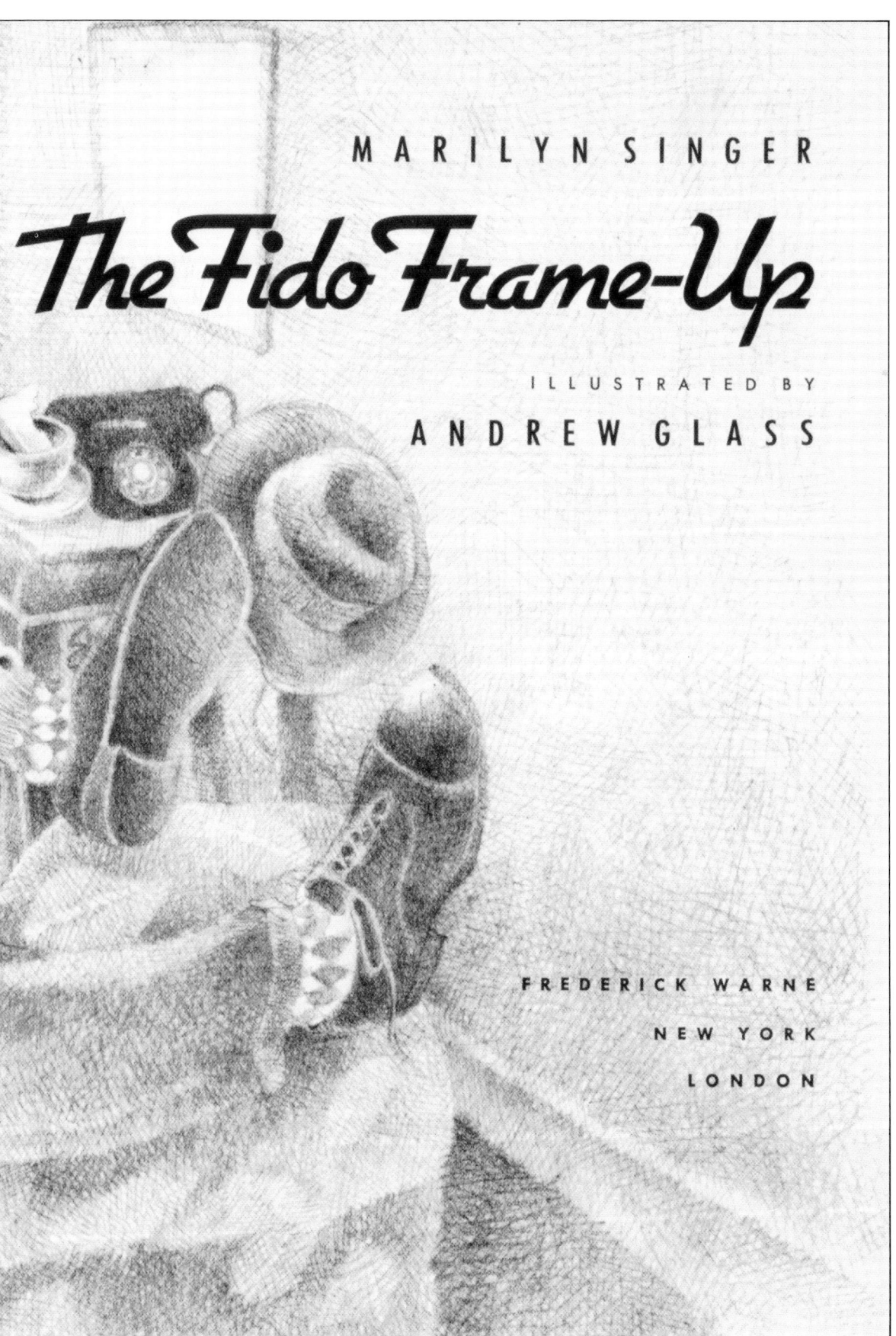

The name's Samantha. Samantha Spayed. But you can call me Sam. ■ (From *The Fido Frame-Up* by Marilyn Singer. Illustrated by Andrew Glass.)

SIDELIGHTS: "I was born in Manhattan and lived in the Bronx until I was five—when my sister was born. Then my family moved out to North Massapequa, Long Island. My childhood was affected strongly by heart surgery I had at the age of eight. My novel *It Can't Hurt Forever* is based on that event. I was also affected by my Rumanian grandmother who lived with us. She told me incredible stories that I remember to this day.

"I lived on Long Island until I was twenty (except for my junior year of college when I went to Reading University, England). Then I moved into New York City with a roommate and started my teaching career. I taught English and speech in city high schools. In 1971, I married Steven Aronson. He and I moved to Brooklyn in 1973. That year I quit teaching full-time because I was too 'avant-garde' for the public school system. I continued to teach as a substitute for one year after that, but I disliked it and left the teaching profession altogether.

"I had no idea what I was going to do for a living. I vaguely thought that I'd write for magazines. Then, my husband got me some work writing teacher's guides, program notes and catalogues on film. One day, while sitting in the Brooklyn Botanic Garden, one of my favorite hang-outs, I began to create some stories based on talking insect characters I'd made up when I was eight years old. I liked writing those stories and kept on doing more of them with other characters. Out of those came *The Dog Who Insisted He Wasn't,* my first published book. I was as surprised as anyone to realize I'd found my career—being a children's book writer. But I sure was pleased.

"I still am. I have written more than twenty children's and young adult books, including novels, picture books, and nonfiction. I draw on my childhood experiences on Long Island, my travels around the U.S. and Europe, my dreams, interests and studies to write my books. I have also been influenced by many writers, especially by my favorite writer, William Shakespeare. I wrote *The Course of True Love Never Did Run Smooth* because I'm such a fan of his—and of *A Midsummer Night's Dream,* the play on which my book is based.

"I believe that I write because writing helps me explore all sorts of areas of myself, including painful ones. I like writing for children because I think that's the most honest kind of writing there is. Recently, besides the realistic novels and picture books I've been writing for a while, I've been working on two mystery series and several fantasy novels. I've been an avid reader of mysteries for a long time, so it's only natural that I'm now creating my own. As for the fantasies, I think that in part my involvement in meditation and esoteric practices has led to my writing them. I also credit 'Star Trek' with opening me up so that I can 'bop around the universe' in my books.

"I think writing is more fun for me these days—although it's also still hard work. Anytime I can see things in a fresh way, I feel I've grown a little younger. That's one of my goals in life—to grow younger while I grow wiser. I believe writing children's books will help me accomplish that goal."

It Can't Hurt Forever has been published in Dutch, Norwegian, and Swedish.

HOBBIES AND OTHER INTERESTS: Studying Taoist meditation and exercise (Chi Kung, T'ai Chi), Hatha yoga, classical Chinese herbology, avant-garde and independent film, bird watching and caring for animals, tap dancing, singing, baseball, Japanese flower arranging.

SMITH, Susan Vernon 1950-
(Carrie Enfield, Susan Mendonca, Rosemary Vernon)

PERSONAL: Born June 6, 1950, in Harrow England; came to the United States in 1957; daughter of Vernon Leonard (a research engineer) and Phyllis (a homemaker; maiden name, Hunt) Smith; divorced; children: Trina, Cory. *Education:* Attended Cabrillo College, 1967, and Patricia Stevens College, 1968-69. *Home and office:* 537 East Fourth St., Brooklyn, N.Y. 11218. *Agent:* Chris Tomasino, RLR Associates, 7 West 51st St., New York, N.Y. 10019.

CAREER: Writer, 1973—; has worked in various positions, including wetsuit designer, secretary, clerk, teacher of writing courses.

WRITINGS: Changing Places (young adult fantasy), Scholastic, 1986.

Young adult; under name Susan Mendonca: *Tough Choices* (novel), Dial, 1980; *Broken Dreams* (romance novel), Scholastic, 1983; *Once Upon a Kiss,* Scholastic, 1985.

Young adult; under pseudonym Rosemary Vernon: *The Popularity Plan,* Bantam, 1981; *The Problem with Love,* Bantam, 1982; *The Popularity Summer,* Bantam, 1982; *Dear Amanda,* Bantam, 1983; *Love in the Fast Lane,* Bantam, 1984; *Language of Love,* Bantam, 1984; *Questions of Love,* Bantam, 1985; *First Comes Love,* Berkley, 1985; *With All My Heart,* Berkley, 1985.

Young adult; under pseudonym Carrie Enfield: *Songbird,* Silhouette, 1981; *Secret Admirer,* Silhouette, 1983; *Picture Perfect,* Silhouette, 1983.

Work is represented in anthologies, including *Freedom Is an Inside Job,* Pacific Press, 1978, and *Discovery on a Summer-Ripe Day,* Pacific Press, 1978, both edited and compiled by Pat Horning. Contributor of articles and stories to magazines, including *Guideposts* and *Parents'.*

WORK IN PROGRESS: Two series for eight- to twelve-year-olds to be published by Simon & Schuster; a collaborative fiction project whose main characters are six very different couples.

SIDELIGHTS: "I began writing seriously when my first child was ten months old. Possibly having an infant in the house made me realize the value of my time, and in that first year I sold twenty pieces to various magazines. The second year I earned over a thousand dollars at writing, of which I was quite proud. Then I had another baby and wrote a book.

"Producing children seemed to have a positive effect on my writing (I think that attitude could work up to a point, but I didn't want to push it, so I stopped at two kids). I wrote another, *Tough Choices,* which was inspired by a situation I found myself very close to.

"The rest of the books followed on the heels of the first, all of them young adult novels, which seemed a natural vehicle for me. In the past year I've begun to make inroads into adult fiction, and have recently completed a large proposal in collaboration with another writer. I have found that it is not very different writing adult fiction—adults have longer, more complicated histories, that's all. They're not as transparent as children—or at least they like to think they're not.

"Too often we forget that we all started out as children, without sophistication, without masks and facades—a condition which is quite refreshing. Childhood is an inherent part of adulthood—it doesn't fall away like dead skin once you 'grow up.' And because childhood and adulthood are actually inseparable and intertwined, they are together (or should be) in all writings, as the basis for character and motivation in fiction and reality.

"What I try to do is write what pleases me, addressing issues that are essentially universal. Since I believe that every story has been told before, my gift is doing it my way. If I've done it right, the reader should find it not too forgettable."

FOR MORE INFORMATION SEE: Horn Book, August, 1980; *Santa Cruz Sentinel*, October 10, 1980.

SNYDER, Gerald S(eymour) 1933-

PERSONAL: Born June 4, 1933, in New York, N.Y.; son of David and Minnie (Beenstock) Snyder; married Arlette Amsellem, August 2, 1961; children: Michele, Daniel. *Education:* Missouri School of Journalism, B.J., 1958; Middlebury College, Graduate School of Spanish at University of Madrid, graduate study, 1961-62.

CAREER: Religious News Service, New York City, writer, 1958-60; free-lance writer, 1958—; United Press International, New York City, reporter and writer, 1962-66; National Geographic Society, Washington, D.C., writer, 1966-71. *Military service:* U.S. Army, 1954-56. *Member:* Lewis & Clark

(From *Is There a Loch Ness Monster? The Search for a Legend* by Gerald S. Snyder.)

Trail Heritage Foundation. *Awards, honors:* Feature writing award from Sigma Delta Chi, 1958.

WRITINGS: In the Footsteps of Lewis and Clark, National Geographic Society, 1970; *The Computer: How It's Changing Our Lives*, U.S. News & World Report, 1972; *The Religious Reawakening in America*, U.S. News & World Report, 1972; *Let's Talk about Computers*, Jonathan David, 1973; *Your Car: How to Buy It, Take Care of It, and Save Money*, U.S. News & World Report, 1973; *1994: The World of Tomorrow*, U.S. News & World Report, 1973; *The Right to Be Left Alone: Privacy in the United States*, Messner, 1975, new edition, 1976; (editor) Wallace Stettinius, *Management Planning and Control: The Printers Path to Profitability*, Printing Industries of America, 1975; *The Right to Be Informed: Censorship in the United States*, Messner, 1976, revised edition, 1978; *The Royal Oak Disaster*, Kimber & Co., 1976, Presidio Press, 1978; *Is There a Loch Ness Monster? The Search for a Legend*, Messner, 1977.

Are There Alien Beings? The Story of UFOs, Messner, 1980; *Human Rights*, F. Watts, 1980; *Test Tube Life: Scientific Advance and Moral Dilemma*, Messner, 1982. Contributor to national magazines, including *National Observer*.

WORK IN PROGRESS: Three books dealing with World War II events: on the Philippine resistance movement on German submarine missions on Palestine.

HOBBIES AND OTHER INTERESTS: Raising children, collecting stamps, watching sports, reading.

STAHL, Hilda 1938-

PERSONAL: Born September 13, 1938, in Chadron, Neb.; daughter of Jay (a ranch hand) and Zelma (a housekeeper; maiden name, Fehrenholz) Clements; married Norman August Stahl (a supervisor), August 1, 1959; children: Jeffery, Laurie, Bradley, Mark, Sonya, Evangelynn, Joshua. *Education:* Wayne State Teachers College (now Wayne State College), Normal Degree, 1956. *Politics:* Republican. *Religion:* Undenominational Faith Church. *Home:* 5891 Wood School Rd., Freeport, Mich. 49325.

CAREER: Rural school teacher in Winnebago, Neb., 1956-57; writer, 1968—; Happy Time Nursery Pre-School, Hastings, Mich., teacher, 1971-72. *Member:* Society of Children's Book Writers, Mystery Writers of America; Romance Writers of America.

*WRITINGS—*For young people: *Melody of Love*, Moody, 1975.

"Elizabeth Gail" series; all published by Tyndale: *Elizabeth Gail and the Mystery at the Johnson Farm*, 1979; . . . *and the Secret Box*, 1979; . . . *and the Teddy Bear Mystery*, 1979; . . . *and the Dangerous Double*, 1980; . . . *and the Trouble at Sandhill Ranch*, 1980; . . . *and the Strange Birthday Party*, 1980; . . . *and the Terrifying News*, 1980; . . . *and the Frightened Runaways*, 1981; . . . *and Trouble from the Past*, 1981; . . . *and the Silent Piano*, 1981; . . . *and Double Trouble*, 1982; . . . *and the Holiday Mystery*, 1982; . . . *and the Missing Love Letters*, 1982; . . . *and the Music Camp Romance*, 1983; . . . *and the Handsome Stranger*, 1983; . . . *and the Secret Love*, 1983; . . . *and the Summer for Weddings*, 1984; . . . *and the Time for Love*, 1984.

"Tina" series; published by Tyndale, except where indicated: *Tina's First Love*, Moody, 1972; . . . *Dangerous Secret*, 1980;

... Elusive Enemy, 1981; *... Reluctant Friend*, 1981; *... Unwelcome Intruder*, 1982; *... Secret Rival*, 1982; *... Eighteenth Summer*, 1983; *... Surprise Romance*, 1983.

"Teddy Jo" series; all published by Tyndale: *Teddy Jo and the Terrible Secret*, 1982; *... and the Yellow Room Mystery*, 1983; *... and the Stolen Ring*, 1983; *... and the Strangers of the Pink House*, 1983; *... and the Strange Medallion*, 1983; *... and the Wild Dog*, 1984; *... and the Abandoned House*, 1984; *... and the Ragged Beggars*, 1984; *... and the Kidnapped Heir*, 1984; *... and the Great Dive*, 1985; *... and the Magic Quill*, 1985; *... and the Missing Portrait*, 1985; *... and the Broken Locket Mystery*, 1985; *... and the Missing Family*, 1986.

"Tyler Twins" series; all published by Tyndale: *Surprise at the Big Key*, 1985; *The Swamp Monster*, 1985; *Pet Show Panic*, 1986; *Tree House Hideaway*, 1986; *The Latchkey Kids*, 1986.

"Wren House Mystery" series; all published by Accent Books: *The Mystery at the Wheeler Place*, 1986; *The Disappearance of Amos Pike*, 1986; *Tim Avery's Secret*, 1986; *Newspaper Caper*, 1987.

Contributor of more than four hundred stories to religious and educational journals.

WORK IN PROGRESS: An adult mystery; books for young people; a new children's series for boys.

HILDA STAHL

Teddy Jo caught Carlie around the legs and they sprawled to the grass. ■ (Cover illustration from *Teddy Jo and the Ragged Beggars* by Hilda Stahl.)

SIDELIGHTS: "As I was growing up in the Nebraska sandhills with my three brothers and five sisters I never thought about writing books or stories. I never thought of doing anything with my life. We were poor and lived in the country, and I was shy and timid. When I was married and moved to Michigan I began to realize that I wanted to accomplish something with my life, but at that time we had three children and I didn't want to leave them.

"One day I saw an ad in *TV Guide* for a correspondence course in writing, and I signed up. I sold my first short story to *Instructor* in 1968, and I knew that writing was for me. I wrote on the kitchen table with babies at my feet and on my lap. I wrote every spare second until the seconds turned into minutes and the minutes into hours. Now, my oldest child is twenty-five and my youngest, fourteen, and I have several hours during each day to write. I always have a work in progress. It usually takes me two weeks to write a book.

"One winter day I started to write a short story and it grew into a book. Suddenly I found that I enjoyed book writing more than short story writing. I have learned to write an outline of my story and from that to write the book. I very seldom rewrite—except in my head. I try to write so that the reader can't put down the book until he or she has finished it. From all over the world I receive fan mail from girls, a few boys, and some adults who love my books. They always beg for more and, of course, it keeps me going.

"In my writing I want to entertain as I teach, and I always have a happy ending. I want the reader to *know* that my books will leave them feeling good, and feeling that life is beautiful even if there are negative situations that must be faced. I like writing for adults as well as children. Mystery and romance are my favorite genres.

"Often I visit schools to talk about writing to elementary school children. I enjoy sharing with them that a shy, country girl became a writer, and if they have a dream and want to see it come to pass, they can accomplish anything they work at.

"I like to write series because I can follow the character and see her grow. When I write a book it's almost as if a movie is running through my head. I write what I see and hear and smell and feel.

"Reading is important to me. I read several books a week, usually in the genre in which I'm writing. Reading what other authors write helps me to improve my skills, I think, and I love to read, but mostly I love to write."

STREATFEILD, (Mary) Noel   1897-1985 (Susan Scarlett)

OBITUARY NOTICE—See sketch in *SATA* Volume 20: Born December 24, 1897, in Amberley, Sussex, England; died September 11, 1986, in London, England. Novelist, biographer, and author of children's books, Streatfeild began an acting career with a Shakespearean repertory theater in England, later appearing in theatrical productions in South Africa and Australia. She turned to writing in 1930, using ten years in the theater as background knowledge for her first adult novel, *The Whicharts*. Following several more adult novels, Streatfeild wrote her children's book, *Ballet Shoes,* which proved to be an immediate success. Among Streatfeild's more than fifty books for children are *Tennis Shoes* and *The Circus Is Coming,* winner of the Carnegie Medal. She also produced a three-volume autobiography (*A Vicarage Family, Away from the Vicarage,* and *Beyond the Vicarage*) as well as twelve adult novels published under the pseudonym Susan Scarlett. Streatfeild was a book critic for *Elizabethan* magazine, lectured on children's books, and made appearances on British television's first children's books programs.

FOR MORE INFORMATION SEE: The Junior Book of Authors, H. W. Wilson, 1951; *The Who's Who of Children's Literature,* Schocken, 1968; *Contemporary Authors,* Volumes 81-84, Gale, 1979; *Twentieth-Century Children's Writers,* 2nd edition, St. Martin's, 1983; *The Writers Directory 1986-1988,* St. James, 1986. Obituaries: *Publishers Weekly,* October 17, 1986.

SUSSMAN, Susan   1942- (Susan Rissman; Art Rissman, pseudonym)

PERSONAL: Born April 22, 1942, in Chicago, Ill.; daughter of Emanuel A. (a judge) and Edie (Leavitt) Rissman; married Barry Sussman (a president of a fabric company), September 21, 1963; children: Sy, Aaron, Rachael. *Education:* University of Illinois, B.A., 1963. *Religion:* Jewish. *Residence:* Evans-

ton, Ill. *Agent:* Jane Jordan Browne Multimedia Product Development, Inc., 410 South Michigan Ave., Room 724, Chicago, Ill. 60605. *Office:* Noyes Cultural Center, 927 Noyes St., Evanston, Ill. 60201.

CAREER: Free-lance writer, 1963—. Associated with Noyes Cultural Center, Evanston, Ill., 1982—. *Member:* Children's Reading Round Table, Midwest Authors Guild, Society of Midland Authors, Writer's Bloc (president, 1983-86), Illinois Art Council, Evanston Arts Alliance, Romance Writers of America, Off Campus Writers Workshop (chairman of sales), Society of Children's Book Writers. *Awards, honors:* Nominated for the Jewish Book Council's Best Children's Book, 1984, for *There's No Such Thing as a Chanukah Bush, Sandy Goldstein.*

WRITINGS: (Contributor) Margaret Branson and Evarts Erickson, editors, *Urban America,* Scott, Foresman, 1970; *Hippo Thunder* (juvenile; illustrated by John Wallner), A. Whitman, 1982; *There's No Such Thing as a Chanukah Bush, Sandy Goldstein* (juvenile; illustrated by Charles Robinson), A. Whitman, 1983; *Casey the Nomad* (juvenile; illustrated by Joelle Shefts), A. Whitman, 1985; *Don't Say Goodbye,* Dell, 1985; *Sweet Talk,* Dell, 1986; *Night after Night,* Dell, 1986; *Just Friends,* Ballantine, 1986; (with Robert James) *Lies (People Believe) about Animals,* (juvenile; illustrated by Fred Leavitt), A. Whitman, 1986.

Also author of "Let's Go for the Record" (children's musical; music by Elaine Burke) produced in San Francisco, Calif., 1986, and "One for You—One for Me," released by Disney, 1987. Author of "Notes from the Locker Room," a column in *Racquetball.* Contributor of articles and stories to magazines and newspapers (sometimes under name Susan Rissman or pseudonym Art Rissman), including *Ellery Queen Mystery.*

WORK IN PROGRESS: This Used to Be a Candy House, a nutrition book for children; *I Can't—I Can,* a preschool picture

SUSAN SUSSMAN

My goodness, beeg boy. Are you in for some wild sorts times. ■ (From *Casey the Nomad* by Susan Sussman. Illustrated by Joelle Shefts.)

book; a book for junior high school girls; research for a book for junior high school boys; a mystery romance dealing with the silk industry; *The Boy Who Hated Hebrew School,* a book on ways to enchant children rather than alienate them; *I Am Princess Zappo from Zarquart,* a book about a thirteen-year-old extraterrestrial; two series, one for pre-schoolers and one for sixth graders; four juvenile non-fiction animal books; a mainstream adult novel; a one-act play.

SIDELIGHTS: "The reasons I give for writing vary according to the date, time, and temperature. What it all boils down to is I have tried *not* writing and I became no good to anyone. I received my first rejection slip when I was eleven years old from the *Saturday Evening Post.* I had sent them a poem saying I wanted the honor of having it rejected by the *Saturday Evening Post.* They were most obliging. I can still recite the poem and think the rejection slip—which some extremely kind editor personalized—is still around.

"I wrote throughout my grade and high school years, including some radio and television scripting for children's shows. I sold my first magazine article while I was a senior in college and I pretty much stayed with newspaper and magazine work from 1963 until I entered the book market in 1982. I expect to continue writing books since they are much less aggravating than articles and tend to stay around a while longer. Occasionally, however, a short story or a one-act play barges in and stands looking over my shoulder until I pay attention.

These ideas won't give me peace until I write them out and send them off. I write about what concerns me, whether it is the problems faced by Jewish children at Christmas time, or the reason there are no professional female baseball players.

"I am most happy when writing for children. Their world is so intense, their problems so much 'bigger-than-life,' their humor so delightfully wacky, that I feel this is where I want to spend most of my writing time. Unfortunately, children's literature is the poorest paying of all the markets and I do other work to supplement this.

"I have moved all my life, living in Chicago, Los Angeles, back to Chicago, California again, southern France, back to Chicago. My book *Casey the Nomad* was born from my interest in the amazing geographic movement of today's children and all the problems involved. Everything I experience in life winds up somewhere in my writing. There is so much I want to say that I doubt I will ever have enough time. Writer's block is foreign to me. Writing is hard work, always, but I can't imagine not having ideas to put down. I have found a regular creative pattern to my life and have managed to schedule my work so the tough work is done during periods of high creativity, and rewrites are saved for the low energy times.

"I can think of no way I'd rather spend my days than writing. My mind writes constantly, even when my body is away from the computer. When people ask if writing isn't lonely work, I have no idea what they mean. My mind is racing from the moment I come into my office at eight in the morning until I (reluctantly) leave at five.

"My family actively affects my work: Sy, my oldest, is creative director of Yale University's children's theater and I am hoping to write a performance piece for him. Aaron, my middle child, is an engineering student at the University of Michigan and has dragged me, screaming and kicking, into the computer age . . . for which I am forever in his debt. Rachael, my youngest, is an energetic, dynamic, fifteen-year-old who eagerly and openly shares all the facets of her life. She and her friends have become my most valuable writing resource. Barry, my husband, is bright, funny, and—luckily for me—a superb editor."

SWEETLAND, Nancy A(nn)   1934-
(Nancy A. Rose)

PERSONAL: Born May 6, 1934, in Chamberlain, S.D.; daughter of Milton Leroy (a farmer) and Helen (an artist and musician; maiden name, Matson) Mortensen; married Robert J. Rose (a salesman), September 13, 1952 (divorced, May 31, 1977); married Robert Sweetland (a director of marketing communications), July 20, 1979; children: (first marriage) Randy, Julie, Kenton, Bruce, Stewart, Melissa, Philip; (stepchildren) Cyndee, Cathy, Carol, Christine, Brian. *Education:* Graduated from University of Wisconsin, 1983. *Home:* 215 Oak Hill Dr., Green Bay, Wis. 54301.

CAREER: Free-lance writer for local and state newspapers and copywriter for advertising agencies, 1962—; Institutional Writing Program in Wisconsin prisons, Green Bay, Fox Lake, Taycheedah, and Waupun, Wis., director, 1969-75; Brown County Mental Hospital, Green Bay, librarian, 1967-75; Northeast Wisconsin Technical Institute, Green Bay, teacher of writing, 1975—; private teacher of writing, 1975—. *Member:* National Federation of State Poetry Societies, Wisconsin Regional Writers Association (member of council, 1984—),

NANCY A. SWEETLAND

Wisconsin Fellowship of Poets, Green Bay Writer's Club, Scripters Manuscript Group (leader, 1970—), Allouez Writers (director, 1971), Harlequin Players, Inc. *Awards, honors:* Wisconsin Regional Writers' Jade Ring Awards, 1967 and 1973, for juvenile fiction, 1970, for adult fiction, and 1976, for poetry; Indiana University Award, short story division, 1971; National Writer's Digest Short Story Awards, 6th place, 1974; Council for Wisconsin Writers' Awards, 3rd place, 1978, for published short fiction. Prize winner in other regional and national contests, 1971—.

WRITINGS—All under name Nancy A. Rose: *Funny-Talk Freddy,* Denison, 1970; *Yelly Kelly* (illustrated by Robert L. Sweetland), Denison, 1970; *Dragon of Cobblestone Castle,* Denison, 1970; *Motherless Bug,* Denison, 1971. Editor under name Nancy A. Rose, "The Artist's Notebook," a weekly newspaper column, 1970-71. Contributor of over 300 stories, articles and essays to magazines and newspapers, including *True Experience, True Story, Women's Day, Green's Magazine, Snowy Egret, Space and Time, Highlights,* and *Press-Gazette* (Green Bay, Wis.).

WORK IN PROGRESS: Two adult novels, one a romance, *A Door to Love,* and one a mystery, *The Virgin Murders;* a young adult novel, *Angel and Me and DDD;* a series of simple, humorous mysteries for the very young reader.

SIDELIGHTS: "My writing for children was put on 'hold' for a while during divorce and subsequent commercial writing for income and is hopefully back on track now with a switch to writing for the older child (nine and up) with *Angel and Me and DDD.* I write about feelings and emotions more than stories for stories' sake with fiction my first love.

"As a child growing up on a farm without a lot of outside contacts, I was a voracious reader; my mother read to us every night before bed until we were old enough to read ourselves.

It was a tradition I continued on to my own seven children. I always wanted to be a writer, but it wasn't until after I began to write for young children that I really enjoyed it, and it became more fun than work.

"I was not financially able to continue on to college after high school, subsequently I went to work as a secretary until I had my family. It wasn't until I was forty-nine years old that I finished my college degree. I did attend many writers' conferences and wrote constantly, always reading the writers' magazines and keeping abreast of the market. The *Horn Book* has been particularly helpful for me in seeing what's being published and by whom. I guess there was no particular outside influence that turned me into a writer—it was always an inner drive.

"As most writers will tell you, experiences have been the background of all my work. My own children and those of others I know have given me lots of ideas. One of the greatest pleasures has been to talk to children in schools about writing and about my books, and to have them tell me how much they like the characters—'he's just like me!'

I have had a number of short stories for children published in various magazines and this past February 'The Year Ground Hog Wouldn't Tell about Spring' was published in *Highlights for Children;* I'm very pleased about that.

"I am presently developing a series of simple, humorous mysteries for the very young reader. I feel that the younger a child is when he or she finds out that reading is the best answer to boredom and that the whole world can be opened up between the covers of a book, the more rounded and interesting a person that child will become. I want to be part of that development."

HOBBIES AND OTHER INTERESTS: Piano, tennis, golf, and theater (acting and directing).

FOR MORE INFORMATION SEE: Press-Gazette (Green Bay, Wisconsin), October 1, 1967, July 20, 1972.

SWITZER, Ellen   1923-

PERSONAL: Born October 18, 1923, in Germany; daughter of Ernst and Stella (Kugelman) Eichenwald; married Gilbert Harvey Switzer (an architect), January 1, 1947; children: Michael, Jeffrey. *Education:* Smith College, B.A., 1945; Columbia University, graduate study, 1946. *Residence:* Madison, Conn. *Agent:* Curtis Brown Ltd., 575 Madison Ave., New York, N.Y. 10022.

CAREER: Time, New York City, researcher, 1945-47; *New York Herald Tribune,* New York City, stringer in Turkey and the Middle East, 1959; free-lance writer. *Awards, honors:* American Association of Anesthesiologists Journalism Award, 1970; *Our Urban Planet* was chosen as an honor book by the New York Academy of Sciences, 1981.

WRITINGS: (With E. R. Wasserman) *Random House Guide to Graduate Studies in the Arts and Sciences,* Random House, 1967; *There Ought to Be a Law,* Atheneum, 1972; *Where Democracy Failed,* Atheneum, 1977; (with Jerome Singer) *Daydreams and Fantasies,* Prentice-Hall, 1980; *Our Urban Planet* (illustrated with photographs by Michael Switzer and Jeffrey Switzer), Atheneum, 1980; *Dancers! Horizons in American Dance* (illustrated with photographs by Costas), Atheneum, 1982; *The Nutcracker: A Story and a Ballet* (illustrated by Costas and Steven Caras), Atheneum, 1985; *Lily Boop* (illustrated by Lillian Hoban), Crown, 1986.

Contributor to *Glamour, Vogue, McCall's, Woman's Day, Reader's Digest,* and *Redbook.* Contributing editor, *Family Circle.*

SIDELIGHTS: "As a writer, I have always considered myself primarily a journalist, which means that non-fiction is for me the best way to convey ideas as well as facts. My books generally have a specific theme that can be illustrated best by presenting it in terms of factual material.

"I write for teenagers because I have confidence in their ability to think through material and to come to their own conclusions, based on the facts presented to them. Adolescents are just rebellious and independent enough not to allow anyone, including an author, to preach to them, and at best, they bring something of themselves to what they see, hear and read."

HOBBIES AND OTHER INTERESTS: Medicine, law, education, politics, women's rights, ballet.

TAYLOR, Paula (Wright) 1942- (Harriet Lake)

PERSONAL: Born May 24, 1942, in Fond du Lac, Wis.; daughter of Edgar A. Wright, Jr. (a factory owner) and Marie F. Wright; married Robert G. Taylor, June 20, 1964 (divorced, 1978); married Cyrille E. DeCosse (an artist and in business), May 21, 1983; children: (first marriage) Claire E. *Education:* Carleton College, B.A. (magna cum laude), 1964. *Address:* 4835 Penn Ave. S., Minneapolis, Minn. 55409.

CAREER: Junior high school teacher of English and German, Fond du Lac, Wis., 1966-67; teacher of English to adult education classes and of German to University of Maryland extension classes, Keflavik, Iceland, 1967-68; teacher of English at a private language laboratory and editor, Amsterdam, Netherlands, 1972-73; Creative Education, Mankato, Minn., freelance writer, educational researcher and projects consultant, 1974—; author of books for young people, 1978—. Writer, Cy DeCosse & Associates (publisher), 1977-78; director of Creating Futures Project, Minnesota Council on Quality Education, 1978-81; director, U.S.-U.S.S.R. Youth Art Exchange, 1984—; editor and publisher, *Youth Link* newsletter, 1984-85; co-director, CONNECT (a Minnesota-based citizen's initiative group forming a cultural exchange between Minnesota and the U.S.S.R.), 1986. *Awards, honors:* Fulbright Scholarship to study Icelandic, 1968; Eddy Award from the Council on Quality Education, 1981, for the Creating Futures Project.

WRITINGS—All juvenile; all published by Creative Education, except as indicated: *Bob Hope: Master of Entertainment* (illustrated by Harold Henriksen), 1974; *Elvis Presley* (illustrated by Dick Brude), 1974; *Johnny Cash* (illustrated by John Keely), 1974; *Coretta Scott King: A Woman of Peace* (illustrated by H. Henriksen), 1974; *Elton John* (illustrated by J. Keely), 1975; *Henry Kissinger: World Statesman* (illustrated by H. Henriksen), 1975; (with Norita Larson) *Walter Cronkite: This Is Walter Cronkite* (illustrated by H. Henriksen), 1975; *Frank Sinatra* (illustrated by J. Keely), 1976; (under pseudonym Harriet Lake) *On Stage: Frank Sinatra*, 1976; (under pseudonym Harriet Lake) *On Stage: Jackson Five*, 1976; *Carole King* (illustrated by J. Keely), 1976; *Pelé* (illustrated by J. Keely), 1976; *World's Daredevil: Evel Knievel*, 1976; *Mark*

PAULA TAYLOR

Spitz (illustrated by H. Henriksen), 1976; *Roberto Clemente* (illustrated by H. Henriksen), 1976; *Basketball's Finest Center: Kareem Abdul-Jabbar*, 1977; *Golf's Great Winner: Jack Nicklaus*, 1977; *Gymnastics' Happy Superstar: Olga Korbut*, 1977; *Cancer*, 1978; *Capricorn*, 1978; *Gemini*, 1978; *Leo*, 1978; *Sagittarius*, 1978; (with Pat Eldred) *Easy Money Making Projects*, (illustrated by Jon Dahlstrom), 1979; *Pythons: Giant Snakes*, Scholastic, 1979; *Cats Big and Small*, Scholastic, 1982; *The Kids' Whole Future Catalog*, Random House, 1982.

Also the author of teacher guides and educational projects. Contributor of articles to periodicals.

SIDELIGHTS: "I grew up in the small town of Fond du Lac, Wisconsin. During my childhood, my family moved just once— to a new house a block away from the old one—but after I was married in 1964, my husband and I lived in eight different cities in ten years. Graduate school, the Navy, and various job opportunities led us first to California, and then to Georgia, Iceland, Minnesota, The Netherlands, Illinois, and finally back to Minnesota. Minneapolis has been my home since then. I was divorced in 1978, remarried in 1983 and now live with my husband and daughter, Claire, my best critic.

"When I graduated from college, I intended to be a high school English teacher, but because of our frequent moves, I had a more varied career than I'd expected. My first job was in a junior high school, teaching eighth and ninth grade English and German. During the Vietnam War, when my husband was sent to Keflavik, Iceland, I taught German through a University extension program on the naval base there. Later, when

Diana Ross' phone call started the transformation of the Jackson Five from local heroes to international superstars. ■ (From *One Stage: Jackson Five* by Harriet Lake. Photograph courtesy of United Press International.)

we lived in Amsterdam, I taught English as a foreign language at a private language laboratory.

"After returning to this country in 1974, I found that teaching positions were hard to come by and decided to look for another sort of career. That year I started working as a free-lance writer for a small publisher in Mankato, Minnesota, and, during the next four years, I completed twenty-three books for them (mostly easy-to-read biographies aimed at high school students with reading difficulties).

"I've become increasingly involved in future studies. In the fall of 1978, I was invited to direct a futures project initiated by a teacher at our neighborhood school and funded by the Minnesota Council on Quality Education, an agency created by the Minnesota Legislature to promote cost-effective innovations in education. As project director, my task was to conduct a future studies program for 200 first through seventh graders at our school and to develop curriculum materials which might be used by teachers in schools around the state. The curriculum materials which emerged from the Creating Futures project (fifty-five activity cards and a teacher guide) are now being used by elementary teachers in Minnesota, in other states, and even in a few foreign countries.

"In addition to my work in the schools, I have also participated in community-wide futures activities. In the spring of 1979, I served on a steering committee which organized a conference for 200 students, parents, teachers, school admin-istrators, and community members. The purpose of the conference was to explore new trends in economics, the arts, technology, and politics, and their implications for the future of education. In the fall, I helped set up an exhibit and present a workshop on ''Futurizing at the Grass Roots Level'' at the World Future Society-Education Section conference. In 1980 I helped to plan and present a city-wide conference on 'Space: The New Frontier.'

"My initial interest in futurism was sparked by Buckminster Fuller in a speech he gave at a conference here in Minneapolis in 1977. Dr. Fuller emphasized the need for people to coop-erate for the good of everyone on the entire planet. He warned that the next twenty years might well be the most critical period in world history—that our very survival might depend on how we react to the ever-more-pressing problems of hun-ger, overpopulation, war, and ecological destruction. He stressed that continuing to view these problems in the same old way would probably lead toward disaster but that by working to-gether to find global solutions, we might create a world of social harmony and material abundance surpassing anything we can now imagine.

"Shortly after hearing this speech, I read an article on chil-dren's perceptions of the future. The article stated that large numbers of grade school and high school students felt that there would *be* no future—that the planet would probably be destroyed by nuclear war before they reached adulthood. I found this article extremely disturbing. For, after all, children *are* our future. A few years from now, they will be the world leaders who will determine political, social, and economic policy. If they grow up feeling that the world's problems are insurmountable, their vision of disaster might someday be-come a self-fulfilling prophecy.

"As I mulled over these ideas, I became more and more con-vinced of the urgent need to help children form more positive images of a future world. *The Kids' Whole Future Catalog* evolved as I searched for a way to counter the doom and gloom of the daily news reports with the more hopeful long-term possibilities foreseen by Bucky Fuller and by biologists, phys-icists, psychologists, computer scientists, and other experts— ideas which, until the recent birth of *Omni, Science 82* and other futures magazines aimed at the general reader, were re-ported mostly in scholarly journals and which, even now, mainly appear in articles which are too difficult for younger kids to understand.

"I worked on the book for almost three years. During that time I contacted literally hundreds of people in fields ranging from holography to peace studies, from robotics to ESP re-search. These experts generously shared their journal articles, papers, press packets, and photos. In sifting through the moun-tains of material I collected, I identified three main strands of futuristic thinking—technological innovation, ecological con-cern, and expansion of human potential (personal and social transformation). I have tried to weave these various strands together within the book, and I hope that the result is a rela-tively balanced—if not totally coherent—whole. One of my main frustrations was that there was so much interesting ma-terial available and so little space for it. I decided to include book reviews and things to send for so that readers who were particularly interested in any of the topics could delve deeper on their own.

"Some people may criticize the book as being overly hopeful and idealistic. But, as Buckminster Fuller once said, 'The world has become too dangerous for anything less than utopia.' I feel it is urgently important to encourage children to envision and

In his zany stage act, Elton John may be making up for all the fun he missed as a child. He wasn't Elton John then. His name was Reginald Kenneth Dwight. ∎ (From *Elton John* by Paula Taylor. Illustrated by John Keely.)

Elvis was one of the greatest recording artists of all time. During his lifetime he had sold over 500 million records. ■ (From *Elvis Presley* by Paula Taylor. Illustrated by Dick Brude.)

work toward a more just and peaceful world. I hope that *The Kids' Whole Future Catalog* will be at least a first step in this direction.''

When writing for children Taylor feels that the writer must keep the material interesting. ''Most of the words you would normally use in writing for adults can't be used when writing for children. You have to know all the technical information you would need to write an adult book and then you have to forget it all in a sense and write as if you were a child discovering it all over again.

''For instance, when I was writing the wildlife book, I had a problem with the idea of retractable claws. Most wild cats have them, but one or two don't. I couldn't say 'All wild cats have retractable claws,' because that wasn't true. But saying that most cats have them opens up a new series of questions that would have to be answered.

''You can't get by without being interesting when you are writing for kids. If you're not interesting, the kids will toss your book away without finishing it.'' [Barbara Reinhold-Harvey, ''Writing for Kids Is Challenging, Fun,'' *The Reporter*, January 4, 1981.]

HOBBIES AND OTHER INTERESTS: ''Biking, bike touring, gardening, music and travel.

FOR MORE INFORMATION SEE: The Reporter (Fond du Lac, Wis.), January 4, 1981.

THOMAS, Art(hur Lawrence) 1952-

PERSONAL: Born July 8, 1952, in Cleveland, Ohio; son of Anthony L. (an electrician) and Anne L. (Rinkus) Thomas. *Education:* Baldwin-Wallace College, B.A., 1974; Kent State University, M.A., 1987. *Politics:* Independent. *Religion:* Roman Catholic. *Home:* 12500 Edgewater Dr., Lakewood, Ohio 44107.

CAREER: Cleveland City Schools, Cleveland, Ohio, teacher of English, writing, and drama, 1975-80; author, 1975—;

ART THOMAS

Brooklyn City Schools, Brooklyn, Ohio, teacher of English, writing, and drama, 1980-83; St. Ignatius High School, Cleveland, Ohio, teacher of advanced placement English and composition, 1983—. Business manager of New Mayfield Repertory Cinema, 1975-85; member of advisory board of Pioneer Drama Service, Denver, Colo., and board of directors of Ohio City Players Theater. *Member:* International Thespian Society, Mensa, National Council of Teachers of English, United States Institute of Theater Technology, Music Box Society, Cleveland Critics Circle.

WRITINGS: All juvenile, except as noted: *Recreational Wrestling* (adult), A. S. Barnes, 1976; *Wrestling Is for Me* (self-illustrated with photographs), Lerner, 1979; *Bicycling Is for Me* (self-illustrated with photographs), Lerner, 1979; *Volleyball Is for Me,* Lerner, 1979; *Theater Publicity Handbook,* Pioneer Drama Service, 1979; *Backpacking Is for Me,* Lerner, 1980; *Fishing Is for Me,* Lerner, 1980; *Merry-Go-Rounds* (illustrated by George Overlie), Carolrhoda, 1981; (with Emily Blackburn) *Horseback Riding Is for Me* (self-illustrated with Tom Galvin), Lerner, 1981; *Archery Is for Me* (self-illustrated), Lerner, 1982; (with Laura Storms) *Boxing Is for Me* (photographs by Robert L. Wolfe), Lerner, 1982; *Fencing Is for Me* (photographs by Julia Sheehan-Burke), Lerner, 1982.

Author of ''Theater in Review,'' a column in *West Life,* 1982—, and of an art review column in *Photojournal Press,* 1986—. Contributor of travel and creative articles to magazines and newspapers, including *West Life.*

WORK IN PROGRESS: A series of theater books for elementary, junior, and senior high school students; a study of the educational aspects of theme parks and their role in the entertainment industry.

SIDELIGHTS: ''My first experience with writing came when I was in college and forced into the position of entertainment editor of our newspaper. I had no previous experience, but this broke the barrier of 'mysticism' associated with writers. Since my major was English and theater, the college newspaper experience helped a great deal in terms of my career choice.

''I was prepared to teach at the high school level, and in an education course found a statement to the effect that 'anyone who thinks that he knows something about a topic should be forced to write a book on it.' Because I was an entertainment editor, I selected a field far removed from my specialty, and my first book was a sports book. That seemed to put me in a 'rut' of writing sports books.

''Like most writers, I find it difficult to force myself to sit at the typewriter for the length of time it takes to get started. For me, almost an hour passes before I actually start writing. I try to keep in shape by writing shorter articles for newspapers.

''I suppose that one of my reasons for writing is to achieve a kind of immortality. Someone once said, 'If you can't be immortal, why bother?' Like an actor, I enjoy the audience response. It's nice to receive letters from children who have read one of my books.

''I enjoy travel and try to fill every day, especially when on vacation. Because I am single, it is sometimes difficult to find a traveling companion who is willing to share a frantic vacation schedule. I like to visit amusement parks and am a real fan of roller coasters. I also try to see what's happening with live theatre whenever I travel.

I first became interested in archery because every day on the way to school I passed a shooting range. ■ (From *Archery Is for Me* by Art Thomas. Photograph by the author.)

"We all seem to respect those who do things that we don't and I have a special regard for playwrights and novelists. Although I teach creative writing, I seem to lack the patience and skill to create in these forms."

HOBBIES AND OTHER INTERESTS: "My spare time is spent bicycling through the summer months, and acting in and directing for community and semi-professional theatres in the Cleveland area, and in magic, juggling, and the occult."

TOWNSEND, Sue 1946-

BRIEF ENTRY: Born February 4, 1946, in Leicester, England. Townsend, who left school at age fourteen, had "very little" education "but read a lot." She writes "because I always have," she said. "It legitimizes what could be taken to be (by other people) my extreme curiosity about people." *The Secret Diary of Adrian Mole Aged 13 3/4* (Methuen, 1982) and its sequel, *The Growing Pains of Adrian Mole* (Methuen, 1984)—

published together as *The Adrian Mole Diaries* (Methuen, 1985)—were immediately popular in England, inspiring a play, a song book, diaries, and computer games. In these comic, candid books, Adrian innocently describes the incidents of his adolescence—his parents' fighting and affairs, falling in love with a new girl at school, his friendship with eighty-nine-year-old Bert Baxter, and the British Broadcasting Corporation's consistent rejection of his poetry. "Adrian's wry observations, entertainingly convoluted adventures, and indefatigable decency are captivating and funny," said *Booklist*. Townsend's other works include *The Great Celestial Cow* (Methuen, 1984) and *Bazaar and Rummage, Groping for Words* [*and*] *Womberang* (Methuen, 1984), three plays. She contributed to the London *Times, New Statesman,* and other periodicals, and has done radio work for the BBC. *Agent:* Giles Gordon, 43 Doughty Street, London, England.

TWETON, D. Jerome 1933-

PERSONAL: Born May 8, 1933, in Grand Forks, N.D.; married in 1957; children: three. *Education:* Gustavus Adolphus College, B.A., 1955; University of North Dakota, M.A., 1956; University of Oklahoma, Ph.D., 1964. *Office:* Department of History, P.O. Box 8096, University of North Dakota, Grand Forks, N.D. 58202.

CAREER: Dana College, Blair, Neb., 1959-65, began as assistant professor, became professor of history; University of North Dakota, Grand Forks, 1965-71, began as assistant professor, became associate professor, 1965-71, chairman of the history department, 1965—, professor of history, 1971—. Visiting scholar, General Beadle State College, 1967. *Member:* American Historical Association, Organization of American Historians, Economic History Association, Western History Association, Agricultural History Society.

WRITINGS: The Marquis de Morès: Dakota Capitalist, French Nationalist, North Dakota Institute for Regional Studies, 1972; (with Daniel F. Rylance) *The Years of Despair: North Dakota in the Depression,* Oxcart Press, 1973; (with Theodore B. Jelliff) *North Dakota: The Heritage of a People* (young adult), North Dakota Institute for Regional Studies, 1976; *Depression: Minnesota in the Thirties,* North Dakota Institute for Regional Studies, 1981.

URE, Jean
(Ann Colin, Jean Gregory, Sarah McCulloch)

PERSONAL: Surname sounds like "ewer"; born in Surrey, England; daughter of William (an insurance officer) and Vera (Belsen) Ure; married Leonard Gregory (an actor and writer), 1967. *Education:* Attended Webber-Douglas Academy of Dramatic Art, 1965-67. *Religion:* None. *Home and office:* 88 Southbridge Rd., Croydon, Surrey CR0 1AF, England. *Agent:* Maggie Noach, 21 Redan St., London W14 0AB, England.

CAREER: Writer. Has also worked as a waitress, cook, washer-up, nursing assistant, newspaper-seller, shop assistant, theatre usherette, temporary shorthand-typist, translator, secretary with NATO and UNESCO, and television production assistant. *Member:* Society of Authors, Vegan Society, Animal Aid. *Awards, honors: See You Thursday* was chosen one of American Library Association's Best Books for Young Adults, 1983.

WRITINGS—Juvenile: *Dance for Two,* Harrap, 1960; *See You Thursday* (Junior Literary Guild selection), Kestrel, 1981, Delacorte, 1983; *A Proper Little Nooryeff,* Bodley Head, 1982, published in America as *What If They Saw Me Now?,* Delacorte, 1984; *If It Weren't for Sebastian,* Bodley Head, 1982, Delacorte, 1985; *Hi There, Supermouse!* (illustrated by Martin White), Hutchinson, 1983, Penguin (U.S.), 1985, published as *Supermouse* (Junior Literary Guild selection; illustrated by Ellen Eagle), Morrow, 1984; *You Win Some, You Lose Some,* Bodley Head, 1984, Delacorte, 1986; *The You-Two,* Hutchinson, 1984, published in America as *You Two* (illustrated by E. Eagle), Morrow, 1984; *After Thursday,* Kestrel, 1985, Delacorte, 1987; *Megastar,* Blackie, 1985; *Nicola Mimosa,* Hutchinson, 1985, published in America as *The Most Important Thing* (illustrated by E. Eagle), Morrow, 1986; *Swings and Roundabouts* (sequel to *Megastar*), Blackie, 1986; *A Bottled Cherry Angel,* Hutchinson, 1986; *Brenda the Bold,* Heinemann, 1986.

Adult: *The Other Theatre,* Corgi, 1966; *The Test of Love,* Corgi, 1968; *If You Speak Love,* Corgi, 1972; *Had We but World Enough and Time,* Corgi, 1972; *The Father Off from England,* Corgi, 1973; *Daybreak,* Corgi, 1974; *Marriage of True Minds,* Corgi, 1975; *All Thy Love,* Corgi, 1975, large print edition, Thorpe, 1985; *No Precious Time,* Corgi, 1976; *Hear No Evil,* Corgi, 1976; *Early Stages,* Corgi, 1977; *Dress Rehearsal,* Corgi, 1977, large print edition, Thorpe, 1984; *All in a Summer Season,* Corgi, 1977, large print edition, Lythway, 1978; *Curtain Fall,* Corgi, 1978, large print edition, Thorpe, 1981; *Bid Time Return,* Corgi, 1978; *A Girl Like That,* Corgi, 1979, large print edition, Thorpe, 1982; *Masquerade,* Corgi, 1979.

Adult; under pseudonym Ann Colin: *Doctor Jamie,* Corgi, 1980, large print edition, Lythway, 1983; *A Different Class of Doctor,* Corgi, 1980, large print edition, Lythway, 1983.

JEAN URE

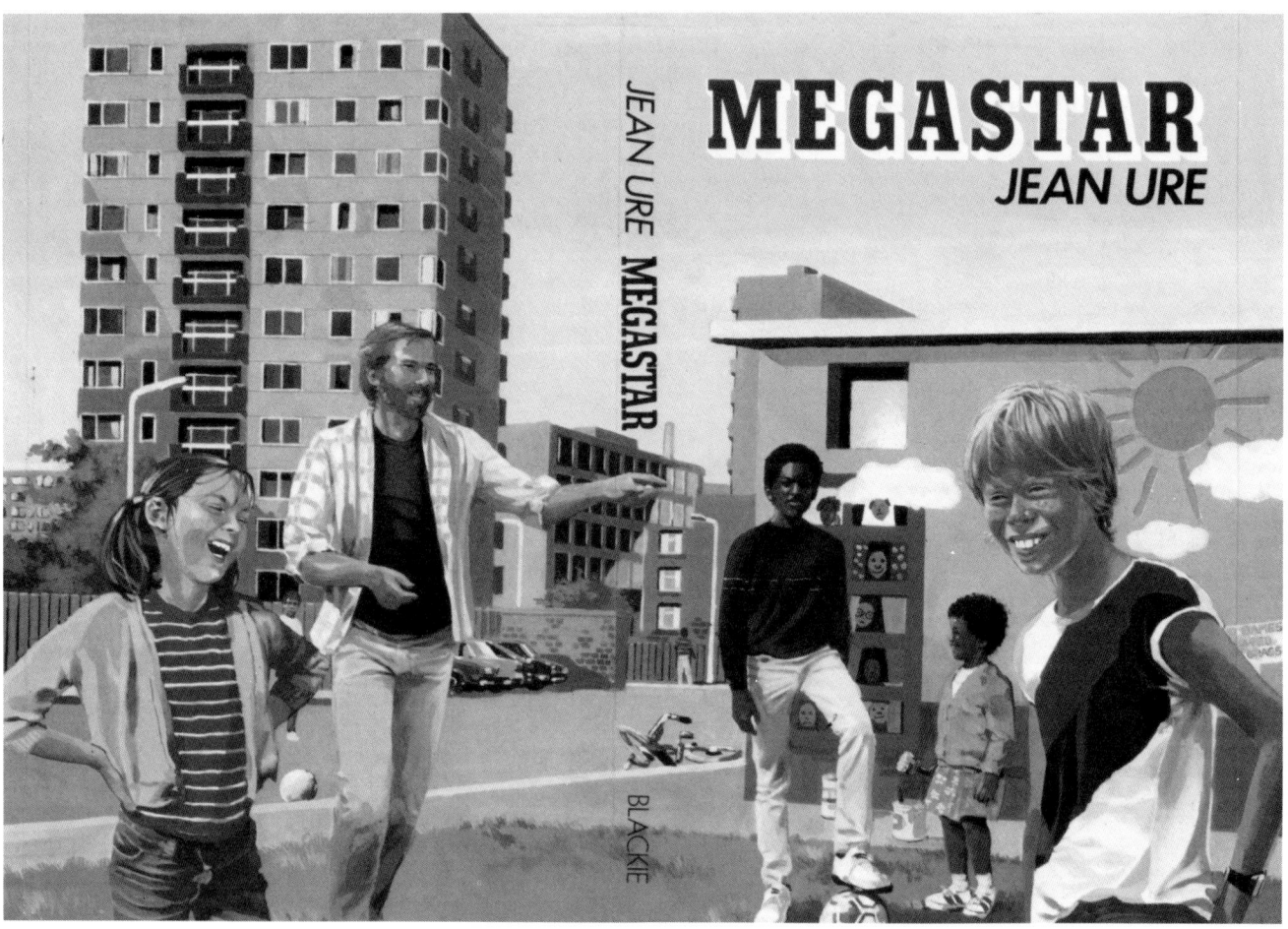

(Jacket illustration by Bob Harvey from *Megastar* by Jean Ure.)

Adult; Georgian romance novels; under pseudonym Sarah McCulloch: *Not Quite a Lady,* Corgi, 1980, Fawcett, 1981, large print edition, Lythway, 1983; *A Lady for Ludovic,* Corgi, 1981, large print edition, Lythway, 1983; *A Most Insistent Lady,* Corgi, 1981, large print edition, Lythway, 1983; *Merely a Gentleman,* Corgi, 1982; *A Perfect Gentleman,* Corgi, 1982.

Adult; under pseudonym Jean Gregory: *Love Beyond Telling,* Corgi, 1986.

Also translator of books from the French. Contributor of articles to periodicals, including *Vegan* and *Writers' Monthly.*

WORK IN PROGRESS: A novel, *Tea Leaf on the Roof,* to be published by Blackie; a young adult book, tentatively titled, *One Green Leaf.*

SIDELIGHTS: "I started writing just about as soon as I could write and have continued nonstop ever since. I'm a compulsive writer in that I live through my books and write 'from the inside out'—drawing from within myself rather than from external sources. To this extent, therefore, I am a writer who does not need to travel and rarely needs to do any special research (though I did research extensively for my five 'Georgian' novels).

"My first book, *Dance for Two,* was written while I was still at school and was a pure 'wish fulfillment' book. I walked out of school early, against all advice to the contrary, declaring that I was going to 'be a writer'—hence years of trouble and despair and a long series of dead-end jobs, culminating in a

very happy and fulfilling two years at a London drama school where I met my husband. Time spent working in Paris perfected my French (now, alas, back to school standards!) which led to a series of book translations for Corgi Books, which in its turn led to a long association with Corgi during which I polished my style and technique writing so-called 'romantic novels'—I say so-called as they weren't really very romantic. More what you would call realistic. Thus their sales were far from startling, but the years of apprenticeship paid off and laid the groundwork for what has come later.

"I turned to writing for children and young adults in 1980, feeling that my views on life had become too jaundiced to allow me to continue to write froth for adults. Childhood, however, is a time of hope and freshness; I draw constantly on my own childhood experiences in my writings for present-day children and would hope to be able to give to those of them who need it, and who are capable of taking it, the same solace and excitement which the books of *my* childhood gave to me. I have extremely positive views on society and the way in which we organise it but have no wish to 'indoctrinate.' If there is one main aim I have in my writings, it is to make my readers question received prejudices, question accepted values—above all, to *think.*

"I became a vegetarian six years ago on the grounds that I had no wish to participate in the torture and slaughter of living creatures in order, quite needlessly, to fill my gut. Further thought on the subject has now led me to veganism.

"My politics are more a matter of philosophy than of 'party politics' as I do not subscribe to any of the major political parties in this country, or indeed in any other. At heart I am an anarchist—I would stress nonviolent—inasmuch as I believe we should organise ourselves to have government over *things* rather than as at present, government over *people*.

"Ideas for future books are brimming over, but basically all my books are concerned with relationships—of people to themselves and of people to each other. Until I have lived with my characters internally for some period of time and can actually hear them talking, I am not ready to capture them on the page. As soon as they come to life, I note down all the conversations that they have, plus any little bits of illuminating description which come to me. Ultimately I have to sit down and wrestle with the hard technicalities of plot—*how* things happen, *where* things happen, *when* things happen. What is the time scale to be? What time of year? From whose viewpoint do I tell the story? I then divide my plot into chapters, and from my (usually quite large) accumulation of notes I make a selection for the various chapters, for example, 'this conversation would take place in Chapter 1,' 'this bit of description would fit very well into Chapter 2,' and so on. Thus, when I come to the actual writing, a good fifty per cent of the hard work has been done. I revise continuously, both as I write, after I've finished each chapter, after I've finished the whole book, after I've typed out the whole book (a task I would never let anyone else perform for me as I find it an essential part of the creative process) and yet again after my editor has read it. Most editors, I usually find, have very useful and perceptive comments to make.

"Finally, I would say that for me writing for children and young adults is far more interesting than writing for adults. If one is to make a living by one's pen—and as a compulsive writer who could never find satisfaction in doing anything else, I need to make a living—then one has of necessity to write 'genre' books if one is to write for adults. These all impose their own restrictions. In the field of children's books, however, there are virtually no restrictions. One is free to choose what subject matter one will and to treat it as one wishes, only bearing in mind the likely level of experience of one's readers."

HOBBIES AND OTHER INTERESTS: "My main leisure interests are reading, writing letters, walking our two fox terriers, playing with our two white cats, listening to music and horse-riding."

FOR MORE INFORMATION SEE: Stephanie Nettell, "Escapism or Realism? The Novels of Jean Ure," *British Book News*, March, 1985.

VOIGT, Cynthia 1942-

PERSONAL: Born February 25, 1942, in Boston, Mass.; daughter of Frederick C. (a corporate executive) and Elise (Keeney) Irving; married first husband September, 1964 (divorced, 1972); married Walter Voigt (a teacher), August 30, 1974; children: Jessica, Peter. *Education:* Smith College, B.A., 1963. *Politics:* Independent. *Residence:* Annapolis, Md. *Office:* The Key School, 534 Carroll Dr., Annapolis, Md. 21403.

CAREER: J. Walter Thompson Advertising Agency, secretary, 1964; teacher of English at high school in Glen Burnie, Md., 1965-67; The Key School, Annapolis, Md., teacher of English, 1968-69, department chairman, 1971-79, part-time teacher and department chairman, 1981—; author of books for young readers, 1981—. *Awards, honors: Homecoming* was selected

as a Notable Children's Trade Book in the Field of Social Studies by the joint committee of the National Council for Social Studies and the Children's Book Council, and was an American Book Award nominee, both 1981; *Tell Me If the Lovers Are Losers* was selected one of American Library Association's Best Young Adult Books, 1982, *A Solitary Blue* was chosen, 1983; *Dicey's Song* was selected one of American Library Association's Best Children's Books, 1982, and received the Newbery Medal, 1983, "for the most distinguished contribution to American literature for children"; Edgar Allan Poe Award from the Mystery Writers of America for the best juvenile mystery, 1984, for *The Callender Papers;* Newbery Honor Book, 1984, for *A Solitary Blue.*

WRITINGS: Homecoming (juvenile), Atheneum, 1981; *Tell Me If the Lovers Are Losers* (young adult), Atheneum, 1982; *Dicey's Song* (juvenile; ALA Notable Book), Atheneum, 1982; *The Callender Papers* (juvenile), Atheneum, 1983; *A Solitary Blue* (juvenile; ALA Notable Book), Atheneum, 1983; *Building Blocks* (juvenile), Atheneum, 1984; *The Runner* (young adult), Atheneum, 1985; *Jackaroo,* Atheneum, 1985; *Izzy, Willy-Nilly* (juvenile), Atheneum, 1986; *Come a Stranger,* Macmillan, 1986; *Stories about Rosie* (illustrated by Dennis Kendrick), Atheneum, 1987.

SIDELIGHTS: Voigt was born in Boston, Massachusetts in **1942,** the second of five children. She has two sisters, and twin brothers, thirteen years her junior. "Our family is not big by my mother's family standards. Most of my cousins come from families of eight or nine. I actually remember very little of my childhood, which makes me think it was quite happy. I suspect it might have been very close to perfect." Voigt's childhood was spent in rural southern Connecticut. "We lived in houses surrounded by spacious yards."

"Because my older sister was *thought* to be painfully shy, my parents decided to send us to nursery school together. I was a

CYNTHIA VOIGT

Jeff wasn't fine and he knew it. ■ (Jacket illustration by James Shefcik from *A Solitary Blue* by Cynthia Voigt.)

little young, but they felt I would be able to help her through. When it came time for the nursery school play, however, she was Miss Muffet, and I was the Spider. Later, when we got to dancing school—she was a Sweet Pea, and I was a Head of Cabbage.

"My grandmother lived in northern Connecticut, in a house three stories high; its corridors lined with bookcases. I remember reading *Nancy Drew, Cherry Ames, The Black Stallion,* and the Terhune book. One day, I pulled *The Secret Garden* off one of her shelves and read it. This was the first book I found entirely for myself, and I cherished it. There weren't any so-called 'young adult' books when I was growing up. If you were a good reader, once you hit fourth grade, things got a little thin. I started to read adult books, with my mother, making sure what I had chosen was not 'too adult.' I read Tolstoy, Shakespeare, Camus and many classics, except for *Moby Dick,* which I finally read in college. It knocked me out. I came to Dickens and Trollope later in life."

Attended Dana Hall School in Wellesley, Massachusetts. "My mother and father had attended boarding schools and continued the tradition by sending their children as well. Dana Hall, a private girls' boarding school, gave us a great deal of intellectual as well as physical freedom, and I loved it. We could go downtown on our own, which in the fifties in a girls board-

ing school was just this side of licentious. Knowing the school trusted us, I believe, helped us to grow up.

"I decided in the ninth grade that I wanted to become a writer. At first, I wrote mostly short stories and poetry. I didn't even know the word 'submission' then, let alone the subtler vagaries of publishing."

Attended Smith College in Northampton, Massachusetts. "I took creative writing courses in college but considered them real bombs. Clearly what I was submitting didn't catch anyone's eye. I never had a bad teacher like my character, Mr. Chappelle in *A Solitary Blue*. There were a few male teachers at Smith who resented teaching women, feeling themselves too good for the position. We had very little patience with that attitude. Mr. Chappelle grew primarily out of my own experience as a teacher. I've never seen anyone quite as extreme as my character, but writers only need to see the edges of a situation to be inspired to make it come alive."

Following graduation, Voigt moved to New York City where she worked for the J. Walter Thompson Advertising Agency. "New York was the place to go after college. It seemed that it took an eternity to find a job, but in fact it took only two weeks. I could type, but didn't know shorthand. I have a great memory, however, and was able to take dictation. I worked for a wonderful woman in public relations, who at the time

(Jacket illustration by Michael Garland from *The Runner* by Cynthia Voigt.)

was putting together a centennial history. She had led a very interesting and exciting life. A vaudevillian, her best act was tap dancing while playing the xylophone blindfolded!

"I moved into a tiny apartment in Greenwich Village, spending half of my monthly earnings on rent. The lady next door owned killer German Shepherds and was in the habit of talking to herself and answering herself while her dogs leapt savagely against her windows. It was a fun year.

"I married in 1964 and moved with my first husband to Santa Fe, New Mexico. I was to work as a secretary to help support us while he was in school. But even with my New York experience it was difficult to find a job. I drifted into the Department of Education one day, and asked what I would have to do to qualify myself to teach school. They learned that I'd attended Smith College, and signed me up for accrediting courses at a Christian Brothers college. Within six months I met the terms of certification. I vowed I would never teach when I left Smith, and yet, the minute I walked into a classroom, I loved it.

Divorced in 1972, Voigt settled in Annapolis, Maryland. "I had been writing throughout college, but during most of my first marriage, I didn't write much at all. My *not* writing was in many ways a symptom of what was wrong in the marriage. I was living alone with my daughter, which is in a sense like living alone, because a small child is simply an extension of

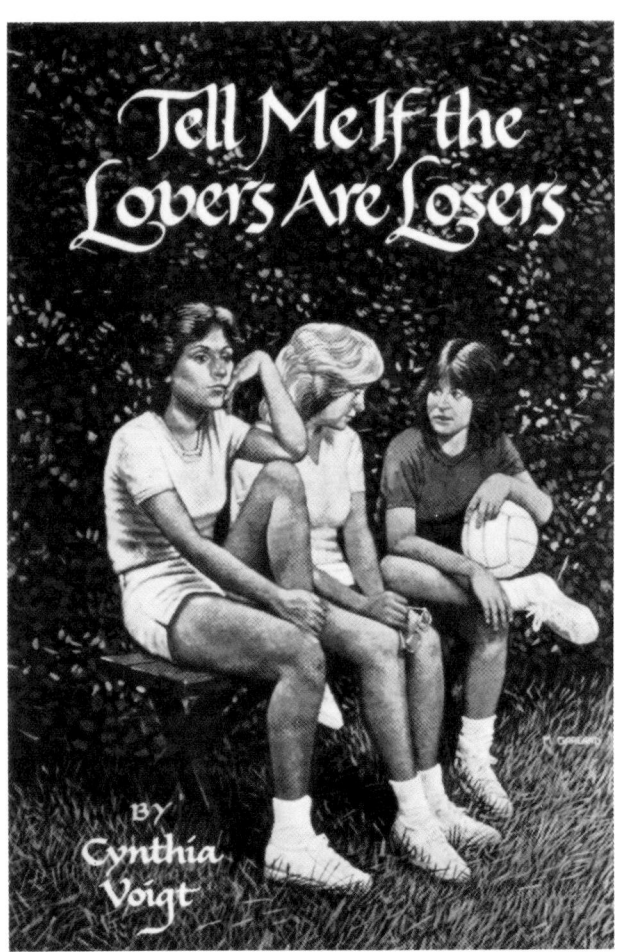

Ann's head turned from one to the other. "Yes, I think I'd better take volleyball. With you." ■ (Jacket illustration by Michael Garland from *Tell Me If the Lovers Are Losers* by Cynthia Voigt.)

Dicey was feeling edgy and not really like herself. ■ (Jacket illustration by James Shefcik from *Dicey's Song* by Cynthia Voigt.)

yourself. Like many women, as soon as I was separated, I found myself washing floors regularly, keeping the house nice, just to prove to myself that I was really okay! I also began writing again. To support us I worked as a tutor. I kept a regular schedule so that I could have an hour to write at the end of each day."

Taught English at the high school level in Glen Burnie, Maryland. "I was writing stories that have either been lost or are at the bottom of a box somewhere. I was by this time teaching in the public school system. After three years, I took a job with The Key School in Annapolis, where I still teach. They were so happy with my performance they allowed me to bring my baby daughter Jessica into the classroom with me for a year, after which, she went to day care.

"I was assigned to teach English in second, fifth and seventh grades. The second graders were a kick and a half. I assigned book reports to my fifth graders. I would go to the library and starting with the letter 'A' peruse books at the fifth, sixth, and seventh-grade age level. If a book looked interesting, I checked it out. I once went home with thirty books! It was then that I realized one could tell stories which had the shape of real books—novels—for kids the age of my students. I began to get ideas for young adult novels and juvenile books. That first year of teaching, and *reading* really paid off in spades! I felt I had suddenly discovered and was exploring a new country.

"My future mother-in-law, who was enrolled in a library science course in children's literature, recommended two books

She wore a shapeless blouse over a long, shapeless skirt. Her feet were bare. ■ (Jacket illustration by Ted Lewin from *Homecoming* by Cynthia Voigt.)

to me: *Harriet the Spy* and *Dorp Dead*. Though there are many books I bring into the classroom year after year—*Mrs. Frisbee, Book of Three, The Gammage Cup* and the short stories by Elaine Konigsburg—*Dorp Dead* has become my favorite teaching tool.

1974. Married Walter Voigt, a teacher of Latin and Greek at The Key School. "I was teaching full time, but was able to continue the writing I'd begun while I was living alone by sticking to my regime of one hour a day.

"I became pregnant and decided to teach part time. One of the things I wanted was more time to write. The summer I was pregnant I wrote the first draft of *The Callender Papers.* When my son, Peter, was an infant, I took him to school and taught with him in a 'Snuggli.' When he was a year old, I wrote *Tell Me If the Lovers Are Losers,* and the next year (he was in a playpen in the faculty lounge next to my classroom), I began *Homecoming.*

"One day while I was writing *Tell Me If the Lovers Are Losers,* I went to the market and saw a car full of kids left to wait alone in the parking lot. As the electric supermarket doors whooshed open, I asked myself 'What would happen if nobody ever came back for those kids?' I made some jottings in my notebook, and let them 'stew' for a year, the way most of my ideas do. When I sat down to write the story that grew from

my question (and this is typical of my process) I made a list of character names. Then I tried them on to see if they fit. I knew Dicey was the main character, but was not sure precisely *who* she was. The more I wrote about her, the more real she became to me. I'd planned a book about half the size of *Homecoming.* But a few chapters into the novel, the grandmother became central and I began to see that there was a lot more going on than would fit in one book."

About the creation of her character, Grandmother Tillerman, Voigt commented, "I was writing chapter three of *Homecoming* and out of the darkness of the typewriter, she leapt fully formed, like Athena. I could hear what she was saying, and began making notes. She was always very clear to me, and in some ways is a mirror image of her granddaughter, Dicey. I sometimes think that Dicey is the type of kid I would have liked to have been, and grandmother is the kind of old lady I would like to be.

"The idea of 'holding on, reaching out, and letting go' which runs through *Homecoming* was part of the rhythmic building of the book. I structured the novel around these three pieces of advice, and as each problem was solved, the next one would crop up. In the end, of course, there is no one right answer."

1981. *Homecoming* published. "When I signed the contract for my first book, I looked at the time schedule with some

I studied this note. Its firm handwriting sloped forward without curlicues and fanciness. ■ (Jacket illustration by Judith Gwyn Brown from *The Callender Papers* by Cynthia Voigt.)

surprise, realizing that in those same months I could produce two babies.''

1982-1983. Published two earlier novels, *The Callender Papers,* and *Tell Me If the Lovers Are Losers* with Atheneum. "I had read many gothics and decided to try *The Callender Papers* as an exercise in plotting, which I felt was a distinct weakness in my writing. I finished, but didn't submit the novel. Then one day Jessica, who was feeling bored, came to my study and picked up the manuscript. She read the book standing up—just as she read her beloved *Nancy Drew* books. 'Gee, I guess *The Callender Papers* works,' I thought to myself. Of course, the book went through major revisions before it was finally published.

"Though *Tell Me If the Lovers Are Losers* is not what I would call autobiographical, it was in some ways inspired by my own experience at Smith College. The book is not in any way factual; rather, it is *suggestive,* capturing the tone, the feeling of my years at college. In the same way, *The Callender Papers* is not a historic novel. Some of the details are accurate, and the diction is evocative of the period, but it is not a carefully researched historical piece, and is more a product of having read many gothic novels.

"When I finished *Homecoming,* I knew I wasn't finished with the Tillerman family, and wrote *Dicey's Song.* After *Dicey's Song* I wanted to explore Jeff's story, and wrote *A Solitary Blue.* The character 'Bullet' in *Building Blocks* had been in my mind since *Homecoming.*"

"When I submitted *Dicey's Song* to my editor, it was with the firm conviction that they would probably not want to publish it. My cover letter read something like: I don't know that you will want this, but I think you will love reading it." [Cynthia Voigt, "Newbery Medal Acceptance," *Horn Book,* August, 1983.[1]]

"*Dicey's Song* is a book about problems and solutions that are not a function of the plot. In a book like *Dorp Dead,* the problem/solution structure controls the plot. *Dicey's Song* is much more internal, and I was afraid it was too indirect for the market. I saw *Dicey's Song* as the natural ending to *Homecoming,* and had no thought, as I worked, of the marketplace.

"It never crossed my mind that a reader might have a problem reading *Dicey's Song,* without having read *Homecoming.* But after I had submitted the book, my editor, Gail Paris, asked me to write an introductory piece to give the reader some background. I was upset; I had written a killer first line and did not want to bury it with the introduction. However by this time I had learned to trust Gail, and so I wrote it. When I saw how the book was typeset, I realized that though I hadn't said a word, Atheneum knew as well as I did that the first line was important. Some readers have started from *A Solitary Blue* and worked their way back to *Homecoming* and it seems to work for them. I can't separate the three books.''

1983. *Dicey's Song* was selected as an American Library Association Best Children's Book and won the Newbery Medal. "When I first heard that *Dicey's Song* had been awarded the Newbery Medal. I entered into a state of massive incoherence. I have not yet completely emerged from this state and suspect now I may never, but one of my first sensible thoughts during the time was: 'I did not know good news could pack such a wallop.' I didn't know good news could keep you awake into the night, distract you so effectively from all appointed tasks, make it difficult, when you confronted it head on, to breathe properly.

"... Forty-eight hours after the famous phone call, during which time the house had been reverberating with the words Newbery and Los Angeles, we went out for a family celebration dinner. [My son] Duffle leaned forward to announce to his grandmother the big news: 'We are going to Chicago, because Mommy won the Blueberry Award.' ... Duffle ... keeps my feet on the ground.[1]

"Writers need readers as they develop a new work. My husband is a wonderful reader, and my daughter has also become a very interested reader. She read the first three chapters of *Homecoming,* and by her reaction, I knew I had begun something worthwhile. Usually I write a rough draft then pull a fair copy off of that when I'm sure the chapter will stand as is. I let my husband read each chapter in its rough form, and then Jessica reads the fair copy. I also let Gail Paris read work in progress. Either I've become very fluid about letting people read my rough drafts, or my editor—lucky woman—has been taken into the family!''

"... I have a long, rhapsodic speech about editors in me. ... The editor works upon, works over the manuscript, to enable it to be the best it can. An editor must be, more than anything else, dexterous, able to cover the territory between the publisher and the writer as well as the records of music, stories and song. They not only make available but also give space and forms to responses.[1]

"Every revision has been slightly different for me. *Homecoming* needed to come down in length by nearly two hundred pages. *The Callender Papers* was not well written in the first draft; all of my characters sounded exactly the same to me, and overall, the language needed polishing. So I went over the manuscript again and again. *Tell Me If the Lovers Are Losers* took thematic revision, because the ideas were not clearly worked out.

"I need to focus on one book at a time. I don't submit ideas, I submit manuscipts. Because I revise a lot, even in the early stages of a book, I prefer not to submit until I'm certain what I have will work.

"I usually begin a book with a character, or, less often, an idea. Once I have the character and some notion of plot, the theme becomes apparent to me.''

Voigt has found several of her characters mysterious and elusive. "It was difficult for me to cook up a reason why a woman would leave her children—something which happens in both *Homecoming* and *A Solitary Blue.* I don't think it is easy for women to leave their children, and that's one reason why I had to make the mother in *Homecoming* crazy. There seemed to me to be no other conceivable way that a woman would leave her children. Melody, Jeff's mother in *A Solitary Blue* was a very hard character to write. I was interested in capturing the kind of person who tends to be long on charm, but is absolutely false. Melody wants to take care of the entire world, a common human failing—it is so much easier to concern ourselves with other people's problems while our own personal world is neglected and goes to hell.

"No, it's not the same to write about a girl going through the sexual changes of puberty as it is to write about a boy going through them. But I feel quite comfortable with my male characters. I believe there are real differences between the sexes, but we are all human beings and so have a lot in common; it seems to me that shared *humanity* is crucial in storytelling.

"I don't shelter my characters from the world any more than I would keep them from going to the bathroom. The Depression and World War II were experiences that shaped and informed me while I was growing up, just as Vietnam has influenced kids growing up today.''

Most of Voigt's stories take place in Maryland. ''Maryland is lovely, and spacious, with a lot of flat land and a huge expanse of sky overhead. It reminds me in some ways of the Southwest, which is also wonderful country.''

Voigt has won many awards, but considers the acceptance of her first manuscript, *Homecoming*, ''the most important award I've won. . . . After years of working on my own, I was suddenly encouraged and accepted by others. Awards are external, they happen after the real work has been done. They are presents, and while they are intensely satisfying they do not give me the same kind of pleasure as being in the middle of a work that is going well.

''I like to have my mornings for writing. Often, I'll work four hours and then go off to teach. But some mornings I use my time to take a walk, pick flowers. Writing is something I need to do to keep myself on an even keel. It's kept me quiet; it's kept me off the streets.''

Voigt still teaches English part time at The Key School. ''My personal theory about teaching is that when you teach you mimic those who taught you well. I had several excellent teachers along the way and when I teach, I remember them and sometimes even hear myself echo them.''

When Voigt teaches writing, she emphasizes ''structure as well as free and honest individual expression. I tell my students that writing is not a comparative act—each student's 'best' writing will be very different.''

Her advice to young writers is to ''Do it, not for awards, but for the pleasure of writing. And remember that publication is often a matter of chance. *Homecoming* was turned down by three of the five editors to whom I submitted the first three chapters.''

Besides writing, Voigt enjoys, ''going out to dinner, shopping with my son or daughter and in the summer, trips to our island in the Chesapeake Bay where we enjoy the beach, go crabbing, read together, wash dishes. I'd love to have a house in Maine someday. It's so beautiful and quiet, and there are so many stars in the sky. When I see something I like, I always want to try and write it—that makes it *mine*, you see. It's almost as good as buying property—I put something in a book, and I almost own it. I suppose I'll have to write a book about Maine, perhaps that will make the dream come true.''

Voigt also enjoys walking in cemeteries. ''There are so many stories in the tombstones, and cemeteries are eternal places. I especially love the place where William Butler Yeats is buried, as well as the cemetery at the foot of Edinburgh Castle.''

FOR MORE INFORMATION SEE: New York Times Book Review, May 10, 1981, May 16, 1982; *School Library Journal*, November, 1983; *People*, December 19, 1983; *Horn Book*, August, 1983.

Children are entitled to their otherness, as anyone is; and when we reach them, as we sometimes do, it is generally on a point of sheer delight, to us so astonishing, but to them so natural.

—Alastair Reid
(from *Places, Poems, Preoccupations*)

WEINBERG, Lawrence (E.) (Larry Weinberg)

BRIEF ENTRY: An author, playwright, and lawyer, Weinberg has written several books based on films, including *Star Wars: The Making of the Movie* (Random House, 1980), *Dragonslayer: The Storybook Based on the Movie* (Random House, 1981), and *The Legend of the Lone Ranger Storybook* (Random House, 1981). Two picture books, *The Forgetful Bears* (Clarion, 1982) and *The Forgetfuls Give a Wedding* (Scholastic, 1984), depict the difficulties the Forgetfuls encounter while having a picnic and arranging a wedding. In the first book, the Forgetfuls forget the food, leave Grandpa at home, lose the car, and become separated from each other—all before reaching the picnic area. Making wedding arrangements for a niece poses similar problems. Curtains are sewn instead of a wedding gown, the bride forgets where the wedding is taking place, and the groom forgets where to meet the bride. *Publishers Weekly* called the Forgetfuls ''an extended family of bears who will keep children shouting with laughter.''

Weinberg's fast-paced young adult novels, many of which are included in high/low series, deal with moral issues and convictions. For example, *Hooded Avengers* (Bantam, 1983) relates the dilemma of a recent high school graduate who is tricked into joining a Klu Klux Klan-like group. When the Hooded Avengers decide to murder a black family, young Ben must decide whether to help the family or remain silent. ''Weinberg has placed realistic characters in a rough setting,'' noted *School Library Journal*, ''to show how the irrational seeds of hate can quickly and easily sprout into terrifying violence.'' Among his other young adult novels are *The Cry of the Seals* (Bantam, 1984) and *War Zones* (Bantam, 1985). *Residence:* Woodstock, N.Y.

WHITNEY, David C(harles) 1921-

PERSONAL: Born March 8, 1921, in Salina, Kan.; son of William R. and Jerusha F. (McCartney) Whitney; married Elizabeth J. West, January 31, 1943 (died, 1978); married Merrie Robin Vaughn, February 23, 1980; children: (first marriage) Ann G., Katherine W., Jane P. (deceased), West Martin (deceased), Peter A., Lynn M. *Education:* University of Kansas, A.B., 1942; attended Columbia University, 1946.

CAREER: United Press Associations, New York, N.Y., feature writer and overnight news editor, 1945-51; *World Book Encyclopedia*, Chicago, Ill., assistant managing editor, 1952-54, managing editor, 1954-64, editorial director and vice-president, 1964; *Encyclopedia Americana*, New York, N.Y., editor-in-chief and vice-president, 1964-65; Cowles Education Corp., New York, N.Y., president and editor, 1965-68; UEC Inc., New York, N.Y., vice-president of educational systems division, 1969-72; David C. Whitney Associates, Inc., Chappaqua, N.Y., president and editor, 1972—. President, Board of Education, Illinois School District 110, 1956-61; mayor, Deerfield, Ill., 1961-64; president and trustee, Chappaqua (N.Y.) Public Library Board, 1975-80. *Military service:* U.S. Naval Reserve, 1942-45; became lieutenant senior grade. *Member:* Authors Guild, Mayflower Society, Association for Supervision and Curriculum Development, New York Academy of Sciences, Royal Society of Arts (London; Benjamin Franklin Fellow), Sigma Delta Chi.

WRITINGS—Juvenile; published by F. Watts: The First Book of Facts and How to Find Them (illustrated by Edward MacKenzie), 1966; *Let's Find Out about Addition*, 1966; *Let's*

Find Out about Milk (illustrated by Gloria Gaulke), 1967; *The Picture Life of Lyndon Baines Johnson*, 1967; *Blueberry, the Bloodhound*, 1967; *Willie and Winnie and Wilma, the Wicked Witch*, 1967; *Let's Find Out about Subtraction* (illustrated by Eva Cellini), 1968; *Let's Find Out about the President of the United States*, 1968; *The Picture Life of Dwight D. Eisenhower*, 1968; *Skippy the Skunk*, 1968; *Ann's Ann-imal*, 1969; *The Easy Book of Multiplication*, 1969; *Limpy the Lion*, 1969; *The Easy Book of Fractions* (illustrated by Sheila Granda), 1970; *The Easy Book of Division*, 1970; *The Easy Book of Sets* (illustrated by Tony Forde), 1972; *The Easy Book of Numbers and Numerals* (illustrated by Anne M. Jauss), 1973.

Other: *Founders of Freedom in America*, J. G. Ferguson, Volume I: *Lives of the Men Who Signed the Declaration of Independence and So Helped to Establish the United States of America*, 1964, Volume II: *Lives of the Men Who Signed the Constitution of the United States and So Helped to Establish the United States of America*, 1965; *The American Presidents*, Doubleday, 1967, 6th edition, 1986; *The Trials and Triumphs of Two Dynamic Decades*, J. G. Ferguson, 1968; *Latin Amer-*

ica, Golden Press, 1968; *U.S.A.*, Golden Press, 1968; (editor with Francine Klagsburn) *Assassination: Robert F. Kennedy, 1925-1968*, United Press International and Cowles, 1968; *The People of the Revolution: The Colonial Spirit of '76*, J. G. Ferguson, 1974; *The American Legacy: A Pageant of Great Deeds and Famous Words*, 3 Volumes, J. G. Ferguson, 1975; *Write Better, Speak Better*, D.C.W.A.I., 1981.

Editor, *Reader's Digest Almanac and Yearbook*, 1972—. Contributor to *Teachers College Record*, *Chicago Daily News*, and *Educational Technology*.

FOR MORE INFORMATION SEE: New York Times Book Review, November 6, 1966; *Library Journal*, October 1, 1975.

WINTER, Paula Cecelia   1929-

PERSONAL: Born October 26, 1929, in New York, N.Y.; daughter of Henry and Marie (Heynen) Winter; married Harold Berson, July 2, 1958. *Education:* Attended Cooper Union, 1952-55. *Home:* 172 Stanton St., New York, N.Y. 10002.

(From the animated filmstrip "Sir Andrew." Produced by Weston Woods, 1977.)

(From *The Bear and the Fly* by Paula Winter. Illustrated by the author.)

CAREER: Fashion illustrator and painter. *Exhibitions;* Group shows at galleries in New York, N.Y., 1950-62, including Eggleston Gallery, 1951, and Leonard Hutton Gallery, 1960. *Awards, honors: The Bear and the Fly* was named one of *New York Times* Best Illustrated Books of the Year, one of Child Study Association's Children's Books of the Year, and Best Children's Book of the Season by *Saturday Review*, all 1976, and was included in Children's Book Council's Children's Book Showcase, 1977.

WRITINGS—Self-illustrated: *The Bear and the Fly* (wordless picture book; ALA Notable Book), Crown, 1976; *Sir Andrew* (wordless picture book), Crown, 1980.

Illustrator: Jan Wahl, *Crazy Brobobalou*, Putnam, 1973; *Where's Your Baby Brother, Becky Bunting?*, Doubleday, 1979; Lawrence Weinberg, *The Forgetful Bears*, Clarion, 1982; L. Weinberg, *The Forgetfuls Give a Wedding*, Scholastic, 1984.

ADAPTATIONS: "Sir Andrew" (filmstrip; with teacher's guide), Weston Woods, 1977; "The Bear and the Fly" (filmstrip), Weston Woods, 1985.

WORK IN PROGRESS: The Cat Man, a wordless picture book for children, for Four Winds Press.

SIDELIGHTS: "I live in Manhattan, a place I find endlessly fascinating and have also spent a lot of time traveling, doing on-the-spot drawings wherever I go. There's nothing like drawing something to really see it. . . . I'm crazy about good art books and illustrated children's books." [Lee Kingman and others, compilers, *Illustrators of Children's Books: 1967-1976*, Horn Book, 1978.[1]]

"My main interests are people, art, animals, and traveling. I've been very fortunate in having been able to travel extensively and to have seen a lot of art. My desire to see people and animals treated humanely is harder, if not impossible, to do anything about."

HOBBIES AND OTHER INTERESTS: Travel (Europe and North Africa.)

FOR MORE INFORMATION SEE: Lee Kingman and others, compilers, *Illustrators of Children's Books: 1967-1976*, Horn Book, 1978.

Childhood shows the man as morning does the day.
—John Milton

WOODWARD, (Landon) Cleveland 1900-1986

OBITUARY NOTICE—See sketch in *SATA* Volume 10: Born June 25, 1900, in Glendale, Ohio; died in 1986, in Spanish Fort, Ala. Artist and illustrator. A biblical illustrator for fifty years, Woodward also painted portraits and landscapes. He co-founded the Cape Cod Art Association in 1948, served on the board of directors of the Eastern Shore Art Association, and was an advisor and instructor in oil painting at the Eastern Shore Academy of Fine Arts. Woodward lectured in biblical art at schools and museums. His works have appeared in exhibitions in Cincinnati, Nashville, Philadelphia, St. Louis, and Cape Cod. Among the books he illustrated are Henry Van Dyke's *The Other Wise Man*, Miriam MacMillan's *Kudla and His Polar Bear*, and *World Bible*. Obituaries: *Detroit Free Press*, June 3, 1986.

WRIGHT, Betty Ren (Revena)

BRIEF ENTRY: A former children's book editor, Wright is now a full-time writer who edits on a free-lance basis. She has written more than thirty picture books, some under the pseudonym Revena, including titles like *Jim Jump, Poppyseed, Snowball, Mr. Moggs' Dogs*, and *Willy Woo-oo-oo*. In addition, her short stories have appeared in periodicals such as *Redbook* and *Ladies' Home Journal*. Also the author of novels for middle-grade readers, Wright combines mystery with a close look at familial relationships in both *The Dollhouse Murders* (Holiday House, 1983) and *Ghosts Beneath Our Feet* (Holiday House, 1984). In *The Dollhouse Murders*, twelve-year-old Amy Treloar seeks escape from the responsibility of caring for her younger retarded sister. She arranges to spend some time with Aunt Clare in the old family mansion, where the discovery of a dollhouse in the attic leads to strange occurrences. *Booklist* called the novel "a gripping, at times gruesome, mystery," while *Horn Book* noted that it "provides insight into the conflicting emotions besetting families forced to cope with the problems of retardation." Similarly, *Ghosts Beneath Our Feet* unravels the mystery of a mining accident that took place thirty years earlier while examining the ties between Katie, her widowed mother, and her rebellious stepbrother, Jay. Wright's other novels include *Getting Rid of Marjorie* (Holiday House, 1981), *The Secret Window* (Holiday House, 1982), and *Christina's Ghost* (Holiday House, 1985). In 1986, *The Dollhouse Murders* received both the Mark Twain Award and the Texas Bluebonnet Award. *Residence:* Kenosha, Wis.

WYLIE, Betty Jane

PERSONAL: Born in Winnipeg, Manitoba, Canada; daughter of Jack (a physician) and Inga (Tergesen) McKenty; married William Tennent Wylie, June 7, 1952 (deceased); children: Elizabeth, Catherine, John, Matthew. *Education:* University of Manitoba, B.A. (with honors in English and French), 1951, M.A., 1952. *Politics:* Conservative. *Religion:* United Church of Canada. *Residence:* Toronto, Ontario, Canada. *Agent:* Nancy Colbert, 303 Davenport Rd., Toronto, Ontario, Canada M5R 1K5.

CAREER: Free-lance writer. Wrote and presented "Betty Jane's Diary," a daily radio program, syndicated by Berkeley Studio of United Church of Canada, 1978-82. Script consultant to

Puppeteers of America, 1966-73; member of board of directors of Bereaved Families of Ontario, Investors' Syndicate, and the Writer's Union of Canada. *Member:* Canadian Association of Publishers, Authors, and Composers, Periodicals Writers Association, Playwrights Union of Canada, Writers' Union of Canada (national council, 1986-87), Association of Canadian Television and Radio Artists, Dramatists Guild. *Awards, honors:* Icelandic Canadian Poetry Prize from Icelandic Canadian Poetry Association, 1974; Canada Arts Council grant, 1982-83; Smile Company Contest, first prize, 1982, for play, *A Place on Earth*, and third prize, 1983, for play, "Blind Spot."

WRITINGS: (Contributor) *The Clear Spirit* (biography collection), University of Toronto Press, 1966; *Beginnings: A Book for Widows*, McClelland & Stewart, 1977, 6th edition, 1985, Ballantine, 1984, published as *The Survival Guide for Widows*, Ballantine, 1986; *Encore: The Leftovers Cookbook*, McClelland & Stewart, 1979; *No Two Alike* (a collection of interviews), Image Press, 1981; *Betty Jane's Diary: Lessons Children Taught Me*, Image Press, 1981; *Tecumseh* (young adult; illustrated by Phil McLeod), Black Moss Press, 1982; *John of a Thousand Faces* (young adult; illustrated by Thomas McNeely), Black Moss Press, 1983; (with Lynne MacFarlane) *Everywoman's Money Book*, Key Porter, 1984, revised edition, 1987; *The Betty Jane Wylie Cheese Cookbook*, Oxford University Press (Toronto), 1984; *The Book of Matthew*, McClelland & Stewart (Toronto), 1984; *The Best Is Yet to Come: Planning Ahead for a Financially Secure Retirement*, Key Porter, 1985; *Successfully Single: How to Live Alone and Like It*, Key Porter, 1986.

Published plays: *The Old Woman and the Pedlar/Kingsayer* (juvenile; one-act; contains "Kingsayers," first produced in Winnipeg, Manitoba at Manitoba Theatre Centre, November, 1967, and "The Old Woman and the Pedlar," first produced in Toronto, Ontario at Young People's Theatre, September, 1977), Playwrights Press, 1978; *Mark* (two-act; first produced in Stratford, Ontario at Stratford Festival Theatre, July, 1972), Playwrights Press, 1979; *Don't Just Stand There—Jiggle!* (puppet plays), Black Moss Press, 1980; *The Horsburgh Scandal: The Man and the Play* (two-act; first produced in Toronto at Theatre Passe Muraille, March, 1976), Black Moss Press, 1981; *A Place on Earth* (one-act; first produced in Toronto by Toronto Workshop Productions, 1982), Playwrights Press, 1982.

Unpublished plays: "An Enemy of the People" (three-act adaptation of play by Ibsen), first produced in Winnipeg at Manitoba Theatre Centre, December, 1962; "George Dandin" (two-act musical adaptation of play by Moliere), first produced in Winnipeg at Manitoba Theatre Centre, May, 1964; "I See You, I See You" (one-act), first produced in Stratford, Ontario at Stratford Festival Theatre, August, 1970; "Size Ten" (two-act), first produced in Waterloo, Iowa at Waterloo Playhouse, May, 1976; "Beowulf" (two-act rock opera), first produced in New York, N.Y. at AMAS Repertory Theater, December, 1977; "Soap Bubbles" (two-act musical; based on her newspaper soap opera serial), first produced in Gravenhurst, Ontario, at Muskoka Summer Theatre, August, 1979; (with Michael Cole) "Double Swap" (two-act comedy), first produced in Gravenhurst at Gravenhurst Opera House, March, 1979; "Blind Spot" (one-act), 1979; "The Second Shepherd's Play" (juvenile; one-act; poetic translation), first produced in Toronto at Cosmus Theatre, 1981, (prose translation and musical adaptation), music by Quenten Doolittle, produced in Calgary at Storybook Theatre, 1982; "Double Vision" (one-act; for young people), first produced in Toronto at Theatre Direct, January, 1986; "Time Bomb" (two-act), first produced in Waterloo, Iowa at Waterloo Community Playhouse, January, 1986.

Author of "Summer Soap," a daily column on soap operas in *Toronto Star,* 1979. Contributor of articles and poems to magazines, including *Maclean's, Chatelaine, Homemakers, Leisureways, Toronto Life, Quest,* and to newspapers.

WORK IN PROGRESS: "The Hookers of Lethbridge," a musical play with composer Ken Nichols; "My Best Friend's Wife/Husband," a musical revue about the perils of friends' spouses with Dave Carley and composer Victor Davies; "Steps," a comedy about a widow's readjustment to living alone; *Mirrors,* a novel about a woman artist's relationship with her mirror (and her family); "The Pact," a play about Karen Blixen's last love affair.

SIDELIGHTS: "*Tecumseh* and *John of a Thousand Faces* are children's books, the two versions of 'The Second Shepherds' Play' are ideally suited for a young audience, though the play appeals to all ages, and the play 'Double Vision' though written for a young adult audience is equally effective with adult audiences, for lunch-time theatre (it's short).

"*Tecumseh* is a history of the Indian chief who played a key role in Canadian-American history during the War of 1812-1814, written for grade three and four readers. I didn't hoke it up with imagined scenes, except for the possible romance the man had with a woman—never confirmed. I did use my playwriting skills to set the scenes and break up the speeches— we have a very complete record of the speeches Tecumseh made, and he was, apparently, a fiery orator. I also speculated on the mystery of the exact circumstances of his death and the disappearance of his body, all based on historical evidence.

"*John of a Thousand Faces* was inspired by and written for my third child, first son, John, just as my play *Kingsayer* was given its spark by and written for my two daughters. I arranged for one of John's best friends, Thomas McNeely, an artist, to illustrate the book. This book actually began as a requested children's film, but the money disappeared. It was impossible to translate to the stage because it had so many cinematic effects, but my publisher thought it had possibilities as a children's book, so I turned it into narrative.

"The fact that it began as film explains the initial image. I was thinking of the fairy tale about the princess who made horrible faces at people and who was warned that she would be stuck with a face if the wind changed. (It did and she was.) I was at an art gallery opening watching a visiting celebrity being photographed and realized that photography was a twentieth-century version of the wind changing and freezing one's face, catching it forever in a smile or a grimace. So the boy who had a thousand faces—day-dreaming, teasing, fighting, feeling resentful, sorry for himself, and so on—has his face 'caught,' frozen by a street photographer, and has to solve the riddle on the man's card first to find the photographer and then to get his face back. All to do with film, you see. Very visual but still, as my work tends to be concerned with a search for identity.

"*The Book of Matthew* is a biographical account of my youngest child, second son, Matthew, who is brain damaged. His life reads like a tacky soap opera but he is a survivor, a strong personality and a delightful human being. The musical theatre piece "Boy in a Cage," still unfinished, unproduced, is for him, and the image is his.

"Another theatre project I did is related to Matthew as well. Ontario Arts Council has an Artists-in-the-Schools program, whereby a creative artist collaborates with a teacher and class to produce something—poetry, visual art, musical, or in my case, a play. I had done one of these projects for an inner-city

BETTY JANE WYLIE

grade one/two class, producing a puppet play with the children.

"One of the ways that I eke out my living is by doing readings from my plays in the schools. A provincial (and occasionally national) program is administered by the Playwrights' Union and subsidized by the Ontario Arts Council and Canada Council. Not many playwrights, we have discovered, are willing to do the elementary schools, preferring high school and college level audiences. It must come from my years of teaching Sunday School, but I really enjoy very young people as well. I have developed, along with the readings, a presentation based on my knowledge of puppetry and playwriting designed to stimulate the children's creative imagination. My idea is that you don't have to have a puppet to have a puppet. I use found objects for puppets (a wooden spoon, a feather duster, a dish mop, and so on) and show my audiences how to play 'what-if' to create stories of their own. I also improvise with them to show them how dialogue develops and how to create a play from action and reaction.

"When my son Matthew was in a special private school for handicapped children, I received another Artists-in-the Schools grant to create a play with and for these kids. The result was magic, a genuine theatrical piece. A VTR film was made of a live performance, on file with Ontario Arts Council.

"I wrote an account of these two experiences which was published in a special Children's Theatre issue of *Canadian Theatre Review,* and realized how much I had to say. I'd love to do a book describing the experiences and the process, together with the two scripts that emerged. One keeps looking for sympathetic publishers.

''I consider myself primarily a playwright, and do all my other writing to support my habit. I am what you might call eclectic. I have had a modest success in a number of different media, but with a low profile, such that I call myself a very prolific unknown. Just as well—I'm afraid of typecasting. The idea comes first, then the form. There is a through-line, of course. I am my common denominator. The book *Beginnings,* about widowhood, and my children's play, 'The Old Woman and the Pedlar,' both ask the same question, in different forms: 'Who am I?' and 'Where am I going?'''

CUMULATIVE INDEX TO ILLUSTRATIONS AND AUTHORS

Illustrations Index

(In the following index, the number of the volume in which an illustrator's work appears is given *before* the colon, and the page on which it appears is given *after* the colon. For example, a drawing by Adams, Adrienne appears in Volume 2 on page 6, another drawing by her appears in Volume 3 on page 80, another drawing in Volume 8 on page 1, and another drawing in Volume 15 on page 107.)

YABC

Index citations including this abbreviation refer to listings appearing in *Yesterday's Authors of Books for Children,* also published by the Gale Research Company, which covers authors who died prior to 1960.

Author Index

The following index gives the number of the volume in which an author's biographical sketch, Brief Entry, or Obituary appears.

This index includes references to all entries in the following series, which are also published by Gale Research Company.

YABC—*Yesterday's Authors of Books for Children: Facts and Pictures about Authors and Illustrators of Books for Young People from Early Times to 1960,* Volumes 1-2
CLR—*Children's Literature Review: Excerpts from Reviews, Criticism, and Commentary on Books for Children,* Volumes 1-11
SAAS—*Something about the Author Autobiography Series,* Volumes 1-3